THE
MAKING OF
AN HISTORIAN

The Collected Essays
of J.H. Plumb

THE
MAKING OF
AN HISTORIAN

The Collected Essays
of J.H. Plumb

The University of Georgia Press
Athens

© 1988 J. H. Plumb

Published in the United States of America in
1989 by The University of Georgia Press,
Athens, Georgia 30602

First published 1988 by
Harvester·Wheatsheaf
A Division of
Simon & Schuster International Group

Printed and bound in Great Britain by
A. Wheaton & Co. Ltd, Exeter

Library of Congress Cataloging in Publication Data

Plumb, J. H. (John Harold), 1911–
    The making of an historian: The collected essays of J. H. Plumb
    p.   cm.
    Includes index.
    ISBN 0–8203–1095–6
    1. Plumb, J. H. (John Harold), 1911– . 2. Historians—Great
Britain—Biography.   3. Great Britain—Historiography.
4. Historiography—Great Britain.   5. Great Britain—History.
I. Title.
DA3.P57A3 1989
941'.0072024—dc19
                                                        88–17290
                                                        CIP

Contents

Preface

When I was asked by the Harvester Press if they might publish my collected essays, it appeared to be an impossible task and so I put off the decision. My essays stretch over fifty years chronologically and their subjects are exceptionally diverse from a short piece on Colonel Robert Walpole's addiction to the turnip to a discursive essay on human history from the Neolithic Revolution to the present time. Also, despite the fact that I had lost nearly ten years through war, the number was startlingly large, running to nearly a million words.

The task seemed so formidable and too incoherent that I let the project simmer for a year to two and began to draft a kind of intellectual autobiography. Then I realised suddenly that the two projects might be compatible, so long as the Harvester Press would agree to four volumes and I could find a first-rate research assistant.

Harvester agreed and I was lucky. Simon Smith has been invaluable – patient, willing to spend hours in dusty attics; always perceptive; a good and thoughtful critic. It is difficult to see how it would have been possible to have collected these essays without his help.

I have also had the wise judgement of Dr Joachim Whaley, not only judgement but also encouragement for there were times when the project seemed too complex and too large. Without his support I may easily have put the project aside. I owe also a debt to my secretary, Mrs K. Serby, who has been locked in battle with my handwriting for five years.

These first two volumes deal with my life as a professional historian and attempt to explain the problems with which I was preoccupied and discusses the historians who helped or hindered my career – not perhaps as fully as I might for I had to preserve the balance of the book. A fuller treatment of my experience of history, of Cambridge, of my college and of the intellectual life of Britain and America I hope will follow in a few years' time.

J. H. PLUMB

Acknowledgements

I wish to thank the following editors and publishers in whose journals or books of collected essays, these articles and reviews were first published:

Cambridge Historical Journal, Conference of British Studies, *The English Historical Review*, *Horizon Magazine* (USA), Hutchinson PLC, *New Republic*, *New Statesman*, *New York Times Book Review*, *Observer*, *Paperback Review*, *Past and Present*, *Prism*, The Royal Historical Society, *Saturday Review*, *Spectator*, *Sunday Times*, *Times Literary Supplement*, *Times Educational Supplement*, *Victoria Histories of the Counties of England*, *Washington Post*: also, the Encyclopaedia Britannica for permission to reprint 'History and Tradition' from *Great Ideas of Today, 1974* and Doubleday, Inc. and Penguin Books Ltd for 'Churchill the Historian' from *Churchill: Four Faces and the Man* (Penguin Books, 1969) copyright © The Dial Press, 1968, 1969; and 'The Historian's Dilemma' from *Crisis in the Humanities* (Penguin Books, 1964) copyright © Penguin Books, 1964.

PART ONE

NAMIER VERSUS TREVELYAN

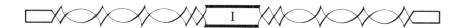

The Road to Professional History

It is nearly sixty years ago since I decided to try to become a professional historian, little knowing, of course, anything of the life of professional historians. Indeed I doubt whether I bothered much about the adjective – basically I wanted to write historical books and the only way I could do so was by joining the academic profession. By 1934 I had only met five professional historians, four men and one woman, who lived by teaching or writing history and two of these for only a few minutes. It seems scarcely credible now, for I was 23 years of age.

I was one of three students who obtained, in 1933, first class honours in history as an external student of London University and I had been awarded a year later a Post-Graduate Studentship by London University – one of six available for all subjects in science as well as in the humanities. There must have been historians on the interviewing board but I did not recognise them nor did they make themselves known. (Many years later I heard that R. H. Tawney was one.)

Of the five historians whom I had met by 1934, the two most important were those who taught me at University College, Leicester. For my first two years as an undergraduate there was only one member of the staff – G. E. Fasnacht, a sad Oxford MA who taught everything from Greek Political Thought to Nineteenth-Century European History: indeed, some six papers in all. His lectures were tedious, drawn from his old undergraduate lecture notes or an obvious textbook. He entered the empty room in gown and mortar-board, saying as he reached the rostrum 'Good morning, gentlemen,' in a low, sepulchral voice. With three in the class, it was too cruel to stay away without making sure that the other two would be there – usually each of us would cut one or two lectures a week. Actually Fasnacht was a kindly man with great personal dignity and no hope. For my last year as an undergraduate Dr Rosalind Hill came from Oxford to teach me medieval history. She probably saved my career. She was very shy but spirited, and emotionally

3

and imaginatively committed to medieval history, and that commitment she could convey in her breathless exciting lectures. Also; she did more than give me a life-long interest in medieval history which I have always read with pleasure: she was fresh from the Schools and she knew what the standards of achievement were likely to be. She nourished my ambition to get a First and helped breed the confidence to succeed. For Fasnacht his profession was a gloomy burden, almost a cross to be borne with dignity, but for Rosalind Hill it was an excitement and a delight. For her work was joy.

These were two professional historians whom I knew well, the only ones. But through C. P. Snow, who had gone from Leicester to Cambridge, I met Christopher Morris, a young Fellow of King's, who was just embarking on his own career as an historian. Through gossip with Christopher what had been mere names – Pickthorn, Temperley, Clapham, Reddaway – became characters against whom perhaps one might measure oneself. And, of course, there was more than gossip, for we discussed a great deal of history as well as the machinery of the Faculty – the ladder of preferment; how appointments were made; all matters, of course, of which I was totally ignorant. Christopher Morris was the first person, not in a teaching relationship with me, with whom I could share ideas and explore research possibilities (if I could get to that stage). But I met him only very occasionally, perhaps a couple of times a year between 1930 and 1934 when I settled in Cambridge.

Before I got to Cambridge I also met G. N. Clark, through the good offices of Fasnacht, for ten minutes in 1933 in his study at All Souls. I was terrified at the thought of the interview but he proved to be a kindly, short, heavy, tank-like man who assured me that my research topic, *Elections to the House of Commons in the Reign of William III*, was a good one and that I did not need to know Dutch. Although I was very awed, he treated me with the courtesy and interest of one scholar talking to another. When I left his study I felt almost as grave and as dignified as Clark himself. By contrast my brief meeting with Namier which I had engineered for myself lasted for two minutes on the steps of the British Museum where he asked me to meet him promptly at midday. He hardly bothered to listen as I quickly described my planned work on the House of Commons in William III's reign. I said that I hoped to follow his techniques to which he snapped 'How else could you do it?' and turned back abruptly to the Museum. Of course, at that point in 1933 he was no longer interested in eighteenth-century politics; his formidable powers were concentrated on diplomatic history and I must have been an irrelevant interruption. It never occurred to me that I should ever meet either of these two distinguished historians again.

It was a curiously innocent apprenticeship and I doubt whether any historian of this century has reached the age of 23 and met so few of his profession. Had I known more about the historians and the way history was developing, I would very likely not have taken the next steps in my career.

Once I knew that I could go to Cambridge to take a PhD, I wanted to be supervised by G. M. Trevelyan – after all, my topic lay at the heart of his own interests and I admired *England Under the Stuarts*, and the volumes on Queen Anne's reign which were just appearing; also G. M. Trevelyan was Regius Professor, the head, I believed, of his profession and I was quite clear-eyed about what my position in Cambridge would be. No one was likely to take much notice of a post-graduate student from an almost unknown and certainly despised University College. If I could prove myself to Trevelyan, I thought, I might have a chance of a Fellowship with his backing and support. I received two very terse notes from him; one telling me that I had to apply to the Board of Graduate Studies to be accepted as a research student; the second some weeks later that the Board having accepted me he would supervise my research. I arrived in Cambridge and waited; after about ten days I was summoned to West Road – the large ugly Edwardian house at the corner of Grange Road, as ugly within as without. His study was dark, the furniture hideous and uncomfortable, and he sat in the corner almost obscured. He remained silent. Frozen by nerves, I took in the lantern jaw, long nose, grey flecked moustache, wire spectacles and tough thatch of greyish hair swept back from a noble brow. Too nervous to speak, the silence became almost unsupportable. What I did not realise was that Trevelyan had never had a research student before and had not the slightest idea what to do, and was probably as nervous as I was. At last, he asked me what I was going to work on. Rapidly I sketched out my programme: the sources I wanted to cover, the weekly visit to the PRO or British Museum. I suppose in my nervousness I went on for ten minutes; at the end silence again. And then he barked in his harsh grating voice 'Good. Quite good. Good.' Then he rose from his chair, 'Come and see me at the end of term. If you have any problems let me know.' With that he escorted me courteously to the door and as he opened it asked me whether I was living in college or not. And that was that. I walked away in utter disappointment. I realised that I was just as much on my own as I had been the previous year when I had wandered from Oxford to London and back again collecting material for my research but discussing it with no one.

The term passed and I still failed to meet any professional historians – even the one at Christ's, A. B. Steel, who was infuriated because I had been given entrance to the college without any consultation with him. It had been arranged by C. P. Snow with his friend, the Senior Tutor,

S. W. Grose. Also Steel was rightly worried. He had just secured his first
outstanding pupil – Arthur Hope Jones, a brilliant young economic
historian, deeply admired by Sir John Clapham, the Professor of Economic History – and he did not want even a dark horse to come into
competition with him. He need not have worried. I was so dark as to
be invisible. I had not only got the wrong supervisor, I had got the
wrong college – but it was only in my second year that I fully realised
my position, because by then I had begun to meet some professional
historians and know what academic professional history was about.

In the academic year 1935/6, there was a revolt in Newnham College
amongst the historians. They demanded a new supervisor in English
history and through the good offices of Christopher Morris, three girls,
brilliant, beautiful and wilful, became my pupils. Through them I made
friends, one of whom, Adam Watson, was a great admirer of Butterfield,
and it was not long before I was going to coffee at Butterfield's house
on Belvoir Terrace and arguing with him until the early hours of the
morning. He was brilliant, exasperating, devastating, mischievous,
mixing in equal quantities malice and generosity. He dragged his principles before my enraged and bloodshot eyes with the skill of a matador.
He forced me to reconsider every idea that I had; I got better at defending
myself, and through Butterfield I gradually knew that I would never
truly belong to the profession of history. I loved yet distrusted Butterfield's impish qualities, his almost electric versatility at times daunted
me but his major principles – the deep belief in the role of Providence
(Christian of course) in human history – left me, in the end, bored as
well as disbelieving. We disagreed too on the function of history. I
believed then as I believe now that history must serve a social purpose
no matter how limited – to try to teach wisdom about the past and so,
perhaps, no more than perhaps, about ourselves and our times. Butterfield thought historians should suspend all judgement about history. He
valued what he called technical history, the careful and precise evaluation
of documentation: indeed he valued it so much that, alas, it inhibited,
indeed froze, his own work. His best work ironically was when he wrote
broad surveys – *The Whig Interpretation of History, The Origins of
Modern Science, Man on His Past* – where documentation was negligible, and the judgements explicit. In many ways we were ambivalent
towards each other, possibly deeply antipathetic characters, but there
were areas of agreement, particularly on how history should be taught.
And he was extremely generous on passing back to me the praise of my
new pupils.

We took delight in each other in differing ways – Butterfield had a
passion, like myself, for literature and we spent almost as many evenings
sharing that delight as in ferocious argument. But my memory, of course,

is mainly of argument because our discussions often spilled over into politics.

Butterfield was a Methodist in religion and a Liberal in politics. He said that he always voted Liberal; it was hard to believe. He was critical of the Spanish Republicans, sympathetic, very, to Franco: he seemed to be completely neutral to Hitler whom he feared far less than the Russians; indeed, when I met him on Cambridge railway station in July 1941, he said, 'Wouldn't it be wonderful if neither the Germans nor the Russians won!' At times he seemed almost deliberately to heighten his right-wing position in order to provoke the inevitable outburst, for deep down he loved to shock, to be contrary. And about politics, even more than about history, his arguments were devious, often radical – but always conservative in conclusion.

His views of his fellow historians were usually guarded: he admitted, of course, admiration for his patron, Harold Temperley; if I mentioned a name he might smile and say nothing, refusing to be drawn for mostly he criticised by silence, only towards Kitson Clark of Trinity and Frank Salter of Magdalene was he openly hostile. He thought they conspired against him on the Faculty Board and that they supported all that was second-rate and that they could not recognise what he called 'the electricity' of a first-rate mind. Any suggestion which Kitson Clark made was treated with the utmost suspicion. It was an enmity which grew deeper with the years and was to have a profound influence on the development of history in Cambridge. It was deepened, too, by Butterfield's personal success – Professorship, Mastership, Fellowship of the British Academy and finally Vice-Chancellorship. (True he had to wait for the Fellowship until he was in his sixties and until Namier was dead, for Namier was adamant in his opposition, quoting with relish a few of Butterfield's scholarly blunders as if they were sins against the Holy Ghost.) But Kitson Clark got nowhere, a mere Readership, not even the Vice-Mastership of his college and never the Academy. And that rankled. The results of this deep personal antipathy I will come to later.

Curiously enough, I met no young historians at the small argumentative parties at Butterfield's – some very clever young men, such as Adam Watson, but no young historians. I joined, on Christopher Morris's advice, the Historical Society but the meetings were usually dull and I wandered about at tea, speaking to no one at all and no one ever speaking to me. Trevelyan attended but as he was in the Chair he rarely had more than a few minutes with the speakers before he sat down and conducted the proceedings with his curious manner of barking shyness.

Slowly I was getting to know him better. We never met for discussion more than twice a term for a quarter of an hour or so, but he became more encouraging, more at ease and more interested in my work. On occasion he would give me materials which one of his copyists at the British Museum had prepared for him in beautiful copperplate handwriting, usually Parliamentary Division Lists, that he thought would be of value to me. I was also slowly beginning to appreciate the qualities of his nature. He possessed an inherent sadness that sprang from his sense of the tragic plight of humanity and the inevitable isolation of the individual in Time. His integrity was rock-like, based on an unshakeable belief in the values which he thought lay at the heart of England's historical experience. I began, slowly, to feel myself to be in the presence of a very great man: a feeling which I have never had for any other Cambridge historian, except David Knowles, but one which grew as the years passed, and I knew Trevelyan better.

In those early years Trevelyan barely noticed any other historians – certainly none in Cambridge except Kenneth Pickthorn whose books on Henry VII and VIII he admired. Outside he spoke with great warmth of Winston Churchill, especially so of his *Marlborough*. He approved highly of Arthur Bryant and tried, though without success, to get permission for me to see the Shakerly papers which were in Bryant's custody. If he spoke of historians, as he often did after he began to ask me to lunch, just before I took my PhD in 1936, he would urge me to read Lecky and Ranke, Macaulay and Gibbon, even Carlyle and Froude. Acton he regarded as a brilliant non-starter. After he had seen the draft of my thesis, our relationship became closer and he kept me much longer in his study. He loved to take a paragraph of mine and polish it – usually just one – breaking up a sentence, modulating the rhythm or deleting an adjective. He became totally absorbed and I realised what deep joys writing gave him, joys I found easy to share, for to be a writer had been the great ambition of my life since I was a boy of eleven – novelist, poet, historian. Circumstances had made me an historian, but the road was still long and full of pot-holes, some of a cataclysmic nature.

I secured my PhD in 1936, my examiners Professor Temperley of Cambridge and Professor Keith Feiling of Oxford. Feiling showed himself to be a generous scholar for I had spent several pages of my thesis making a mockery of some of his scholarship – the inaccuracies of his quotations, his use of suspect evidence and the inadequacy of his analysis of party. He was very generous because my thesis was faulty – not in material or argument, but in presentation. I was insecure, leaving too much for footnotes, placing too little extended argument in the text; also the structure was poor and the writing far too rapid and unconsidered – at times careless. Above all it lacked the essential quality of authority: partly I now think because I failed to tackle Namier's methodology head-on. I was too frightened of my future career to take on such a giant. It took me the best part of twenty years, more than half of my academic career, to get Namier and his works into true perspective.

And there was another complicating factor. Butterfield and Namier were locked in a kind of mortal combat. Namier hated Butterfield, a hatred that deepened year after year and became a kind of obsessional rage. He spoke of him with sneering bitterness, arranged for his books to be savaged by anonymous reviewers and wrecked his reputation whenever opportunity offered. As for Butterfield, he was rather frightened of Namier. He rejected Namier's historical work but not directly. He fenced at Namier, throwing in a dart whenever he could, and danced away from the missiles Namier hurled at him. Yet Butterfield never talked to me about Namier, never interested himself in my work to see whether or not it helped his case against Namier. In a very odd way Butterfield always ignored my historical work, until I produced Walpole. Until then his usual question was to ask me if I was writing a novel! Yet I am sure the endless years of delay of Butterfield's major work, *George III, Lord North and the People* was due to his fear of Namier. Their conflict, however, probably made me over-cautious.

As for Trevelyan, in spite of the one warm review he had given him, Namier was not regarded as a serious competitor. Walking round his beautiful dene at Hallington he stopped and barked out: 'Namier – a great research worker but no historian.' Unfortunately Namier was central to my working life. In the scholarly world at large Namier was *the* historian of eighteenth-century politics, a man whose reputation grew and did not diminish for a great deal of my working life. So this collection of my scholarly articles must be prefaced by my final assessment of his work after his death in 1960, strengthened by the remarkable insights into his character, derived from his biography, written by his wife.

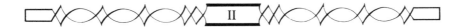

II

Sir Lewis Namier

All of my professional work, the little published before the war, and the major part which came after, was always written with Namier in mind. I appreciated his immense qualities; the industry, the precision, the insight into politicians and their actions. For many decades, until his late marriage, I pitied him as a man – lonely, deprived, hungry for love. I thought, also, that in many aspects his work was wrong and his methods not creative but destructive of historical understanding. So it is appropriate to begin with him: first a review of the extraordinary biography published by his wife Julia in 1971 in which she lay bare the seismic faults in his character through which his passions boiled and tumbled. An anguished man, indeed. The other is an assessment of his work made after he died.

Julia Namier, Anguished Historian: Lewis Namier, a Biography

The most disturbing feature of this book is the photograph of Sir Lewis Namier on the jacket, for in spite of the smile of pleasure that is just beginning to illumine his face, the eyes and the set of the mouth betray years of pain, anguish and, perhaps, fear, not of a physical but a spiritual kind.

That face we saw often enough but few noticed the anguish as they listened to Namier's harsh voice recounting his adventures with eighteenth-century records, or expounding the shortcomings of his professional colleagues, or explaining the tangled diplomatic skein of the pre-war years. He could be boring, he could be obsessive, but always one felt oneself to be in the presence of a great man of quite uncommon intellectual gifts. His memory was enviable, for it possessed extraordinary range and great exactitude: his arguments were always powerful

10

and sharp-edged; he could from time to time phrase his ideas in telling images.

And yet all of his work had an unfinished quality – brilliant, suggestive essays that seemed to promise books that would rival those of the greatest historians. They were never written. And this extraordinary book by Lady Namier helps us to understand why. Behind that careful scholar, so seemingly dominated by intellectual considerations, raged a torn and tormented man, obsessed, guilt-ridden, a character who might have stepped straight from the novels of his favourite author, Dostoievsky.

Namier was born into a family of Polish-Jewish landowners, who were rapidly ceasing to be Jews: indeed Namier rarely, if ever, entered a synagogue until he was an adult, and his family seemed to have maintained absolutely no Jewish customs or ritual at all. So there was Namier's first burden – how could one be a non-Jewish Jew? His family in the end became Catholic, but he refused, although he was already a Christian: indeed Lady Namier maintains that he was probably a Christian in belief as early as his first years at Balliol.

Although no longer practising Jews, Namier's family were not accepted by the Polish aristocracy and landowners as true gentry: furthermore, Namier deliberately rejected his future as a Polish land-owner by drifting to the West, taking British citizenship and quarrelling very sharply with his father. Yet he was cut to the marrow when he discovered on his father's death that the Polish estates had gone to his sister and not himself.

Jew and not Jew, Pole and not Pole, landowner and not landowner: to these contradictions Namier added another – a married man who lived for most of his life as a bachelor. Powerful sexuality was a part of his nature, but often the objects of his love, at least until he reached middle age, were totally unsatisfactory. His first wife – a mysterious and shadowy figure in this book – seems to have been totally unsuitable. She deserted him for another man, but only long after he had deserted her spiritually. And as with all the sorry scrapes that Namier got himself into, he bore a great burden of guilt, knowing his responsibility.

His outer life was little better than his inner. The passionate loyalties that he created were outweighed by the furious enmities. His judgements about his own career were rarely sound, and so he flitted from job to job – academic, journalistic, Zionist organisations, and even commercial, until he landed up in the unlikely post of Professor of Modern History at Manchester, due ironically to a favourable review by G. M. Trevelyan in the *Guardian*. And there he stayed. Distinguished as he was, other and older universities kept their doors closed – envy and fear and mean-mindedness had their triumph, and thereby hardened the least attractive part of Namier's nature — his savagery towards professional rivals and the remorseless vindictiveness that led him to stalk his prey for decades.

In such a life there could be little harmony and less peace. Indeed it is not surprising that Namier's life was riddled with insomnia and psychosomatic illnesses, including semi-paralysis of his right hand. He turned hungrily for support to Christian belief, to daily prayer, to a variety of psychoanalysts. He remained burdened to the end with a sense of men's evil and with the gravity of his own guilt.

Lady Namier tells the story of this extraordinary man — titanic in feeling as well as in intellect — with candour; indeed at times with surprising candour. Naturally her sympathies are always with 'L' and she does, I think, minimise the sadistic streak, more destructive of himself than others, that ran through his nature. The earlier part of his life is derived from notes dictated by Namier before his death: at times it reads very much as an *apologia pro vita sua*, but even if it is, how many of us could be so candid as this?

Certainly, whatever revisions subsequent biographers may make, this will remain the basic study: an inseparable part of the Namier story. What still has to be explored is the connection between his creative work and the passionate drives and obsessive complexities of his nature. Work obviously was an anodyne but it was more than that: it was also a search for security, which until the last decade of his life he had never known.

The Atomic Historian

There have been more popular historians in this century than Sir Lewis Namier but none, except perhaps for F. W. Maitland, who has achieved such adulation from his professional colleagues. There were always far more reservations felt about the work of R. H. Tawney, who came in for a scholarly battering late in life of an intensity that Namier never had to face. There have been other historians of high quality whose work has received, and rightly so, great admiration from fellow scholars — Powicke, Stenton, Clapham, Knowles — to name but the obvious, yet great scholars as they were, they were never attributed such originality as Namier, nor were they believed to have created a new technique in historical investigation or founded a school of historians. Nor, one might add, were their careers so fissured as Namier's. Their reputations moved steadily forwards: Namier's was much more erratic.

Namier's professional reputation was not easily made. He moved from an insecure academic post at Balliol to insecure business appointments in New York. He took great personal risks in the 1920s, never playing safe but pursuing relentlessly his scholarly obsession with the first years of the reign of George III. Two major books appeared in 1929 and 1930, *The Structure of Politics at the Accession of George III* and *England in the Age of the American Revolution*, brilliantly authoritative but, as we shall see, utterly misleading titles. Their reception was mixed, and the second book had a somewhat poor press. The impression they made, however, was effective enough for Namier to be elected to the Professorship of Modern History at Manchester, the only established academic post that he ever held. He occupied it for 22 years. He continued, however, to live in London, travelling up each week to do his necessary academic chores. As a Jew, Namier was naturally profoundly disturbed by the conflicts of the 1930s. He worked actively for the Jewish National Home in Palestine and attempted to expose the folly of appeasement. He had long-standing links, through earlier work in the Foreign Office, with government circles. Naturally he was drawn to the group which clustered about Churchill, Eden and Duff Cooper. Although profoundly anti-German, there was in Namier an equal hatred of all forms of radicalism. For him, Britain's social structure was as near to perfection as corrupt men might get. No one could speak to him for ten minutes without realising the depth and strength of his conservatism or his veneration for monarchy, aristocracy and tradition. Public affairs preoccupied him and it was not until the late-1940s that Namier's interest in the eighteenth century revived. During his last few years at Manchester he helped to resuscitate the project, moribund since before the war, of an authoritative *History of Parliament*, financed by public funds. For the next ten years he dedicated his life to his section of this history. These were the years when his reputation took flight and all the long-delayed honours came pouring in – honorary degrees, knighthood, and above all the adulation from younger professional historians. The years of neglect were over, and he savoured his triumph. Even Oxford paid him tribute.

A chequered career for a man of great ability usually argues either a difficult personality or times inappropriate for his ideas. Namier carried the double burden. Namier was blessed, or cursed, by an enormous weight of temperament. Even if he sat still and said nothing, his presence could almost be physically felt. His eyes were sharp, guarded, watchful: his mouth thin, firm and somewhat cruel. He possessed a heavy powerful body and a strong bone structure that was noticeable in his jaw and forehead. He had very little natural charm, no small talk, his wit was intellectual and laced with razor blades, his conversation obsessional. He revered accuracy and allowed no conversational slip to pass uncorrected. He never hid his contempt for colleagues whose standards fell below his own either in scholarship or intellectual clarity. He enjoyed both an enemy and victim, yet he could easily be touched by kindness. Like many savage men, he possessed a streak of sentimentality. G. M. Trevelyan represented in his books all that Namier thought, professionally speaking, well-nigh worthless – yet he never spoke anything but kindly of Trevelyan and generously avoided reviewing his works. And nearly twenty years afterwards he constantly referred, with a kind of wonder, to what he considered to be Trevelyan's generosity – namely his review of his second book in the *Guardian*. After all, Trevelyan's father, Sir George Otto, was one of Namier's major targets, an historian who had totally misunderstood the politics of the 1760s.

To those who had identified their work with his, who had given him loyal discipleship, Namier became formidably attached. So long as they were unswervingly his, he was entirely theirs. Words of praise, rare jewels in his prose, gleamed in his reviews of their works. Namier could make reputations as well as break them. In both cases his judgements tended to excess.

The difficulty of his temperament had certainly held back his career in the 30s. Although a man of far-ranging intelligence, his major preoccupations were confined, narrow and deeply obsessional. Indeed he was a curious mixture of the fine Talmudic specialist, excited by the minutiae of historical investigation, ravished by detail, and a creative artist, alive to the nuances of human psychology. Once people came into his ken, his mind moved into a different dimension: imaginative, perceptive, at times daring, capable of using and accepting techniques that bordered on the bogus and gullible. The psychology of the unconscious fascinated him and so did graphology. He believed implicitly in the latter and, it is said, listened with reverence to the opinions of a Viennese graphologist, whether the handwriting were Charles James Fox's or the applicants for a post in the *History of Parliament*. Be that as it may, there was this remarkable contrast. The exact scholar who was obsessionally concerned about the day-to-day machinations of Mr Basset at Penryn in Cornwall, who savaged the slightest error in detail, who, above all, scorned historical theories or broad analysis of historical situations and circumstances, who, indeed, believed that the history of ideas was not worth the paper it was written on, and the *littérateur*, for whom all psychological theories were fodder: such a mixture of myopia and imagination is rare in historical scholarship. In Namier, it had singular results.

First, let us take the myopic scholarship by which in the end Namier's reputation will survive or die. What exactly did he do? And what was the famous Namier method?

When Namier set to work in the 1920s, there was a traditional interpretation of the English past which was called the Whig interpretation of history: not entirely accurately, for many Tories accepted it.

This dealt with the growth both of political liberty and of party. For this interpretation 1760 was a vital date, a watershed, as Sir Keith Feiling called it in his *History of the Tory Party*. George III, according to this view, educated on a diet of Bolingbroke's *Patriot King*, not only wished, but set about reassuming the powers of the royal prerogative which his grandfather and great grandfather had lost. To do so, he had to break the great Whig families who had imprisoned the Crown. This he did by restoring Tories to favour and by buying support through a lavish use of pensions and patronage. His remorseless use of the King's Friends and the insistence on his own policies led to the follies of the Wilkes' crisis and the disasters of the American War of Independence and, above all, to a revival of the Whig party under its leader Rockingham and its prophet Burke, who exposed George III's attempt at personal rule and secured a return to constitutional monarchy.

Namier blew this sky high: not by polemics but by patient, detailed investigation of each and every Member of Parliament – this was Namier's famous method. First he investigated who the Members of Parliament were in 1761 and how they got there. What was their ancestry – Whig or Tory? Did they get their seats through government influence or Court money? Who and what had their loyalty – the Crown, Whig magnates, Tory leaders, Whig principles or what? Exact, patient, tiresome and boring, this type of research needs to sift endless correspondence and a myriad of books on local and family history. About 1000 or so men need to be known in precise detail. Only by rigorously defining and pursuing fixed and limited goals can one hope to dominate this daunting plethora of facts. So Namier kept to the House of Commons in 1761, indeed restricted his investigation there to carefully selected areas where the Crown influence might be regarded as permanent, such as in the Cornish boroughs or where it might be weak, as in Shropshire. And then he investigated George III's secret-service fund, item by item. And he analysed how the Duke of Newcastle lost in 1763 so easily power which he had held for a lifetime. A painstaking biographical analysis was undertaken to discover just who voted for and against Wilkes or the Stamp Act. The larger problem of George III's constitutional or unconstitutional behaviour was left: first of all, Namier insisted, the detail must be truthfully discovered and exactly described. The result, stated simply, was this. All George III's ministers were overwhelmingly Whig: government money for elections was, in terms of the total budget, trivial: the Whigs dominated Parliament on all the benches and they voted on either side on all the great questions: principles counted for little, accommodation between Tories and Whigs everywhere abounded: loyalty to group leaders was great and so was loyalty to the throne. In short the established interpretation was nonsense. There was no great party of King's Friends, there was no revival of the Tory Party, and Namier went on to claim that George III, uneducated in Bolingbroke's ideas, behaved with constitutional propriety. Here was no pseudo-Stuart, but a hardworking, deeply conscientious man of low intelligence and small experience. The errors and follies of Wilkes and America were those of his Whig ministers, not his.

Yet much of this remained buried in the highly detailed essays that formed Namier's first two books. He was, however, incensed when his work was blithely ignored, as it was initially, not only by Feiling, but also by a host of others; even more incensed when the honours of the academic world went to the exponents of the time-honoured, if false, interpretation. Also the times themselves were unpropitious for Namier. The 1930s were riven by ideological strife: political ideas, the conflict of classes, the aspirations of the masses appeared to be the true political realities. All historians writing of self-interest, of the ineffectiveness of ideas in relation to the realities of political power, of status, or of inherited position had little appeal. And Namier himself did not follow up his books. His Ford Lectures, given in 1934, remained unpublished. By the end of the war, it seemed as if Namier's work on the eighteenth century was over, and that he would be appreciated only by a small band of constitutional historians working in that field.

But from 1950 his reputation flared into prominence. The times had become appropriate. In America the consensus school of historians, who maintained that the political conflicts of America were illusory and that the bulk of American people had always been united in their aspirations, were dominant and highly regarded. Not only were ideologies folly, they were even worse — ineffective, delusions which never really motivated political men, who were more concerned with self-interest, power and loyalty to the pack. The mood of the 1950s was deeply conservative: altruism wore the air of absurdity. Hence Namier's pointillism, his insistence on studying each politician in isolation seemed very relevant. The eighteenth-century world which he depicted was barren of issues, ideas, deep conflicts or warring classes, and party meant nothing. His work revealed universal truths about politics, not only the truth about politics in the 1760s. Applied to other times, Namier's surgical method would, doubtless, expose similar hypocrisies in politics.

So his reputation climbed; yet there were critics, principally Sir Herbert Butterfield, whom Namier had always treated vindictively. Their skirmish, however, was mainly about secondary matters; Butterfield attacked the limitations of the Namier technique, not Namier's whole approach to political history. Yet he was very vulnerable. Namier's titles always claimed far more than the books contained. *The Structure of Politics* ignored the House of Lords, refused to consider the politics of London, or Westminster, paid no attention to the interrelationship of the City, Treasury, and the formation of policy. Public opinion might not have existed, and there was no consideration whatever of the power of the press, either metropolitan or provincial. By studying one not very typical election, Namier managed to throw eighteenth-century politics out of focus. He ignored not only most of the electorate, but also the political nation, which was far more extensive than the electorate itself. The growing antipathy of the public to the politics he described did not seem significant to him. The *Structure* was a collection of essays on limited subjects with a great deal of the politics of the 1760s left out.

Namier was the victim of his obsession with detail. Politics cannot be understood in terms even of a decade. There was no need to attack Namier's method: his omissions were far more serious and damning. Yet scarcely anyone challenged him on these lines.

Namier himself was not without intimations of this limitation of vision. He was aware that the system of politics he had described for the early 1760s did not last long and that parties, reborn in the American conflict, soon rose again in effectiveness: a subject which he always hoped to treat but never did. In an admirable essay, *Monarchy and the Party System*, he exposed the complexities as well as the hypocrisies of party labels at Westminster, but also discussed, even if he did not explain, their realities in the provinces. He delighted in exposing the cant of politics, and God knows there has always been a surfeit of it, but his scepticism about political issues and their public support was too strong. Eighteenth-century England was riven by political issues, issues which divided families and friends as much as Suez or appeasement, and these were not only the great issues – Wilkes and America, but also the less obvious, such as the role of monarchy or the reform of institutions. These questions agitated a considerable part of the nation and the powerful debates that ensued influenced the development of English politics and the position of the monarchy over the next half century. Namier provides a classic example of an historian who can get every detail correct, indeed write nothing false, yet by exclusion create a misinterpretation of an age as misleading as the one that he was trying to replace.

Professional historians engaged on eighteenth-century subjects are paying less and less attention to Namier's methods or his results. No one now would seriously argue that his technique and his conclusions have any relevance either to the early or to the late eighteenth century. In his own precise period, interest is now returning to the ideological conflicts which he ignored – for example, the strong roots in English politics of the political attitude adopted by the American colonists in the 1760s. Again the growth of a sense of political and social identity in the West Midlands, in the Scottish Lowlands, in Lancashire and Yorkshire, which was to influence profoundly the growth of politics in the nineteenth century, is of more fundamental importance than the Duke of New-castle's secret-service list. Of equal importance is the revitalisation of the electorate, a matter nearer to Namier's field, yet, of course, ignored by him. These, and many cognate problems, will add fresh dimensions to the understanding of mid-eighteenth-century politics, and bring back the dimension of time that Namier carefully excluded.

So where does Namier stand? At, I think, the crossroads of his repu-tation. He will remain a cult hero of conservative historians, and that means the bulk of the historical profession. His animus towards altruism, his cynicism towards human motivation, his reverence for inherited status, his belief in the authority of possessions, his near-idolatry for the English landed classes and for parliamentary monarchy will ensure a respectful and laudatory public within the establishment.

To those historians working in the field, whether it be the huge one of English politics between 1660 and 1832, or the narrower one of the politics of the 1760s, his limitations will for some time become more apparent than his contribution. This will be salutary, so long as it does not go too far, for his achievements are positive and will endure. For the wide general public that reads history, that still delights in Gibbon and Macaulay and in, say, Neale and Taylor in the present, he must seem a minor figure. Namier never mastered the art of narrative. Indeed, he never wrote a history book in its true sense; only essays. And his style, often praised, is too often gritty, overloaded with quotations and his prose poorly constructed: indeed not very readable – this is particu-larly true of his longer essays, less so of his shorter ones. And Trevelyan's terse comment 'great research worker, no historian' seems appropriate.

His incursions into the diplomatic history of the twentieth century have already begun to fade into oblivion. This will never happen to his eighteenth-century work. Within its limitations, which to my mind are serious, it is both brilliant and final. No one can ever talk about party again, as they did in the pre-Namierite days, for the first two decades of George III's reign. The simplicities are over, replaced by a far more sophisticated, realistic and factually grounded picture. And I would go further than this – the imaginative side of Namier, his intuitions about people, strike me as being brilliant, profound and original. He was a master of the miniature biography – read his vignettes of George III or Daniel Pulteney, and there are scores of others. For me he is one of our best historical essayists. He lacked the large literary gifts that make a Gibbon or a Ranke, but within his narrow compass he has few rivals.

His weakness lay in his attitude to history and to life. He eschewed too rigorously the problems of historical and social change; indeed, he largely evaded the problems of time and its effect on human institutions. His obsessive nature and his deep suspicion of generalisation drove him into narrow confines and history cannot, will never, be understood when limited to hours, days and months.

It is a matter of decades and centuries. A comparison with the greatest historian of Namier's generation, Marc Bloch, places Namier in focus. Bloch possessed the same meticulous care for detail, the same almost obsessive interest in precision, but Bloch possessed a far, far greater compassion for humanity itself than Namier, if less for individuals. And it was this larger vision of mankind, so sensitive to social structure and the nature of historical change, that made Bloch the finer, the nobler historian. And it was his wide love of man that turned Bloch into a radical: his compassion was fortified by his experience as an historian. Namier for most of his life was more conscious of malice, evil and double-dealing, which drove him into conservatism and a narrow, seemingly unassailable specialisation. As Bloch once said, no one can be a really great historian without loving life, an attitude which Namier would have thought absurd. Humanity for him was both too corrupt and too ridiculous to love. His own nature was too fissured. Namier was the victim of his temperament. He could hate, and he enjoyed his cruelty; he was rarely magnanimous; all of which argues an aching, bruised and slightly fearful inner life. In obsessional scholarship Namier found relief and security. Only in the last decade of his life did success and personal happiness mellow his spirit a little. But it was too late, had it even been possible, to fuse his remarkable gifts and so turn him from a brilliant research worker into a great historian.

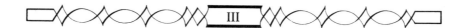

The Persistence of Political Attitudes

When Sir Lewis Namier's reputation was reaching its greatest height in the 1950s, there was a scholar, Dr Caroline Robbins of Bryn Mawr, whose ruggedness of temperament and elephantine stamina was working on a massive volume which ran totally counter to Namier's work. It is doubtful if she could have written and worked in Britain on her project, certainly not with the same support or with the same approval which she was given by perceptive American scholars. Her position is made clear in my Introduction to her collected articles but a little needs to be added.

Apart from myself I do not think that there was one British historian of the eighteenth century who realised the importance and value of her work. Namier behaved monstrously towards her. She applied for a D.Litt at her old University, London, and he was appointed assessor. He failed her totally and damningly – a fact in which, alas, he took pride: Butterfield who, after all, had worked on cognate subjects (particularly in *The Englishman and His History* 1944), remained exceedingly circumspect, avoiding all discussion of her work. Namier's view was that her book was a non-subject. He could not believe that a few pamphleteers and newspapermen had the slightest influence on the pursuit of political power. The book he thought badly constructed and worse written. Certainly it is not easy reading, but equally certainly very rewarding to do so.

When writing my life of Sir Robert Walpole, I had been struck by the kind of books which his father and grandfather bought; they betrayed their worries and bafflement about the nature of political society; about the divine nature of kingship and the political order; about the importance of law, the corruption of constitutions, the morality of political action, the virtues of republics. And their book rooms could be matched by others of men like them caught up by wars and constitutional experiments of seventeenth-century Britain. Never before or since have the

English gentry been so cogniscent of political, moral and religious philosophy or read so much of it. Of course, this habit did not vanish with William III and Mary II ensconced in Kensington Palace. It made sense to see the debates lingering on and on, as Caroline Robbins had first suspected and then revealed. *Cato's Letters*, written to denounce Walpole in a specific political situation, not only resonated with the past but rang out to the future, to America and to a revival of radicalism. Political men might seek power, but even in the 1760s it could be for a political purpose. There was no one more self-seeking than Edmund Burke. Much of his so-called political policy was devised for a particular situation, but what he devised could have a philosophical meaning for other times and for other men. Following the Introduction to Caroline Robbins, therefore, is an earlier review about Edmund Burke – the eighteenth-century philosopher whom Namier, and his assistant John Brooke, loathed: loathed because they thought him an over-valued hypocrite – his ideas a mere fig leaf.

Caroline Robbins, Introduction to Absolute Liberty

For much of her professional life, Caroline Robbins was a lonely historian for her work ran counter to what was then fashionable. This might not have mattered so very greatly in many areas of British history but the field that Professor Robbins chose was the political culture of eighteenth-century England in which the giant scholar, Sir Lewis Namier, ruled with baleful eye and acid wit. And Sir Lewis did not believe in political ideas; he did not believe much in continuities in politics. Politics, he thought, were to be found in the corridors of power, in the interplay of personalities at the centre, or in the expediencies which events, at times, forced on politicians. He dismissed Edmund Burke as a humbug; allowed that Hume was shrewd up to a point but, for him, the clear-eyed political realist was John Robinson, the Secretary of the Treasury who knew the men of power in constituencies, in government and out of government; he rarely, if ever, bothered to ask himself what the political orientation was of any man. He preferred to know what was wanted in money, office, patronage. He was as indifferent to political ideas and traditions as Namier himself. One of Namier's favourite metaphors was that politicians were like packs of hounds chasing the same fox (power and profit); packs which took up issues like strong scents only to drop them if they failed to lead to the quarry.

Professor Robbins was not interested in short-term political action. Her instinct for the realities of human behaviour led her to believe that

politics could only be understood over time; that time was an essential
feature of political activity as well as day-to-day political action. And,
of course, she was right. The overwhelming weakness of Namier's work
is that it ignores the dimension of time and this led him naturally enough
to ignore not only the persistence of ideas but also the persistence of
traditions of political behaviour or that the way to political power might
for some men lie through a political ideology. Or, put in less grandiose
terms, in political concepts which appealed to men and women because
they seemed just and rational and inherent in British political history.

Although Caroline Robbins's apprenticeship as an historian was spent
editing an important parliamentary diary (by John Milward) of the
1660s, she had no intention of limiting her interests to a decade or even
a reign. She has taken the period from the English Civil War to the
American War of Independence as her bailiwick and the question which
she had sought to answer not only in her books but also in a stream of
articles, has been – how far did the ideas of the seventeenth-century
political philosophers and pamphleteers, particularly those who wrote
to support the idea of commonwealth, influence both the American
politicians who were in favour of independence and also those Britons
who supported the American claims and were responsible for the revival
of radicalism in Britain during the second half of the eighteenth century?
And all that she has written over a very long professional life has related
directly or indirectly to this question.

Between the death of John Locke and the emergence of Edmund
Burke, the British scene seemed curiously devoid of political philosophers
of any stature. Bolingbroke had some claim but his writings owed, it
seemed, little or nothing to the seventeenth-century radicals neither did
the sharp and pertinent essays of Hume. But Caroline Robbins was
shrewd and realistic enough to realise that climates of ideas, even the
continuity of political attitudes and concepts, often owes little to the
giants of political philosophy and a great deal to lesser men – pamphleteers, journalists, publicists of all kinds. Her great book which Namier,
I suppose, never bothered to read, *The Eighteenth Century
Commonwealthman* (Cambridge, Mass., 1959), gave new life to half-
forgotten men – Molesworth, Toland, Gordon, Trenchard, Thomas
Hollis and Brand Hollis and demonstrated how the ideas of the seventeenth-century Commonwealthman – particularly men such as March-
amont Nedham and Henry Neville who believed, with the intensity of
Locke, in the inviolability of property – persisted throughout the early
eighteenth century and began to enjoy a revival in the 1750s and 1760s.
This work, not greatly appreciated when it first appeared, has now
established itself as one of the most important and seminal monographs
on eighteenth-century political culture published since the war. Its influ-

ence has been very great, particularly on the work of Bernard Bailyn whose *Origins of American Politics* owes much to Caroline Robbins – indeed, there is no political historian of eighteenth-century Britain or America who is not deeply in her debt.

Although this major book is the foundation of Caroline Robbins's reputation, she has been a very productive historian, considering the burden of teaching, lecturing and administrating which she bore for so many years at Bryn Mawr, much to her pupils' profit. One might have wished for more books; one longed for a life of Andrew Marvell to whom she has dedicated so much thought and scholarship: indeed, as with other creative and stimulating historians, there are many books one would have wished to have had. Nevertheless the corpus is impressive. After *The Eighteenth-Century Commonwealthman, Two English Republican Tracts* is perhaps her most important contribution to the history of political thought because Professor Robbins prefaced her edition of Henry Neville's *Plato Redivivus* and Walter Moyle's *An Essay Upon The Constitution of the Roman Government* with a long introduction which surveyed the republican thinking of seventeenth-century England. But underpinning this book there was a very solid foundation of articles that stretched back over decades.

Caroline Robbins possesses formidable equipment as a scholar – immense industry and a scholarship that is exceptionally wide-ranging, indeed rare in a modern professional historian. One has only to turn to the very first article in this volume to read Professor Robbins at her best. William Popple is a typical subject for her. Ignored by almost all historians, he was, nevertheless, a very important figure in the circle which gathered about John Locke. He was the nephew of Andrew Marvell and the friend of William Penn as well as Locke whose *Letter Concerning Toleration* he translated. As a believer in the absolute liberty of conscience in relation to religion, he is a part of the great tradition of radical thinkers. To give him substance, Professor Robbins needed to chase him first from the East Yorkshire Record Office at Beverley to the notarial records of the Gironde, via the manuscript depositories at the Bodleian, British Library, the Public Record Office, the National Archives, Paris, to say nothing of a side-step to the Huntington Library, California. And the range of printed sources is equally impressive. Nor is this mere antiquarianism for Professor Robbins brings out Popple's close link with Isaac Papin who, until converted to Catholicism, played a very important role in preaching religious toleration in Rotterdam, Danzig, Hamburg and Berlin, particularly against the strict Calvinists. Indeed the article lays bare a section of the European republic of letters that was important in the beginnings of the European Enlightenment. The article also deals with the Lockeian circle, The Dry Club, that was concerned to debate the problems of religion, as well as Popple's involvement in the Board of Trade: indeed the article is as rich as a plum pudding and many a professional historian would have been very happy to turn it into a short monograph. Of course Miss Robbins can illuminate the well worn fields of scholarship as well as the obscure. Her short article on the influence of Machiavelli displays how acute her perceptions are whatever the subject may be. Nor must Professor Robbins be regarded as a mere British historian; her contributions to our understanding of Revolutionary America have been of great importance. Indeed the whole thrust of her work has been towards a deeper understanding of the men of the American Revolution, steeped as they were in England and its history.

Edmund Burke and his Cult

The world of political ideas is an odd world to move around in, and none odder than Russell Kirk's *Conservative Mind*, in which Edmund Burke is revealed as the great prophet of Anglo-American conservatism. Throughout this book, the implication is that radicals are addicted to non-realistic, richly sentimental, over-optimistic abstractions, whereas conservatives are down-to-earth men, whose ideas are firmly anchored in a hard-headed appraisal of human nature and a deep sense of the history of mankind. Quaint, indeed, to think that 'equality' is more abstract that 'tradition', that 'moral essence' should mean more than 'human need', that reverence for the past should have a higher moral value than hope for the future. Above all, there is the monumental self-deception of the conservative that anti-rationalism is wisdom. Russell Kirk quotes Keith Feiling with solemn approval: 'Every Tory is a realist. He knows there are great forces in heaven and earth that man's philosophy cannot plumb or fathom. We do wrong to deny it, when we are told that we do not trust human reason: we do not and we may not.' Distrust of reason: here is the self-revealed core of conservative belief and so, as we might expect, a few sneering asides are made by Kirk about a 'world smudged with industrialism' and 'corrosive intellectual atomism'. And it comes as no surprise that at the end of his essay on Burke he should drool about 'the tidy half-timbered inn, the great oaks and the quiet lanes of Beaconsfield' and sneer at the villas, housing estates and light industry that have bitten deep into Buckinghamshire countryside since Burke's day. Here is Tory realism with a vengeance: like the half-timbered inn, it is largely phony. The rationalisation of prejudice, the sanctification of the status quo, the attribution of historical inevitability and Divine Providence to inequality and human suffering certainly acquired its most persuasive apologist in Burke and so, perhaps, it is not surprising that he is rapidly becoming a cult.

As well as a cult, Burke is a serious historical figure. The mass of his papers and the variety of his correspondence, to say nothing of the devious nature of his life, have, however, made him a professional historical problem of the first magnitude. Professor Copeland has organised a team of dedicated Anglo-American editors, and the volumes of his correspondence are flowing from the press, beautifully and skilfully edited in the highest traditions of American scholarship. This type of task is so much more professionally and skilfully accomplished by American editors: and British scholars would never have achieved so definitive an edition if left to their own devices. After the correspondence, one can only hope that the papers will follow and then a critical edition of the published works, for after all Burke is one of the founders of European conservatism and no matter how silly and self-deceiving his views may be, they deserve, historically speaking, a proper treatment. They require understanding but not an idolatrous revival.

Many scholars will regard Carl Cone as being immensely venturesome in producing a long two-volume life of Burke before the essential work of editing is completed. Burke was, rightly from his own point of view, extremely sensitive about many of his activities, particularly those which involved money and his relatives. His namesake, William, whom he called cousin, was an adventurer devoid of any sense of financial morality, whose sole aim in life was to make a fortune by any means that came handy. Although a fortune eluded him, he bore his burden of personal debt (£20,000 alone to Lord Verney) with indifference, if not panache, and lived the life of eighteenth-century affluence. Burke was not only devoted to him but also involved in many of his dubious financial transactions. Burke's relations with his brother, Richard, almost as devious as William, remain equally obscure, and far more light on the more disreputable side of Burke's life may yet be forthcoming. It will not, however, alter the essential picture. The vast amount of detail about Burke's life and politics, already known, make this huge biography very well worth while. Delay would not have improved it. Again, like the edition of Burke's correspondence, this biography is typical of much sound American professional scholarship. There is little analysis, little judgement, but a steady, accurate, comprehensive narrative of Burke's life, interspersed with an excellent précis of what he said and wrote. As an account of Burke's life it will survive many generations. For an interpretation of Burke's character, however, it will have to be supplemented by the brilliant, brief biography which John Brooke contributed to the *History of Parliament*.

Brooke and Namier have been castigated for their treatment of Burke, for taking a low view of his character, for dismissing so many of his ideas as self-deceiving humbug, and for accusing him of creating the absurd mythology which has clouded so much of the history of George III's reign. Wrongly, it seems to me. Burke was not a simple man. His nature demanded action and constant justification for what he did, intended to do, and even hoped others might do. Rationalisation was a deep psychological need, so his pursuit of power and fame required to be justified in moral and philosophic terms. Hence his concern lay rather with political attitudes than political action. He was led to those attitudes by the necessities of his own life – money, patronage, status. Yet no matter how self-seeking the motives, or self-righteous the implications, the views which Burke adumbrated must be judged as views, as ideas, as political attitudes. Although it helps us understand his character to juxtapose his ardent advocacy of the economical reform of the Royal Household with his avaricious demand when in office for places, sinecures and pensions for his dependants, this does not invalidate his arguments. There is no essential contradiction between Burke as a great political philosopher and the character of him drawn by Brooke.

There is a need to know his character and circumstances to appraise the emotional force of his ideas and why they have struck such a sympathetic echo in the unconscious minds of generations of men: for, in many ways, Burke persuades by rhetoric rather than by argument. As Namier and Brooke have been quick to point out, Burke's exceptionally difficult family life deeply influenced his attitude to authority and power. His mother was neurotic, possibly she suffered from mental illness; his father was tyrannical. Rejecting his father's plans for his career, Burke arrived in London with little but his wits to sustain him. Although a gifted and ambitious man could move about eighteenth-century English society with ease, he could never hope to feel that deep sense of belonging that came naturally to those born within it. An alien adventurer of remarkable literary gifts, perceptive insight into human nature, powerful if disturbed character, and a greedy ambition for affluence, Burke needed patrons as he needed roots: he wanted to find the security that as a child he had never known, and as a man would always elude him.

This sensitivity to the needs of his own security was generalised and projected with great subtlety by Burke not only into political action but also into political thought. Insecurities in all their varied forms riddle most human lives creating needs for habits, rituals, shibboleths, even historical tradition. And it was in this area that Burke's own personal compulsions fused with the needs of mankind, and he possessed the gifts of thought and language that could give a sense of inevitable destiny to this urge for security. And yet, of course, this alone could not have been responsible for his vast reputation with ensuing generations. In Burke's world insecurity was growing – the revolt of America, the stirrings in Ireland, the onslaught of the French Revolution, the turmoil in India, all threatened the security of eighteenth-century society. But insecurity went deeper than this, and continued to grow: new forms of wealth in commerce and industry challenged the supremacy of those great landed families whom Burke liked to picture as the great oaks of England. Graver still were the growing threats of violence from the lower classes, interlaced with cries for liberty: and the ever urgent demands for reform and a wider democracy. In Burke's day the voice of the *sans-culotte* echoed round the seats of power and made their occupants nervous. To natural psychological insecurities which beset men were added, therefore, fears for wealth and authority. And as these insecurities grew with the developing social and industrial revolutions of the nineteenth and twentieth centuries, so grew the veneration for Burke. What for him had been largely a psychological need became a philosophy of anti-democratic greed.

Burke, throughout his life, operated in many dimensions, but two are of major importance – his contribution to the political structure of eighteenth-century England and his general political philosophy. The former is a bone of contention between scholars. What he tried to do, and his motives here are of no great importance, was to give a greater unity of principle and a firmer consistency in action to the Rockingham Whigs, to transform them in their own and in other people's estimation from a faction to a party. In the highly personalised politics of eighteenth-century England fragmentation of political groups took place with ease and frequency, making it so much easier for an active monarch, such as George III, to influence policy and decision. So Burke tried to weld the Rockingham Whigs into a party of known principles which would act consistently in opposition and enter office as a body on their own terms, which they finally achieved in 1782. Certainly this crusade of Burke's helped to revitalise politics and helped to create the sense that opposition should be based on political and intellectual alternatives to the government in office rather than mere factional warfare. Although much of Burke's own analysis of the contemporary political scene was biased and wrong, nevertheless he remains one of the most significant figures in the constitutional history of Britain in the late eighteenth century, and this aspect of Burke's career is exhaustively and admirably dealt with by Professor Cone.

However, Burke's major dimension lies in his role as the founder of modern conservatism – now the object of a special and dedicated lobby among American historians, who are steadily pushing Burkeian studies into political philosophy courses as a means of propaganda. Burke believed that wisdom was instinctive and religious rather than rational

or intellectual. Time and Providence, the slow revelation of moral law
and moral purpose, human wisdom gradually accreted over the centuries
like a geological sediment, the poverty of reason compared with the
Divine Plan which mysteriously binds past, present and future together,
the idea that there is an order, sanctified by God and History, that keeps
things (and men) fast in their place – these concepts litter Burke's works
and speeches. Reason, or enlightenment, these are figments of dreams,
delusions, fairy lights in the scarcely knowable mysteries of human
society. These the wise man scoffs at. In phrases such as these, often
rhetorized into paragraphs and pages of compelling eloquence, Burke
gave an air of virtue, morality and godly wisdom to an attitude that was
anti-intellectual, and dominated by the meaner and more aggressive
aspects of human nature. It is extraordinary that such lucubrations
should be regarded as having any intellectual value whatsoever –
emotional value for those who need them, perhaps, but intellectually
most of Burke's political philosophy is utter rubbish, and completely
unhistorical.

There is no room to argue the case against Burkeian conservatism
fully here but the nub of the matter would seem to lie in this. Why
should a rationalist, intellectual approach to the problems of human
organization seem either wicked or stupid or both, when such problems
as man has solved – control of power, the diminution of diseases, etc.
have been achieved by their application? Why should a reliance on
intellect be regarded as foolishly optimistic or wildly idealistic and an
addiction to tradition, ancestral wisdom, and the mysteries of Providence
be the hallmark of sound judgement? Burke clothed in the eloquent
language of religion and ethics the nakedness of private greed and public
oppression. He himself was too complex, his needs too conflicting for
his thoughts and actions to be synthesised in a few sentences, but
certainly that has been his value for the generations of conservatives
who have revered him. As an outsider who never got in, Burke often
felt himself drawn to the oppressed, the wronged, the impotents of
society: and alongside Burke the conservative there was also Burke the
reformer who gets scant attention. As Professor Cone illustrates again
and again Burke is often far more complex, far more fascinating in
action than when his pen flows with piety and gets lost in the meaningless
verbiage of political theology.

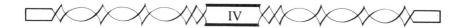

First Step

After securing my PhD in 1936 I set about publishing what I considered to be its most important discovery. It was this: the strength of the committed Whigs and Tories in the Convention Parliament of 1689 which settled the fate of James II and conferred the crown on William III and Mary II was finely balanced – contrary to all previous belief. I had obeyed Namier. I had laboriously studied each member of the Convention Parliament and delved wherever possible into the nature of his political experience and action. About one third of the Commons were men without political experience or known commitment. They held the balance of power. There is no doubt that the compromises which smudged the nature of the Revolutionary Settlement, the rejection of doctrinaire ideology of either party, was due to their presence. Nevertheless party politics remained a vital element and political decisions about the constitution were taken as freely as decisions could be taken in seventeenth-century parliaments. However, Namier's techniques had revealed a world remarkably different from that of 1761. Indeed the possibility that Namierian analysis was limited to a very short period of political history, and was atypical of the eighteenth century as a whole, was growing in my mind, and I began to extend my researches into the reign of Queen Anne and beyond when, in 1939, all work had to cease for seven years.

The Elections to the Convention Parliament of 1689

The election to the Convention Parliament of 1689 was one of the most important ever held, but singularly little attention has been paid to it.[1] A detailed examination has revealed a number of factors which cast fresh light on the state of the country during the Interregnum and on

29

the composition of the Convention Parliament. In this article I intend to restrict my attention to three aspects of the election: firstly, the effect of James II's preparations upon the composition of the House of Commons; secondly, the effect of the preparations of William III and his supporters; thirdly, the manner in which this election was fought in the various constituencies.

I

There has never been any detailed examination of the effect of James II's lengthy preparations for a Parliament on the personnel of the Convention. There is far more material dealing with James' preparations than for any other aspect of this election. He was going to attempt to push the repeal of the tests through Parliament and for this it was necessary to have a House of Commons more subservient than that which had met in 1685. For a year before William's invasion he had been making very careful preparations. James had three methods.

The first, the purging of corporations, had been started by Charles II after the Rye House Plot. It was simple and effective an idea, but in practice it was difficult and dangerous. James II remodelled a number of corporations and intended to continue to do so, until each corporation could be depended upon to support him. The King in his new charters usually reserved the right to elect the major officials; at the same time, the corporations would be filled with men whom he could trust. This led immediately to the intensification of party jealousy; ejected members of the corporations were naturally opposed to those in office.[2] Some corporations refused to surrender their charters, as Winchester and Buckingham had done,[3] but the case was then usually taken to the lawcourts and in the end James won.[4] His intention was to impose his own nominees for Parliament upon these remodelled corporations, but they occasionally found this too much. At Reading. Sudbury and other places, the King's agents desired a further regulation, otherwise, they said, the King's opponents would succeed at a general election.[5] As late as September 1688, Ipswich, Wells, Taunton and many other boroughs required to be regulated before the success of the King's interest could be counted upon.[6] In only a small proportion of electoral boroughs did the corporations return Members to Parliament, but in most cases they played an important part.[7]

Some elections were, however, beyond the control of James and the Duke of Beaufort states this very succinctly, when writing to the King, after he had surveyed Wales with a view to nominating members there. 'The election having been by prescription, could not be regulated by the new Charters and placed in the magistrates, but continues still in the freemen which are very numerous and not subject to be put in or out

at the King's pleasure.'⁸ He could not control the county seats, nor
boroughs with a wide franchise, nor burgage boroughs where the patron
or owners of the burgages were opposed to his policy.⁹ He could only
have controlled them if he had remodelled the whole basis of parliamentary representation, and this he clearly dared not do.

His second method was to secure reliable men as local officials. This
is illustrated by the number of times he changed his Lord-Lieutenants
in 1688 and by his famous three questions to deputy-lieutenants and
magistrates, concerning the Penal Laws and Test Act. The replies to
these, together with the suggested alterations in the magistracy, have
been printed by Sir George Duckett and to James they must have been
extremely disappointing, for he received practically no support except
from Catholics or Dissenters.

The third method might be called the emergent combination of the
former two. In September the King sent out a number of agents into the
counties. These men were under the control of the Board of Regulators
and were armed with secret instructions. These give a clear indication
of James' thoroughness.

> 'You are likewise', the instructions run, 'to consider what Mayors and Sheriffs
> in being are active in his Maties service, and to be depended upon, and which
> of them are fitt to be removed before the Election, either in order to their
> being chosen to serve in Parliament, or to promote the Election of others, and
> to engage the Sheriffs to attend in person at the Election, not only in the
> Counties, but in each respective Corporation, and to take care of the Returns,
> and also to give an account of the inclination and behaviour of the respective
> Town Clerks, Clerks of the Peace, and Sub-Sheriffs whose places render them
> capable of his Maties service in case they be right, but otherwise dangerous
> and prejudicial thereunto.'¹⁰

Another instruction, intended to make the magistracy as useful as
possible, finishes by advising them to use 'any other method or expedient'
that will help to promote good elections.¹¹ James, too, realised the value
of propaganda, for his agents were instructed to spread about a number
of books and pamphlets with which they were provided in order to
refute the ideas made current through Fagel's letter.¹² The agents were
also to inform those that they conversed with 'that *Liberty of Conscience*
hath been the cause of the Hollanders great trade, riches and power'.¹³
Nor did James forget his own servants, for the agents were to investigate
'the behaviour of the officers of the several branches of His Majesty's
revenue in relation to elections whether they promote His Majesty's
interest as they ought to do'.¹⁴ His own servants were not to be trusted
completely, for the agents reported that many of them were not indus-

trious for the King. Several, including a number of postmasters, were averse to his policy.[15]

By September 1688, the agents had surveyed all the boroughs of England and Wales and they sent the results to the King.[16] There are a number of indications that their reports were over-sanguine. In almost every borough the agents saw the certain success of the King's men, yet they often claim as 'right' men who were, as we know from the returns to the three questions, opposed to James' policy. A glaring example of this occurs at Richmond where the agents welcomed the certain success of the Hon. John Darcy. Darcy had been removed from his appointments, owing to his votes in the Parliament of 1685, and had been forbidden the King's presence. Also earlier in the year he had given a categorical refusal to James' three questions.[17]

One of the results of these investigations was the issue of letters of recommendation to patrons and corporations by the Earl of Sunderland.[18] Unfortunately the collection as it now remains is incomplete, for it does not contain letters to all of the Cinque Ports where James, as Lord Warden, had a right to nominate one member, nor is there a letter to Portsmouth which is known to have been waiting for the King's recommendation. A number of well-known patrons of boroughs such as the Earls of Clarendon, Pembroke, Bath, Radnor and Rochester are not included either. Sunderland hoped to recommend 102 members; to make the computation anything like accurate, it is necessary to make an increase of 40 per cent, bringing the total to 143 members, which is a large number but not so large as might have been expected after the years of preparation. It still left 372 members for whose choice James had to depend on the goodwill of their patrons or electorates. After this great effort, James' control over his Parliament could not have been certain and this may have been partly responsible for his vacillating policy in regard to the issuing of the writs in the months of November and December 1688.

The invasion by William had two serious effects upon these preparations. In October, James returned to boroughs and cities all charters surrendered since 1681, with the result that where there had been loyalty before, there was now bitterness and confusion, for numbers who had been turned out hastened to get back into the corporation.[19] Naturally they had no love for the men who had helped to turn them out, nor for James whom they thought to have been responsible.[20]

A serious consequence of William's invasion was the loss of the support of the dissenters. They played a large part in James' scheme, for he believed that they would be willing to give their support in return for religious toleration. The election agents were instructed to 'acquaint yourselves with the preachers of Dissenting Congregations and encourage them to employ their interest, for the abrogating these *Laws and Tests* and if you find any of them dissatisfied enquire who they correspond with in *London* and give notice of it'.[21] In consequence of this in Buckinghamshire five reputed dissenters were encouraged to stand for Parliament and received the support of the government.[22] These men, Richard and John Hampden, Edmund Waller, Richard Beake and Thomas Lewis were from old Buckinghamshire families with a tradition of opposition to royal tyranny and to them political freedom was as dear as religious toleration. It was quite natural for them to break their uneasy partnership with James and rally to the support of William who offered them religious toleration together with constitutional practice.

These two factors had serious results and in themselves would have seriously hampered the preparations James had so carefully made. Worse was to follow. The sequence of events is well known. James vacillated until it was too late; his army melted away and he himself suffered from severe physical disorders of a nervous nature. All of his power disappeared and he had to flee ignominiously to France. The forces of exclusion had triumphed and Shaftesbury's friends were returned to the Convention; Harbord, Hampden, Lee, Wharton were back on the front benches and Anchitel Grey's diary is full of their speeches. Yet James' hope of success had largely depended upon these men.

From a list of the front-bench speakers in the Convention, it would not have been surprising if the settlement had been much more profoundly Whig. The middle course adopted by the Convention has been explained in a number of ways but never satisfactorily. It has been argued that the result was due to the compromise of parties, but party divisions were as strong as they ever had been. Others have said that the Tory party was divided, which is true, and that the Whigs had a policy which triumphed, which is not true, for Whig policy had stood for the headings of the first Bill of Rights which were whittled down in committee, until what might have been a definition of the constitution became nothing more than the expression of a pious hope. Another explanation has been that the Whig House of Commons was controlled by the Tory House of Lords. There was less chance of controlling votes in the Commons in January 1688–9 than there had been for many years, and the Commons' proposition was the one which was ultimately passed in the Lords. The famous vote of 28 January and the Bill of Rights, both of which originated in the Commons, are the real basis of the settlement which has so often been praised for its moderation. Why were the Commons so moderate? No one could call Lee, Birch, Sacheverell and the Hampdens moderate men, and these were the men who led the Commons. Was the House of Commons as Whiggish as almost every historian who has written about the Revolution has maintained?

Contemporaries were not so definite about it as later writers have been. Richard Sarre, who was closely connected with Dr Charlett, the Tory Master of University College, Oxford, and his circle which included Harrington, the Tory pamphleteer, could write: 'The country generally makes a good choice of representatives.'[23] By 21 March, another observer states that the Church of England had a majority in both Houses, although 'they knew their strength no sooner'.[24] The list of Whig defeats, too, during this year is not a small one. They failed in the matter of comprehension and they failed over their great bills concerning indemnity and corporations. No satisfactory reason has been given for this. If the Commons consisted of a large Whig Party, why could it have happened? On the other hand, it is possible that contemporary observers were nearer to the truth, and, in finding a majority for the Church of England party, they were not seeing what they wanted to see, but seeing the real state of affairs. To divide the Commons rigidly into party, Whig and Tory, is not possible. Four men who voted against the vacancy of the throne, voted eleven months later for the most flagrantly Whig measure of the Parliament, namely, the Sacheverell clause of the Corporations Bill.[25] Over less controversial matters, changes were no doubt more frequent. Yet there were parties; contemporaries recognised the fact, and it is quite obvious that they were right. Also in a body of 513 some rough estimate should be possible. There is one piece of evidence, not enough in itself, but sufficiently definite to use as an indication, that alters the accepted conception of the constitution of the Commons. 151 voted against the vacancy,[26] 174 for Sacheverell's clause:[27] these men with a few exceptions must have been confirmed Whigs and Tories and the disparity between the two numbers is not great. It seems most probable that the Whigs had but little superior strength in the Commons and that the greater majority which they enjoyed in the first months of the Parliament was due to the trend of events rather than to their own numbers.

The strength of the opposition can be tested more conclusively by an analysis of the success of James' preparations, and secondly by considering what members of the Exclusion Parliaments sat in 1688–9, and how many members of the 1685 Parliament were there. Both methods have certain disadvantages, but taken together they do give a clearer idea of the reasons why the revolutionary settlement came to be what it was.

Of Sunderland's nominees about 45 of the 102 obtained seats in the Convention, although frequently for boroughs to which he had not recommended them.[28] This indicates that, although they had political influence independent of Sunderland and the government, this influence was not completely destroyed by his fall and James' flight.

In analysing the returns of the King's agents there are one or two factors which require notice. The men whom the King's agents thought would be returned were not always people whom they considered firm supporters of James; and sometimes men whom they thought would support him, did not.

In Yorkshire, the government had very little influence, confined almost to the one rather odd case of the Queen Dowager's right to nominate to one seat at Boroughbridge.[29] At Hedon, Henry Guy and Charles Duncombe had control of the borough, and as they were usually in the employment of the government, it was a safe government seat. Their influence, however, was personal and not dependent upon the government.[30] Government could also influence the Scarborough election but not conclusively enough to nominate. In Yorkshire, therefore, James had had to depend almost entirely upon the goodwill of the local magnates. Out of 30 seats, the king's agents thought thirteen men would be elected who would be supporters of James' policy. This was optimistic, for they counted John Darcy and Sir Jonathan Jennings, both of whom had opposed the suggested removal of the Penal Laws and Test Act. Five men were looked upon as doubtful but not doubtful enough to be objected to, whilst ten others were passed over in silence, which, from a consideration of the other counties, indicates that they were not favourable to James. For the remaining two seats which were those for the county, the agents had no idea who would be elected. Out of their list of 28, thirteen succeeded in being returned to the Convention: six supporters and seven doubtfuls. Of the six supporters two were, however, confirmed friends of dissenters if not dissenters themselves.[31] Also out of this thirteen, only one voted against the vacancy of the throne, Sir Jonathan Jennings, a supporter of Danby.[32] The two county members were Sir John Kay and Thomas Lord Fairfax; the former had Whig affiliations, the latter was one of the Tory group led by Danby.[33] It is, I think, fair to say that men who were willing to support James in September were inclined to the right in politics. Of this type, Yorkshire sent twelve to the Convention.[34] Yorkshire was, however, greatly influenced by the Tory Earl of Danby in its sympathies and his power may have counted for a great deal, and it is necessary to investigate other types of counties.

Suffolk at this time was free from any dominating interest, although Lord Huntingtower had considerable interest at Orford and Lord Cornwallis at Eye which had a very bad reputation for elections.[35] It also illustrates how this method of approach must be used with caution, for although ten out of eighteen members voted against the vacancy, the King's agents forecasted correctly the election of only two members whom they thought would be willing to serve the King and both of these were friends of dissenters. Two members whom they thought 'not right' were elected but one of them proved to be loyal to James.[36] Another, Sir Thomas Barnardiston, whom they thought was right, was returned, not for Suffolk county, but for Great Grimsby. One borough, Orford, was not accounted for, being left to the discretion of Lord Huntingtower. In fourteen cases the King's agents were quite wrong. In Suffolk, it would appear that James' preparations broke down quite completely; the men whom he wanted returned were not elected. Yet the breakdown of his arrangements did not lead to a triumph of his enemies; on the contrary, men were elected who were loyal to him although they had not received his support.

In Hampshire, the electoral system was much closer to that which we associate with the unreformed Parliament and through its servants in the navy, the government had a very large interest in a number of seats. In such a county James' preparations could be much more thorough. Hampshire had 26 seats and in September eight had no nominees, although four were expected to be filled by whomsoever James should recommend.[37] At Christchurch, Lord Clarendon had a commanding influence and his candidates were expected to be loyal.[38] They were. Of the remaining sixteen, the agents suggested that the numbers elected would be: eleven who would be for James, one who was a moderate man and four who are passed over in silence. Of the sixteen, nine were elected: two were members of the Whig group who had supported James II,[39] one was a moderate,[40] and one had been passed over in silence, but voted against the vacancy.[41] Seven supporters were elected and to these may be added the two for Portsmouth; two from Christchurch; and one from Andover,[42] making a total of twelve out of 26 seats.

These analyses show that, although the returns of the King's agents are not completely reliable, they do give some idea of the strength of the political party of the right and show how far it was successful at the elections; checked and corrected by the lists of those who voted against the vacancy and for the Sacheverell clause, they become more reliable and the inference is very plain. Out of a total of 74 members investigated, 34 were men who inclined very definitely to the right. This suggests that the House of Commons was not, as many have supposed, overwhelmingly Whig. there was the possibility from the earliest days of a real and solid opposition to Whig principles. James' long preparations for a Parliament had some success; as has been shown previously, there was a considerable difference between the Parliament that might have been elected on the first issue of the writs and the Convention Parliament, but a sufficient number of confirmed Tories (i.e. supporters of James) were able to maintain their interest, in spite of the events of December to January 1688–9, to form the basis of a solid opposition in this assembly.

In 1685, James had opened a Parliament devoted to him and to his house; nearly 200 of these members were sitting in the Convention and they numbered slightly more than those who had sat in the Exclusion Parliaments. All the members of the Parliament of 1685 were not High Church and Tory, for both Richard Hampden and Thomas Wharton were members. The same, however, is true of the Exclusion Parliaments for a number of the King's friends retained seats even in those inauspicious days. The actual numbers are worth quoting:

Members of the Convention who were members in
1661–78	80
1678/9–79	164
1679	187
1680/1–81	192
1685	196 (99 of these had sat 1678/9–80/1)
Newly elected members	183

Of the 99 members who were members both in Charles' Parliaments and in 1685, about 60 were members of the Court Party.[43] This analysis, which has a number of obvious drawbacks, gives a rough total of 160 members who were of Tory principles, or at least had been so previously. In any case they must have been there in at least equal numbers to the old exclusionists.

Another interesting fact emerges from this analysis and that is the relatively high proportion of newly elected members: 183 men had never been to Parliament before, which is about 40 above normal number. This is quite extraordinary, because at such a crisis one would have expected the electors to turn to experienced men; with the two parties very nearly balanced, these new and inexperienced men must have had a deciding influence upon the course of events; unallied as yet to any political party, they probably followed not principles, but the necessities of the time, and because necessity was Whig during the troubled days of January 1689, they were probably Whig, too, but, as the pressure of events was eased, the house, to at least one observer, swung more to the right.[44] This was due to the large numbers both of inexperienced and moderates who sat in this Parliament.

II

These were the results of James' lengthy preparations, but during this time William and his supporters were not idle.

It is not necessary here to review the events of the Revolution, but, I think, William's attitude to them has not been portrayed with much truth. After each development, William seized all the opportunities implicit in it. It is only necessary to consider what he made both of the first flight and the conference at Hungerford, in order to see what an admirable tactician he was.[45] He had a quick and penetrating insight into political problems and, from what we know of his character, it seems certain that by indirect methods he would do what he could to obtain a satisfactory membership in Parliament.[46] He could not employ the method of James, for, in his declaration, he had said that 'he would refer all to a free assembly of the nation, in a lawful parliament'.[47] Also, although the administration was in his hands, after James' flight, his main concern was to maintain order, raise money and win over eminent men like Nottingham and Godolphin who were only half-heartedly devoted to his cause.

An examination of two sets of boroughs under government influence, namely the Cinque Ports and the Isle of Wight, gives little further light except of a negative kind. The government could control fairly thoroughly both of these groups of boroughs.[48] The Lord Warden of the Cinque Ports had a right to nominate to the seat at each port, but the Lord Warden was James II himself, so in January the office was vacant.[49] No nominations to the Cinque Port seats seem to have been made. This is partly confirmed by the correspondence of Thomas Papillon, who became a member for Dover. He was a Whig and had been in exile in Holland since 1684.[50] He afterwards became First Commissioner for Victualling the Navy, for he was a loyal supporter of William. Here was a suitable member, but the government did nothing to support his candidature.[51]

The Isle of Wight had five seats under the control of the Governor,[52] who usually acted upon nominations received from the government. Sir Robert Holmes was Governor in January 1689.[53] He had been a loyal servant of James II, but was to serve William with similar loyalty. In September 1688, he had received nominations from the Earl of Sunderland in view of the forthcoming Parliament;[54] two of these obtained seats in the Convention. The government influence at Newport was not very secure, and for the Convention the town returned two local men, Sir Robert Dillington, bt., and Sir William Stephens, kt.[55] Of the other two, one was the Earl of Ranelagh, at that time a loyal Tory, but afterwards Paymaster of the Forces and a Whig who was expelled from the House of Commons for peculation.[56] The other was Fitton Gerard, a confirmed Whig, son of the Earl of Macclesfield, who never obtained a seat without great difficulty, and it is impossible to see how he was returned for a seat in the Isle of Wight without government support.[57] It is probable, too, that the Earl of Ranelagh may have been suggested, for he was an official of the government, Tory, but, like other officials, willing to serve William, and a useful man to have in the Commons. The most probable course of events was, I should think, that Sir Robert Holmes was asked to find a seat for Gerard, and perhaps for Ranelagh – although this is doubtful – and then left to his own devices.

Apart from these close preserves of the government, it also possessed a great deal of influence through its servants in the customs and excise, and especially through the navy in other boroughs, chiefly seaports. The shipyards at Chatham had a great influence on Rochester elections.[58] Apart from the fact that the corporation unanimously elected Sir Joseph Banks, bt., the London merchant, and Sir Roger Twisden, kt., a local country gentleman, nothing is known about the Rochester election to the Convention.[59]

Another borough in which the government had considerable interest was Portsmouth where, throughout the reign, admirals or admiralty officials were usually elected. The Earl of Dartmouth was in charge of the fleet and the Admiralty during the Interregnum and to him Francis Gwyn addressed two letters, asking to be recommended to Portsmouth if Colonel Norton should fail to stand. He also recommended Henry Slingsby, an alderman of the town, to the Earl. As Norton stood, Gwyn did not, but his recommendation was accepted, for Slingsby was returned. Here government interest was left to the discretion of the man, appointed by James, who was still in charge. He directed the election upon the advice of his friends. It is interesting to note that Gwyn was a confirmed Tory, but that he did not suggest turning out Norton, whom he calls a Presbyterian.[60]

For Harwich, another admiralty borough, which was less secure, there is, thanks to the indefatigable Samuel Pepys, a great deal of evidence.[61] Pepys was defeated by a local country gentleman, John Eldred, but the correspondence concerning the election is very detailed, and a number of important indications can be found in it.[62] The most striking, perhaps, is the absence of any direct corruption. Pepys does not ask for pressure to be brought on government servants nor is there any hint of direct bribery. He stresses only the benefits that would naturally accrue from having him as a member. Perhaps more important than this, is the absence of any help from above; Pepys sends no recommendation from the Prince nor from any of the more important officials.[63] The administration of James had broken down and in a sense there were no officials at the Admiralty higher than Pepys himself, yet one would have thought that a letter from Dartmouth, or even from Danby or Shrewsbury, would have been useful. It is clear from this example that the Prince did not embark on a policy of recommendation and coercion in boroughs where the government interest was strong. The civil servants that became, or attempted to become, members of Parliament did so upon their own initiative. This was due, I think, not specifically to the desire of the Prince to avoid any but the freest of elections, but to the fact that the administration was in a chaotic condition. The Prince was too busy to do it, and the men around him were not sure of their official positions.

This is all the knowledge we have of interference by the Prince or of influence used in boroughs where the government had some control over the election. Compared with subsequent government interference under William the discrepancy is not very great, but, compared with the control of borough elections which James II planned, the difference is apparent and remarkable.

Although the provisional government did little, its supporters did a great deal. Apart from close boroughs, a number of peers and commoners exerted a wide territorial influence. The Earl of Danby had a considerable influence in most of the Yorkshire elections, especially those for the East and West Ridings. From the calendar of the Leeds papers, it is obvious that he exerted himself to influence the elections not only in Yorkshire but also in Lincolnshire.[64] One method employed by Danby has, I think, no parallel in electioneering. Sir John Kay proposed to offer himself as a candidate for Yorkshire but this met with the disapproval of Danby and his party. In consequence the following letter, signed by 22 of them, was sent to him:

Sir,
  Being desirous that the union and good correspondence in this county of York may be continued, the effect of which has much contributed to the good success of our cause in these parts, and very much doubting that so great a contest as is likely to be in the election of representatives for this county may beget great heats and animosities therein, amongst friends and neighbours, we do request and desire you to forbear your pretensions to be Knight of the shire in this county, at this time, and we shall upon the consent thereto declare ourselves to be with much obligation,
Sir,
  Your most affectionate friends and servants.

Sir John Kay, however, was undaunted and called their bluff. He was returned to Parliament without, it seems, a contest.[65] This letter gives some indication of the intensity of feeling which was aroused and in itself would be enough to alter the view that the elections for the Convention were smooth and pacific.

Farther north in Westmorland and Cumberland, there were two houses of great territorial influence. Sir John Lowther of Lowther supported the Revolution[66] His opponent was Sir Christopher Musgrave, a high Tory, loyal to James.[67] In December, before the first flight, Musgrave had hoped to control the election in two boroughs, Carlisle and Appelby, and that for Westmorland county. This had infuriated Sir John Lowther, who wrote: 'I proposed a compromise in vain. I have determined, therefore, to stand myself with Lord Wharton's son, whose family have a great claim, not only on account of their great estates, but, much more, for their well deserving upon this great occasion from all good Protestants.'[68] On the same day, 5 December, Lowther sent out an address on Henry Wharton's behalf in which there is no mention of his political principles but a great deal about his religious beliefs.[69] Musgrave went ahead, giving out that he would not spare money for elections and his prospects at Carlisle were so promising that John Aglionby, Lowther's agent, wrote despondently: 'Before I got to town they had given a great treat to the most considerable men of the corporation and 'tis said have carried on their business a great way so that by way of what I can yet learn it will be a matter of much difficulty and expense to prevail for a new man.'[70] The height of Musgrave's success came on 16 December when, after much manœuvring, he obtained control of the garrison at Carlisle which put his supporters in a truculent frame of mind.[71]

It was unlikely that the news of James' first flight had reached the north and, when it came, Musgrave's prestige crumbled. By 11 January Sir Christopher Musgrave had retired from his candidature for the county 'in order to prevent the heats and animosities which a contest would occasion at this unseasonable time'.[72] Out of the six seats which he hoped to control in December, he obtained one at Carlisle for himself and one at Appleby for his son, Philip. This offers a striking instance of the way in which the influence of families was transformed by the success of William and of the way in which the credit of James' supporters sank.

More important perhaps than this is the conclusive evidence it offers of the way in which William's supporters worked on his behalf. In later Parliaments, the Lowthers and the Musgraves in general respected each other's right to one of the Westmorland county seats, but on this occasion Lowther refused to compromise.

Examples could be multiplied of the way in which William's partisans tried either to get suitable men elected or to obtain seats for themselves. William Harbord, whose eagerness to enter Parliament, together with his passionate attachment to William's cause, so disgusted the Earl of Clarendon,[73] made so sure of his election that he was returned for three boroughs. Considering the importance of the events which were taking place, it was only natural that men should be eager to be returned for Parliament.

A number of conclusions emerge from this detailed study of territorial influence. The most obvious is that wherever possible the adherents of William did whatever they could to influence elections in his favour.

This does not mean that the Convention Parliament was partly packed. It does not mean that the elections were unfair and biased, any more than they were at other times. No historian can with any justice apply 'fair and unbiased' to any election of the seventeenth century. All of William's supporters considered that they were only exercising their legitimate rights, and although to us many of their activities would seem to invalidate the election, yet to them it was 'a free and lawful assembly'. James' supporters did likewise and where their influence was absolute, they met with success, except in one outstanding example.[74] On the other hand, their territorial influence diminished as James' credit fell.

III

Although patrons and peers with wide influence played an important part in elections, so did that more numerous and more silent body of men, the voters. One of the most interesting problems of this election is the manner in which it was fought.

As one reads through the materials for this election, one is amazed by the absence of any reference to the political issue which was the foremost question in January 1688–9, namely, what was to be done with the King? A great number of pamphlets were written about it,[75] and men in the immediate entourage of the Prince were obviously exercised by the problem, for at the end of November, or in the early days of December, Burnet had considered the pros and cons of deposing the King. He had decided that the best thing would be for the King to live in Italy whilst the country was ruled by a regency.[76] By 18 December events had moved ahead of theory and the Prince's friends at Windsor were talking of a 'cession of the throne',[77] by 22 December a newsletter writer was able to describe the variety and difference of parties on this issue.[78] When one turns away from the centre of activity to what was happening locally at election times, there is a marked and obvious change. Sir John Knatchbull's diary gives the only known reference to the effect on the fate of an election of the candidate's political views in respect of the abdication. The case in question is that of Sir William Twisden, who was defeated at the election for the county of Kent because he had not signed the Association. It was rumoured that the Corporation of Newcastle refused to recognise the validity of the Prince's letter and that Sir Ralph Carr and Sir William Blackett finally elected themselves, but I have found nothing to substantiate or disprove this.[79] In no other election which has come to light was there any direct mention of the immediate political issue. In the long and detailed correspondence of Samuel Pepys to his supporters at Harwich, he never says, nor is he asked, what his views are about the settlement of the crown. He does say that we will be for the 'Protestant religion as by law established',[80] but High Tory or Low Whig could say this with equal conviction and sincerity.

The wider religious question was occasionally of some force. Robert Price, candidate for Weobley, thought that his chances were being jeopardised by the report that he had been for the removal of the Penal Laws and Test Act.[81] This had, of course, been one of the most widely discussed questions of the day and every country gentleman of importance had been forced to consider what views he held. It was this question, not the dynastic one, that had a great deal to do with the choice and success of candidates.[82]

The problem of the settlement could not, I suppose, have been absent from the elections for Southwark nor Middlesex, for the voters there must have read the pamphlets which poured from the press. Boroughs, close to London, were possibly affected, too, by propaganda, although it must be remembered that at Maidstone, which is not very far from London, an observer states that a supporter of William lost the election because his agent lost his temper and called the voters 'rabble'.[83]

If the elections were not about political matters, then what were they about? Although there is no explicit mention of the immediate political issue, in most elections, between the candidates there was an implicit division of opinion. At Abingdon, for example, the contest was between Sir John Stonhouse and Thomas Medlicot. There is no mention of politics, but Stonhouse was a well-known Tory, opposed to James, yet loyal to the Church,[84] whilst Medlicot, the Recorder of Abingdon, had been turned out of his office by James II, no doubt owing to his sympathies. After his election he made a few Whiggish speeches in the House of Commons.[85] On 6 May, this election was declared void, on Stonhouse's petition against Medlicot, and a vigorous by-election took place between Southby, a man very well known locally as being in favour of dissenters, and Stonhouse, who ultimately obtained his seat by petition.[86] Stonhouse was a staunch supporter of the Church of England whilst Medlicot and Southby had affiliations with dissenters. This division on broad and general lines can be illustrated in a number of other elections but not in all.[87] At Stamford, for example, the contest was almost entirely personal. The candidates were the Hon. Charles Bertie, Capt. William Hyde and Sir Pury Cust, who was defeated. Cust was connected with Brownlowes of Belton, Lincolnshire,[88] and was a country gentleman of solid Church of England principles. Bertie and Hyde were of a similar class.[89] In general, the motives for contesting an election were similar to the motives which made men contest elections for other parliaments. In many places a contest was avoided, but at others, personal or party strife in its wide sense, or the desire to be present at Westminster, overrode the sense of emergency and brought about a contest. Even so it is remarkable that the dynastic issue played such a small part in the brief election campaign which preceded the Convention Parliament. It was not very long since the countryside had been disturbed by the passionate harangues of Shaftesbury and his followers about Exclusion. The reason why a similar campaign was not instituted in the Interregnum is most probably to be found in the common conviction of all parties, excepting a tiny minority, whatever the differences which separated them in other matters, that James II could not be recalled. It was not necessary to arouse the electorate over the niceties of the constitutional problems involved in his so-called abdication: that was a matter for the wisdom of those that ruled at Westminster.

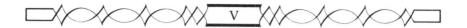

V

Beginning Again

After the war was over Cambridge became full of undergraduates and the teaching load of dons was extremely heavy, especially as many, beyond the retiring age, gave up as soon as hostilities ceased. In my first year back, I had to do over twenty hours' teaching, some on subjects such as American History about which I knew practically nothing. At the same time I was appointed a temporary faculty lecturer. The first year I had to prepare forty lectures, the second year forty more as I was required to undertake a special subject on *Sir Robert Walpole and the Opposition 1722–37.* I calculated that I wrote in these two summers nearly 250,000 words of lectures; I was reading day and night to keep up with the earnest, mature and dedicated scholars who returned from the war. I had had practically no holidays during the war and usually worked a 70-hour week: I worked even harder from 1946 to 1948. There was no time for archival research, none at all, but publication was important if I was to make my temporary grade permanent. Fortunately, I was asked by Allen Lane to write a short history of England in the eighteenth century for Penguin. For this the lectures which I had written in 1946 were useful and the book was finished by April 1948. I remember very vividly writing the last paragraph. I was at Ascott House, the guest of Anthony de Rothschild. I put my pen down and stretched back in the beautiful Chippendale desk chair in which I was sitting: it shattered in pieces. Tony behaved impeccably. 'Don't worry,' he said, 'Partridge will fix it,' and Partridge did. I didn't know until then that beneath the glittering display of the Bond Street shop worked some of the finest cabinetmakers in the world: they could resurrect any antique.

It took two years, however, to get the book published owing to paper shortage and when it came out, all printers were on strike, so it was never reviewed. Fortunately, G. N. Clark, then Regius Professor at

Cambridge, read it, approved highly and I sailed into the more secure waters of an assistant lectureship.

I was still heavily burdened with college and university teaching – the thrust of my future research undecided but inclining towards a life of Sir Robert Walpole. In the autumn of 1948 I was asked by the editors of the Victoria County History to write an essay on the *Political History of Leicestershire, 1530–1885*. This was peculiarly useful, for my family home was in Leicester: I had worked on the Rutland MSS at Belvoir for my PhD. Much of the archival material was easily available to me. It was a way of getting back to some archival work and also a challenge in the handling of narrative and analysis. The narrow compass of the chapter was a god-send for an historian who had been out of detailed research for a decade.

And it brought me back to the problems of British politics in the eighteenth century. The oligarchs certainly dominated Leicestershire politics – up to a point. Yet political attitudes strengthened at times of crisis and they were never absent at any time: party issues might lie moribund for an election or two but Whigs remained Whigs and Tories Tory. And there could be no doubt either that such attitudes were strengthened by religion – High Church Toryism in the eighteenth century like hatred of Rome in the nineteenth century were factors of significance in Leicestershire politics. It was clear that Namier's methods and Namier's interpretations were not fully adequate.

The Political History of Leicestershire, 1530–1885

From the Reformation to the last quarter of the nineteenth century the political history of Leicestershire maintained, except at times of national crisis, a constant pattern. Political activity was confined almost entirely to parliamentary elections when broad issues of national policy were rarely debated. Elections were very largely settled by arrangement between the leading families, aristocratic and gentle, and when contests took place they were as much the result of family feuds and quarrels as of differences on political issues. It was natural that the families with the greatest influence at Court, or in the nineteenth century in the government, should dominate local politics. Until the Civil War the Hastingses, Earls of Huntingdon, and from the Civil War to the end of the nineteenth century the Mannerses, Dukes of Rutland, had the dominating voice in Leicestershire politics.[1] But in this the political history of Leicestershire differs very little from that of other Midland counties. The political power of the Dukes of Devonshire in Derbyshire and of the Dukes of Newcastle in Nottinghamshire was commensurate with that of the Rutlands in Leicestershire.

The Reformation had singularly little effect upon Leicestershire politics; the great families, whatever their differences with each other, moved conformably with the times. Even Edward Hastings, Lord Hastings of Loughborough, the ardent supporter of Queen Mary and her executor, took the Oath of Supremacy, after a taste of the Tower, and died a Protestant. The upshot of this was to add to the political tranquility of the county, and recusancy never became a problem in Leicestershire.

The Parliament called in 1536 was vital for the development of Thomas Cromwell's attack on the monasteries and care was taken to secure Members of Parliament who 'for their worship and qualities be most meet for the purpose'.[2] The writs for Leicestershire have been lost, but William Ashby of Quenby was certainly one of the members. He wrote effusively to Thomas Cromwell, thanking him for his letters of recommendation to the Earl of Huntingdon and others, and he assured Cromwell that he would do his best to serve the King. He was appointed Commissioner to survey the monasteries of Leicestershire on 24 June 1536 along with Sir John Nevell, John Beaumont, George Gyfford, Robert Burgoyn, and Roger Ratclyff. And he did not fail in his duty. The writs for the Parliaments of 1539 are also missing, but for the penultimate Parliament of Henry VIII summoned on 16 January 1542, Sir Richard Manners, the brother of Thomas, the 1st Earl of Rutland, was elected as the senior Knight of the Shire. The powerful influence of his brother at court, strengthened by the active part he played in defeating the insurrection of the northern rebels in 1536, would have made his election certain. He was the first of his family to represent Leicestershire. The Christian name, Thomas, alone survives of the junior Knight of the Shire, but he may well have been Thomas Hastings, who represented the county in 1553 and 1554 (twice), the second son of George, 1st Earl of Huntingdon, who, like the Earl of Rutland, was a great favourite of Henry VIII and was instrumental in helping to defeat the Pilgrimage of Grace. The names of the representatives of Leicestershire in the last Parliament of Henry VIII's reign are not known, but for the first Parliament of Edward VI, called in 1547, Sir Edward Hastings was the senior Knight and Sir Ambrose Cave the junior. They also represented the county in Edward VI's second Parliament.

Unlike most of his family, Sir Edward, afterwards Lord Hastings of Loughborough, was a strong Catholic. He took part in the invasion of Scotland with Protector Somerset in 1547, but his political triumph came with Queen Mary's accession; apart from his religious convictions, it was natural enough for him to support her, for the hereditary enemies of the Hastingses, the Greys, were deeply involved in Northumberland's bid to obtain the crown for Lady Jane Grey. Their defeat was Hastings's triumph. In spite of his opposition to Mary's marriage with Philip II, offices were showered on him. He became a Privy Councillor, Master of the Horse, and finally Lord Chamberlain (1557). Honours and land came his way as well as office. He was made Knight of the Garter in 1555 and Lord Hastings of Loughborough in 1558: the manors of Market Bosworth, Loughborough, and Creech St Michael (Som.) were bestowed on him. Nevertheless, he remained 'given to melancholy': justified, as events turned out, for at the accession of Elizabeth I he was disgraced, imprisoned, and made to abjure his religion. But when such a man was proposed for the county, backed as he was by the weight of Hastings' family, there was nothing for the gentry to do but accept him. In the political circumstances of the time opposition was inconceivable.

His colleague, Sir Ambrose Cave, was far closer to their kind. The Caves, who were to play an important role in Leicestershire politics for the next three centuries, were more typical of those Leicestershire gentry of the sixteenth century who were making money fast out of monastic lands. His brother, Sir Thomas, had purchased the manor of Stanford (Northants.), belonging to Selby monastery (Yorks.), for £1,194 3s 4d. Sir Ambrose's father had married into the Fieldings of Newnham Paddox, afterwards Earls of Denbigh, the most powerful family just across the Warwickshire border. In such ways they built up their territorial influence until they completely dominated south-west Leicestershire. Sir Ambrose himself was wise and discreet. He hitched his wagon to Burleigh's star. Burleigh brought him into the Queen's Privy Committee and no doubt was responsible for making him Chancellor of the Duchy of Lancaster in 1563. The alliance was cemented, as Tudor alliances were wont to be, by marriage, for Sir Ambrose's nephew, Roger, married Burleigh's sister. Nevertheless, Sir Ambrose Cave may be regarded as truly representing the gentry of Leicestershire. Although the writs for Mary's reign are defective, it is clear that the gentry managed to retain their hold on at least one seat. The junior representatives in her four Parliaments were Henry Poole of Countesthorpe, George Turpin of Knaptoft, William Skeffington of Skeffington, and George Sherrard of Stapleford. Of these, all but Poole came of families long established in Leicestershire, and all, including Poole, were deeply concerned in accumulating land, tolerant of inclosure, tolerant of depopulation, men in whom the Leicestershire gentry and yeomanry could put their trust. In the last of Mary's Parliaments the gentry managed to capture both seats, for George Vyncent of Peckleton, a newcomer to the county, was surprisingly enough elected as Senior Knight of the Shire. But for the other Parliaments of Mary for which the return exist, a Hastings held the senior seat.

These years required great circumspection, for Leicestershire gentry were involved in more dramatic political activity than the choice of parliamentary representatives. Throughout the forties and fifties of this century the country was involved in war, rebellion, and threats of invasion, all of which touched the lives and fortunes of Leicestershire men. In 1544 Henry VIII called on Leicestershire to provide him with 54 carriages, 8 ox-wagons, and 340 horses. For the projected invasion of France 2,534 men were mustered, and the list of gentlemen responsible reads like a roll from a Tudor Debrett—Villiers, Grey Haslerigg, Digby, Skeffington, Vyncent, Turvill, Shirley, Cave, Beaumont — all are there and their status can be judged by what is demanded of them. Sir John Villiers undertook the heavy burden of providing four horsemen and 106 foot, completely furnished with arms.

The next year the same demands were made and by June 1545 500 Leicestershire men had been sent to Boulogne. In 1546 another group of 400 was dispatched to Dover, to be followed later in the year by similar groups. Kett's rebellion in 1549 aroused but slight sympathy amongst the Leicestershire peasantry, and the Council thanked Henry, Marquess of Dorset, for the quietness of the shire. Yet some sympathy there was, for in September 1549 the Earl of Huntingdon had been hanging peasants in Rutland for intended rebellion and he proposed to deal subsequently with the men from Leicestershire.

On the death of Edward VI in 1553, Leicestershire was involved in more spectacular events. Henry Grey, 3rd Marquess of Dorset, whose wife was a granddaughter of Henry VII, was made steward of the manors and lordships in Leicestershire belonging both to the Crown and to the duchy of Lancaster, and in the same year was created Duke of Suffolk.[3] His daughter, Lady Jane Grey, who was born at Bradgate in 1537, was married on 21 May 1553 to Guildford Dudley, and on 10 July 1553 entered the Tower as queen. Warrants were issued in her name to her followers to 'assemble muster and levie all the povere that ye can possible make', but the men of Leicestershire waited on events. It was enough for the Hastingses to know that the Greys were involved with Northumberland; that alone made certain that they would support Mary as soon as they were able. Sir Edward Hastings, brother of the Earl of Huntingdon, ignored Jane's commission but responded at once to Queen Mary's appeal. A further reason is to be found in the fact that Cardinal Pole, Mary's closest adviser, was a relative of the Hastings family and it is to him that their success in her reign is due.

Northumberland's attempt quickly failed and Mary had little difficulty in securing her throne, but it was more seriously jeopardized by her proposal to marry Philip of Spain. Wyatt's rebellion of 1554 presented Suffolk with an opportunity to re-establish his position. He dashed into

Leicestershire with his brothers and issued a proclamation calling people to take up arms against the foreigner.

The men of Leicestershire gave him no support; he fled to Warwickshire where, ironically enough, he was captured by the Earl of Huntingdon. Death and disgrace followed for his family; he himself, his brother Lord Thomas Grey, his daughter Lady Jane, and her husband Dudley were all executed. Had it not been for this last act of folly it is unlikely that his daughter would have lost her life. By all reports she was a young woman of singular intelligence and accomplishment: she had spent almost all her life at Bradgate, which will always be associated with her name.

The accession of Elizabeth I did little to upset the balance of political forces in Leicestershire. Catholicism was not strong, and the Hastings family quickly swung back to its natural alliance with puritanism. The Greys therefore failed to make much capital out of the religious revolution, although one small triumph was the capture of the senior seat for the young husband, Adrian Stokes, of Suffolk's widow. The junior knight was Francis Cave, a relative of Sir Ambrose Cave. But the political history of Leicestershire in this reign is largely the history of the Hastings family. By 1584 Henry, 3rd Earl of Huntingdon, had secured a dominant position in the politics of the county, or rather had re-established the Hastings interest, which had weakened during the reigns of Edward VI and Mary, at the expense of the gentry, but not, it would seem, without a struggle. Evidence is scant but the names of the members elected indicate a contest for power. Nicolas Beaumont of Coleorton and George Turpin of Knaptoft were elected Knights of the Shire in 1562. In the Short Parliament of 1571 they were not returned; Francis Hastings, 'the meanest beagle of the House of Huntingdon', younger brother of the earl, and Adrian Stokes sat in place of them. This has every appearance of an alliance between the great families of Hastings and Grey to keep out the gentry. At the next election in 1572, the gentry reappear in the persons of Nicholas Beaumont and Sir George Turpin. But it was a short-lived triumph. From 1584 until the end of James I's reign the gentry could never be certain of holding even one seat, and this is an extremely rare situation in county politics. In those counties whose social and political life was dominated by a great family, it was usual for that family to share the representation with the gentry. Certainly the stranglehold of the Hastingses bred resentment, but the resentment was never strong enough to become effective.

The head of the Hastings family was Henry, the 3rd earl, an ardent and devout Puritan, although his mother was the niece of Cardinal Pole. Through her he had a claim to the succession, and had Elizabeth's attack of smallpox in 1562 proved fatal he would have been, as Professor

Neale has pointed out, the ardent Protestants' candidate.[4] He was Lord-Lieutenant of Leicestershire in 1559 and of Rutland in 1569, Knight of the Garter in 1570, and Lord President of the Council in the north in 1572. As Lord President he was responsible for the custody of Mary, Queen of Scots, whose joint guardian he had been made in 1569, and for a time his castle at Ashby was considered a suitable place for her imprisonment. He had raised forces in Leicestershire to help suppress the rising of the northern earls in Mary's favour and this had probably helped him to his Garter. His position in the county was further strengthened by his brothers, all active men, all Puritans, all resident in Leicestershire. His two deputy-lieutenants were his brothers. His influence in Leicester, of which his family held the stewardship, was also very great, and his nominees sat for the borough. In Leicestershire no one could compare with the Earl in social prestige or political influence; there was no one, even, strong or powerful enough to make capital when, for a short time, he fell out of favour with the Queen. Election followed election and the Hastings monopoly was not challenged; the gentry took their seats when the Hastingses did not want them both, and a Turpin, a Beaumont, or a Skeffington was occasionally seen at Westminster. But in 1601, at the election for Elizabeth's last Parliament, a challenge was made. It would seem that there was a growing faction in the county which disliked the Hastings monopoly, for the earl's influence was directly challenged in Leicester itself. There George Belgrave managed by guile and chicanery to gain a seat, although he was described as a noted enemy of the Earl. Belgrave was the heir of William Stokes, the brother of Adrian, and so distantly connected with the Greys. In the county itself the challenge came from Sir John Grey, who wrote asking for the help of the Earl of Rutland, whose brothers he had befriended when in his custody after the rising of the Earl of Essex. But it was to no avail. As yet Rutland's power in Leicestershire was negligible.

The strongest protest against the Hastings influence came in the election of 1621. Once again both seats were demanded, this time for Sir George Hastings and Sir Henry Hastings. The election was held at Leicester Castle and 1200 freemen declared for the two Hastingses but, although they had a clear majority, the Sheriff, Sir Alexander Cave, took legal advice, and refused to return Sir George Hastings on the ground that he was a non-resident and returned Sir Thomas Beaumont, the defeated candidate, in his stead.[5] Naturally the Hastingses petitioned the House of Commons against this decision, and as the legal question involved – the right of a non-resident to represent a county – raised important constitutional issues, the case was extensively debated in the House. Sir Thomas Beaumont was allowed to be represented by counsel. Inevitably his petition was dismissed, for its acceptance would have led

to the unseating of many members. Sir Thomas Beaumont was so infuriated by the result that he threatened to sue Cave for damages and he
was only saved by the protection of the House of Commons. This result
so encouraged the Earl of Huntingdon that, in 1625, he was writing
about the county as an eighteenth-century peer might have written about
a pocket borough. 'I pray you speak,' he wrote to Thomas Wright from
St. Albans, 'to the freeholders of Leicestershire to vote for my brother,
Sir George Hastings, at the election on 5 May. At my coming home you
shall know who I desire should be the other Knight of the Shire.' But
times were not so easy for the Hastingses; one seat went to Sir Wolstan
Dixie of Bosworth, who was closely related to the Beaumonts, and Sir
George had to be content with the Hastings seat at Leicester itself. The
senior county seat went to the Earl's son Ferdinand, Lord Hastings,
who, since he is not mentioned in the letter of 5 May, must have been
rushed in at the last minute. This was done perhaps to still criticism
about the non-resident Sir George and to make certain that at least one
county seat was procured for the family, for the Earl's son and heir had
almost a prescriptive right.[6] Although the Hastings family maintained a
hold on the senior seat until 1640, they never again monopolized both,
and the stand taken at Leicester Castle in February 1621 by a Beaumont
and a Cave seems to have effectively rallied the Leicestershire gentry.
Nevertheless, from the Reformation to the Civil War, the political life
of Leicestershire was dominated by the Earls of Huntingdon; there was
no power comparable to theirs, and their relatives and clients represented
both county and borough almost continuously in Parliament.

We must, however, return to Elizabeth's reign. National events had
their repercussions in Leicestershire; the threat of a Spanish armada
rendered more acute differences in religion. From 1585 commissions to
take recusants were issued to the leading gentlemen of the shire, and
George Shirley of Staunton and Robert Brooksby were taken into
custody. In February 1588 the Sheriff, William Cave, proceeded against
Roman Catholic women and youths but complained that some had fled
from their habitations before the arrival of his officers. Compared with
other counties, however, the amount of recusancy in Leicestershire seems
to have been small and caused little trouble to the local authorities. The
fear of a Spanish invasion was more alarming and the military resources
of the country were strained to the utmost. In December 1587 the Lord-
Lieutenant, Henry, Earl of Huntingdon, was ordered to 'select and equip
500 men in Leicestershire to be in readiness to serve on any sudden
occasion'. The full force of those liable for service was called out and
sent to Tilbury; in addition to the 500 footmen raised according to his
instructions, the Earl gathered together a band of 500 private soldiers
which was maintained by his family for many years.

The foreign policy of Elizabeth's latter years made further demands for soldiers from Leicestershire. She supported the French Huguenots with troops and in 1591 150 able-bodied men from the shire were ordered to be sent to Normandy for the succour of the French king. They were soon recalled, 'the Queen not being minded that they should be out of the realm above 2 months', but in the following year more Leicestershire men had to do a term of service overseas.

Provision of men for the army in Ireland, however, was to prove a more severe strain than help to the French. The hardships of guerrilla warfare made constant reinforcements necessary; in 1595 35 men were ordered from Leicestershire for service in Ireland 'furnished with coates of good stuf and to be lined to preserve them better this winter season'. Further men were called for in April and more contingents, fully furnished with arms, were required in 1596 and 1597 to fill up the decayed bands already in Ireland. So desperate was the resistance of the Irish that Elizabeth, 'fynding her gracyous dispocycon to reduce the rebells of Ireland by some peaceable means to obedyence doth not take effecte', ordered fresh levies in 1598 and 1599. Money was collected in the county for the relief of the sick and disabled who returned. Their tales of suffering in Ireland made it very difficult to obtain any but undesirable men for the service, and the Council complained to the Earl of Huntingdon in 1600 that the Leicestershire levies 'have and do contyneuallie either runne awaie before they comme to embarque, or abandon their service very soone after their comming into Ireland'. The defeat of Tyrone by Mountjoy in 1603 put an end to this strain on the county's military resources.

But peace may have been a dubious blessing, for at least the Irish war had been one way of getting rid of the violent and the discontented, who seem to have been particularly rife in the early years of the seventeenth century. There was a fierce riot at Cotesbach in 1607, a part of the bitter and widespread Midland protest against inclosure.[7] In 1606 fears of peasant discontent had led the Earl of Huntingdon to order two barrels of gunpowder to be used to 'compel the inhabitants to desist from assembling to lay open enclosed ground'. A gibbet which had been erected *ad terrorem* had been demolished by a turbulent mob and the chamberlain and the mayor, Robert Herrick, were confined to their houses by the order of the Earl of Huntingdon. This was rough treatment, since the Herricks had been lending the Hastingses money. Not only the peasantry but the gentry were restless. Henry, 5th Earl of Huntingdon, was very conscious of the great political power which he wielded in the county and he did not hesitate to use it in the most forthright manner. The tone of his letters is always peremptory and often aggressive. This in itself cannot have endeared him to the Leicestershire gentry, some of whom, moreover, may have been alienated by his rabid puritanism and somewhat tyrannical handling of county elections. Whatever the cause, there was considerable plain speaking about his character in 1628 and two Leicestershire gentlemen, Sir Henry Shirley and Sir Anthony Faunt, were severely punished for their aspersions; Shirley was imprisoned in the Fleet by the House of Lords and Faunt was heavily fined in the Star Chamber. But this, together with the fact that after 1621 the Hastingses were never able to dominate the county elections and occasionally found the town itself intractable, shows that their political domination was far less secure than it had been in Elizabeth's reign. The jealousies and animosities of the gentry towards them were to be more important in the political crisis which led to the Civil War than the violent and sporadic outbursts of the peasantry.

Indeed, the personal and family feuds were notorious; Leicestershire was described as 'like a cockpit, one spurring against another'. Clarendon believed that the whole county was violently divided between Greys and Hastingses, 'a notable animosity' without the addition of any other quarrel. The personal nature of the quarrel may have had an important bearing on the strategy of the war, owing to the reluctance of Henry, Earl of Stamford, to move his forces from Leicestershire and so leave the county at the mercy of the Hastingses. From the lists of parliamentarians and royalists, compiled from the State Papers, it is possible to discover the allies of these great houses amongst the gentry.[8]

A rough geographical division is discernible. The bulk of the royalists were drawn from the country lying to the north and west of the Fosse Way with the addition of the spur of highland which runs up to Belvoir, an outlying bastion of royalist strength. Most of Grey's supporters, on the other hand, were drawn from the south and east of the county. The parliamentarians had a clear majority of the leading families amongst the gentry. Behind Henry, Earl of Stamford, were ranged the following families: Ashby of Quenby, Babington of Rothley, Cave of Stanford, Dixie of Bosworth, Faunt of Foston, Hartopp of Buckminster, Hazlerigg of Noseley, Herrick of Beaumanor, Packe of Prestwold, Palmer of Wanlip, Pochin of Barkby, Smith of Edmundthorpe, Villiers of Brooksby, Winstanley of Braunstone. Many of these were relatively new families. Some, like the Caves, Babingtons, and Ashbys, had done particularly well out of monastic land; others, like the Herricks and Dixies, had made their money as merchants and had then turned landowners; but the Faunts and the Villierses were old-established families, as old as any on the royalist side. In general the royalists were more impressive in lineage than wealth. Shirleys, Turvilles, Skeffingtons, Turpins, Skipwiths, Poulteneys, and the Beaumonts of Gracedieu had deep roots in Leicestershire and were not unprosperous, but the majority of royalists were small squires such as Farnham of Quorn or Wright of Barlestone. Nor had the royalists, apart from the leading families, the same experience of politics and administration, for, apart from the Hastingses, only one royalist family, Staresmore of Frolesworth, had produced a Knight of the Shire since the great disputed election of 1621, whereas a Hazlerigg, a Hartopp, and a Dixie had sat in the Commons. At the two critical elections of 1640, the Hastingses failed to retain their hold on the county and both seats went to supporters of Parliament's cause – Sir Arthur Hazlerigg and Lord Grey of Ruthin.[9]

There were three major strategic points in Leicestershire – the town itself and the castles of Ashby-de-la-Zouch and Belvoir.[10] Belvoir, with Newark, was a serious threat to the communications of the parliamentary forces in East Anglia and Yorkshire. Ashby was extremely important, not only as a stronghold for guerrilla raids but also as a fortress protecting the royalist communications between the south-west and the Duke of Newcastle in Yorkshire; in consequence the skirmishes in Leicestershire were of considerable importance to both sides, and it was not by chance that the decisive battle of the war was fought at Naseby on the borders of Leicestershire.

The first real trial of strength came in March 1642 in the struggle between Stamford and Henry Hastings, the militant royalist son of the Earl of Huntingdon, to obtain control of the militia and of the magazine, kept at the Newarke, Leicester. The Commons were determined to put an end to the king's control over the militia, which he exercised through the appointment of the Lord-Lieutenant, and to this end, on 5 March 1642, both Houses of Parliament nominated Stamford Lord-Lieutenant of Leicestershire. He was also empowered to call together all His Majesty's subjects in Leicestershire 'that are meet and fit for the wars, and them to train, exercise and put in readiness, and them . . . from time to time to cause to be arrayed and weaponed and to take muster of them'. Power to appoint deputy-lieutenants and officers was also conferred on him, and he used his forces 'for the suppression of all rebellions, insurrections and invasions that may happen, according as they . . . shall receive directions by his Majesty's authority, signified unto them by the Lords and Commons assembled in Parliament'.

The King could not agree, for such an act would have destroyed the whole basis of his military power, but the Parliament passed the Militia Bill as an 'ordinance of Parliament' and the lord-lieutenants were directed to act according to its provisions. In response, the King issued a proclamation forbidding the raising of levies except by his express command. To counter this the two Knights of the Shire, Sir Arthur Hazlerigg and Lord Grey of Ruthin, were sent by Parliament to Leicester to see the Militia Ordinance put into force, and Stamford was given authority to call out the trained bands for June. Stamford had an enthusiastic welcome in Leicester and an attempt, probably by Hastings, to stop him executing his warrant was brushed aside.

The royalists had not been idle under these provocations and Leicester-shire was the first county to receive a commission of array from the King (12 June). Hastings issued warrants for assembling the trained bands of foot and freeholders' bands on 22 June but he was so doubtful of Leicester that he appointed the Raw Dykes as the place of assembly and persuaded the Mayor of Leicester, Thomas Rudyard, to ignore Stamford's order and not call out the town bands. It was Hastings's intention to seize the magazine of the county at the Newarke, but in this he was frustrated by Stamford, who removed most of it to Bradgate. Stamford, however, either had second thoughts or the royalist forces were strong enough to compel him to change his mind, for by 7 July Charles was complimenting Hastings on its return to Leicester. Hastings had been appointed High Sheriff on 25 June in place of Archdale Palmer, who was a parliamentarian, and he was instructed to use the magazine 'as there shall be occasion'. In addition, Hastings's royalists were preventing considerable numbers of men from obeying Stamford's summons, particularly in north Leicestershire. It was doubtless because of the success of Leicestershire royalists that Hastings, Sir Richard Halford, Sir John Bale, and John Bate were impeached by the Commons, on the grounds that by acting under the King's commission of array they had disturbed the peace of the kingdom and betrayed the liberties of the subject. The Commons wished to intimidate royalists in other counties from following the prompt and energetic action of Hastings, who had arrested the parliamentary commissioner sent down to declare his actions illegal, and who was taking great pleasure in harrying his old enemy Stamford at Bradgate.[11]

Nevertheless, Stamford, Hazlerigg and Grey of Ruthin were doing what they could to rally the parliamentary forces and they reported excellent response at Broughton Astley, where appeared on 14 June 'above 100 volunteers and trained and private men'. The next day Kibworth made 'a good appearance' and further recruiting meetings were held at Copt Oak, Melton Mowbray and Queniborough, where the appearance was considered particularly good 'considering how many great Papists and ill-affected people live there-about'. But much as the parliamentary propagandists made of this response, it was far less spec-tacular and heartening than the forays of Hastings. Charles decided to visit Leicester himself in order to consolidate the admirable effect which the royalists were having.

The King entered the town on 22 July and was received with warm expressions of loyalty by 'ten thousand of the gentry and better sort of inhabitants of that county'. Charles appealed for help, if help were needed, but the King hoped that such help would not be necessary as he thought that Parliament could not reasonably refuse his latest proposals. But if occasion should arise, 'I know you will bring horses, men, money and hearts, worthy of such a cause'. Apart from an offer to raise and maintain six-score horses and horsemen, the appeal did not receive much response, for, as Clarendon realised, 'if the King were loved there as he ought to be, Parliament was more feared than he'. Indeed, the King was promptly presented with a petition which expressed regret at his long estrangement from his 'highest and safest council of Parliament', complained of Hastings' actions and of the honours bestowed on him, and requested the King to leave the magazine and militia in the hands of the Earl of Stamford – a bold demand, since the King had already declared Stamford a traitor. But worse was to follow on the next day, when a further petition was presented which called for an immediate settlement of the question of the control of the magazine. Three demands were made that the magazine might be distributed to the several hundreds of the county, that it might never be 'reassumed' but by a legal power, and that the keepers of it might have liberty and protection for discharging their trust. No doubt the Mayor and Corporation, caught between the conflicting demands of Hastings and Stamford, felt their position to be invidious and desired protection. None was forthcoming; the King merely replied that if the keepers of the magazine had done what was warrantable they needed no protection but the law. It was, however, decided to distribute the magazine through the six hundreds of the county. The King left Leicester on 26 July but returned for a night on 18 August before proceeding to Nottingham, where he set up his standard on 22 August 1642.

The declaration of war spurred Hastings to increased patrol activity, in which he was helped by Prince Rupert, who was quartered at Leicester with 800 of the King's horse. They found each other congenial company and they attacked Bradgate, carrying off some of the arms stored there by Stamford. They scared the household and had boisterous fun with the chaplain, for they took away his clothes and spoilt them. But Rupert overstepped his instructions in September when, short of ready money, he roughly demanded £2,000 in the King's name from the Mayor and Corporation of Leicester, threatening in his postscript to appear before the town with horse, foot, and cannon to teach them that it was safer to obey than to refuse the King's demands. The town hurriedly provided £500. They did not, however, have to find the rest, for the King heard of Rupert's rash action, disowned it, and discharged the Corporation from obedience to Rupert's demands on the ground that he only wished for voluntary loans from his subjects. It is not known whether the

Corporation took this broad hint, but it does not appear that the money paid was returned. Fortunately for Leicestershire Rupert was called away to the west: Hastings accompanied him and fought with great bravery at Edgehill on 23 October.

During the winter Parliament took measures to strengthen its position in Leicestershire and the Committee for the Safety of the Kingdom received orders in April 1643 to provide Lord Grey with six guns, 1000 muskets, and ammunition. During this winter the parliamentary forces seem to have obtained a secure grip on Leicester itself. But the royalists continued to consolidate their position, and their most striking victory during the winter was the taking of Belvoir Castle in January 1643 by Colonel Gervase Lucas, High Sheriff of Lincolnshire. Lucas was made Governor of the castle and had the revenues of Framland hundred for his support, 'which Lord Loughborough takes ill'. In February it was rumoured that the parliamentarians intended to recapture Belvoir but no action resulted. Throughout the county conditions were anarchic and Hastings attempted to secure some sort of order by declaring that he would use his utmost endeavour to prevent the plundering of those who had obeyed the ordinance of Parliament for the militia, upon a similar promise from Lord Grey to those who had appeared for the King. It is not known whether Lord Grey responded to his request.

Both Ashby and Belvoir were exceptionally strong and well-fortified, both admirable bases for marauding raids on Roundhead territory, and many skirmishes took place between the Ashby and Belvoir royalists and the Roundheads from Leicester during the next two years. Indeed, the strength of Ashby and the riotous royalism of its soldiers became topics of the London press. It was reported that there are as 'debased wicked wretches there as if they had been raked out of hell' and that 'they have three malignant priests there, such as will drink and roar . . . and swear and domineer so as it would make ones heart ache to hear the country people to relate what they heard of them.'[12]

Fear of Lord Loughborough at Ashby and Colonel Lucas at Belvoir immobilized Lord Grey of Groby, who was unwilling to move his forces. Oliver Cromwell's plan to unite his own forces with Grey's and with those of Sir John Gell, the Roundhead leader of Nottingham and Derby, was thus completely frustrated, and he was unable to go to the relief of the Fairfaxes, hard pressed by the Duke of Newcastle in Yorkshire. 'Believe it,' Cromwell wrote, 'it were better, in my poor opinion, Leicester were not, than that there should not be an immediate taking of the field.' He persuaded Grey to go as far as Nottingham but no farther. In consequence of this and of Hotham's treachery the Fairfaxes were decisively defeated by Newcastle at Adwalton Moor.[13]

Grey had little ability, 'a young man of no eminent parts', as Clarendon described him, and the initiative in Leicestershire remained with the Royalists. In November 1643 Colonel Lucas, in command of a strong force from Belvoir and acting in concert with a troop of horse from Newark, caught the Roundheads unawares at Melton Mowbray, and took 300 prisoners, three members of the Leicester Committee among them. Much valuable booty – 300 horses and 400 weapons – was also taken, a loss which had to be made good by a parliamentary vote of £500 and 400 arms on 7 December 1643. But some relief was given by the aggressive action of Sir John Gell, who later in the winter captured 120 horses belonging to Hastings, together with some prisoners. Further sharp skirmishing took place round Hinckley church in March 1644. Loughborough, returning from a successful ambush of Covenanters on the way to Leicester, had locked up his prisoners in the church. a relief party was summoned partly from Leicester and partly from Bagworth. The prisoners were rescued, but most of the Cavaliers escaped safely to Ashby.

These minor successes, however, did little to allay the concern which Parliament felt for the military situation in Leicestershire. In July 1644 the principal parliamentarian inhabitants of the county were formed into a new Committee for the Militia whose duties were to 'raise forces, suppress the enemy, to assess taxes, to pay the troops, to appoint officers and suppress revolt'. But the new committee was soon at loggerheads with Lord Grey, and the 'gentlemen, freeholders, and best affected of Leicestershire' petitioned Parliament to compose their differences and complained that the best men of the county were left out of the new committee. They wanted 'the now dishevelled soldiers' to be collected under the command of Lord Grey so that 'we may be able again to give limits to the now unbounded enemy'.[14] Attempts were made throughout the summer of 1644 to destroy or to reduce the marauding forces of Ashby and Belvoir, and, although some success was achieved, it was insufficient to repress the royalists; the Roundheads' most important achievement was the victory of the parliamentary forces under General Fairfax and Colonel Gell in the Vale of Belvoir, but the expected consequence – the fall of Belvoir – did not ensue. Moreover, this success was quickly overshadowed by a brilliant royalist cavalry victory at Melton Mowbray, where Sir Marmaduke Langdale, on his way north to relieve Pontefract Castle, overcame Colonel Rossiter, who tried to intercept him.

As yet no serious warfare had touched Leicestershire and there is a very amateur air about the skirmishes and ambushes between the Hastingses and the Greys, but in 1645 more serious events were at hand. It was suspected that the royalists were planning an attack on Leicester itself, the state of whose defences gave cause for alarm. Colonel George

Booth wrote to Lord Grey from Leicester in April 1645, stressing the weakness of the garrison and the inability of the town to withstand a siege – '500 resolute well-managed soldiers could at any time make themselves masters of this town'. The defenders consisted of ill-disciplined men; the townsfolk were dissatisfied with the government, for the 'Grand Masters' (presumably the members of the Leicester Committee) fortified their own houses in the Newarke but left the rest of the town undefended. This letter provoked the Committee of both Kingdoms to advise the Leicester Committee to put their defences in order. This they tried to do but time was denied them.[15] Charles was forced to take action in order to draw off Fairfax, who had begun to besiege Oxford, and having joined his army with Rupert's he was strong enough to tackle Leicester. On 27 May the King was at Ashby, on the 28th he spent the night at Cotes, the home of Sir Henry Skipwith, on the 29th he was at Aylestone, and the siege began. The royalist forces numbered about 5520. There is no very reliable figure for the garrison, but probably it was fewer than 2000.

On Thursday, 29 May the main body of the King's army approached and a skirmish took place, but the Leicester forces had to withdraw to the town. On Thursday night or Friday, Rupert set up a battery of six guns directed on the weak places in the defences. These were pointed out by royalists who had escaped from Leicester during the night.[16] On the same day Rupert sent in generous conditions of surrender, considering the disparity of the forces. While the Leicester Committee were still discussing their answer the time allowed by Rupert ran out, and he commenced the bombardment of the town at three o'clock on Friday, 30 May. By night wide breaches were made in the walls, 'which by the industry of the men and women of the town were some of them made up again with Wool-packs and other materials'. The repairs were inadequate; the breach considered practicable; at midnight twenty companies of the Royalist infantry advanced against the town. A desperate defence of great valour was conducted by Sir Robert Pye and Major Innes at the Newarke, Captains Babington and Hacker at the West Bridge, and Colonel Grey and Lieutenant-Colonel Whitbrooke at Eastgates and St. Margaret's churchyard. The resistance was finally concentrated at the Newarke breach. Here, as one of the defenders afterwards wrote,

was the fiercest assault, the enemy there comming to push off Pike, four times they attempted and were as often repulst, our men taking two of their Colors from them. Captain Hacker and Captain Babington with their horse and a cannon from a corner of the wall made a miserable slaughter of them; amongst the rest Colonell St. George in a bravery came up to our cannon, and was by it shatter'd into small parcels, and with him many more, for after the manner of the Turks, the horse forced on the foot to fight, they being beaten upon by our Musketteers, great slaughter was made of them.

About the same time the royalists by use of hand grenades forced an entrance at the Eastgates and 'the horse being come in they rid with a full career in a body of about 600 up the streets, clearing them as they went, and so to the Newarke, and coming upon the backs of our forces there, they fighting gallantly and defending the breach, there was no way left but to submit upon quarter, which they did'.

In the heat of victory the royalists sacked the town, and exaggerated reports of the carnage were rapidly circulated. Charles I, in one account, was described as urging his troops on to greater bloodshed, and White-locke wrote that 'they gave no quarter but hanged some of the committee and cut others in pieces. Some letters say the kennels ran down with blood'. One newspaper, however, reported that it was the Irish who were the most desperate assailants, though, it was added, they did no more hurt than 'what was done in a heat'. Also, a Puritan pamphleteer wrote, 'give the divell his due, there was indeed many slaine at the first enterance and some that made little resistance and some women and children amongst the multitude, by the rabble of common souldiers, but I cannot learne of any such order to destroy all, as is said by some.' Nevertheless carnage there was, for Clarendon reports that it was 'exceeding regretted' by Charles.

The plunder was vast; 140 cartloads of goods were sent off to Lich-field, Belvoir and Newark, and at their own estimate the parliamen-tarians admitted losing nine pieces of ordnance, 1000 muskets, 400 horses, and about 50 barrels of powder. The King was elated, for the prestige of the victory was very great, and, much to the consternation of Parliament, the parliamentary garrisons at Bagworth, Coleorton, Kirby Bellars and Burghley House promptly deserted their posts. Recrimi-nations of prophetic intensity were hurled at the wretched Leicester Committee. Fairfax promptly abandoned the siege of Oxford, and strengthened by the addition of Cromwell with 600 horse marched north to engage the King.

The decisive battle of the war was nearly fought in Leicestershire. Having reprovisioned Oxford, the King occupied a strong defensive position on carefully chosen ground at Market Harborough. When Rupert's scouts, however, reported that Fairfax, who was encamped six miles away at Gilsborough, was retreating, Charles incautiously moved into Northamptonshire, to find himself at a disadvantage of ground at Naseby. Parliament's victory was total, and 'magnanimous Lieutenant General Cromwell pursued their horse with a full carrier about 12 or 13 miles at least, even within 2 or 3 miles of Leicester, the longest pursuite that ever was since this unhappy Warre began'. According to tradition the King and Prince Rupert stopped in their flight at Wistow Hall, the home of Sir Richard Halford, in order to obtain plain saddles which would not betray their rank. They left their richly decorated ones behind, to be a memento in the Halford family of faithful service and loyal hospitality. The King made a short stop at Leicester to see that the wounded were being cared for and then made his way to the Welsh border.

The parliamentary forces rapidly overran south Leicestershire and invested the town, whose royalist governor, Lord Loughborough, had done all in his power to strengthen the defences. But he had only been in command for a fortnight, and, apart from enlisting 400 recruits from the county for garrison work, little had been done. On 16 June Fairfax demanded the surrender of the town but Hastings resolutely refused. Fairfax proceeded to use the siege guns which he had captured at Naseby and bombarded the Newarke. On 17 June Hastings realised that the position was hopeless and asked for a parley. Colonels Rainborough and Pickering were sent in to treat and Hastings accepted their terms. On Wednesday, 18 June, Hastings marched out at the head of his force, but only the cavalry officers were allowed to take out their arms. Hastings was bitterly criticized for surrendering all the guns, arms, ammunition, and provisions at Leicester, an act which led to great rejoicing in Parliament, who voted a day of public thanksgiving, observed on the 19th. A collection was ordered in London churches for the relief of those people of Leicester who had suffered most from the ravages of the royalists.

Although the King's cause was lost, neither Ashby nor Belvoir tamely surrendered to Parliament. Both Lord Loughborough and Colonel Lucas, with their gallant garrisons, were determined to fight to the last. In October Belvoir was besieged by Colonel Pointz. On 21 November he summoned the castle to surrender, but Lucas replied tersely: 'I was not placed here by the King to surrender to rebels. I will not give one inch of ground I am able to maintain with my sword.' The garrison responded to the bravery of its commander. They defended themselves with great courage, and only after a bitter battle were they forced to give up the stables and outworks. 'The works were the strongest I have seen in England', wrote one of the attackers, 'and gallantly defended, and our men at first discouraged so much that the General, myself, and some other officers were fain to keep the men at the works with our swords.' In January 1646 Lord Loughborough made a sortie from Ashby and attempted to relieve Belvoir. Although he surprised the parliamentarians he was unable to break their hold on the castle. After the loss of his outworks and his fresh-water supply, it was only a matter of weeks before Colonel Lucas was forced to parley with the envoys from Parliament, one of whom was, naturally enough, the Earl of Rutland. His presence probably secured the honourable terms which were allowed to Lucas in order to avoid the destruction which a final assault would have caused.

Only Ashby remained. With the county very largely under parliamentary control, it became very difficult for the garrison to secure supplies. The castle was closely besieged from September 1645, and, although it was reinforced by 600 royalists in October, its fall was only a matter of time. Loughborough finally surrendered to Colonel Needham, the governor of Leicester, on 2 March 1646. The fall of Ashby marks the close of the Civil War in Leicestershire. That was obvious to all men.

What was less obvious was that it also marked the fall of a great family. The surrender terms demanded that the castle was to be 'slighted' and stripped of all means of defence, which was carried out later, in or after 1648. Never again was Ashby to be the seat and stronghold of the Hastings family. Even before the Civil War that family had begun to live more frequently at Donnington Park and afterwards they lived there permanently.[17] Although Loughborough prevented the sequestration of both his own estates and those of his brother, Lord Huntingdon, yet the wealth of both was seriously diminished by subsequent fines. But more than all of this was the loss of prestige. Many of their followers were not so lucky and their estates were lost, and further support of Hastings held out little hope of recovery or reward. It was natural that the Hastingses should be proud of their devotion to the royalist cause and so develop a tradition of uncritical loyalty to the Stuarts. Theophilus, the 7th Earl, was imprisoned for his Jacobite sympathies. This attachment to a lost cause resulted in a steady decline in their political prestige in Leicestershire, and after the Civil War no member of the Hastings family ever represented either the county or the borough of Leicester in Parliament, both of which had been almost their private preserves for a century. Yet in political structure the century which followed the Civil War differed little from that which went before. Aspiring men needed the patronage of a great man or family. The men of Leicestershire turned naturally to the Greys, Earls of Stamford, the successful rivals of the Hastingses, and also, and more effectively, to the Mannerses, Earls of Rutland, who, after the Civil War, devoted far more time to their Leicestershire interests. In 1668 Belvoir Castle was reconstructed and became their chief home, and from that time they began to exercise a power nearly as extensive as that wielded previously by the Hastingses.

The shape of things to come was indicated in August 1648, when Lord Grey of Groby was made Governor of Ashby Castle during the scare caused by the Second Civil War, which did not touch Leicestershire.

Later he was granted £1500 out of Crown lands because he had been 'very zealous in forwarding Parliamentary interests' in Leicestershire. Another £1500 was granted to the Earl of Rutland to recompense him for the demolition of Belvoir.

The invasion of Charles II in 1651 made great demands on the military resources of the Midland counties. Lord Grey was ordered to raise volunteers in Leicester, Nottingham, and Rutland to march against Charles. They were quickly raised and they fought under him at the battle of Worcester, for which Grey received the thanks of the Council of State.

Leicestershire was undisturbed by royalist plots or insurrections during the Commonwealth, and a loyal address was sent to Richard Cromwell from the 'well-affected inhabitants of the county of Leicester' on the death of Oliver Cromwell. But as the Commonwealth dissolved in anarchy, conditions in Leicestershire became more turbulent. In August 1659, when 300 volunteer horse had left Leicester to tackle the rising of the royalists in Cheshire, the Earl of Stamford declared for the King, and Major Babington of Rothley Temple, another Roundhead who had changed his principles, gathered together two or three hundred men in arms. These, however, were easily dispersed by the militia and he himself was taken prisoner. Stamford and Babington had been wise only a little before their time and in less than twelve months (12 May 1660) Charles II was proclaimed in Leicester. The county celebrated wholeheartedly; at Melton Mowbray an ox was roasted in the streets; and 'ringing of bells, volleys of shot, bonfires, music and dancing and all the usual ways of expressing so great a joy continued three days'. But there were few who lost, or gained, by the change. Sir Arthur Hazlerigg, excluded from the Act of Oblivion, died in the Tower. Lord Loughborough was restored to the lord-lieutenancy of the county in 1661 but to little else, and on his death it passed to the Earl of Rutland, in whose family it remained with scarcely a break for the next 200 years.

After the Restoration, the pattern of Leicestershire politics was soon made clear. Lord Roos, the eldest son of the Earl of Rutland, was returned for the county with George Faunt of Foston.[18] This division of representation between the aristocracy and the gentry was usual for the next 150 years, and electoral peace was only disturbed when the aristocracy tried to secure both seats for themselves or on those rarer occasions when party or personal feelings ran so high that a contest became inevitable. In the election of 1679 Lord Roos joined with Lord Sherrard, but they were immediately opposed by Sir John Hartopp of Rotherby. Hartopp had married the daughter of General Fleetwood: he was a known friend of Nonconformists and his Whiggery was far more ardent than that of Sherrard or Roos: indeed, the latter was associated with the Court. Nevertheless, in Hartopp's opposition there was a social as well as a political protest, an expression of the resentment felt by the smaller gentry at the prospect of both seats going to sons of the nobility. The sheriff was cautious and returned Roos and Sherrard, but Hartopp's supporters petitioned against the return. In the House of Commons Roos's election was declared void by 116 to 78 and a new election ordered.[19] The Commons did not bother to consider a counter-petition against Hartopp, who was returned, presumably unopposed, at the subsequent election. Sherrard and Hartopp continued to represent the county throughout the Exclusion Parliaments. The crisis about the succession, and the fears aroused by the Popish plot, appear to have touched Leicestershire but little.

The defeat of Shaftesbury and the Whig débâcle which followed the exposure of the Rye House Plot brought a slight change in political forces. The Earls of Rutland moved quietly and discreetly with events. They were regarded for a time as loyal by James II, but the Earls of Stamford lost face and their position was taken by the Earls of Huntingdon, who enjoyed a brief Indian summer of political influence.[20] At the election of 1685 Hartopp was dropped and his place taken by a young Tory lawyer, John Verney, the son of Sir Richard Verney of Allexton who afterwards on his son's advice claimed and obtained the dormant barony of de Broke.[21] Passionately royalist as the Parliament of 1685 was, it was nevertheless not royalist enough for James II, who began to develop the political revolution started by his brother. Both Charles II and James II realised that they could never secure complete toleration for Roman Catholics until the control of local government was in the hands of their supporters. Borough after borough was made to forfeit its charters – Leicester's went in 1684 – and the new ones issued usually reserved considerable powers of appointment to the Crown and the right of election of a Member of Parliament restricted to the corporation, which was easier to control.[22] The turn of county government followed; the method employed was to remove strong Whig justices of the peace and replace them by Roman Catholics or Protestant dissenters. The same was done with the deputy lieutenants. In order to facilitate this process in Leicestershire, the Earl of Rutland, the Whig tradition of whose family made him unreliable, was dismissed from the lord-lieutenancy and replaced by the Earl of Huntingdon, an uncompromising royalist. By the spring of 1688 the process was considered to have gone far enough for James to call a new Parliament, but he was determined to be certain of his members on the issue of toleration. The lord-lieutenants were instructed to question all their deputies and justices as to whether they would support the repeal of the Test and Penal Laws. If they answered unfavourably they were to be dismissed from office and every step taken to prevent their election to Parliament. Huntingdon carried out this investigation for Leicestershire in February 1688 and made his return to James. His deputy-lieutenants, Sir Thomas Burton of Stockerston, Sir Henry Beaumont of Stoughton, Sir William Holford of Welham, Richard Roberts of Thorpe Langton and Henry Nevill of Holt, all carefully chosen for their loyalty, agreed, but apart from one justice, Dr William Foster, little other support was forthcoming from the county gentry. Many such as the Abneys, Verneys, Noels, and Packes were discreetly absent from the county during the inquiry; but Sherrards, Babingtons, Hazleriggs, Boothbys, de la Fontaines, and others flatly refused. There could be no doubt that the most powerful political families in the county were steadfastly opposed to James's policy.

It was the removal of so many country gentlemen from the bench and the militia which made the Revolution of 1689 inevitable and success easy for William III. Stamford, Rutland, Ferrars, and Sherrard all attended in November 1688 on the Princess Anne as she passed through Leicestershire on her way to join the northern lords at Nottingham. In the county the Revolution was accomplished easily but not without incident. Fears of the Irish put the county in a state of alarm on 12 December 1688, and so disturbed were conditions in January 1689 that soldiers had to accompany the collectors of customs and excise. After James II's flight, William called a Convention which after his acceptance of the Crown declared itself to be a Parliament. Elections to this assembly had been rushed and many men were returned who would have been returned had James called a Parliament. This was partly true of Leicestershire. Sir Thomas Halford, an ardent Tory, was returned for the county, along with Bennet, Lord Sherrard. Halford, with Babington, one of the members for the town, refused to vote for the motion offering the Crown to William and Mary.[23]

The Revolution of 1689 opened a new era in Leicestershire politics. From this date Parliaments have met every year, and one of the easiest ways to social and political success has been through service in the House of Commons. The control of membership added greatly to the prestige of the aristocracy, who cultivated parliamentary electors as carefully as their pheasants. This attempt to dominate completely the political life of the county bred resentment amongst the lesser gentry. By mutual support they became powerful enough to win one county seat and to maintain their hold on it. As Leicestershire was poorly provided with seats in Parliament, the borough representation was quickly dominated by the leading county families and the parliamentary politics of the borough were very largely an extension of those of the county. As the king's agent phrased it in February 1688: 'there are none of the Members of the Corporation of Leicester proper to stand for

Parliament men, either for quality, fortune or interest, especially in a County where there are so few Elections. But the corporation did not suffer: members of county families were as attentive to the special interests of Leicester as any corporation member would have been. They were always ready to present petitions on behalf of the town. In the same way, of course, the county members looked after any matter which touched the life of the county, and in return they expected the county to make loyal addresses when the occasion arose so that they themselves would not seem to be lacking in loyalty.[24]

For much of the eighteenth century the politics of Leicester followed a placid course, members and elctors pursuing harmoniously their mutual interests, but there were occasions when there was a sudden flare-up of political strife and this was very common from 1689 to 1722. In 1695 the peace of the county was disturbed, for the Duke of Devonshire considered setting up his son as a candidate. On the other hand, Thomas, Earl of Stamford, was confident that he had secured complete control of both the county and the town. Events proved otherwise. Stamford secured a seat for one of his clients, George Ashby of Quenby, but Rutland was powerful enough to keep his hold on the other for the Hon. John Verney. Devonshire had to place his sons elsewhere. Stamford, although defeated, was determined in 1698 to try once more. 'I find my Ld Stamford', wrote Verney to the Earl of Rutland, 'is resolved to have a poll in Leicestershire again for Mr Bird and Mr Ashby will stand. I am sorry I am like to be the occasion of more trouble to your Lordship having given you more than all my services to you can ever deserve.' At this election the gentry were not prepared to stand by and watch Stamford and Rutland fight it out. They had their own candidate in John Wilkins of Ravenstone, a Tory squire, related through his wife to the Caves and the Villierses, both powerful families among the independent gentry. Rutland managed to secure the election of Verney but Stamford failed with Ashby and Bird.[25] The gentry succeeded with Wilkins. Stamford did not take kindly to his eclipse, and in the next election the county was threatened with a further contest, but in the end the same members were returned. This Parliament lasted but a few months and the county was plunged into a violent contest in which old friends were parted and new alliances made. The trouble began with Lord Roos, Rutland's eldest son. The removal of the family home from Haddon Hall to Belvoir Castle had lowered Roos's interest in Derbyshire, and he was so frightened of defeat that he insisted on his father backing him for Leicestershire. At the mayor's feast at Leicester on 18 November, Roos declared his intention of standing for the county and joined with Lord Sherrard, a young man of 24, who had just succeeded his father and was already Lord-Lieutenant of Rutland. This was an outrageous action on the part of the aristocracy and aroused great anger among the gentry. Verney immediately deserted his patron, the Earl of Rutland, and set up in opposition. He joined with Sir George Beaumont, a sound Tory; Wilkins too was a candidate. The loss of Verney and his friends to the Rutland interest was offset by the gain of George Ashby and Bird, who now became ardent supporters of Lord Roos.[26] Yet so complex were the political alignments of this time that many of Rutland's supporters in the county were very strongly opposed to his choice for the town, James Winstanley.[27] But Rutland was overwhelmingly triumphant; the two lords were returned for the county, and both his clients, James Winstanley and Lawrence Carter, secured the representation of the town. It was the most complete victory ever achieved by the Rutlands, equalling the triumphs of the Hastingses in the days of Elizabeth, but it was never repeated. This aristocratic domination was bitterly resented, and as soon as William III died Verney and Wilkins were busily canvassing the county. Once more Roos joined with Sherrard, but the resentment felt by the squirearchy was too strong for them and Verney and Wilkins were returned. Roos did not venture to contest the county again until 1710 and Verney remained a member until his death in 1707. In 1702 the Rutland interest was partly defeated at Leicester itself, Sir George Beaumont of Stoughton Grange, a firm Tory, capturing a seat from Lawrence Carter.[28] At the by-election which followed Verney's death George Ashby was returned unopposed,[29] but this was because Parliament had almost completed its three years. At the general election of 1708 Ashby joined with Sir Gilbert Pickering, Bt., another Whig, related to the important clan of Wortley Montagu. Although Pickering was successful, Ashby was defeated and Geoffrey Palmer of Carlton Curlieu, a sound Tory, was elected in his place. A petition attacking Palmer for bribery and corruption was presented by Ashby's supporters, but the House of Commons refused to take cognizance of it. In 1710 Lord Roos, by that time Marquess of Granby, decided to quit his pocket borough of Grantham and stand once again as Knight of the Shire for Leicestershire. In order to facilitate his election Pickering stood down, the Tories were not challenged for the other seat, and the county was spared an election contest. Granby, however, spent only a few months in the Commons, for his father died in 1711 and he removed to the Upper House as the 2nd Duke of Rutland. The Tories decided that there was a chance of obtaining the second seat and they pressed Sir Thomas Cave of Stanford to accept nomination. He did so only to find that another Tory, Captain Tate, was already in the field. 'I must confess', wrote Sir Thomas, ' 'twould be unhappy to have the Church interest once divided which would be difficult to unite.' Fortunately for Sir Thomas, Tate realised that he lacked influential backing and withdrew. In 1713 the

Tories retained their hold, Lord Tamworth, the eldest son of Earl Ferrers, who had been a strong supporter of Cave in 1711, taking the other seat. The Tories had taken advantage of the violent revulsion from the Whigs, caused by the Sacheverell trial, and also of the preoccupation of the Duke of Rutland with his family affairs. But it was inconceivable to the Whigs that the Tories should be allowed to control both seats and a determined challenge was made to defeat them in 1715. Tamworth had succeeded his father as Earl Ferrers and Sir Thomas Cave was joined with Sir Geoffrey Palmer. The Whigs adopted George Ashby and Thomas Bird, who was strongly backed by the Duke of Rutland and Lord Sherrard.[30] The election took place at Leicester Castle on 14 February 1715. The sheriff, Sir John Meeres, was a Whig. He prevaricated and made the election as difficult as possible for the Tories and then refused to make a return on the ground that it was not possible to conclude the election owing to 'tantas riotas, routas, affraias, tumultus, et perturbationes'. The sheriff's refusal caused a great stir in London and filled the newspapers.[31] To try and strengthen their position the Whigs petitioned the Commons, maintaining that William Baresby, the under-sheriff and a Tory, had refused over 600 of their votes. Eager as the House of Commons was in 1715 to secure the return of Whig members, the behaviour of the sheriff had been so outrageous and the evidence for Cave and Palmer so strong that the best that they could do for Ashby and Bird was to order a new writ for a fresh election.[32] The Tories hoped to avoid a new contest, but Ashby and Bird demanded a poll, which lasted three days. Lord Keeper Wright stayed in Leicester throughout the contest 'lest tricks should be played'. He was an ardent Tory who 'protests to spend his blood and estate before this country shall be nos'd by any Duke in Christendom'. The county agreed with Wright, and, when the poll was cast up, there were 2251 votes for Sir Geoffrey Palmer, 2203 for Sir Thomas Cave, 1639 for Bird, and 1630 for Ashby. Undoubtedly the desire of the Duke of Rutland and Lord Sherrard to dominate Leciestershire politics caused widespread resentment. But it was difficult for the Tories to maintain this success. The great Whig nobleman had a great attraction for the ordinary freeholder. The nobleman could oblige the freeholder in 101 different ways. He could also be a dangerous enemy.[33] When Sir Thomas Cave suddenly died in 1719, Lord William Manners was put up to represent the Rutland interest. To oppose him was a more audacious act than to oppose candidates merely supported by the Duke of Rutland. In consequence the Tories failed against him and although they petitioned the Commons on behalf of Francis Mundy, accusing the deputy-lieutenants, justices of the peace, and the sheriff of corrupt, arbitrary, and illegal proceedings, they had so little faith in their own case that they asked the Commons to allow them to withdraw their petition.[34]

At the election of 1722 a curious situation arose. Between 1689 and 1705 Leicester borough elections had been partly controlled by the great county families, but the decision of the Commons in 1705 to allow non-resident freemen a vote increased the electorate considerably and made the elections more difficult to manage. Until 1768 the town returned ardent Tories, unsympathetic to the Whig aristocratic families. Leicester, of course, had many freeholders who had a vote in the county, and in 1722 they put up their own Tory candidate, James Wigley, in opposition to Lord William Manners and Edmund Morris. Wigley only had backing from the town and the sheriff refused a poll, probably on the ground that the issue of the election was clear from a view of the voters. The sheriff's refusal resulted in a petition by the corporation's most ardent Tories — Gabriel Newton, Samuel Bull, and Thomas Johnston — but it is interesting that none of the Tory gentlemen of standing in the county supported them.[35] The gentry had been content to divide the representation with the Whigs, for Morris was a Tory. No doubt it was resentment at this deal which had caused the Tories of the borough to run their own candidate.

Amicable arrangements between Whig and Tory, alternating with attempts by one side or the other to capture both seats — this represents the pattern of Leicestershire politics until the end of the century. There were contested elections in 1734 and 1741; at the latter an Ashby still forlornly battled against a Cave.[36] After that there was peace until the by-election of 1775 when the Duke of Rutland and the Earl of Huntingdon ran opposing candidates — William Pochin, Whig, and John Hungerford, Tory. A bitter contest ensued but the Tory finally carried the day. For the general election of 1780 the Duke of Rutland made great efforts to secure agreement between the parties in order to avoid the expense of an election. This was done, and Pochin and Hungerford were returned.

But times were changing. Throughout the eighteenth century the Whig aristocracy and the Tory squirearchy had used the grievances and prejudices of the working class for their own purposes. Very frequently the Rutlands, Stamfords, and Harboroughs had allied themselves with the stocking-frame knitters against the Tory corporation of Leicester. In fact this had become the tradition of Leicestershire politics. It was broken in the first place by the French Revolution; according to a contemporary, 'the Whig families and landowners of this county soon surrendered all their former notions of liberty, and joined the Tories in supporting the old governments in their abuses'. But an equally important factor in breaking up this traditional pattern of politics was the change caused in the balance of social forces by the widespread development of stocking-frame knitting[37] and the increased exploitation of the Leicestershire coalfield. These two factors created industrial villages in the county and gave rise to a class of capitalists, bankers, merchants, and manufacturers such as the Pagets, Pareses, Frewens, or Coltmans. This new class looked to liberalism and radicalism, to free trade and Free Church, to solve the problems of the dangerous social ferment of the early nineteenth century.

The first effect of the change in county elections was to make both the aristocracy and the squirearchy unwilling to allow their differences to go to the length of a disputed election, and a contest did not take place until 1818. During these years the military history of the county is of greater interest than its parliamentary politics.

The fears of an invasion from France in the Seven Years War led to a revival and reorganisation of the national militia, which had been neglected during the long period of peace. The new militia law of 1757 fixed a quota of 560 men for Leicestershire to be raised by ballot. After a reluctant start the militia by 1760 was fully constituted and formed into two companies under the command of the lord-lieutenant, the Duke of Rutland.[38] But the fears of the French Revolution and of Napoleon led to far greater military activity in the county. During the invasion scare of 1803–4 there was very great enthusiasm for the Volunteers. The Leicestershire Yeomanry was formed. The Duke of Rutland offered to raise a corps of infantry, 'The Belvoir Castle Volunteers', consisting of four companies of 100 men. Not only did Leicester and the main market towns raise companies of infantry but many smaller villages such as Earl Shilton did likewise. In case the Volunteers should be called away to the coast, the Mayor of Leicester wished to form a local corps for the 'preservation of peace' in the thickly populated districts. The mayor was far-sighted, for the training acquired during these years was to be of great value to the gentlemen of Leicestershire during the turbulence of the Luddite and Chartist agitations.

Leicestershire came comparatively lightly out of the Luddite riots. Conditions throughout the Napoleonic Wars had been getting steadily worse for the working classes. The high price of food and the unstable conditions of the stocking-frame trade had led to very frequent distress. In 1800 the Duke of Rutland and the Earl of Stamford were making large donations for the relief of the Leicestershire poor; soup kitchens were opened in Hinckley, but this did not prevent serious riots, in which bakers' shops were attacked. It was these scenes of turbulence, as much as the fear of Napoleon, that encouraged the middle class to volunteer for the yeomanry. By 1812 conditions had deteriorated badly in the Midlands. Changes in fashion, over-production, particularly of shoddy goods, and excess labour created conditions of great difficulty in the

hosiery trade, and serious frame-breaking manifested itself in Nottinghamshire. It did not spread seriously in Leicestershire, though a few
frames were broken, and a correspondent of the *Leicester Journal*
boasted that 'in several large village halls the stockingers themselves
have come to a resolution that they will have no Ludd's men'. The main
activity of the Luddites in Leicestershire was the extortion of money for
the support of their cause. In December 1811 collectors were active
in Osgathorpe, Hugglescote and Ibstock. Often the Luddites protected
themselves by forcing the sale of copies of the Framework Knitters Act.
At the Assizes in March 1814, David Walker, Thomas Thorne and
William Plant were found guilty of extorting money in aid of frame-
breakers and transported. The secretary of the Committee of Framework
Knitters, Thomas Allsop, sent a letter to a leading manufacturer, threatening him with death in the name of Ned Ludd. And finally on 14 May
1812 there was a considerable riot at Loughborough, arising out of a
protest about food prices. Only the prompt action of Colonel Boot and
the militia prevented serious destruction. The yeomanry was called out
until this part of the county was peaceful again. Colonel Keck, MP for
the county, commanded the yeomanry. With the prospect of an election
before him, he used the opportunity to address his men on the state of
the county and the necessity of maintaining law and order, if need be
by force.

For the next four years Leicestershire was free from any serious
trouble, but on 29 June 1816 a grave disturbance occurred in Loughborough, at the factory of Heathcote and Bodenz, important bobbin-
lace manufacturers. The employees at this factory, whose wages had
recently been greatly reduced, suggested to the Loughborough committee
of the stockingers that the factory should be attacked. The Loughborough committee borrowed £40 from the 'Warp Lace Committee' of
Nottingham, in order to hire what was in effect a semi-professional team
of frame-breakers.[39] At one o'clock in the morning,

> The large Bobbin Lace Manufactory of Mr Heathcote at Loughborough in
> this county was beset by about 100 men, armed with blunderbusses. One of
> the six watchmen by which the place was guarded snapped his pistol at them
> and was immediately shot through the neck; the ball, however, is extracted
> and he is considered out of danger. They then secured the remainder of the
> watchmen and compelled ten men who were at work in the factory to lie
> down with their faces towards the ground, whilst they destroyed upwards of
> 50 frames in the short space of 40 minutes. The damage, including the lace
> cut and burnt, is upwards of £5000, independent of the loss of business and
> above 300 hands, in consequence, out of employ.

This was the most daring and destructive outrage of 1816. The government acted promptly; dragoons were sent to Loughborough and a reward of 500 guineas offered for the apprehension of any of the Luddites. The ringleaders were quickly arrested. They included James Towle, who had previously been acquitted on a charge of frame-breaking at Nottingham. Towle was extremely popular among the framework knitters and the authorities took great care at his trial at the summer assizes at Leicester. There were threats of disturbances and it was reported that ten men were paid to attempt to kill the judge.

Towle was condemned and, later in the year, executed. His death did nothing to stop the Luddites; indeed, his brother William organised destruction for revenge. But he too was caught and he followed James to the gallows. With him were executed four other Luddites, and three others were transported for life. This mass execution proved a grim and effective warning and it marks the end of Luddite activity in Leicestershire. Trade was improving and at the same time there was a growing hope that conditions would be improved through more orthodox methods of political agitation and negotiation.

At first the new spirit in politics did not touch the county elections. Those of 1790, 1796, 1802, 1806, 1807, and 1812 were decided according to the old pattern – a client or relative of Rutland taking one seat, a Tory the other. In October 1812 there is a letter from Lord Robert Manners to his fellow candidate, George Anthony Leigh Keck of Stoughton Grange, which discusses the election in purely eighteenth-century terms. Lord Robert writes that the only possible danger to either candidate is that his father may have to put up Pochin, because the Duke is obliged him to for the part he has played in recent considerable sales of property. Lord Robert intends to send his freeholders into Leicester – 'if you have no objection, to give these freeholders a dinner and supper in a plain way at Stephenson's'. Also his two sons will be there for canvassing; they should have 'some weight with the ladies at heart, being both very tall and very handsome youths'. The dinner and the youths were both unnecessary, for both candidates were returned unopposed. In the correspondence and in the letters of thanks published by the newly elected members there is no mention of the growing turbulence of the county and of the difficulties which faced the lower classes.

In 1818 the election did not run so smoothly. Naturally Keck and Manners stood for re-election. Thomas Babington of Rothley Temple, who had represented the borough for fourteen years, was also adopted. But unexpectedly C. M. Phillipps of Garendon Park was nominated. His supporters were the Pagets, which indicated that his attitude to politics was likely to be independent and liberal. Shortly before the election Keck withdrew on grounds of ill health. Nevertheless a spirited election, 'as determined a contest as the County has ever witnessed', was expected.

The election started on the Saturday, and on Monday, 28 June, 'carriages of every description from the elegant barouche to the humble dung cart were put in requisition and came rattling in from all quarters' to Leicester Castle. During the weekend, however, Babington thought better of it and decided to retire from the contest. Anti-Catholic feeling was extremely strong in the county and Babington's vote in favour of the admission of Roman Catholics was held against him. It is true that Phillipps was a Whig, but he was believed to be sound on the Catholic issue.[40] At the chairing of the successful candidates there were scenes of considerable violence. 'The populace', it was said, 'appeared to be seized with a fit of revolutionary frenzy, and upon Lord Robert Manners appearing in the Chair, commenced a most brutal attack upon his person, by a discharge of almost every species of missile accompanied with the most furious gestures and diabolical language.' By the time Lord Robert reached his committee room he was battered, bleeding, and coated with filth. It was one of the few ways open to the unenfranchised to express their attitude to Lord Robert's reactionary opinions. Phillipps regarded his election as a portent, which in some ways it was. He said at the hustings: 'man is no longer the same passive machine he once was; ignorant, unlettered, uninformed. He has begun to think, reflect and reason; and what is knowledge but power? Woe to those who shut their ears to the popular expression of the public voice? His election cry was *'vox populi, vox dei'*. The election of 1818 indicates that the structure of Leicestershire politics was changing. Old rivalries were giving way to new, and coveys of freeholders could not be driven so easily to the polls to vote for their landlord's choice. Even though Phillipps did not feel strong enough to contest the elections of 1820 and 1826 against Keck, now recovered in health, nevertheless both Keck and Lord Robert Manners could no longer ignore the working classes as they had done in the past. In their election addresses they went out of their way to express sympathy with the distress which was, at this time, the unhappy lot of manual workers.

With the mounting excitement occasioned by the question of parliamentary reform, the radicals decided once more to attack the county seat. At the election of 1830 Thomas Paget was the candidate but he was unsuccessful against the two die-hard Tories, Keck and Manners, both supported strongly by the Duke of Rutland.[41] Nevertheless Lord Robert Manners's bitter and determined opposition to any reform of the constitution whatsoever lost him considerable support throughout 1831. After 32 years in Parliament Keck did not fancy a violent contest in which, owing to the agitation for reform, his chances of success were slender and he retired. Phillipps was nominated in his place, and on Manners's withdrawal the second seat went to another Liberal, Paget.

The demand for parliamentary reform was widespread – 7000 persons in Leicestershire signed a petition in favour of the Reform Bill. Meetings of thanksgiving were also held when the Bill was before Parliament. But Leicestershire was largely free from the disturbances which were common in the rest of the country during the passing of the Reform Bill. In October 1831 there was a riot at Loughborough which had to be suppressed by the yeomanry. This led to active recruiting of the yeomanry and to the building-up of armament at Belvoir in case of further trouble; but none materialised.

The Reform Act divided the county into two parliamentary constituencies, North and South – a division which lasted until 1885.

Leicestershire returned two Tories, Lord Robert Manners and Henry Halford, and two independents, Charles March Phillipps and Edward Dawson, to the first reformed Parliament. Of the two independents Dawson was the more radical and was the first to go in 1835; he retired from the contest on the advice of his district committees – the first hint we have of Liberal organisation in the county. It was almost certainly *ad hoc* and not permanent. Phillipps, although in favour of the Reform Bill, was far less radical than Dawson and he was completely sound on the Church issue, which was one of the most burning political questions in the county. In his election address in 1835, Phillipps made it quite clear that he would not vote for any further change in Church or State, and particularly stressed his disapproval of Lord Althorp's Church Rate Bill and of the suggestion to allow dissenters into the universities.[42] Nevertheless he did not last and in 1837 he was replaced by another Tory, C. W. Packe. Leicestershire continued to return four Tory members for more than twenty years. This was partly due to the superior organisation of the Tory Party; a permanent conservative society was established in the southern division of the county, where the Liberal danger was greatest. The society held monthly meetings and paid great attention to the register. But the main Tory strength was derived from the hatred of free trade which was naturally widespread in a community which believed that the Corn Laws were the bulwark of agrarian prosperity.[43] Moreover, there is no doubt that many freeholders in Leicestershire voted consistently Tory because of their fear that a Liberal government was bound to undermine the established Church. They had a real horror of both Roman Catholicism and Protestant Dissent and could not tolerate the idea of any concessions to either party. In July 1847 a public meeting of freeholders and parliamentary voters was held at Melton Mowbray at which the following resolutions were passed:

1. That payment of public money to Roman Catholic clergy, Jesuits etc. ought not to be allowed.

2. That Roman Catholicism subverts souls and the Pope is a foreign ruler not to be obeyed.
3. That the Crown takes oaths to protect Protestants and to abjure Popery.
4. That if Britain tolerates Roman Catholicism she will fall as a nation.
5. That the displeasure of God will be incurred.
6. That all reasonable toleration for Roman Catholics was allowed by previous legislation.

At the same time the *Leicester Journal* strongly criticised the votes given by Lord Charles Manners and Sir Henry Halford, two of the county members, in favour of the Maynooth Grant, which they considered to be an unwarrantable concession to Roman Catholics. One of the reasons for the bitter opposition to Roman Catholicism was the fact that north Leicestershire, where Roman Catholic parishes were already established at Shepshed, Whitwick, and elsewhere, was one of the most fruitful fields for Roman Catholic missionary enterprise.[44]

Both the Corn Laws and the Roman Catholic question agitated politics of mid-nineteenth-century Leicestershire, but the most critical political issue lay just outside formal politics. This was the question of the Charter and Chartism. Throughout the 1830s the peace of the county was frequently disturbed by riots caused by the wretchedness of the conditions of life of the working class, particularly the stockingers.[45] At each general election in the 1830s distrubances were expected at Hinckley, Loughborough, Shepshed, and other centres of framework knitting, and special constables were enrolled and regular troops temporarily quartered there.[46] In 1837 a detachment of the 10th Hussars was sent for, post-haste, from Nottingham, in order to quell a serious riot at Loughborough, where trouble seems to have arisen from the detestation in which the working class held the new Poor Law.

The Chartist agitation itself falls into two distinct periods: from 1839 to 1840 and from 1848 to 1849. In the former period the industrial villages of the county were more disturbed than the town; in the latter period the town was the centre of the agitation. In January 1839 Loughborough was in a very unsettled condition. Inflammatory leaflets were being distributed, and early in February it was reported that arms for Chartists were being made at Shepshed as well as at Loughborough. The wealthier inhabitants became thoroughly alarmed and besought the Home Secretary to send metropolitan police officers, or to permit them to form an armed association for the protection of life and property. Finally, they sent a deputation to the Home Office to stress the expediency of stationing a permanent military force at Loughborough in a new barracks to be built for the purpose. Apart from Loughborough the most serious disturbances, or threats of disturbance, were in the Hinckley district, which, after Leicester and Loughborough, was the most important centre of the hosiery trade. The first signs of political activity on the part of the Chartists occurred in June, when they distributed handbills in Earl Shilton and Hinckley calling for a mutiny. The magistrates were immediately alarmed and sent for cavalry from Coventry. This, or lack of success, intimidated the Chartists, who postponed their meeting for a month. During the summer several demonstrations and meetings were held, but there was no physical violence, only impassioned and inflammatory language. Throughout the winter of 1839–40 Chartists' meetings were held in the industrial villages, creating alarm of an almost hysterical intensity amongst the magistrates and the manufacturers, some of whom remembered the Luddite outrages. The reason, of course, for their fear was the almost complete absence of a police force. The Hinckley magistrates pointed out to the Home Secretary in August 1839 that they had no police force at all. The only method they had of keeping law and order was by intimidation, by the ostentatious use of the yeomanry and militia. There is no doubt that the lack of police made the whole situation more dangerous, but Home Office agents also magnified the danger of Chartist agitation. In fact the Chartist leaders in Leicestershire, Smart, Skevington, and Cooper, were cautious men and their following was small. After 1840 the agitation died away and the county authorities were less concerned about public order, but occasionally there was a clash. In 1842 a meeting of Chartists at Mowacre Hill was roughly broken up by the police and this fracas achieved some notoriety in Chartist circles as the 'Battle of Momecker Hill'. But with growing demand for the repeal of the Corn Laws and for the Ten Hour Act, the support for Chartism dwindled and faded; dissensions among the Chartists themselves were also responsible for their temporary eclipse.

In 1848 there was a sharp revival of Chartist activity. Again Loughborough was a focal point and the Chief Constable of Leicestershire was worried by Chartist meetings held there on 3 April. The Home Office immediately took steps to provide Loughborough with arms and ammunition in case the civil authorities should have to be strengthened with army pensioners. A troop of dragoons was also sent to the town. A largely attended meeting was immediately followed by a parade of the dragoons through the principal streets, followed by extensive drill in the market-place. Skevington, the Chartist leader, refused to be provoked and acted with elaborate courtesy towards the commanding officer. A Chartist camp, to last several days, was set up at Loughborough on Sunday, 9 April, and Chartists from Leicester and Nottingham and their surrounding villages poured into the town. The civic authorities took elaborate precautions but there was no danger until a rumour spread that twenty Chartists had been arrested. A protest meeting was called and quarrymen from Mountsorrell, armed with their hammers, rushed into the town, but the magistrate, C. M. Phillipps, persuaded Skevington to put an end to the meeting. This he did after a few skilful sarcasms about the past liberalism of Phillipps, who had been an ardent supporter of the Reform Bill. During the next few weeks rallies, meetings, and canvassing campaigns were held in the district; Feargus O'Connor was cheered as he passed through the railway station on his way to Nottingham. In May Chartists at Loughborough were being enrolled in the National Guard. But elsewhere, apart from Leicester itself, the county was quiet and Chartist agitation at Hinckley and Wigston was not very effective. At Loughborough, however, the authorities were sufficiently worried to ban a meeting of Feargus O'Connor and elaborate precautions were taken in case of trouble; dragoons were brought into the town and army pensioners enrolled; as it turned out the protest meetings and processions were broken up without disorder. Later in the summer Chartist meetings became more numerous and widespread. There were riots at Countesthorpe, and at Earl Shilton Chartists were thought to be drilling at night and to be in possession of pikes. There was also trouble at Stoney Stanton and Sapcote. By the end of September the county was quiet.

For the next thirty years the political life of Leicestershire is concerned with formal politics, with the struggle between ever-growing Liberalism and the traditional Tory attitude of the county, and this struggle is focused on the general elections. As the number of voters grew the representation of the county ceased to be a matter for arrangement between the leading families and the gentry, and there developed a need for party organisation, for committees, local societies and election agents. Members themselves were forced to state their attitude on a far greater variety of topics than would have been considered decent by their fore-runners in the eighteenth century. But after years of uncontested elections, the first contest which took place in the Northern Division of the county in 1857 was more typical of eighteenth-century politics. C. H. Frewen, who had a highly developed sense of the value of independence, objected to the hold of the Manners family and so set himself up in opposition. He was easily defeated. In 1859 E. B. Farnham, who had represented his division since 1837 decided to retire, and his brother-in-law, E. B. Hartopp of Little Dalby, was promptly nominated in his place, possibly to exclude Frewen. Hartopp was a fanatical Anglican, bitterly opposed both to Rome and to Protestant Dissent.[47] But more important than these personal objections was the feeling that no notice was being taken of the opinions of the electors. A meeting of Liberals was held at Melton Mowbray and strong denunciations were made of the influence of the Manners family; as a protest it was decided after all to run C. H.

Frewen as an independent candidate. Frewen was not a Liberal, but a somewhat eccentric Conservative. His major support, however, came from radical and advanced circles and at the ensuing election, which he lost, it is interesting to note that he polled more votes than his opponents at Loughborough and Syston only. There was no doubt too that he had some sympathy amongst the gentry, who disapproved of the high-handed way in which nominations were made, but the serried ranks of the Rutland tenantry carried the day. But this election is still remote from modern political conflicts.

The first county election which has, in any way, a modern air is the by-election for South Leicestershire in 1867. At the general election of 1865 the borough had returned two Liberal members, and this encouraged the Liberal Party to challenge the Tory hold on South Leicestershire when C. W. Packe died. The Liberal Party chose Thomas Tertius Paget of Humberstone Hall, an important Leicester banker, as their candidate. The Conservatives put forward Sir Henry Halford's son-in-law, Albert Pell, an owner of extensive property in East London. A fierce campaign ensued. Central headquarters of both parties were in Leicester; there was door-to-door canvassing in villages; the candidates toured the countryside, or, as Paget put it, 'the whole energy of the Tory party has been called forth from Burbage Wood to Easton's lonely vale'. But the Liberals caught the Tories by surprise. Their party organisation was far superior, and this undoubtedly gave Paget his narrow margin of victory. He beat Pell by 39 votes.

This seriously disturbed the Conservatives. They blamed their own apathy, their defective register of voters, and grumbled because residents in Leicester had a vote in the county, a fact which to them seemed unjust. Immediately after the defeat they set to work to prepare for the next election.[48] They had not long to wait, for the parliamentary reform carried through by Disraeli in 1867 necessitated a speedy election. The county occupation franchise was lowered to the £12 limit, but voting was still open and many tenants-at-will were frightened to vote against the wishes of their landlords.[49] Paget lost his seat after a hard-fought contest. The final figures of the poll were: Lord Curzon 3223, A. Pell 3111, and T. T. Paget 2839. In the Northern Division Frewen again challenged Lord John Manners, who was joined by S. W. Clowes, Hartopp having been discreetly dropped. Frewen, however, only polled 1751 votes against 3200 cast for Manners and 3095 for Clowes. In 1870 Lord Curzon succeeded his father as Earl Howe. This caused a vacancy in South Leicestershire. Paget stood once more and the Conservatives put forward W. U. Heygate, a member of an old Leicestershire family with large agricultural and industrial interests. Heygate had a majority of 712 and Paget's poll declined to 2570, the most considerable fall being in Leicester itself. This was the last open-voting election to be held in Leicestershire, for in 1872 the ballot box was introduced. The change was expected to reduce the influence of the landlord. Perhaps because of this, at the general election in 1874, the Liberals decided to fight both constituencies; Henry Packe challenged Lord John Manners and S. W. Clowes, and Paget stood once more for South Leicestershire. But Leicestershire naturally followed the wave of popular opinion which swept Disraeli into power, and all four Conservatives were elected. In 1880 both divisions of Leicestershire remained loyal to their traditional politics. In 1885 there was a further modification of the franchise. House-holders in the county were given a vote and the parliamentary divisions reorganised. North and South Leicestershire, which had been in existence since the Reform Act of 1832, were abolished and replaced by four single-member divisions: Melton, Loughborough, Bosworth, and Harborough.

This reorganisation marks the end of the old political structure of Leicestershire, for no longer were there any Knights of the Shire; with the coming of the ballot, too, the direct influence of the great landed families disappeared. The strong party organisations, by now well rooted in the market towns of Leicestershire, brought an end to the unopposed elections which had been such a feature of Leicestershire politics for centuries. Gradually the names of the great political families – Curzon, Cave, Halford, even Manners – disappear, and are replaced by those of semi-professional politicians. By 1885 the political life of Leicestershire had ceased to be the intimate, personal affair of the nobility and gentry from which the working classes were excluded. It had become impersonal, democratic, a cog in the vast national party machinery in which local issues were frequently submerged. But, perhaps, most important of all was that the working classes, organised in trade unions and possessing a vote, exerted for the first time a powerful political influence.

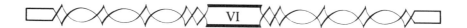

VI

Government at Work

From 1950 I was more or less securely established at Cambridge. In 1946, after much heart-searching, I moved back to my old college, Christ's, where there was a great chance of becoming its leading historian. By 1950, I was appointed a university lecturer, a tutor of the college and its Director of Studies in History. So that I could give time to research and writing, I sacrificed one-third of my university salary and did no lecturing in the summer term; apart from college teaching and committees, I was free from early March until October for creative work. I had also decided that to pursue the Namier model, whatever its validity for the election in 1761, was a blind alley for the period 1689–1740 in which I was interested. The success of my first book, *England in the Eighteenth Century* (1950), the interest I had discovered in handling structure and narrative, combined with the dominant passion of my early life which had led me to write novels – the endless variety of human experience – turned me towards historical biography on the one hand and a study of history and historians on the other.

I decided to write about Sir Robert Walpole and the politics of his age – to try to comprehend how the political turbulence of the time of his youth and early manhood had become political stability by his middle age. I wanted to know more about the nature of oligarchy. There were other huge themes – the effect of 25 years of war; the revolutions in finance, diplomacy, toleration; the easing of theological terror and fear: all were waiting to be explored.

I felt growing confidence and a deeper sense of having found at least the road along which I wanted to go. As I waded through the vast archives of Walpole's age I naturally made one or two startling discoveries – the most important of which was three remarkable sets of memoranda about cabinet meetings which provided an incomparable insight into how executive action was taken in the reign of Queen Anne: a subject which at that time was in a chaotic muddle due to

an incompetent American historian, E. R. Turner, who misunderstood
everything which he read. The result was a paper on Queen Anne's
cabinet for the Royal Historical Society but not given until I had finished
the first volume of Sir Robert Walpole's life. Namier, for once, was
generously enthusiastic about this paper. Although it cleared up a
problem once and for all, pointed out what further research could be
done and the value of these memoranda for all political historians of
Anne's reign, nothing much has followed. I should have turned the
article into a book, but such technical history − written purely for other
historians − was not the history which I wanted to undertake. It was
amusing to write an article during a hot summer holiday in Dubrovnik,
but anything longer would have been wasting my creative life. After all
I had lost the best part of ten years in the war.

The Organisation of the Cabinet in the Reign of Queen Anne

I

The purpose of this paper is twofold; first, to draw attention to hitherto
unknown manuscript materials of great value for the diplomatic, military, political and administrative history of Queen Anne's reign, and
secondly, to demonstrate by the use of these manuscripts how the cabinet
was organised at that time.[1] The manuscripts in question are memoranda
made by three successive secretaries of state. Robert Harley made notes
of 372 meetings of the cabinet or lords of the committee from 21 May
1704 to 8 February 1708; Charles, 3rd Earl of Sunderland, of 236 from
13 December 1706 to 4 June 1710; and William, 1st Earl of Dartmouth,
of 168 from 18 June 1710 to 17 June 1711.[2] These memoranda cover
the majority of the meetings of the highest executive bodies of the English
government during the most vital years of the War of the Spanish
Succession. Not only do they show the gradual formation of policy and
the development of strategy, but they also throw a great deal of light
on the influence both of the Queen and of the leading statesmen of her
time. These documents vary, of course, in quality. They consist of notes
made by the secretary for his own use; sometimes they are little more
than mnemonics. A memorandum of Sunderland's on the meeting of the
cabinet on 26 Mar 1710 runs: 'Board of Ordnance, & Com. of Ireland to
attend on Tuesday morning eleven a clock',[3] which is not very revealing.
Sunderland, however, was rather a lazy man, but fortunately most of
his notes are fuller than this. Harley, on the other hand, loved information for its own sake. He often made notes of when members of the
cabinet came in to the meeting, and frequently jotted down who spoke

to a given question. On 25 June 1704, when the cabinet, at Windsor, debated whether or not to continue Meinhard Schomburg as commander of the English forces in Spain, Harley's notes are sufficiently full to permit the reconstruction of the opinions of those cabinet ministers present. Dartmouth's notes, although not so full as Harley's, are richer than Sunderland's, and fortunately they are better preserved, as a series, than either of the other two. They form a continuous record for those meetings at which Dartmouth was present, whereas there are gaps in both Harley's and Sunderland's.[4] It must be stressed that these notes are not formal cabinet minutes, and they do not cover the entire business discussed at a meeting of either the cabinet or lords of the committee. Some of Harley's and Sunderland's notes refer to the same meeting, but they cover different aspects of the business, and this factor must be kept clearly in mind, particularly when the nature of the business which came before the cabinet or the committee is under discussion. Nevertheless, scrappy and incomplete as they are, these documents are of vital importance, and should not be neglected by any historian of Queen Anne's reign, for they add to our knowledge of the strategic and diplomatic preoccupations of her government. For example, before Port Mahon was taken, its retention at the peace had been considered and decided by the cabinet.[5] Again the interest of the Whig ministry in the expedition against Quebec has been thought to have been perfunctory and somewhat half-hearted. Actually the cabinet and committee spent long hours on the organisation and logistics of this plan, which was only reluctantly cancelled.[6] The detailed arguments between Peterborough and the cabinet about his conduct are to be found in Sunderland's notes, so is the examination of Greg, Harley's clerk who was convicted of treason,[7] and also the investigation of the rumours which involved the Duke of Leeds and his son, Carmarthen, in Jacobite intrigues.[8] Of course, much is known of these matters from other sources, but there is much also that is new to be gleaned from these manuscripts. It is not, however, with what they contain that I am primarily concerned but with what they demonstrate in relation to the organisation of cabinet government.

II

About forty years ago there was considerable controversy about the nature of cabinet government in Queen Anne's reign.[9] E. R. Turner in his book *The Cabinet Council* attempted, without great success, to settle the problems which this controversy had raised. Wolfgang Michael put forward in the third volume of his great history of the eighteenth-century views which were at variance with Turner's.[10] The most recent English historian of the cabinet, E. Trevor Williams, relied principally on Turner and gave his views a wider currency.[11] The points at issue were briefly these. Were the two bodies, called the cabinet and the lords of the committee, in fact the same body, or was there a distinction between them? If so, was the distinction related to the place of meeting, the personnel, the function of the two bodies or to all of these things? And was there a smaller body still, composed of one or two members of these committees, which dealt with the most secret matters of state? The evidence which these historians had for their arguments was, firstly, some notes of Daniel Finch, 2nd Earl of Nottingham, and a few similar jottings of Bolingbroke's; and secondly, references to meetings of these bodies in contemporary letters and memoirs, and descriptions by foreign ambassadors of the way the English government worked or mention of these bodies in their despatches.[12] The major part of this evidence was second-hand and it has proved curiously misleading. Michael claimed that the presence of the sovereign was needed before a cabinet meeting could be held; Turner denied this. Turner insisted that the composition of the lords of the committee was more fluid than the cabinet, an opinion which has been endorsed by E. Trevor Williams. Views were also divided on the difficult question as to whether the two bodies were in fact one, or whether they did essentially the same work. It is not my intention to discuss in the light of this new evidence where each historian of the cabinet was right or wrong, for that would require a separate paper, and perhaps it is sufficient at this point to remark that not one of them obtained all the right answers and, considering the nature of the evidence which they had at their disposal, this is not at all surprising.[13]

The 776 memoranda upon which the rest of this paper is based contain the following information in addition to notes on business; the date of meeting, where it took place, and a list of those present (except that Sunderland never states whether or not the Queen was present). Sunderland always states in his heading and in his endorsement what type of meeting was taking place. He makes only one slip in 236 memoranda. Although neither Harley nor Dartmouth distinguish the type of meeting held in their headings or endorsements, they frequently do so in the body of their notes, which makes it quite certain that Sunderland's distinction was not idiosyncratic, but one that was generally accepted.

The distinction made by Sunderland is this. Meetings held in royal palaces are endorsed as cabinet meetings; those held at the Cockpit, usually in the senior secretary's room, or on very rare occasions at the house of a minister, are endorsed as meetings of the lords of the committee. The same distinction is made time and time again by Dartmouth. On 9 July 1710 the cabinet met for their usual Sunday meeting at Kensington Palace and Dartmouth notes 'Letter from Gen Stanhope from Spain of June 22 ordered to be read again upon Tuesday next at the Committee at the Cockpit'. The memorandum for 11 July 1710 of the meeting held at the Cockpit gives the results of the discussion of Stanhope's letter.[14] And similar references to the 'Lords at the Cockpit' or the 'Committee at the Cockpit' run through all of these memoranda. There can be no doubt that the ministers made as clear a distinction between these two bodies as Sunderland. A cabinet meeting always took place in the royal presence, and usually in a royal palace. To this there was one exception: Queen Anne held cabinets at Bath during her visit there in the summer of 1703.[15] The committee was even less peripatetic; it usually met in Whitehall, but could on occasion meet in ministers' houses.[16]

III

The next distinction to consider is the question of membership, and here the memoranda of Harley and Dartmouth are vitally important. These documents show that the Queen and her husband, Prince George of Denmark, were always present at cabinet meetings, but that they never attended committees. For some reason Sunderland never mentions the presence of the Queen, although he always notes the presence of her husband, and it is fortunate that Harley's memoranda deal with many cabinet meetings that Sunderland also annotates, for Harley records that the Queen was present. Apart from the presence of the sovereign and her husband, there is no difference in the membership of the cabinet and committee; members of one appear sooner or later at the other, naturally some were more active than others, and cabinet meetings tended to be better attended than committee meetings. Before turning to a detailed consideration of membership of the cabinet, perhaps a word is necessary on the frequency and regularity of meetings. After her accession, the Queen maintained William III's custom of holding a regular meeting of the cabinet after dinner on Sundays.[17] Sunday meetings proved inadequate for the business created by a great war and there were many weeks when the cabinet had to meet again, and sometimes even twice, in addition to Sunday. The burden on the Queen, as well as ministers, was very heavy. In 1705 at least 64 meetings of the cabinet were held, and one on Christmas day; from 18 June 1710 to 17 June 1711 the Queen attended 62. Committee meetings were held even more frequently; in the later period 106 meetings were held within the year. Often the days of Queen Anne are considered more leisured and more spacious than ours; certainly, they were not for cabinet ministers. They had to work exceptionally hard.

Some, of course, worked harder than others. The burden of work naturally fell most heavily on the secretaries. During the period covered by Dartmouth's notes, Boyle, who was secretary until 20 September, 1710, missed none of the meetings attended by Dartmouth, and St John, who succeeded him, was absent from only ten out of the remaining 146. Dartmouth himself could only have had five days' holiday from 18 June 1710 to 17 June 1711, for that is the longest gap without a meeting in his notes. As Dartmouth's record is the most complete, his figures of the attendance of other ministers may be of interest. I have calculated these, however, from 1 October 1710 when the various ministerial changes of this time were complete, for the summer months were exceptional in that the cabinet still contained Whigs, waiting their dismissal, with junior Tory ministers put in temporarily to counterbalance them.

During the remaining period from 1 October 1710 to 17 June 1711 49 cabinet meetings were held, and 91 committees. The lord keeper, Harcourt, who was only appointed on 19 October, was present at 39 cabinets but only ten committees. The reason for this is simple. The committee met usually in the mornings at 11 a.m. when the keeper was involved in his legal duties. The president, the Earl of Rochester, the Queen's uncle, however, only missed one cabinet and one committee until he was taken ill and died at the beginning of May 1711. The Duke of Queensbury, the secretary for Scotland, and the Duke of Buckingham, the steward of the household, were equally assiduous, the former missing only five cabinets and ten committees, the latter doing even better – four cabinets and three committees. The First Lord of the Treasury, Earl Poulett, only missed two cabinets and nine committees until he was superseded by Harley as Lord Treasurer in May 1711. Until then Harley had been Chancellor of the Exchequer but he had sat in the cabinet, a very exceptional situation when the offices of first lord and chancellor were divided, and a tribute to his political standing. He had, however, already missed sixteen committees and seven cabinets before Guiscard stabbed him on 8 March 1711 which kept him away until 21 May. When he returned as Lord Treasurer, he only attended three out of the remaining eleven committees, but was present at three out of the four cabinets. The only other minister who could compare in activity with these was the Duke of Shrewsbury, the Lord Chamberlain, who, in spite of his well known aversion to business, attended all but three cabinets. He was more daunted by committees and missed 22 of them. There were only three other members of the cabinet at this time: the Lord-Lieutenant of Ireland, who, although only absent from four cabinets, missed 26 committees; the Duke of Marlborough, the commander-in-chief, who attended eighteen meetings, eight cabinets, and ten committees, between 31 December 1710 and 17 February 1711, after which he left for his campaign; and finally, the Duke of Newcastle, the Lord Privy Seal, whose fitful attendance illustrates the uneasiness which he felt about belonging to a predominantly Tory ministry. In the summer of 1710 he stayed in the country very late, only reaching London early in

December; yet the ministry had shown a desire to have him present, for on 30 October they had delayed business in the hope that he might shortly be in town,[18] When he arrived in London, his attendance proved extremely irregular; he was present at only 38 meetings, 20 cabinets and 18 committees.

There were two other great officers of state, both Whigs, who retained their offices yet ceased to sit in the cabinet, although they had done so since the beginning of the Queen's reign. One was the Duke of Somerset, master of the horse, a Whig who, if he could not bring himself to resign his place, deliberately withdrew from the cabinet to mark his disapproval of the ministry.[19] The other was Tenison, the Archbishop of Canterbury, who ceased to attend after 8 September 1710, although he had been an active member of both the cabinet and committee in all other ministries. Whether he himself refused to attend or whether he ceased to be summoned is not known; but Tenison's absence, due to a Tory ministry, pledged to uphold the principles of the Church, marks the beginning of the decline of the Archbishop of Canterbury as an active member of the cabinet. Archbishop Wake attended for a year or two after the Hanoverian succession, but he was soon at cross-purposes with the ministry; after that his health declined and by the time his successor was appointed fundamental changes had taken place in cabinet government and archbishops were permanently excluded from the active part of the executive, if not from the formal cabinet.[20] Of the Whigs associated with Harley's government, only Shrewsbury gave it wholehearted support and worked devotedly for the administration. These attendance figures show how dangerous it is to maintain that Harley's ministry was a typically mixed administration, because one or two Whigs remained in office, for they underline Somerset's antipathy and Newcastle's uneasiness; only one Whig, Shrewsbury, supported him consistently in the cabinet.

There is one further question relating to membership which remains to be answered. How many offices automatically carried with them a seat in the cabinet? Cabinet government, by Anne's reign, had not developed many settled conventions, but there are lines of division between office holders that are already discernible. The Lord Chancellor, or Lord Keeper, the Treasurer, the President of the Council, the Lord Privy Seal, the Lord-Lieutenant of Ireland, the commander-in-chief, and the two secretaries (three after the Union with Scotland in 1717) were automatically members of the cabinet. If the Treasury was in commission, then the first Lord sat in the cabinet. They were the office-holders whose presence was regarded as essential; probably until 1710 the Archbishop was in the same category. For the rest, it depended on the quality and influence of the men who held the office. When the Duke of Devonshire died on 18 August 1707, he was succeeded by his son as

Lord Steward. The Queen decided, according to Harley, that 'the new Lord Steward is not to be summoned to the committee till winter, that it may not be pretended to be annexed to places'.[21] Although Henry Marquess of Kent had been Lord Chamberlain of the household from 1704, no ministry had regarded his presence at the cabinet as desirable. When the Duke of Shrewsbury succeeded him, he entered the cabinet at once. The Earl of Orford was summoned as First Lord of the Admiralty, but Sir John Leake, Orford's successor, was not. Then, as now, the politician rather than the office could command cabinet rank.

Before turning to the most important question of the relation of the cabinet to the lords of the committee and the business which each performed, perhaps I may be allowed to make one further comment on the attendance of some ministers. Because of the relatively minor office achieved by some politicians the importance of their influence can be underestimated and so can the difficulties which they created for friends and enemies alike. Some men know instinctively how to use power, and frustrated ambition can make them exceptionally awkward colleagues. Swift in his *Journal to Stella* stresses very frequently his fears of Somerset's influence, fears which now seem out of all proportion to his political importance.[22] These cabinet memoranda provide the clue to Somerset. He was indefatigable in attendance at both the cabinet and committee. He was far more regular than the chancellor, the president, the privy seal, the steward and, at times, the treasurer. Also it must be remembered that he had by far the longest career as a cabinet minister, for Marlborough, who rivalled him in length of time, was frequently absent abroad for periods of many months' duration. Fortunately Harley occasionally made a note of those who spoke on a particularly important question. Somerset, obviously, held strong views, loved voicing them, and could rarely hold his tongue, often speaking three or four times on the same subject.[23] Posterity has neglected him; his contemporaries, no doubt, devoutly wished that they might have been able to do so.

Finally there is the question as to whether cabinets or committees were the more fully attended. Cabinets on the average were better attended than committees. Seven was the lowest attendance for a cabinet, three for a committee. Never once between 1704 and 1710 was there a full meeting of the cabinet, although there were a few meetings in which there was only one absentee; the usual attendance was about nine. Harley's cabinets were slightly fuller – on one occasion all members were present and the average was about eleven. The usual attendance for the committee was five to six. This numerical difference between the two bodies is very important. For it meant this, that work done by the committee was, more frequently than not, reviewed by members of the cabinet who had not taken part in the preliminary discussions. The value of this will be more apparent when the nature of the work done by both bodies has been examined.

IV

It is on the nature of the business performed by the cabinet and the lords of the committee that misconception is greatest. E. Trevor Williams writes, on the evidence largely of Turner, that the committee, 'became, in short, the effective aspect of the privy council, which gave official ratification to its decisions. But it dealt only with conciliar business and had no concern with important matters of policy. Foreign affairs in particular, were outside its sphere of influence.' Nothing could be further from the truth: foreign affairs and the strategy and tactics of war were its main preoccupations. There was no aspect of government business which might or might not be discussed by the cabinet or the committee; the differences between them lay in method and in detail.[24]

In former centuries the privy council had interrogated people suspected of treason. This duty now devolved on the committee. Guiscard stabbed Harley on 8 March 1711 at the Cockpit at a committee meeting. Similarly Greg had been interrogated by the committee in 1708. The cabinet, however, gave authority for these interrogations and often laid down the lines upon which it wished the interrogation to proceed.[25] The committee, even in the discharge of this ancient function of the privy council, was responsible to the cabinet. And this leads to one of the major differences between the two bodies. The committee undertook the entire burden of interviews and interrogations. It held, therefore, joint meetings with a wide variety of persons and committees. The cabinet was an exclusive body to which it was exceedingly rare for anyone to be summoned who was not a member. There were only three regular exceptions. Every Sunday the Prince's council gave a report on the state of the Fleet. This was the first item on the agenda, and, once given, the council left. The Secretary-at-War was also called in from time to time for a specific item of business. And the recorder of London was summoned to attend the cabinet to give a report on malefactors before the Queen's prerogative of mercy was exercised.[26]

On the other hand, the committee rarely held a meeting without summoning other government servants either singly or as a collective body for the discussion of those items of business which concerned them. The commissioners of transport, the commissioners of sick and wounded, the Scottish lords, the Irish lords, admirals and generals either on furlough or about to depart on a new expedition – Rooke, Leake, Vetch, Peterborough, Galway, Stanhope – all of these were frequent visitors to the Cockpit.[27] It is the presence of these members of the government at occasional meetings at the Cockpit which led E. R. Turner into one of his errors. He wrote in his discussion of the two bodies:

> Finally the most important difference between the two bodies lay in the fact that membership in the cabinet was limited strictly to certain great officers whom the King appointed to be his confidential advisers, while the committee of council was a committee of the whole council, and, though usually made up of the great officials and active workers who composed the cabinet, might also include other members of the Privy Council if they chose to attend.[28]

That is inaccurate – at least for Anne's reign. As we have seen, the committee and the cabinet were composed of the same men. No government servant, not even a privy councillor, could *choose* to attend. The committee sent for admirals, generals, and government officials as they required them for particular business. One example will suffice to illustrate precisely this relationship. The Duke of Argyll had been appointed ambassador to Charles III and commander in Spain in January 1711. His instructions were drawn up by the committee and on 14 February 1711 he was, according to Dartmouth, 'sent for in and his instructions read and agreed'. There was no question of Argyll, although a privy councillor, attending the committee as of right even when his own instructions were under consideration.[29]

There were not many committee meetings without the attendance of some junior minister or serving officer or subordinate council, but these were not the only interviews which the committee held. It was also the connecting link between the cabinet and foreign ambassadors, particularly those of our allies. The Queen might see ambassadors formally, the secretaries informally, but the most profitable discussions were those held semi-formally with the committee. In July 1709 the cabinet was considering the future of Minorca and the hope was entertained that a treaty might be drawn up with the Austrians and the Dutch. After the government had settled its policy, the cabinet on 19 July 1709 ordered: 'the Lords to consider of the Treaty of Minorca and to talk with Comte Gallas and Hoffman upon their full powers'.[30] Both Gallas and Hoffmann (and his predecessor Vryberg) were very frequent visitors to the Cockpit, for the complicated strategic and diplomatic situation of the Allies called for close co-ordination between them.

This need for consultation sprang naturally from the work upon which the committee was principally engaged – the detailed direction of war and diplomacy. A consideration of one busy week's business of the committee from 2 to 9 July 1704, taken from Harley's memoranda because they are the richest in detail, will give an adequate idea of the range of the committee's work on these aspects of its business.[31] The main task before the committee in this week was the co-ordination of the expedition to Portugal under Lord Galway. The committee met on Tuesday, Wednesday, Thursday, Friday and Saturday and there were two cabinet meetings on Tuesday and Sunday. Galway was in attendance at each meeting of the committee and he was called in for consultation; he himself had a number of proposals to make to the committee, largely for increased staff – engineers and surgeons and for greater shipping space, one and a half tons per man instead of one and a quarter – all of which the committee accepted.

The committee also had discussions with St John, the Secretary-at-War, who had drawn up two papers covering the military side of the expedition. These were subjected to searching criticism. The committee sent for the officers of the ordnance and enquired in great detail into the provision of firearms. The commissioners of transport and the prince's council were summoned to discuss provision of shipping space and convoy arrangements. The latter were complicated by the question of the convoy from Jamaica arriving in time to release shipping. This led the committee to seek information and assurances from the Board of Trade about its arrangements for the West India trade convoys. Letters for the ambassador at Lisbon, Methuen, and for the Commander-in-Chief of the Fleet, Admiral Rooke, were drafted; the Portuguese envoy was interviewed about the supply of corn in Portugal, so was the Moroccan resident about horses from Barbary. The treasurer gave a report to the committee on the difficulties which would face him in finding the necessary money for the expedition, as the parliamentary vote had been inadequate. Finally a long letter to Stanhope, our ambassador in Holland, was drafted and the main lines of argument to be used with the Dutch envoy (Vryberg), in order to get his government to make a proper contribution of men and money, were sketched out for Harley's guidance. In addition to dealing with the Portuguese expedition, the committee drew up instructions for the new envoy to the Tsar; dealt with the problems of a convoy from the Channel Islands; consulted with the commissioners of sick and wounded about the treatment of a Spanish deserter; and they considered and deferred questions relating to privateers until they had before them the precedents from William III's reign. Finally, they dealt with the correspondence from their envoys abroad. That week they read and considered letters from Stanhope at the Hague, Stepney in Vienna, Wyche at Hamburg, Aglionby at Zürich, and from Chetwynd, who was acting as Hill's secretary, at Turin. If ever a committee or a cabinet deserved the title of efficient, surely it was the lords of the committee at this time. Obviously the committee was exceedingly busy on questions of detail and on questions of policy.

What then was the role of the cabinet? Two meetings were held during

this week, one at St James's at six p.m. on the Tuesday and the other
at Windsor on the Sunday, as usual after dinner, probably about four
p.m. At these meetings the main business was to approve in the Queen's
presence either letters drafted by the committee or decisions taken by
them. For example, on Tuesday evening the letters which the committee
had drafted to Methuen and Byng were approved and signed by the
Queen in the cabinet. An amendment was made to the letter to Methuen;
Byng's letter was merely signed. At the same meeting secretary Hedges
gave the queen a résumé of the work done that morning by the
committee, on the expedition to Portugal, which was approved. The
decision was taken to inform Stanhope and Vryberg. The Archbishop's
order for a thanksgiving service (for victories in Flanders) was likewise
authorised and the secretaries also were given approval for one or two
minor pieces of business for which they needed the Queen's authority,
e.g. that Lord Portland should be instructed to stay in Portugal until
Galway arrived. It is true to say, therefore, that this cabinet did little
more than give final sanction to the work previously done by the
committee. The same is almost, but not quite, true of the meeting at
Windsor on the Sunday. Secretary Hedges gave a long report of what
the lords had done about Portugal, and from this arose a discussion of
the arguments to be used by Stanhope, the ambassador at the Hague,
to persuade the Dutch to do their share. This topic had been raised in
the committee the day before and the main lines of the letter to Stanhope
then agreed. The cabinet took an identical attitude to the committee.
The cabinet, however, went one step further than the committee. It
assumed that negotiations with the Dutch would be successful and gave
the committee authority to discuss with Galway the question of the
command of the regiments which they hoped the Dutch would raise for
the Portuguese service. The decisions on ordnance and victualling were
then confirmed, not without Somerset attempting an amendment to raise
the victuals from six weeks' to two months' supply. Two members of
the Prince's council – Churchill and Clark – were then called in and the
cabinet discussed convoy arrangements. The Prince's council had not
been too helpful about convoy arrangements with the committee – its
quasi-independent position and semi-royal protection made it quite obviously the most dfficult body with which the committee had to deal. To
return to the Sunday meeting, Churchill and Clark introduced a totally
new concept. Throughout the week the convoy arrangements had been
discussed in terms of the ships which would be released by the return
of the West India convoys – now it was suggested that the convoys from
the Oporto trade might be used. The cabinet accepted this proposal. It
is odd that the Prince's council, which had been in consultation with the
committee throughout the week, should not have thought of this before.

The method of the Prince's council, however, will not be unfamiliar to those who have spent long hours on committees; resentment of control can often lead to an unwilling collaboration and a withholding of vital information until the highest councils are reached. The presence of the Queen and the Prince in the cabinet was frequently necessary to enable the lords to extract what they wanted from the Prince's council. In this relationship therefore the cabinet played a more important rôle than that of merely agreeing to decisions already taken. Once the convoy arrangements were settled the work prepared by the committee was completed. It did not, however, conclude the business of the cabinet. There were further naval matters, brought forward by the Prince's council, which may not have been before the committee – arrangements for the Sussex coast, the pardon of some malefactors in Devonshire, and the far more important question as to whether Whetstone, the admiral in the Baltic, should enter foreign ports in order to seize French shipping. Naturally this gave rise to discussion and the cabinet ordered that he was to be instructed to avoid giving any possible offence to Her Majesty's allies, although the ministers agreed that some discretion would naturally have to be left to Whetstone's commanders. One might expect such a matter to have been discussed by the committee first and it may not be fanciful to see in this one more instance of the council's jealousy.

Although this week of July 1704 was a busy week for the government it was in no way exceptional, and it is thoroughly typical of the relationship which existed between the various government bodies which decided and coordinated policy. As far as military planning was concerned, and the diplomatic issues arising from such planning, the 'efficient' body was the committee, in the sense that it carried the greater burden of detailed work. Yet it would be quite wrong to think of the cabinet as a mere rubber stamp, rapidly declining into formal obscurity. It is wiser to regard the cabinet as similar in function to a second chamber, a place of revision and reconsideration before the royal authority was given to ministerial acts and decisions. The committee did the spade work in interviews and discussions and also in drafting of despatches or orders, but the final decision on all of these matters had to be taken by the Queen, sitting in the cabinet. And the decision, once taken, was decisive, and could not be altered except by the Queen in cabinet council.[32] Here stretches a great gulf between the authority of the committee and the cabinet. Unless specific authority was given to the committee by the cabinet, no decisions could be taken by it.

There were, of course, many other matters, apart from military or diplomatic, which came before the cabinet and committee. Any aspect of the life of the nation, no matter how trivial or even ludicrous, might find its way on to the agenda of the cabinet or the committee. The purchase, upkeep and transport of a herd of spotted deer for the Sultan of Morocco agitated the committee and the cabinet, as well as every department of state from 3 October 1710 to 26 April 1711, when they are heard of for the last time. The cabinet decided that they must be despatched in a neutral ship rather than a man-of-war for safety's sake.[33] In these memoranda, Balthazar St Michel, Pepys' wayward brother-in-law, makes his last fleeting appearance, still down on his luck, still begging; naturally his petition was dismissed.[34] On another occasion the committee was deeply exercised by a proposal to introduce an insurance scheme for marriage.[35] Most of their time, when not devoted to war or diplomacy, was, of course, taken up by mightier matters – the problem of the poor palatines, questions relating to Bills before Parliament, to the East India Company, to the plantations; discussions of the charges of the Judges about to go on assize; decisions about proclamations – there were few aspects of English life which did not, at one time or another, demand attention.[36] When the affairs of Scotland were discussed by the committee they usually summoned two or three of the leading peers of Scotland to take part.[37] And, of course, there was a considerable amount of formal and semi-formal business which does not appear in these notes. When Sunderland was indisposed on Sunday, 11 May 1707, Harley had to conduct his business for him and he wrote later:

> The Queen has been pleased to sign all your Lordship's papers but one viz. Mr Chudleigh's case to be ennsigne in the Guards. Her Majestie said she would speak with the Prince about it and then let your Lordshipp know her pleasure.[38]

Obviously these memoranda do not give the full picture of cabinet business, and it may be dangerous to argue from what they do not mention, yet it is worth drawing attention to two notable absences. Treasury business, although not entirely neglected, is rare.[39] The same is true of parliamentary business; Bills are occasionally discussed and, on one occasion, the handling of a debate, but there must have been a far more considerable discussion of such matters elsewhere.[40] Yet faulty and incomplete as these memoranda are, they permit a far more accurate picture of cabinet government to be drawn than has, hitherto, been possible.

Although the broad outline is clear enough, there are one or two obscure matters upon which further evidence would be invaluable. It is probable that there may have been smaller and more secret committees of the cabinet for planning projected military expeditions. On 25 March 1711 'The Queen declared a design of the expedition to Canada to the

Lords and ordered Mr St John to give them an account of the forward-
ness the preparations were in for that service.'[41] The choice of a secret
committee may have been made deliberately by St John to circumvent
discussion in the committee at an early stage, for Harley was thought
not to be sympathetic to the Quebec expedition.[42] The notes made by
Nottingham in 1702 and endorsed 'secret committee' probably refer to
a similar sub-committee for they deal with naval matters only; certainly
they do not refer to the committee, as described above.[43] And, of course,
there were very frequent private meetings, informal in character, at
which these ministers took counsel together; and these should not be
confused with the committee at the Cockpit or with committee meetings
held in the secretary's home.[44]

These secret committees and private committees have done much to
confuse Turner and others, but the greatest confusion of all has been
caused by their attempting to describe a system of cabinet government
which was coherent for not one but several reigns. The system here
described was not the method of cabinet government employed by
William III. A large quantity of cabinet memoranda of Sir William
Trumbull has recently been discovered which shows that William III
played a far more active role than Queen Anne.[45] Similarly this system
of Queen Anne's did not last for long after her death. An admirable and
flexible cabinet organisation had been devised, an organisation which
had directed England's war effort with great success, yet by 1717 the
system had begun to break down, by 1720 another cabinet system was
coming into being. Both these topics are too large to enter in upon
here. There is, however, one important point worth making. The system
described above survived the Hanoverian succession. The memoranda
of Townshend, and others, show that in 1714, 1715, 1716 and the early
months of 1717, George I attended cabinets, accompanied, according to
ancient custom, by his son and heir, the Prince of Wales; the lords of
the committee continued to meet at the Cockpit.[46] For three years at
least the organisation of cabinet government went on as before. What
linguistic difficulties, if any, embarrassed George I and his ministers,
were obviously surmounted.[47] It is not until after 1717 that the great
changes occur and the system which had been so efficient in Queen
Anne's reign gives way to another. The new system does not emerge
into the full light of day until the late 1730s, and much remains to be
done to clear up the process of change.[48] Fortunately cabinet and
committee memoranda are not so sparse for these years as was first
thought, and it should not be long before we possess an accurate picture,
well based on documentary evidence, both of the origins of cabinet
government and of the profound changes which occurred in the reign
of George I.[49] The exceptional richness of this type of document from

1704 to 1711 makes, however, the reign of Queen Anne the most suitable starting point for both enquiries, for here the historian is on solid ground.

Turner recognised that many of his difficulties were due to a lack of evidence which bred obscurity and that his troubles would have been dispelled had he been able to lay his hands on a continuous series of minutes of the cabinet or the committee.[50] The evidence which he failed to find is now abundantly available and it is possible for the first time to establish with certainty the organisation of cabinet government in the reign of Queen Anne.

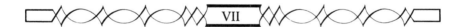

VII

Namier Rejected

By 1950 my ambition as a professional historian had crystallised. The transition of English political life from violence, civil war, riot, plots and executions, bitter religious and political controversies of the late seventeenth century to the comparatively settled world of eighteenth-century politics was a complex and fascinating problem, bridged by the life of Sir Robert Walpole – his childhood, youth and young manhood spent in one, his great political authority achieved in the other. So in 1949 I decided to write a life of Walpole, but at the same time collect material and do some work on the problems of the change from political confusion to political stability. Indeed in 1949, I wrote an article which grew out of a talk to the Stubbs Society in Oxford on *The Growth of Oligarchy 1689–1715*: Richard Pares wanted it for the *English Historical Review* but, perhaps perversely, I put it in a drawer for twenty years. I realised that publication in isolation might help my reputation as a professional scholar but would distort the problems I wished to solve. Yet it was a valuable exercise, giving me insight into the political processes in which Walpole was involved, but by extrapolating it from political debate, I should have been guilty of what I was increasingly criticising in Namier.

About 1950 Namier emerged once again in my life. He had asked me to help him revive the History of Parliament Trust. This was a commission set up and funded by Parliament. It was the brain-child of Josiah Wedgwood who thought the lack of a biographical dictionary of the House of Commons a national disgrace. I had met Josiah Wedgwood, through Trevelyan, and his remarkable wife – both larger than life. She used a silver ear-trumpet and terrified me once on the terrace of the House of Commons, where they were giving me tea. She asked me a question, listened to my answer for a few seconds and then firmly placed her trumpet on the table. To my relief she began to pour tea. The History of Parliament Trust now became Namier's obsession: all political

historians were to be rallied to the cause to produce a dictionary of
Members of Parliament from the Middle Ages to the twentieth century.
He knew what he wanted and he wanted all historians to accept his
views. He came recruiting in Cambridge. Kitson Clark, who, freed from
the burdens of a Trinity tutorship, had taken up historical research once
more, called a meeting on his behalf.

Kitson Clark was a huge man, physically like Namier. He was noisy,
eager to dominate any collection of males; bombastic, voluble, easy to
mimic, easy to deride and he carried what in Cambridge can be a life-
long ball and chain – failure to secure a first in the Tripos. Butterfield
had no doubt that he was second-rate, so did many others in the faculty
– the economic historians, Clapham and Postan, regarded him as mildly
comic; the medievalists suspected that Kitson Clark was not sound on
the curriculum and might sacrifice them for the new subjects which he
vociferously supported – American History and Third World history
(then called Expansion of Europe).

So the meeting in Kitson Clark's rooms above Trinity Great Gate was
a curious confrontation. Namier presumed that Kitson Clark was a
college hack, a chairman who would sit still and listen. Kitson Clark
saw the opportunity as one which he could exploit in pursuit of his
renewed ambition to be an accepted professional scholar. Kitson Clark,
although an indifferent historian, was a tough and realistic politician.
He had chosen the audience carefully – mainly youngsters who might
need his backing. Namier gave a clear exposition of what he wanted
done. In the next three hours he was subjected to a criticism of his views
which quite obviously both startled him and irritated him. There were
harsh critics who said that individual biographies explained nothing –
useful as dictionary, perhaps, but not serious history; reasonable to get
it done if a government was foolish enough to put up the vast amount
of money required. Some argued the project was too large and would
go the way of the Victoria County History at which one or two lonely
scholars were still working, three-quarters of a century after it had been
launched. Whilst these frank criticisms were made, Namier glowered
and Kitson Clark looked increasingly portentous with thought. And then
he spoke. He praised the project as a biographical tool for political
historians (yet regretted the absence of the House of Lords from the
project) but felt that many of the criticisms levelled at it could be met
by a study of the constituencies in a separate volume placed before the
biographical dictionary – this would create political continuity from
period to period and give a new dimension to the project that could be
further improved by additional essays on problems thrown up by work
on the constituencies and on the members themselves. For once in his
life Namier realised that he was out of control of a discussion of his

own project. He had never thought of a constituency volume and failed to marshal any serious arguments against it.

This meeting had two results. Namier became obsessively antagonistic to Kitson Clark and instead of asking Kitson Clark, who was longing for the invitation to join the editorial body of the History of Parliament Trust, he asked me. Namier grudgingly accepted the idea of a volume dealing with the constituencies, largely, I think, in order to seal off what he thought might be a damaging criticism. The serried ranks of Cambridge historians in favour of it had unnerved him. Yet he always remained half-hearted about the constituencies. In the end it increased both work and costs considerably yet achieved little else.

It was strange to be appointed to a body whose purpose I was beginning to doubt, by an historian whose methods, it seemed to me, were increasingly open to criticism. It might have been more honest and honourable to have resigned. Namier, however, still towered over eighteenth-century political studies and I was, at least, tolerated by him. His enmity could be terrible. I let him think that one day I might take on the Parliamentary History from 1689 to 1715, and, indeed, this was less of a remote possibility than it seems now. Had my biographical ventures (*Walpole, Chatham, The First Four Georges*) failed, it was the type of work to which I might have reconciled myself, but even then it would never have been in the Namierian mould.

However about twice a year for three years the editorial committee of the History of Parliament Trust met, and very quickly I was disabused of any lingering admiration I might have had for the project. Sir Frank Stenton was in the chair, Sir John Neale and Sir Lewis Namier argued their way through an agenda of trivialities, with rage on Namier's part, with feline skill by Neale: the audience – Roskell, Aspinal, Sedgwick and myself – made an occasional interjection, almost uniformly ignored. One famous quarrel lasted a long afternoon and was about capitalisation – should it be Duke of Bedford or duke of Bedford, Queen of England or queen of England. Neale argued at length for the lower case; with mounting rage Namier would not have it, his eyes glowed, his voice rasped; Neale pressed and Stenton slept. At last, after an hour or two spent on probable savings in costs, difficulties for proof-readers and other red herrings, Namier growled in his strong Polish-English – 'I will not have my Queen with a small "q". You can show your lack of respect if you like. I will not. The volumes must differ.' Neale's face shone with pleasure and in his gentlest, silkiest voice, he said, 'I am surprised Lewis about that because in your century, historians always used a small "q" or a small "d" for Duke. Don't you recall Archdeacon Coxe's practice?' Namier exploded into noisy but wordless rage. Stenton woke up, blinked and murmured 'I think we ought to get on.' After a desultory word or two (none from Namier), the meeting was adjourned.

Such an utter waste of time depressed the spirits. Nor did any progress ever seem to be made. The Parliamentary grant was too small, secretaries and assistants far too few, office space minimal. No wonder it has taken decades for volumes to appear and for Parliament to get exasperated and reduce its grant.

The project still totters on – not without a certain biographical value but of no real historical importance. By the time I published the first volume of my *Life of Sir Robert Walpole* (1956), my admiration for Namier and his method had become qualified. I hope that I never lost sight of his greatness (badly fissured though it might be) but I was convinced that his methods did not really work. R. R. Walcott, a man of modest talents and considerable industry, toiled for a quarter of a century to produce a slim volume on the politics of Queen Anne's reign: like Namier's own book on George III's politics, it did not live up to its title and it was merely a collection of essays. However, it had been long-heralded, and it had to be dealt with firmly but courteously for Walcott was a kind and generous man, if of limited historical insight. The second review, printed below, on *The Rise of the Pelhams* by John B. Owen is also closely related to political history in the Namier manner. Owen, a New Zealander, had worked for many years as an assistant to Namier on the *History of Parliament*, and *The Rise of the Pelhams* owed a lot to Namier in method and outlook. With John Brooke's *George III*, this is by far the best book written by any of Namier's disciples. Its strengths and its weaknesses stem from that dark, brooding, authoritarian scholar. It received an excellent press; however, alas, few read it.

The last review deals with Namier's contribution to the History of Parliament, finished by his devoted, if ill-paid, assistant John Brooke. Both reviews could have been more savage, more destructive without being untrue, but I was conscious in both cases of the years of toil and the dedication of their authors. None of the three scholars were without uncommon qualities. I rarely, if ever, review what I totally despise: for me Namier still wears the trappings of greatness – a titanic man frustrated by his own nature.

Walcott and the Politics of the Reign of Queen Anne

The title of Professor Walcott's book is a little misleading, for he is concerned, apart from a brief chapter on the session of 1707–8, with parliamentary politics of the years 1701–2. Furthermore, the bulk of his book deals with an analysis of the structure of the House of Commons – its electoral system, its party groupings. The factual basis of these chapters is given in four lengthy Appendices. The discussion of political action is confined to a brief survey from 1660–1700, a more detailed analysis of the general election of 1702, and a case study of the crisis of 1707–8 which culminated in the dismissal of Robert Harley from his secretaryship of state. Professor Walcott has tried, therefore, to do in a very short book what Sir Lewis Namier did for the early 1760s in three stout volumes.

Professor Walcott states his thesis quite clearly in his Introduction. He believes that 'the traditional picture of early eighteenth-century government with two parties contesting for power' is false. And he starts his analysis of politics by ignoring the party system altogether. His study of the electoral system and of the composition of the Commons leads to the definition of a number of groups. 'By correlating scattered data', he writes, 'on the antecedents, economic interests, family and personal relationships of individual Members of Parliament we should be able to identify many personal and family groups.' Professor Walcott identifies seven major connections – two Whig: Junto; Newcastle–Pelham–Townshend–Walpole; one mixed: Court peers (Somerset, Carlisle, Pembroke, Stamford); and four Tory: Marlborough–Godolphin; Nottingham––Finch; Hyde–Granville–Seymour; Harley–Foley. The relative strength of these connections is assessed and their membership is analysed in the Appendices. Having identified these groups, Professor Walcott turns to the election of 1702 and the parliamentary session of 1707–8 and finds in the conflict between these factions a more satisfactory explanation of what happened than the concept of a struggle between two opposing parties. And he concludes:

> the architects of governments and of parliamentary majorities worked within a multi-party framework. This assumption often fits the facts far better than the two-party interpretation, but the party history of the period 1688–1714 has been explained so universally in terms of 'Whig' and 'Tory' exclusively, that the similarities between it and the later eighteenth-century political structure have been commonly overlooked. The more one studies the party structure under William and Anne, the less it resembles the two-party described by Trevelyan in his Romanes Lecture and the more it seems to have in common with the structure of politics in the Age of Newcastle as explained to us by Namier.

Unfortunately for Professor Walcott no archives of the richness of the Newcastle or Hardwicke papers survive for the period of his book. The Harley papers are valuable (it is a pity that Professor Walcott relied solely on what has been printed by the Historical Manuscripts

Commission. The edition of these volumes was highly selective and the unpublished papers at the British Museum and at Nottingham would have been an important addition to Professor Walcott's sources). Nevertheless Harley's archive does not give anything like the same detailed picture of politics which is so readily available for the middle of the eighteenth century. In consequence, Professor Walcott has relied very heavily on genealogical sources and on division lists – perhaps too heavily – and it is a pity that the huge scale of his work prevented him from undertaking the prolonged search for materials which still exist in sufficient abundance to permit a detailed reconstruction of most members' political attitudes. His need to compress his work has led him here and there into a number of hasty conclusions and, at least in one case, to the isolation of a connexion for which there is little evidence but genealogy.

It is very difficult to believe in Professor Walcott's Newcastle–Pelham-–Townshend–Walpole faction. In the correspondence which exists in the Chomondeley (Houghton) MSS between Townshend and Walpole there is only one reference to the Duke of Newcastle in Queen Anne's reign, when Townshend suggested that Walpole might see him to get a friend off being pricked as High Sheriff of Norfolk. As he also suggested the possibility of using the Duke of Somerset, with whom Walpole was much more friendly, no great significance can be placed on this slight evidence. Townshend is to be found lobbying Newcastle with the Junto in October 1708 (G. M. Trevelyan, *Ramillies and the Union with Scotland*, p. 414), and when Newcastle broke with the Whigs in 1710 neither Walpole nor Townshend went with him. It is hard to believe in the importance of a political faction for which there is no evidence that its members ever consulted together or deliberately and consciously acted in unison.

And the list of members of this connection given on pp. 206 and 228 also arouses scepticism. Sir John Holland, a man of wide political influence, was an independently minded Knight of the Shire, and no man's client. Horatio Walpole, uncle of Robert, was an unshakeable Tory who loved to twit his nephew on politics and later tried to betray him. He was always an avowed Tory. The Marquess of Hartington and Sir Thomas Littleton are listed as nominees of Walpole; in fact they owed their seats at Castle Rising to Lady Diana Howard. (cf. my *Life of Sir Robert Walpole*, Vol. 1, p. 100). Mistakes of this kind were, perhaps, bound to occur in a thesis covering such a multiplicity of members and their constituencies and, even if the Newcastle–Townshend–Walpole faction is abolished, Professor Walcott's main thesis still remains. His analysis of the Tory groups carries more conviction and he gives clarity and precision to what others, including Macaulay, had sketched. He also brings out very well the dilemma of all Tory groups. They were much more effective in opposition than in office. Their attacks on placemen, on nonconformists, on the waste and expense of war, drew to them the support of the disaffected back-benchers; a support, however, which tended to melt away once they achieved office. Yet is not this, too, evidence of a deep-rooted cleavage in the political world, and one, perhaps which transcends the tactical manoeuvres of career politicians? And this, again, leads to the larger question as to whether it is entirely wise to consider politics merely in terms of the House of Commons and the struggle for office which must, by the very nature of things, lead to compromise and to the weakening of principle. In the large constituencies and amongst the educated and professional classes no-one who has studied this period can doubt that 'Whig' and 'Tory' represent a vital difference of political attitude and are not meaningless labels. Professor Walcott is perhaps too ready to sneer at older historians, such as Trevelyan and Feiling, who accepted such labels, not always blindly or naïvely (as he infers), but in the realisation that to question them minutely would inhibit the formation of broad general conclusions – conclusions which Professor Walcott's work has not wholly destroyed. Within the broad dichotomy of party there has always been, and always will be, connections and factions, based on common interests, loyalties, and ambitions, but they are only one aspect of political activity.

It is a pity, however, that Professor Walcott presses his thesis too far; just as he is too often ready to attribute a Member of Parliament to a faction on the mere evidence of a family relationship, so also is he too eager to see the wiles of faction in the conflicts and debates of political life. When discussing the parliamentary session of 1707–8 (pp. 136–7) Professor Walcott is at pains to demonstrate the difficulties which the Junto Whigs were causing for the Marlborough–Godolphin administration because they wished to eject Harley and secure more power for themselves. The government's policy in Spain was attacked by the Nottingham–Rochester Tories in the House of Lords, and, according to Professor Walcott, Marlborough, to spike their guns, 'conjured up the vision of a great Spanish expedition, on (sic) the order of 40,000 troops under the command of Prince Eugene which he said was being planned with the Emperor.' Instead, however, of spiking the Tories' guns this, according to Professor Walcott, gave an opportunity to the Junto to embarrass Marlborough.

Unfortunately (he writes) the matter was not allowed to rest there. The grandiose expedition mentioned by Marlborough did not exist as yet except in his own mind. He had mentioned it on the spur of the moment in order to divert the dangerous course of the debate; but in no time at all the Junto leaders gave the idea independent life. After

Somer's motion – 'that no peace can be safe or honourable' which left Spain and the Indies in the possession of the Bourbons – had been passed, Wharton moved that the Lords thank Her Majesty for her pains in planning such an expedition as Marlborough had mentioned; and Halifax added a final motion that the Queen be asked to continue her efforts to induce the Emperor to do his part (p. 137).

These events are capable of a simpler explanation, and one which has little to do with the conflict between Marlborough and the Junto. The 'grandiose expedition' existed not only in Marlborough's mind but also in the Emperor's. He had suggested to Hensius sending Eugene to Catalonia as early as 17 September 1707 (cf. B. van T'Hoff, *The Correspondence of John Churchill and Anthonie Hensius 1707–11*, The Hague, 1951, pp. 345 ff.). Marlborough had taken up the scheme vigorously but, as his enthusiasm grew, the Emperor's diminished. The matter had been several times before the Cabinet and the Lords of the Committee and on 9 September 1707 (N.S.) the Queen had written personally to the Emperor, urging him to agree finally to the expedition (cf. Sunderland's Cabinet memoranda for December, Blenheim MSS, C.I. 16). The motions of Wharton and Halifax were, therefore, quite in tune with the Ministry's policy and can be regarded as helpful rather than embarrassing to the government; indeed they may even have been agreed with the Ministry in order to put yet further pressure on the Emperor, for Sunderland was a member of the cabinet, and in close touch with the Junto, and it is unlikely that either Wharton or Halifax were uninformed of the proposed expedition. In discussing the Junto, it should be remembered that though they wanted more power for themselves, they also held political views which influenced their political action.

Factional strife, as such, is a key to only a part of the politics of Anne's reign. There were large issues – the war and toleration were two – about which men felt deeply enough to act in accordance with their feelings, even at the expense of immediate advantage to their clique. Nor can the wider world of politics be ignored – the political attitudes in the constituencies, in the Church, in the press and, above all, in London, which helped to mould the decisions of the Court, of the Junto and of the Commons. Although it is helpful to stress the similarities between the policies of the early years of Queen Anne's reign and those of 1760, and for this all historians will be in Professor Walcott's debt, the differences are more remarkable and more important.

John Owen: The Rise of the Pelhams

This is a most important book and one which all students of eighteenth-century politics must master. It is based on a wealth of scholarship – Dr Owen has investigated the lives of some 600 Members of the 1741–7 Parliament. Written with great clarity, it presents the thesis that ability in debate and the pursuit of an acceptable policy mattered more in the control of the House of Commons than places or rewards. Furthermore, although no politician could survive without the favour of the King, his support was insufficient of itself; if the House of Commons and the leading politicians were hostile to his choice of advisers, they could not survive. The strongest ministers, such as Sir Robert Walpole and Henry Pelham, were those who could speak in the Closet for the Commons and in the Commons for the King. Weakness, indecision and frequent ministerial changes occurred when this mutual confidence was lacking. This, of course, will be acceptable, in the main, to most students of eighteenth-century politics. It has rarely been better said or more amply demonstrated.

Historians will also be grateful for Dr Owen's masterly analysis of Carteret's failure to make secure the political ascendancy which he enjoyed in 1743. He brings out clearly what many scholars have recently reiterated, that George II was deeply engrossed in English affairs. Dr Owen describes lucidly the exceptional circumstances in which the Pelhams and Hardwicke forced the King to give them his confidence and reject Carteret. He dismisses the concept, so long current, that this defeat of George II placed him 'in toils' and put him at the mercy of the politicians. This crisis, however, might with advantage have been compared to that which faced George III between 1781 and 1784. Then, George III outwitted the politicians and got the servants of his choice, partly because Rockingham and Fox were incompetent in the way they imposed their will on the King and partly because of the obstinacy and political dexterity of George III himself. Newcastle and Hardwicke moved with greater skill and they were aided by the weakness of the King's will; nevertheless George II was forced to part with friends and to accept servants he disliked or hated – and this is in marked contrast with both his father and his grandson and justifies to some extent the Leicester House cry that he was 'in toils'. The constitutional implications of this crisis still need further probing.

Much of Dr Owen's characterisation is excellent. He brings out very clearly and very well Carteret's temperamental weaknesses and demonstrates the shortcomings of his foreign policy which was far less adroit than he arrogantly assumed. And just praise is given to Newcastle. His picture of Henry Pelham is altogether admirable; and there are many deft touches which bring minor politicians to life with equal sharpness.

And finally, on the credit side, there is the large and important fact that Dr Owen, unlike many political historians of the eighteenth century, pays close attention to the interaction of foreign affairs with alignments in the House of Commons; an interplay of forces which his narrative method abundantly demonstrates. It is a pity that he did not pay equal attention to the political feelings and discussions which took place in pamphlet and newspaper during this period. Members of Parliament were not all isolated from the currents of alarm, despondency and hope which ran through their constituents and voters. This influence is difficult to trace, but no one can deny its effect at times of crisis, and it is particularly important at the time of Walpole's fall.

There are, however, one or two points where many will differ with Dr Owen; and there are also one or two gaps which could have been filled with advantage from sources which Dr Owen does not appear to have used. His analysis of the general election of 1741 and of Walpole's fall is excellent as far as it goes, but it does not go far enough. The Bootle letters in the Royal Archives at Windsor show how deeply the Prince of Wales was involved, not only in the elections in Cornwall but also in Sussex and in Yorkshire. More use could have been made of secondary authorities, particularly the excellent work of Dr Cedric Collyer on Yorkshire and Eliott Perkins on the election as a whole. Far too much weight is placed on the unreliable recollections of the Rev Henry Etough, one of the most notorious liars of the eighteenth century. 'Etough repeatedly stresses', Dr Owen writes, 'the little assistance that Walpole gained from the secret service fund in 1741.' The Scrope MSS in the Northamptonshire Record Office, which give details of secret service disbursements, show that there is no substance in Etough's assertions. Dr Owen could with advantage have given greater weight to the effect of Walpole's age. No one, knowing his health, could have expected him to survive the 1741 Parliament. That fact, and the unpopularity of his conduct of the war, must have made many a thoughtful member of the Court and Treasury party decide that he was a bad risk and the sooner replaced, the better.

But more important than any of these things is the question of the influence of place, profit and honours in building up the ministerial party in the Commons. In one long chapter, entitled 'Raw Material', Dr Owen subjects the membership of the House of Commons to a detailed analysis of its political affiliations. Parts of this chapter are exceptionally good – the analysis of Toryism has never been bettered. Dr Owen proves that at this date Tories were born, never made, and that their number was steadily diminishing: there is no example of a Whig becoming a Tory in these years. Equally fine is his elucidation of the hard core of the Court and Treasury party – his 'men of business' upon whose shoulders rested the entire burden of parliamentary administration. To regard their sinecures as anything but salaries is ludicrous. And it is admirable that this should be made abundantly clear. It is also a merit of Dr Owen's book that he should have brought out the vital importance of the independent members. In day-to-day business, it is true, they were not very important, indeed they were often absent, but at times of political crisis their vote could be decisive. No one will quarrel with Dr Owen about their importance, but some scholars will feel that he has been far too generous in assigning members to this category. This partly springs from one of his basic beliefs. He is of the opinion that the pursuit of pension, place, profit or honours was not of prime importance in controlling political behaviour. Except for providing seats and salaries for men of business, he considers government patronage 'had the character of private charity rather than public corruption'. Sir Robert Walpole did not hold this view. At the election of 1741, he needed to defeat Dodington at Bridgwater. He did not hesitate to ask for the votes of Sir Walter Pynsent, a local Tory of great influence, writing to him in these terms: 'I never ask favours, but with a design to acknowledge them, in the best manner I am able, and if you will lay this obligation upon me you shall find I am a grateful man.' Walpole meant what he said and knew what he meant: his charity began at home. His whole life had been spent in making patronage pay political dividends. In the remaining fragment of Walpole's correspondence there are over 50 begging letters from 27 government supporters whom Dr Owen lists as independent country gentlemen. Indeed this list holds some strange names; one of the strangest is that of Sir Roger Bradshaigh, both of whose sons held places at Court, whose attitude can best be judged by the remark of his fellow borough patron at Wigan, when there was a possibility that Walpole's son-in-law, Malpas, might want his seat: 'I told him I knew you to bee soe much Sir Robert's humble servant that if he desired you shou'd resign next election to Lord Malpas, I was sure you would' (quoted from Marjorie Cox, 'Sir Roger Bradshaigh, 3rd Baronet, and the Electoral Management of Wigan' *Bulletin of John Rylands Library*, vol. 37, p. 152).

It is true that Dr Owen can point to the fact that perhaps once or twice in their political lives a few of these men voted against the Ministry, although, even here, some of the evidence is suspect, for the only knowledge of such actions derives from printed division lists that are notoriously inaccurate. But allowing that they did, such votes were often a forcing bid derived from impatience at waiting for further sweeteners or were matters – like Place Bills – where an independent act was rarely frowned on. Here Lord Egmont's diary is immensely revealing. He prided himself both on his conscience and his independent spirit, but his private journal reveals how, time and time again in the early 1730s, his political behaviour was rendered circumspect and conformist by the prospect of favours for his dependants and honours for himself. What finally drove him to independence was this – that he set his price too high; disappointment and frustration enabled him to indulge his conscience more lavishly. Patronage could produce a furious spirit of independence as well as subservience; either way it is a political factor of the greatest importance. It is right that Dr Owen should stress that men of independent mood and judgement were numerous in the House of Commons, but the constant belittling of the effect of patronage, which runs throughout his pages, may, if accepted too readily, be equally as misleading as the view that 'all men had their price'. This aspect of Dr Owen's thesis is the one where further exploration and debate is keenly needed. It is, however, very salutary that he should have raised the issue so sharply.

And two very small matters. It seems a pity that Dr Owen should consistently give manuscript references to documents or parts of documents that are fully printed in P. Yorke's *Life of Hardwicke*. The name of the Tory leader, Sir John Philipps, is consistently misspelt. It is a piquant fact, not noticed by Dr Owen, that he was a cousin of Sir Robert Walpole!

Sir Lewis Namier and John Brooke: The History of Parliament. The House of Commons, 1754–1790

Already there has been considerable public and private criticism of these volumes, some of it unjust, a great deal of it ill-informed and most of it misdirected. That, however, they are open to criticism cannot be denied, but they also deserve a full measure of praise. The sources for parliamentary history for the second half of the eighteenth century are multitudinous, and it required scholars of the calibre of Sir Lewis Namier and Mr John Brooke to master them. Namier brought to their study a mind of exceptional lucidity, a memory of quite remarkable range and an analytical intelligence at once original and acute. He could concentrate his formidable powers on particular issues for weeks, months and years on end. Yet in his scholarship there was always a stratum of obsession that had its attendant dangers, some of which are apparent in these books. In these volumes 1964 lives are covered and only someone who has worked on the biographies of obscure men will appreciate the amount of time and energy, as well as ingenuity, that can be consumed in tracing a birth, a marriage, a death. In some ways Sir Lewis Namier and John Brooke have been more fortunate in this respect than the scholars who will be dealing with earlier periods, for county histories and the like are more reliable for the late eighteenth century. Nevertheless, their task was monumental.

Considering, therefore, the multitude of sources, it is not surprising that these volumes should have taken over twelve years to compile, in spite of the fact that Namier had covered much of the ground between 1754 and 1763 in his earlier work. In consequence, this enterprise has been costly. It would have been more costly still but for a great deal of voluntary help given by many scholars and archivists (it may seem a little churlish to many that two or three pages out of 2000 were not spared to thank many of these by name). The result is a permanent enrichment of eighteenth-century history, for the two biographical volumes will be of great value to all who work in this period. Heavy as the task was, the volumes could probably have been produced both more quickly and more cheaply. There is a case, which need not be argued here, for a thorough overhaul of the History of Parliament Trust. Certainly far stronger editorial direction and control should be called for. In many ways these volumes are too idiosyncratic, too dominated by Sir Lewis Namier's special interests and concerns, and I should have thought they would prove to be an impossible model for other periods to follow and in many cases an undesirable one. But to the volumes themselves.

It is easier to deal with the biographical volumes (Vols ii and iii) first. The aim in these books has been to give a potted version of the bare bones of an MP's life and career, followed by an extended account of his political activity in Parliament. The great statesmen who already have full biographies written about them are dealt with adequately but not extensively, and the avowed purpose was to treat all other members in accordance with their political importance.

The rule, however, seemed easier to lay down than to follow at any level. Both John Wilkes and Lord George Germain (Sackville) have many detailed biographies written about them (Wilkes' not very satisfactory, Germain's far more so): Germain, however, gets thirteen columns (of which one and a half are devoted to his behaviour at the Battle of Minden and Wilkes gets only three and a half. Reformers whom Sir Lewis did not love do not do well. Brass Crosby gets one column, John Sawbridge three. Even Sir George Saville, that pillar of independency, only gets seven columns, the same as the Hon Thomas Walpole, a figure of no great importance. (One dreads to think how many columns Thomas Walpole might have got had the editors been aware of the bulk of Walpole's manuscripts which, perhaps mercifully, they missed.) John

Brindley, who sat for about fifteen months in Parliament for Dover, has over five columns, much more than John Robinson, who played a vital role in politics for a decade. Even odder are the ten and a half columns devoted to Chase Price, amusing adventurer though he was, who gets far more space than Charles Jenkinson or either of the Foxes. A much firmer editorial control was needed. Again, within the biographies too much space is given to electioneering or management of the parliamentary seat, often with extensive quotations, much of which is repeated in Volume I, and too little to the attitude of members to political questions. This is not ignored, and, Mr A. J. P. Taylor's criticism that political attitude plays little or no part in the biographies must derive from a cursory reading; nevertheless, there is an imbalance that stricter editorial control could so easily have put right. However, many of the larger biographies are outstanding pieces of compression, particularly those by Miss Lucy Sutherland, and many of Namier's possess new insights.

The standard of accuracy is high, yet not so high, perhaps, as one might have expected from these two scholars, Namier and Brooke, who have been so notoriously ferocious about the peccadilloes of others. In one particular they are downright slipshod. The decision was taken to list the fact if an MP made the Grand Tour. The result is chaos. Omissions everywhere abound. For example, in the Walpole family both Sir Edward Walpole and the Hon Horatio Walpole, eldest son of Lord Walpole of Wolterton, did the Grand Tour; so did John, Lord Hobart, so did George Treby, so did Lord Mandeville and so one might go on and on. Even a cursory glance at the Horace Walpole–Mann correspondence, in W. S. Lewis's edition, would have saved them from some of the more obvious of these omissions, but only Mr Brooke could have saved himself from the worst howler. In his commentary on the Grand Tour he remarks that no member of the Brudenell family made it, but in his own biography of Lord Brudenell he rightly lists him as having done so.

And one may make one further criticism of these biographies, particularly of those men about whom very little is known: no use seems to have been made of wills. For an earlier period these give valuable material about a Member's economic and philanthropic interests and often factual information about relatives and friends. However, these criticisms are heavily outweighed by the value of the bulk of the biographies; nevertheless, it is to be hoped that, in future volumes, they will be better balanced in regard to both space and material used.

The first volume is the least satisfactory. It contains many good things, one or two impressive ones and much valuable information. But the *intention* of this volume is difficult to discern and for this the editorial board must be held partially responsible. In this volume each constituency is dealt with. When the detailed work of a specialist scholar is available, as Mr Underdown's for Bristol or Mr Brian Hayes's for Norfolk, the result is admirable – not only are elections dealt with, but also the conflicting political forces within the constituency are assessed. When the editors, however, are forced to use their own resources, the result is much less satisfactory. Often too little work has been done and the result frequently is little more than a catalogue of elections which repeats, in a somewhat different guise, not only the material but the language of the biographies. Indeed, this volume is dominated by the major Namierite obsessions – elections, borough management, and the type of men who sat in Parliament; so much so that an unkind critic might say that a monument had been raised to Namier rather than to Parliament.

Half of the introduction in Volume I by Mr Brooke is *The Structure of Politics* writ large and adds little that is new. In an all too brief section Mr Brooke attempts to deal with other parliamentary matters, but he can spare only three pages for legislation and only a paragraph for private legislation which, in the period, is of great constitutional importance. As to any discussion of parliamentary policy – financial or foreign – it is hard to find. Questions relating to parliamentary privilege, to the influence of the House of Lords, to the problem of Ireland, or to dissent and to a host of other matters of the first importance, are not adumbrated. Perhaps the editorial board did not intend these matters to be dealt with; perhaps the intention was to produce merely a biographical dictionary of the House of Commons; if so, Volume I is largely redundant and a great deal of what it contains could have been tabulated in appendices.

These volumes display the strength and weaknesses of Namier as an historian: on the one hand, his obsessive preoccupation with elections, patronage and management to the exclusion of all else; and, on the other, the superb quality, the magnificent dedication, and the incredible comprehension of his scholarship within these narrow limits. He possessed little sense of proportion; he turned his attention too late to both radicals and the constituencies; he remained largely indifferent to the activity of Parliament or to the reactions of men and women outside formal politics to Parliament. Still, in many ways, it is a miracle that these books got written at all and without the selfless dedication of Mr Brooke and the generous help of such formidable scholars as Miss Sutherland, Lady Haden-Guest and Mr Cannon, amongst others, it is unlikely that they would have appeared before the funds ran out. And in spite of faults of planning and some errors of omission, they will be of lasting worth. Nevertheless, further volumes should be much more carefully planned. If what is intended is a purely biographical dictionary, it should not masquerade, even in the title, as a History of Parliament. These volumes are emphatically not that.

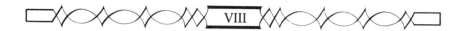

VIII

The Wider Issues of
Eighteenth-Century Politics

The nature of oligarchy leads most historians to overvalue patronage, family relationships, and the pressure of the Crown. These are important, but oligarchy also rests on great riches, traditional and local loyalties, and the committed family traditions. Oligarchs, secure in their estates and in their local authority, can wait for a sympathetic government, if need be, for a generation or two. Oligarchy and independency may be strange bedfellows but at times they embrace each other with passion. Rarely did aristocratic families dominate entirely their localities – there were other men of power, often with different political and religious attachments, who could not be ignored or treated with total indifference without endangering the oligarch's own power and respect. Nor did independency of mind belong merely to the aristocracy and landed gentry: there were clerics, lawyers, doctors, bankers, coal-mine owners, ship owners, monied men of status here, there and everywhere with parliamentary votes. Few such men were 100 per cent reliable generation after generation. Once a pyramid of political power had been created, its preservation could make men more cautious of conflict. That is why all governments detested contested elections and did their best to avoid them. Nevertheless about one-third of all constituencies went to a poll at general elections. (Oddly enough the general election of 1761 – Namier's model – had less contested elections than average; indeed there were fewer than in any election of the eighteenth century.)

Furthermore the size of the electorate of the unreformed Parliament had always been underestimated until I studied it in detail. I demonstrated how it grew in the seventeenth and early eighteenth centuries only to be deliberately contracted after 1715. No government in the eighteenth century lost an election but no government faced a new Parliament without an opposition. And beyond the electorate, beyond the Commons and the Lords was an ever-growing political nation, alive to issues both specific and general, from Cider Tax to toleration for

Dissenters, and able to exert some pressure at Westminster. These are the views expanded in *Political Man* printed below. The more I studied eighteenth-century politics, the more I realised that the election of 1761 was atypical, and that the most important and enduring discovery of Namier was the nature and limits of that royal patronage which Whig historians had so greatly exaggerated.

By 1967 I had largely completed what I wanted to write about eighteenth-century politics. In 1966 I gave the Ford Lectures at Oxford which I had always regarded as the highest accolade that an historian of Britain could win. *The Growth of Political Stability* (1967) was the result. It was based on twenty years' work and could easily have been three or four times longer had I tipped in the filing cabinets. But I wanted it to be read widely, and it was. I was diverted from finishing my biography of Walpole by the invitation to give the Ford Lectures. After that, I started the third and final volume and wrote about a fifth and then put down my pen. I wanted to call the third volume 'The Politics of Old Age', and I decided that it might be best to defer a little until I could summon up enough empathy for the aged. That was the excuse, but deeper down I think I was tired of eighteenth-century politics. Also in the early 1960s I had visited America repeatedly: I became absorbed in its life and culture, fascinated by its historiography and the whole problem of the nature of history began to absorb more of my time. Indeed, it was this preoccupation which first made me brood on one of the most fundamental problems that can occupy an historian's mind. How do ideas become social attitudes? This has been my major preoccupation for the last twenty years.

Yet I still hanker for that third volume of Walpole, largely because younger historians rarely consider the effect of age on individual politicians or work on the demographic problems of the political nation as a whole. In Walpole's day the population was stable, growing but little, and there was little imbalance between young and old, but by the last decades of the eighteenth century youth was rapidly becoming the predominant part of the nation – and youth is more prone to ideological passion and it riots more readily than the middle-aged. Demographic patterns which can be very complex are rarely utilised by political historians or even social historians for that matter. And it is one important aspect of Walpole's later years that I regret not exploring.

The Growth of the Electorate in England from 1600 to 1715

Representative governments have had a very chequered history during the last 400 years of western history: common in the late Middle Ages, they were mostly suppressed or ignored by the second half of the seventeenth century. Their relationship with monarchy and their role in national government have been more closely studied than their social bases. Furthermore, although the idiosyncratic development of England, where the representative assembly strengthened at a time when others had floundered or were floundering, has been noticed often enough, the reasons for that survival have not been satisfactorily explained. Not only did Parliament in England survive in the seventeenth century, but also it fathered a notable subspecies in those colonial assemblies which marked the representative institutions of America. And whatever we may think of seventeenth- and eighteenth-century Parliaments, the men of the Enlightenment regarded them as bulwarks of liberty: a gleam of hope in a Europe dark with oppression.

For a generation the English contributions to social and political liberty have not engaged the attention of scholars, perhaps because such a preoccupation might seem to be tainted with Whiggery and its misguided interpretation of English history. And the essentially English origins of American revolutionary ideology were also politely ignored, a situation now corrected by Professor Bernard Bailyn.[1] There is at last a clearer realisation that the American colonies shared a common political and social culture with Britain. They were parts of the same polity. Moreover, not only were the American institutions of government of the same family as those of Britain, but they suffered the same ills, the same genetic weaknesses. The intention both of Parliament and of the colonial assemblies was for a mixed government in which the competing forces in society were balanced: the representative assembly guarded liberty and insisted on economy, which they knew would be constantly threatened by the very nature of monarchical or gubernatorial government. Parliament preserved those liberties which the world envied all Englishmen. Yet by 1700 these had been constantly threatened for over a hundred years, indeed not only threatened but nearly extinguished by the Stuarts. And the Augustan Parliaments were suffering new and more insidious setbacks from a cunning and power-hungry executive that used places, contracts, honours, promotions and bribes of every kind to undermine the nation's fundamental liberties. And in the early eighteenth century the suspicions which had been focused on the monarchy were being transferred to the ministry. And the same is true in the American colonies: the protection of American interests against exploitation by Britain was felt to depend not only on the burgesses in their assemblies, but also on the voters who sent them there. The ultimate bulwark of the nation's liberties, English or American, was those who exercised the franchise.

You are called [wrote John Trenchard, appealing to the freeholders before the election of 1722] the Mobb, the Canaille, the stupid Herd, the Dregs and Beasts of the People and your interest is never thought of by those men who thus miscal you. . . . For my own Particular [he went on] I cannot give myself leave to despair of you, because I must at the same time despair of old English liberty: You are our Alpha and Omega, our first and last resource and when your virtue is gone, all is gone.[2]

And what political propaganda, written in England, was more popular in America than Cato's letters? The political base of both societies rested on the enfranchised freeholders. And it is this social base of Parliament that has been constantly ignored. Parliamentary relations with the monarchy and the executive were not its only relationships of importance. Parliament, in the seventeenth century, was a representative institution, and representative of a large and constantly growing body of men – the freeholders of England: a body which contemporaries never ignored.

By Trenchard's day the freeholder had, however, been exhorted for generations to avoid the wickedness of men intent on corrupting him and so destroying his true principles. In 1634, John Preston admonished electors and told them 'it is an error among men to think that in the election of burgesses . . . [they] may pleasure their friends or themselves'[3] – implying that if the freeholder voted for godliness, the Commonwealth would be secure. From Preston to Trenchard, the freeholder had been the target of a deluge of pamphlets which urged him to follow his true principles.[4] But 'true principles' ranged from a love of the Church and a loyalty to the monarchy to a passion for liberty and a horror of arbitrary power. What is clear, however, is that everyone assumed that there was a voter to be persuaded or cajoled.

By Walpole's day millions of words had been printed in electioneering pamphlets: they lie thick, dusty and rarely disturbed on our library shelves.[5] Although nominally sold, they were usually given away in bulk by their sponsors to be distributed to taverns, coffee houses and voters of local standing and importance.[6] Now if it is true that, as Namier said, not one in twenty voters exercised his franchise freely, but merely did the bidding of his landlord, or as Professor Walcott would have us believe for Queen Anne's reign, that county elections were more often than not settled by the nobility and gentry between themselves, this pamphleteering would seem to be a fatuous waste of time and a shocking waste of money.[7] Or was there, as these generations of pamphlets would imply, an electorate in 1700 to be persuaded; or a sufficient number of voters whose own private decision on whom to vote for could sway elections this way or that? And if there was such an electorate, when had it come into being, for the sixteenth century witnessed no such propaganda as this? And how had this electorate grown, steadily or by fits and starts? And, more important still, how extensive was it and how free? And, most important of all, what influence did it have on the nature and structure of English politics? It is to such questions as these that I am, with the help of other scholars, now addressing myself.[8] This essay is a first report, very tentative, and one that exposes problems rather than offers solutions.

About the early history of the electorate, whether of boroughs or of counties, we know next to nothing, a field of research which for the fifteenth and sixteenth centuries badly needs cultivating. We know, of course, that the qualification for the county voter was fixed at 40s. freehold in 1429, although the reasons for this and the social standing of those to whom it gave the vote are still somewhat obscure.[9] Certainly by the end of the sixteenth century the forty-shilling freeholder had acquired a semi-sacrosant status, and I know of only one proposal at any time that the qualification should be either raised or lowered, except of course during the Civil War and Protectorate.[10] This qualification was seriously affected by the inflation of the sixteenth century. Initially this aroused, as far as I know, no comment. The reason for this could be that the electorate counted for very little before the 1580s when there are indications of an awareness of the freeholders' potential value. It was not until James I's reign that the gentry realised fully that the freeholder could be a source of power in their ideological disputes and personal feuds.

From the indications that we have, however, the Tudors do not seem to have liked a large electorate. In 1489, the Commons abolished the right of the citizens of Leicester and Northampton to vote in parliamentary elections by Act of Parliament. Also, whenever one can catch an actual glimpse of elections in Star Chambers proceedings, there are strong indications of a similar attitude. When at Chichester in 1584, the candidate of the commoners told a leading member of the corporation that he must please the people, he was rebuked sharply, 'No, no', Edward More told him, 'the people must be governed, not pleased.' Needless to say the commoners' candidate lost the election. These sentiments – fear of the voice of those not within the magic circle of the self-perpetuating oligarchies of the parliamentary boroughs – find numerous echoes elsewhere. In Gloucester in 1584, the city magistrats told the Earl of Leicester 'that experience hath taught us what a difficult thing it hath always been to deal in any matter where the multitude of burgesses have voice'[11] – a difficulty which most corporations took pains to avoid.

By the 1580s there are hints that the potential value of the voter was being realised and also that an increase in their number might help those who desired a more godly commonwealth. In 1587, in a moment of

exasperation, John Field, the ardent puritan, leader of the classis movement, burst out to a colleague, 'Tush, Mr Edmunds, hold your peace.
Seeing we cannot compass these things by suit nor dispute, it is the
multitude and people that must bring the discipline to pass which we
desire.[12] As we know, the Puritans had been exceedingly active in the
elections for the Parliaments of the 1580s, and this is the decade when
we get the first hints of appeal to a wider franchise in order to defeat
the entrenched corporation oligarchies. In one case, Warwick in 1586,
a puritan extremist, Job Throckmorton, forced his election by threatening to invoke the rights of the commonalty to vote.[13]

'Men of the meaner sort' did not in Tudor or Stuart England take
themselves 40 miles across a county in order to vote for a man they did
not know or for men of whose principles they were ignorant. Neither
did humble tradesmen challenge their masters in the Guildhall about
who should represent them in Parliament unless provoked to do so. If
these Tudor freeholders were becoming active, it was because they were
becoming recognised as useful by men who wished to get into Parliament. The electorate, if not created, was at least conjured up. And for
the sake of true godliness even the insecure would take risks and on the
question of godliness even humble men might feel capable of judging
their social superiors, especially when instructed from the pulpit by a
man such as Cartwright, whose presence at Warwick antedated Throckmorton's bid for the election. Also there are hints that, in these elections,
country gentlemen were beginning to marshal their freeholders: indeed
so many Puritans were returned in the 1580s, overturning old loyalties
and established connections, that it is difficult to understand how this
was done without a more skilful exploitation of the electorate than had
been customary.[14] Certainly the hints are sufficiently strong for a closer
study of the Elizabethan electorate to be very much worth while.

When, however, we reach the reign of James I and the early Parliaments of his son, there is no question of hints, no question of scraps of
evidence; the evidence about the electorate is clear and unequivocal. The
floodgates were opened by the Commons victory in Goodwin's case in
1604, a well-known triumph but still underestimated in its importance
for the development of Parliament and the seventeenth-century constitution. Hitherto, disputes about elections had tended to find their way
to Star Chamber; but, owing to James I's foolishness, for he threw away
a strong legal case, the Commons became their own masters, immediately
deciding not only whether a person or a category of persons might sit
in the House, but also the validity of elections.[15] The validity of the
election might have been limited to contraventions of due processes, but
the Commons took upon themselves the more fundamental questions of
parliamentary franchises, the revival of representation in boroughs where

it had lapsed, and even the question of new enfranchisement, matters hitherto regarded as falling within the prerogatives of the Crown. Not many Parliaments were to pass before the Commons were laying down, in their resolutions, general principles about the nature of the franchise. Many attempts were made with varying success to secure a comprehensive Bill to regulate election methods and in 1621 this Bill contained clauses to alter the franchise. Some of these facts have been long known if insufficiently stressed, but what has been totally ignored is the consistency of the pressure by some members of the Commons on matters relating to the electorate, the exceptional vigour of this pressure from 1621 to 1628 and the connection between this pressure and a change of fundamental importance that was taking place in the electorate itself.[16] It was these years which saw parliamentary representation secure a wide social base without which the Stuarts might have had far less difficulty in securing control of the corporations and so reducing the power of Parliament or abolishing it altogether.

There is an irony here that needs to be stressed and to which I will return later. It was the invasion of the gentry into the representation of the corporate boroughs that not only gave these towns larger electorates but also strengthened their constitutional role.[17] Had the usual legal requirements that resident burgesses be elected been rigorously maintained, the Commons would have been a far less formidable body. It was this victory, the snatching of borough representation by the gentry from nominees of courtiers and aristrocratic families and from local merchants and patricians, that gave Parliament much of its strength to oppose the Crown. The struggle for political power was as intense in the electorate as in the Commons.

However, the more precise question of the growth of the electorate must be explored. In the counties inflation produced the voters; so there was no need to create them by other means. Indeed, it would seem that those members of the Commons who were most active in electoral matters, amongst whom Hakewell, Glanville, Henry Poole and Sir George Moore were to the fore, were well aware both of the devaluation of the freeholder qualification and of the injustice of excluding the modest copyholders. In 1621 the Bill to regulate elections contained a clause by which the freehold was to be raised to 80 shillings a year, but copyholders of ten pounds a year by inheritance added. This probably would not have diminished in any way the size of the electorate, but altered its composition. However, the large county electorates were more active than they had been. There were more contests and they were more hotly contested. The Commons made great attempts to secure fair and just elections. They severely rebuked the sheriffs of Cambridgeshire and Yorkshire who refused a poll when demanded, and even insisted that

Thomas Wentworth should undergo another election.[18] Both sheriffs had publicly to acknowledge their fault at Quarter Sessions. Again the Commons resolved that the taking of names of freeholders at the poll was improper, as pressure might be subsequently applied on the freeholder because of his vote.[19] Of course, polls continued to be evaded and lists of freeholders composed, but these resolutions of the Commons express a political attitude. Another aspect of the same mood was the denunciation of letters of recommendation:[20] as Sir George Moore insisted, 'Free Choice, so Free Voice'. Such,[21] however, remained a hope and never became a reality in county elections. Personal influence continued to be rigorously asserted. And the gentry, of course, continued to organise their freeholders,[22] but with one, two, three, sometimes four thousand men present at an election there could be no certainty as to how a contest might go. For the next hundred years contests in the counties were frequent. When as few as twenty or thirty voters might sway the decision one way or the other, there was always the possibility that the most careful organisation of disciplined and committed freeholders might fail. In such situations the influence of political attitudes, of commitment to political and religious ideology became much stronger. Inflation had increased the number of county voters. The gentry organised them and brought them to the poll because the gentry were divided – sometimes on personal issues, sometimes on territorial issues, sometimes on religious and political issues and sometimes on combinations of all three. They mustered loyal men, neighbourly men, like-minded men. The multitudes were conjured up, but once conjured up they created a factor of uncertainty and the final decision as to who should represent the county no longer remained entirely in the hands of the gentry. True, their influence was paramount. They selected the candidates, but the final choice between them could be made by a small body of freeholders. Knowing this it became even more important to convince freeholders on issues as well as personalities.

In the very vital period in the development of the electorate between 1614 and 1628, the increase in county electors and the greater numbers of freeholders involved was only one aspect of what was taking place. There were even more significant changes in the borough electorates – an aspect of parliamentary history which has not been noticed, yet it is of profound significance for the survival and development of representative government in England.

There are two aspects of the growth of the borough electorate in this period: one widely known, the other ignored. The borough electorate had grown since the Reformation Parliaments by the simple process of reviving the representation of boroughs which had sent Members to Parliament in the past, but whose representation had fallen into desuetude, more often than not through poverty, the borough being unable or unwilling to pay the members' wages. Other boroughs had representation granted to them by the Crown. Sir John Neale has analysed this process and demonstrated convincingly that the Tudor gentry, particularly those at Court, were responsible for this growth and that they controlled the representation so granted. Now almost all of these boroughs, revived or enfranchised, were small towns, principally little seaports. Their electorates, in consequence, were very small too. The franchise was usually confined to the important burgesses. More often than not they were expected to elect without question the names sent to them by their patrons.[23] Even these electoral crumbs add to the total number of those involved in sending men to Parliament. However, after 1621, through a cunning interpretation of Goodwin's Case, decisions about enfranchisements or revivals were no longer a matter for the Crown, but for the Commons, and the attitude of the Commons towards the electorate may be judged from what they did. In all the revivals for which they were responsible between 1621 and 1628, the franchise, except in one instance – Weobley – was declared by the Commons to be in the inhabitants paying scot and lot or in the inhabitant householders. This gave to even small towns such as Great Marlow or decayed towns such as Milbourne Port an electorate of 200 or more. There is a remarkable consistency about the franchises of boroughs revived by the Commons: indeed this is also true of those re-enfranchised by the Crown. But it is a totally different principle. All but one of the Crown's – Evesham – were given an extremely restricted franchise. The towns revived by the Commons, it is true, were not selected because they were heavily populated. They were the result of a judicious combination of Hakewell's learning and the desire of the opposition to strengthen itself. Hakewell and his friends acted as ideologists often do, upon the principles in which they believed (that is that the franchise should be in the inhabitants), but also in their own self-interest (it was applied to small market towns where their influence was uppermost).[24] Nevertheless, wide franchises create large electorates, and no matter where they may be sited, large electorates require more care in management, more cajolery, more argument than tiny bodies of twenty or thirty. And the boroughs which the Commons revived had wide franchises and initially they were not easy to manage.

This brings us to the second aspect of electoral growth – that made by decisions of the Commons. Between 1621 and 1628, time and time again the Commons voted in favour of a wider franchise. There is no space here to go through case after case and a few examples must suffice. At Sandwich in 1621, the Commons overrode the Privy Council decision that the right to election was in the Mayor and Jurats and insisted that the commoners had a right to vote.[25] At Chippenham the electorate was widened and taken out of the hands of the thirteen capital burgesses.[26] At Pontefract, a revived borough, it was resolved that, as there was no charter, 'the Election is to be made by Inhabitants, Householders, Resiants',[27] a far wider franchise than freemen. In 1624, the Commons laid down a general principle, arising from their discussions on the contested election at Cirencester,

> there being no certain custom nor prescription who should be the electors and who not, we must have recourse to common right which, to this purpose, was held to be, that more than the freeholders only ought to have voices in the election; namely all men, inhabitants, householders, resiants within the borough[28]

– echoing the decision which they had taken in regard to Pontefract in 1623. Colchester, Boston, Oxford, Warwick are other examples of the Commons widening the electorate.[29] The process was continued in 1640.[30]

The leaders in this development were, of course, lawyers and members who were suspicious of the influence of the Crown and its servants. These decisions demonstrate quite clearly that they felt that an extension of the electorate was in their interest. Their arguments also hinted at natural right, although couched in historico-legal terms.

An even more interesting development, however, was taking place in many towns without the intervention of the Commons. The Elizabethan borough electorates were small and approached in remarkably oblique ways. It is true that already one or two towns had large open electorates,[31] but this type of constituency appears to be rare. Towns such as Lincoln, Exeter, Reading, Oxford, Cambridge, Leicester, Northampton, King's Lynn and many others did not recognise the right of the freemen or inhabitants to vote. The normal process was for the mayor and aldermen to select candidates and for the Common-Council men to approve. There were variations of this process, but in almost all of these major boroughs, the effective electorate was confined to the closely-knit, intimately related borough oligarchies which provided the aldermen and Common-Council men. During the early seventeenth century this method of election began to change: sometimes helped by a decision of the Commons, but often not. Exeter allowed the freemen a voice in 1627 and this was confirmed by the Commons.[32] We know far too little about this process, but the results were remarkable. Although for towns such as King's Lynn and Cambridge the electorate had only risen from 51 to 300 and 24 to 200 respectively, Lincoln, Northampton, Leicester, Exeter had acquired electorates of nearly a thousand, electorates which continued to grow in size during the rest of the century. This movement

in the major cities from a closed to an open electorate is of vital importance, for it was a process that the Stuarts desperately attempted to
reverse. The greatest stumbling block to parliamentary management was
always the counties and the great cities; and the great cities, by and
large, acquired their large and open electorates in the early seventeenth
century, probably many of them between 1614 and 1628.

Why did this happen? We do not know. No historian has hitherto
remarked on this vital development in the growth of the parliamentary
electorate. It will need to be explored in depth. Had this development
been confined to one or two boroughs one might have presumed that it
was the result of purely local circumstances, but the widespread nature
of the change and the comparatively short time in which this growth
seems to have taken place would argue that it was the result of a political
attitude that had become widespread; that there were men, bent on
power, who felt that they were more likely to secure it if the basis of
parliamentary politics was widened. Who were they? As yet we do not
know. We may surmise that those members of the Commons who took
pains in election matters – Hakewell, Glanville, Henry Poole, Sir George
Moore and others associated with them – and who time and time again
demanded far wider franchises, were also active outside the Commons.
This group will need further study. Many were lawyers and they justified
their attitude on grounds of ancient inherent right of freeborn Englishmen. This is clear from the debates in the Commons and their
decisions. The situation in the boroughs is, however, obscure and so far
I have gleaned but few indications. Most local historians have not
noticed the change which took place. However, there are bits of evidence
which point in certain directions. At Exeter, the first signs of pressure
from the freeholders came in 1588 and 1593, when the corporation
conceded that the Common Council had the right to alter their choice.
However, the Common Council accepted what was offered them. The
issue was forced by Ignatius Jourdain, who was Member of Parliament
for 1621 and 1625, but not elected by the corporation in 1626. He,
however, got himself elected in the open county court and he repeated
this performance in 1627, when the House of Commons confirmed his
election. This established the freemen's right to vote; the franchise,
however, was not extended to the freeholder until 1689.[33] Nevertheless
Jourdain's victory extended the franchise dramatically. Ignatius Jourdain, the effective champion of the franchise, was a calvinist and a leader
of the puritans in Exeter. Furthermore, Jourdain was supported by John
Hakewell, sheriff of Exeter and the brother of William Hakewell, MP
one of the leading lights of the committee which dealt with disputed
elections. He had been deeply involved in the abortive Bill for franchise
reform in 1621, another to regulate elections, and of course in the revival

of the Buckinghamshire boroughs in 1624. Members of the Exeter
corporation had stayed with him in London when disputing the Bishop
of Exeter's claim to nominate a justice of the peace for the city.[34] When
further research is done, I think that we shall find that the men active
in opening the franchise were puritans, often lawyers, sometimes
merchants, frequently country gentlemen. Certainly the freemen, and the
freeholders and the inhabitants must have been aroused, organised and
led by some men of influence. It is unlikely that citizens in King's Lynn
or shopkeepers in Reading assembled of their own accord to insist on a
right to vote. But whatever the reasons, the electorate grew, fast between
1614 and 1628. But it did not stop then. The Commons in 1640
possessed a vigorous champion of large electorates in Sir Simon D'Ewes,
who believed as sincerely as any Leveller that the poorest man had a
right to vote unless charter or ancient custom denied him that right.
And in this view D'Ewes had the support of several members.[35] They
were successful in widening several franchises. Not all, however, much
to D'Ewes's chagrin. To the despair of what he called 'the religious and
sound men of the House', Salisbury was lost and Edward Hyde and
Michael Oldsworth seated on a narrow franchise: too many MPs being
swayed, D'Ewes thought, by the fact that Oldsworth was secretary to
the Earl of Pembroke.[36] Indeed, I doubt whether the majority of MPs
were ever very sympathetic to a wider franchise. After all, the Bill of
1621 failed to become law and th' frequent Bills to regulate elections
never did any better than the bills to regulate drunkenness. Success came
from an effective pressure group that was very strong indeed on the
Committee for Privileges and Elections; and they exploited their superior
knowledge (far, however, from accurate) of constitutional precedents
and tried to establish general constitutional principles about the franchise. They had many successes, but they also had their failures. Nevertheless with each parliamentary election in the reigns of the first two
Stuarts, the electorate had grown considerably. By the Long Parliament
it reached down not only to the minor gentry and rich merchants, but
to yeomen, craftsmen, shopkeepers in the majority of towns and all the
counties.

This enfranchisement took place for the sake of political power. The
value of the elector and his vote increased with the growth of strong
ideological differences in the gentry about religion, taxation and the role
of Parliament and the monarchy. To sway his mind, to persuade him to
the hustings, to secure his vote by every art became a vital preoccupation
with all who were concerned with government. Hence the first four
decades of the seventeenth century witness the growth and burgeoning
of strictly political propaganda written to influence voters and the development of broadsides and ballads for similar purposes.[37]

Also there are signs that men of 'the meaner sort' were no longer at the disposal of their masters. The contested elections for county seats occurred occasionally in Elizabethan Parliaments and from the Star Chamber proceedings to which they occasionally gave rise, Sir John Neale has described them to us in detail. They raised violent passions, but the passions were territorial or personal: bitter feuds between families or of different sides of the counties; occasionally, as in Rutland in 1601, a few sharp epithets about religion might be thrown out in the shouting and jostling and general hurly-burly of taking a view of the voters.[38] The personal element, however, was totally dominant. Certainly family conflict had not vanished in 1640 and the most recent historian of Kent maintains that family and clan issues decided the elections both to the Short and Long Parliaments in that county.[39] Indeed there is evidence to support this view, letters of Sir John Sedley to Sir Edward Dering telling of the machinations of neighbours or the promise of others to deliver their tenants. The correspondence between the principal gentry involved in the election scarcely mentions issues. And no one can doubt that clan and family, social and territorial standing, played their parts. There were few families in Kent in 1640 who could aspire to have a Knight of the Shire and their rivalry was acute. But does it really seem probable that a highly populous county, rich in small gentry as well as yeoman freeholders, would totally ignore issues in 1640? Within two years men would be killing each other for issues. As well as leading families, there were voters. Sir Edward Dering knew it. That he canvassed widely is well known. But now we have his personal reckoning of his voters and also his account of the election of 1640, material that has hitherto eluded the historian of this period.[40] Sir Edward Dering's list of freeholders is nearer akin to the lists drawn up by candidates in the Elizabethan period, prior to the day of election, so that they could be checked at the poll, than to a poll book of the late seventeenth century, although it possesses some resemblance to this. It is, however, the earliest embryonic poll book that we have, some 38 years before the next. It lists those who promised themselves to Dering and those who voted for him; lists some who defaulted and some who voted for his rival, Sir Roger Twysden. It is a half-completed document and many parishes are blank: presumably Dering found the task too onerous for his own labour. Fortunately, however, he appended, largely it would seem to relive his feelings, an account of the election and of the reasons which he thought caused his defeat. From the lists which Dering did draw up, it is clear that many who had promised did not finally vote for him: possibly having heard discussions in the groups of freeholders and gentry at Penenden Heath, they changed their minds. Of some there is no doubt: of sixteen freeholders of Smarden Dering noted 'these of Smarden defaulted'.[41] In many parishes it is obvious that promised votes did not materialise at the actual election. This hardly looks as if the gentry could deliver their freeholders *en bloc*. The reasons Dering gives for his failure, apart from the chicanery of what he called 'the warping Sheriff', were that 'The obscure[42] and puritanical that are separatists & lovers of separation did make itt theire cause to have a child of theires in ye House. no paynes was enough for them: and what they will, they will do pertinaciously.'[43] That is the puritans had been earnestly canvassing. Equally destructive were the rumours which Dering said were current about him. He listed them. They were these:

> Entred in opposition to my Lo Chamberleyne.
> Entred in opposition to Sr Hen: Vane.
> Entred in opposition to ye Deputy Leiuten.
> Was a commissioner for ye Knighting money.
> Was ye cause that shipping money was payd.
> Is another Buckingham.
> Will not go up to ye rayles att communion.
> Is a papist.
> Is a patentee for wine.
> Called ministers hedge-preistes.
> Can not endure Bishops.
> Set up first altar in Dover Castle.
> My wife keepes popish pictures.
> Is a courtier.[44]

Although several of these are contradictory, no one could deny that the majority are ideological and that they touch the burning issues – religious and financial – of the previous eleven years of royal rule. In 1640 in Kent, issues were present; the personal position of candidates towards them discussed: and we know that freeholders or the minor gentry who led them, could change their minds. This is undeniable. And Kent is no different from Suffolk, Essex, Norfolk or other counties where the evidence is also clear:[45] an electorate running into thousands could not be mustered like sheep or ignore the world in which it lived.

Dering calculated that 10,000 were present at Penenden Heath, an obvious exaggeration even allowing for hundreds of local sightseers, hucksters and the like, but well over 2000 registered their votes. These were certainly present for a whole day, possibly longer, and it is unthinkable that such a concourse brought together for a political act should have avoided either a discussion of politics or the relationship of the leading personalities to them. Dering quickly recognised the facts of life and not only made his peace but forged an alliance with the Puritan group and at the election for the Long Parliament he succeeded in defeating Twysden's candidate. He discharged this debt by proposing the Root and Branch Bill although he did not stay long allied to the Parliamentary opposition. I would not suggest for one moment that the support of the Puritan element or its withdrawal was the most critical factor in this election.[46] It was one factor. The family connections and alliances of the Derings another. But family connections and alliances were now entangled in political issues that smouldered with political violence. The extent of the electorate, partially swayable by these issues, as well as by loyalty towards or fear of their betters, had become a factor too in county politics. In 1640, the situation in the counties as well as the boroughs had changed out of all recognition from Elizabethan times, and we witness the birth of a political nation, small, partially controlled, but no longer coextensive with the will of the gentry. It could not be called by the most fervent stretch of the imagination democratic, and yet the political system was no longer purely oligarchical. Nor did very many of the gentry view this extension of political interest and activity with a great deal of favour. Their attitude probably chimed with Lord Maynard's, who vowed after the Essex election of 1640 never to appear again at 'popular assemblies whear fellowes without shirts challeng as good a voice as myselfe'.[47] Indeed the gentry of Essex had every reason to fear the yeomen and weavers of Essex, for they had driven the Catholic Lady Rivers helter-skelter out of the county, seized Sir John Lucas, the royalist, before he could quit his house. Their revolutionary zeal, not altogether unwelcome to the House of Commons, had scared the local parliamentarians out of their wits.[48] As in Essex, so in Suffolk and a dozen other counties. The rumblings of the lower classes, bitterly anti-Catholic and anti-Royalist or rather anti-establishment, were too loud for their ears. And yet to survive, as Mrs Pearl has shown in her excellent study of London, the parliamentary forces could not entirely rely on the sympathetic tycoons. They were forced to a wider base – to citizens and apprentices.[49] And once forced to it, they had to indoctrinate, to educate their supporters in politics and in religion. Nor were they alone in discovering either this necessity or its value. The Levellers were soon preaching, exhorting, talking of the rights of the Commons of England, and discussing an electorate so extensive that it made both Cromwell and Ireton wince with horror.[50]

The Civil War was one long, troubled, baffling, political education. And the Commonwealth was but the second act. It should be remembered that between 1653 and 1660 there were more parliamentary elections than there had been for the previous 30 years. The old nexuses of families and interests, if not entirely destroyed, were fractured and broken, enabling new men and their allies to taste the sweetness of social status and political power, and even to weave in some boroughs and some counties a new pattern of obligation and so consolidate a basis of

loyalty, founded on common political attitudes that had not only powers
of survival, but also of growth. The political upheavals of the Commonwealth in counties and in parliamentary boroughs have scarcely been
studied, yet it is here, I suspect at the very grass roots of political power,
that the struggles began that were to lead to the great conflict between
Whig and Tory for the rest of the century.[51] Also what is so often
forgotten in the study of Cromwell is that he attempted to find an
equitable and broad base for government amongst the propertied classes.
Quite contrary to his own political security, he increased to the point
of absolute dominance the Knights of the Shire and abolished the little
oligarchical boroughs with their tiny electorates. Kept firmly in the hands
of the propertied classes, nevertheless within these limits the Cromwel-
lian franchise was quite fairly distributed, even though the franchise was
less, far less, generously interpreted than before the Civil War.
Cromwell's franchise was fixed at a high level – the possession of £200
in real or personal property. It was less than he and Ireton had seemed
willing to concede when at Putney the Levellers had pressed for an
almost universal male suffrage (only conceding the exclusion of servants,
apprentices and beggars). By 1648 the question of the electorate had
become a burning issue, central to the debates about fundamental rights
and questions of sovereignty. When the Levellers demanded a vote for
all inhabitants, this arose from their experience of county elections, from
what they had seen and heard, not from abstract theory. They were
carrying to a logical conclusion the policy introduced by the Puritan
leaders in the House of Commons between 1614 and 1628. A great deal
of debate from 1640 to 1660 revolved about the proper base for political
power, the proper role, that is, for the electorate.[52] The electors were a
fact of political life: the county elections with their thousands of voters
created more than an air of representation and participation. The gentry
had to convince and cajole as well as exert their social authority or
browbeat their poorer neighbours. Those who fought for Parliament
were deeply conscious of the problem of the decayed boroughs and the
influence this might create for men of great property and they were eager
to rationalise the borough system and make their franchises akin to the
counties'. However, the point which I wish to stress here is that the fact
of the emerging electorate, both in the boroughs and in the counties,
helped to create the issue of representation and the debates about it.
The Levellers, as well as Ireton and Cromwell, drew their ideas from
their experience of the facts of political life, particularly elections to the
House of Commons.

The issue of the electorate and of the franchise was central to the
Restoration settlement. Indeed the prospect of that settlement was
certainly eased by the reversion to the old franchise which took place in

1659. The Convention Parliament showed its sympathies for a wide franchise by declaring for it in all disputed elections in which the evidence allowed them the opportunity of doing so, a policy which was immediately reversed by the Parliament which met in 1661.[53] Charles II and more particularly James II knew where the danger lay. They longed, both of them, for a more autocratic and settled form of government. They remained deeply suspicious of Parliament. And neither of them succeeded in managing one for long. They tried out all methods. They had some success, for they never met a Parliament, not even between 1679 and 1681, in which they did not have powerful and numerous allies. Throughout the century the majority of the propertied classes were deeply suspicious of political and constitutional crisis for fear that it would encourage 'the multitude'. Nevertheless to balance the power of the monarchy, some felt that they had to lean towards it. Shaftesbury, who was no democrat, could only hope to overcome the loathing of the King for Exclusion by rousing the mass of the electorate by playing on their twin fears of popery and arbitrary government.

The Exclusion Parliament knew where their safety lay – in the mass of freeholders who turned up to the elections in such numbers that the Tory candidates gave up the contest on sight. Whenever there was the slightest chance the Exclusion Parliaments declared for the widest franchise in the parliamentary boroughs. They knew well enough that beyond the leading gentry families, beyond even the lesser gentry and pseudo-gentry, there were yeomen, husbandmen, craftsmen of every kind – bakers, weavers, stocking frame knitters, butchers, men of small substance – for whom political and religious issues were no longer a matter for their betters. Their political education had not stopped with the Restoration. Pamphlets, newsletters, ballads, the growth of coffee houses and clubs, the development of cross-posts and better stage-coaches allowed ideas to travel fast. There was growing up in England a politically conscious nation, not co-terminous with the population, but far wider than the large-property-owning classes, far wider even than those who exercised the franchise, great though this was becoming.[54]

After the Revolution of 1688, the situation changed dramatically. General elections became very common indeed, averaging in Queen Anne's reign about one every two and a half years. Contested elections in every type of borough became commonplace. Some constituencies were contested far more frequently than their equivalents in the nineteenth century. As we know, party passion ran high, and the struggle between Whig and Tory became a bitter one. To control electorates became a matter of vital importance. The methods by which this was achieved and their effect on politics I have described elsewhere. One development which I noticed in *The Growth of Political Stability* was the printing of poll books.[55] The poll book served a variety of purposes. One was that it was sometimes difficult to challenge freeholders willing to swear to their freehold at the poll, whereas once their names and villages were in a candidate's possession, he could study them at leisure and use what he discovered to challenge the result at the Bar of the House of Commons if he could afford to do so. More importantly these books demonstrated to the organisers of both parties where their strengths and weaknesses lay; where more canvassing might be needed for future electoral contests. They also showed whether promises had been kept or broken. Indeed by Queen Anne's reign they had come to be regarded as almost essential for every constituency with a large electorate. We know of the existence of 101 poll books for Queen Anne's reign alone and there are probably many, many more to be discovered, for, unless they were printed, which was usual only for the counties and not always even for them, they tend to survive in a single copy. Although they have been known, they have never been systematically used: indeed they have scarcely been glanced at. But through them we can investigate the nature of the electorate in detail, get through to the actual voters and discover how they cast their votes in election after election.

The size of the electorate is astonishing. In 1640, Suffolk had an electorate of approximately 3000, very large by the standards of the time; by 1710 this electorate had grown to 5500 or more – in fact the electorate had nearly doubled, and perhaps some 500 voters were added in Queen Anne's reign.[56] Such a growth is typical of the electorate as a whole. From preliminary calculations the electorate rose, at a conservative estimate, from 200,000 in William III's reign to 250,000 by the end of Queen Anne's. It may indeed have been much larger than this, for reasons which I will return to later. However, a quarter of a million voters, using Gregory King's figures for the total population, gives a percentage of 4·7 who possessed the vote, whereas after the Reform Bill only 4·2 per cent did so. In 1832 the spread of the electorate was, of course, somewhat more equitable, but that is another consideration. As a percentage of adult male population, of course, the figure would be far higher: probably about 15 per cent or above. Obviously it is extremely important to know who constituted this electorate. One would like to know how literate it was, how much it was under the control of the landlords and gentry. Was it, as it were, born to its political commitment, voting Whig or Tory election after election, or can one discern commitment to leading families and figures that over-rule other considerations? How deep into the population did the electorate penetrate? Many of these questions cannot be answered yet and we shall be many years before we can give solid, statistical answers, for the amount of material is huge and no work of any sort has, to my knowledge, been done on it. It will need many hands and many hours of computer time to make this material yield all of the information that is buried within it. And, of course, the evidence is uneven – for Suffolk, for example, we have a splendid series of poll books for 1701, 1702, 1705 and 1710, whereas for Devonshire or Berkshire there are none. Again, in the boroughs, we have an excellent series for burgage boroughs, particularly Cockermouth, where there is a poll book for every election.[57] The owners of burgages wished to make sure that their dependants had cast votes as promised and also they needed the poll books to decide on possible points of attack, for at this time burgages in most boroughs were in many hands. Other types of borough, however, vary. Most large boroughs such as Norwich or Nottingham fortunately have one or two poll books.[58] Norwich poll books have the added interest that they give the occupation of the voters, so that we know, for example, that the overwhelming majority of the Norwich weavers were consistently Whig in politics, but that the butchers stayed Tory. The material, scattered as it is and sparse as it is, for some regions and for some types of borough, is I am sure sufficiently rich to yield an insight in depth into the political life of the nation such as no other source can give. These poll books will also, quite probably, throw considerable light, too, on the structure of the population as a whole, for, so far, the demographers have ignored these poll books as a source for the reconstruction of parish life, yet they list a large section of the middle and lower middle classes.

However, certain features of the electorate emerge from quite a cursory study of a sequence of poll books. Let us glance for a moment at Suffolk.[59] One is immediately struck by the number of voters who vote in one election only. This is true of the small villages as well as the market towns of the area. Let us take the tiny village, little more than a hamlet, of Westhorpe in the heart of Suffolk. In the four elections for which we have a record, eighteen freeholders voted, but ten of them in one election only. Only two freeholders voted in all four elections, one of whom was the richest man in the village, William Boyse Esq. One man voted in three elections and five in two. Boyse's votes are interesting. In 1701 he voted Tory, in 1702 he voted Whig, Whig again in 1705 and back to Tory in 1710. here indeed was a floating voter. I suspect Boyse was a patriot who rallied to the Whigs and the war and grew in the end disgruntled with both. The other regular voter was Thomas Rodwell. He was an immovable Tory, voting for the two Tackers in 1705. He was, of course, the village parson. Of the one who voted in three elections and the five who voted in two, all but one remained true to their allegiance and cast their votes for the same party. It is also interesting that most of the single voters occur in the 1705 election when the question of the Tack was a burning issue. Twelve freeholders, seven

Whigs and five Tories, left Westhorpe for Ipswich in 1705, whereas only four voted in 1701, eight in 1702 and six in 1710. However, this high proportion of single voters is common elsewhere: it is quite clear that it is a phenomenon of the electorate of this time. What, as yet, one cannot be sure about is that the Tack brought these Westhorpe men to make the journey to Ispwich. It could have been the result of intensive canvassing at this election. It is just feasible that their presence is the effect of high social mobility. We may discover these freeholders at other elections, living in different Suffolk villages. Personally I think this very unlikely. I believe it was issues and canvassing that got the voters out then, as it does now. Other evidence would seem to support this view. Single election voters are extremely common in all villages and towns and may provide as much as twenty per cent of the electorate at any given election which would give an almost lunatic rate of social mobility. Single election voters is one strange and important fact to emerge. But these books provide other evidence that is equally interesting. It is exceptionally rare to discover any village where the same voters go to election after election voting for the same party *en bloc*. Most villages were divided on party lines. I would estimate that over 90 per cent of villages in Suffolk were divided in politics. Even in areas dominated by great landowners such as Sir Robert Davers, the high Tory Knight of the Shire, villages still have their Whigs. Thomas How and George Cocksedge in Davers's own village of Rougham insisted on voting against him. Of course the leading gentry could deliver a large number of votes from their tenantry, through loyalty, common interest and, at times, fear, but there still remained a great number of voters who could not be dragooned, who insisted on going their own way. In almost every village there were committed party men, Whig and Tory: their reasons for being so will have to wait until we know far more about them.[60]

If we turn from the villages to the towns we find a similar picture. A large number of townsmen in Suffolk possessed a county vote and again we find the pattern of a small committed core on both sides, Whig and Tory, who vote in election after election and a large number of freeholders who turn up for one election only. In the three elections of 1702, 1705 and 1710 for Suffolk, 91 freeholders of Eye voted; 46 voted in only one election. This may be slightly too high, for there could be freeholders who voted in 1701 whom I have listed as one-timers for 1702; so the figures for 1705, eleven out of 51 voters, and 1710, seventeen out of 45, are more reliable, but even this confirms what we have noticed before that there were many freeholders who were stirred to vote once but not again. And the reasons for this will need investigation, but it hardly looks like landlords driving their tenants to the poll. Of the more regular voters at Eye, there were five Tories who voted three times, ten Whigs who voted three times for their party and two Whigs who voted Whig in 1702 and 1705, but who changed their party in 1710. Of those who voted twice, twelve were Tories, seventeen were Whigs, but again two of the latter deserted to the Tories, one in 1705, the other in 1710. From this it would seem that Whigs were more active. The single voters were split pretty evenly between Whigs and Tories — about ten in each election — so the slight margin which the Whigs maintained at Eye was due to the coherent and regular voting of the committed Whigs. There are signs, too, that a few Whigs grew disillusioned with the war and what drift there was in 1710 was from Whig to Tory. In the counties and large boroughs, a cursory inspection of the poll books indicates a considerable division on party lines, important floating voters, and less landlord control than has been suggested. The importance of the poll books diminishes somewhat as one moves from the counties and the great boroughs to the small corrupt boroughs of the south-west, but they still convey important and difficult facts. We get the same indication of growth and not contraction — that comes later, after 1715. Small boroughs, such as Cockermouth, Pontefract and Weymouth all more than doubled their electorates and most of the Cornish seaports added voters during the late seventeenth century. What, however, is more interesting is that often these small electorates were not, as one might expect, very constant in their make-up: for example, at Mitchell in Cornwall 40 voted in the election of 1705, 56 in 1713, but there were only eighteen voters common to both elections. This may, of course, be explainable by specific circumstances at Mitchell, although it is difficult to see what they were.[61] The most surprising factor to emerge from our preliminary investigation of the electorate between 1689 and 1715 is for me this large turnover of voters in counties and boroughs, great or small. In boroughs as small as Mitchell, we may be able to solve this peculiar problem fairly quickly and the solution may throw insight on the larger problem of the counties.

From the poll books so far investigated it is clear that every constituency of any size had committed party men who voted in elections with the same regularity as many MPs did for their party at Westminster. They were life-time Whigs or life-time Tories. These were the most active and effective part of the constituency, turning out election after election. It is also clear, however, that some voters lost their faith and changed sides. There was a floating vote that could swing a constituency from Whig to Tory.[62] What is surprisingly rare in Suffolk, considering the size of the electorate, are voters splitting their votes, giving one to a Tory the other to a Whig, as one might expect if clan or family issues were dominant. Single voters, plumpers, are rare too at least in Suffolk.

It would, however, be quite wrong to think of this electorate as being totally free: quasi-feudal relationships still counted, men acknowledged their social leaders and followed them, bribery and threats were far from unknown. All the arts of persuasion and cajolery were centuries old by 1700. The evidence for that is voluminous, well known and incontrovertible. How effective it was needs to be tested by the evidence of the poll books. The fact remains that, as ministers, party leaders and the gentry well knew, there was an electorate to be managed and one for which issues and political ideas carried weight. And it was by this electorate that the liberties of Englishmen were protected and secured, for they decided who should represent them, for this was the period when constituencies, great and small, frequently found themselves at the hustings.

As I have shown elsewhere, the very fact of a large electorate and the frequency of contests subtly influenced the nature of politics in the period.[63] The aim of the Whig leaders when married to the Hanoverian succession, was to evade it, diminish it or control it.[64] The gradual strangling of the elctorate by the executive did not pass unnoticed. There was a powerful feeling that the fundamental liberties of Englishmen had been betrayed and that the foundations of parliamentary government had become worm-eaten: a situation that had many echoes with the political situation in the American colonies, so that *Cato's Letters* had the same ring of truth in New York or Norfolk. The freeholder had become in seventeenth-century England a political animal. No country in Western Europe had experimented so deeply as England with a qualified democracy and when men talked of the liberties of Englishmen, it was not idle rhetoric. It meant that tens of thousands of them, a very significant proportion of the male population, had the right to choose their governors after 1688: opportunities were frequently available for them to exercise that right in contested election after contested election. By the middle of the eighteenth century much of that birthright had been lost, hence both the bitterness of the *Craftsman* and the growth of a movement for reform.

We historians have been, perhaps, too concerned with the politics at the centre, with methods of manipulation and influence, and ignored the politics at the grass roots in the constituencies, where between 1688 and 1715 the voice of the electorate was able to make itself heard in many places. And it is now being realised, too, that this experience, in all its complexity, influenced the politics of America profoundly. I hope that before very long we shall know far more about this electorate: there is much to learn and we have a key, even though a most complicated one, in the poll books. One of the odder results may be to show that England was far more democratic between 1688 and 1715 than immediately after 1832, and much more dominated by party issues.

Political Man

Most of the cultural and intellectual activities of Englishmen in the eighteenth century enjoyed an extension of public participation – art, music, literature, as well as theology, philosophy and history reached deeper into the nation: books, magazines, pamphlets, newspapers tumbled from the presses; and certainly there were far more literate men and women, aware of the great issues of the day, than there had been. Did, however, the political life of the nation run counter to this general development? Was the individual excluded more and more from political activity by the extension of the life of Parliament from three to seven years, by the decline of party, and by the growth of oligarchy? A narrow view of politics, a myopic concentration on the mechanics of parliamentary elections, might lead one to believe so, but politics and political issues still reached beyond the confines of Westminster. They were of paramount interest to a nation whose liberties, no matter how oddly institutionalised, were the object of envious admiration among the liberal philosophers of Western Europe. Consider for a moment the fury unleashed by the Excise Bill, or by the attempt to permit Jewish Naturalisation or even by the Cider Tax: to say nothing of Wilkes, America and the rest, and one cannot doubt the widespread participation of Englishmen in politics. True these outbursts were partly engineered, and they were but tornadoes that swept the surface, for the basic structure of eighteenth-century politics was very stable, steel-like in its strength, even if it bent in the wind. The political experience of the seventeenth century was not obliterated over night, either by the Glorious Revolution or the Septennial Act: radicals and Tories existed even in 1750. Politics was never merely a matter for the politicians.

In the seventeenth century in order to win their victories against the Crown, the gentry and their aristocratic allies had called into being a large parliamentary electorate, and one which from time to time exercised the powers of choice. Between 1700 and 1715, eight general elections for Parliament were held, a far greater number than have ever been held since in a comparable time-span. Also, during this period only a handful of parliamentary boroughs avoided a contest, even those with very small electorates.[1]

In order to understand the relationship of the individual to the political institutions by which he was governed in the eighteenth century, it is very necessary to look at this early period more closely, for it deeply influenced all subsequent political history of the Hanoverian period.

There are a number of elementary factors to remember about politics in the reign of Queen Anne which are sometimes overlooked. One I have already mentioned, the exceptional frequency of general elections, and, at these elections, contests in all types of constituency were rarely avoided for more than an election or two. Counties went very frequently to a poll, involving, except in such tiny counties as Rutland, thousands of freeholders. Some counties where divisions went very deep, such as Essex, were fought time and time again. As with the counties, so with the great boroughs: Westminster, Bristol, Norwich, Coventry and their like were battle grounds for – and I have no hesitation in using the word – party. Nor did the tiny boroughs avoid contests: a few did, but even some of the smallest corporations possessed their party divisions, and often the defection of one or two voters could swing the town from a Whig to a Tory patron. Frequent elections, contests and party, Whigs versus Tories – these are the three major ingredients of the politics of this period: factors which enabled most gentlemen and a number of freeholders and burgesses to exercise a free political choice.[2] And this was England's vast singularity, a unique situation amongst the major powers of the world at this time.

The issues were clear, and understood by thousands of voters, if not all, and men in the heart of borough politics watched closely and with passion what was happening at Westminster. The choice of the Speaker of the House of Commons in 1705 was a vital test of party strength: John Smith was supported by the Whigs and the Court, William Bromley by the Tories.[3] Smith got home, in spite of a defection of seventeen Tory placemen to Bromley. (They paid for such insubordination later when fifteen of them lost their places.)[4] The contest had been avidly followed back in King's Lynn by Robert Walpole's Whig supporters. One of the leaders of the Lynn Whigs wrote off at once: 'the Choice of your Speaker is very pleasing to all honest men, but on the contrary a great Mortification to the High Church papists and atheists.'[5]

It was not only the great issues that these local politicians watched: they were keenly aware of the twists and turns of party tactics. Another Turner, John, the nephew of Charles, and Robert Walpole's least inhibited supporter in Lynn, wrote to him on 7 December 1705:

> I cannot tell what to judge of your condition when last Votes I saw[6] you were outmustered by 29 in the Agmondisham election.[7] I never thought to find S Edward Seymour [the Tory leader] a prophett, as our parsons will certainly represent him to be, for they encourage themselves with a saying of his that 205 volunteers will beat 248 prest men, so they still think to get the better of you.[8] But I cannot see they misse a man and I am sure you had a great many absent but if they will not appear, they ought to be reckoned as cyphers. If you were not more hearty yesterday, I expect to heare you are baulkt at Norwich too.[9]

Politics mattered. And the number of people involved was very considerable. Take Norwich, which worried John Turner. In 1705, about 2500 men voted: probably about 25 per cent of the active male population, and only 150 votes separated the Whig and Tory candidates. The principles were clear-cut: on the part of the Whigs support for Marlborough's war (Turner had been terrified that there might be a reverse before the election), and opposition to the High Church party; dislike of high taxes, dissenters and courtiers on the part of the Tories.

Throughout the land, the electorate was divided. Small boroughs or large counties were both prone to attacks of party fever. So long as the Tories had prospects of office, their guineas could ring as true as a Whig's: in the pressure of circumstances, doubtful voters, wobblers uncertain of their own or the world's future, could float one way, then another, and often upset the certainties of machine politics. This is why, on occasion, the influence of Lord Wharton in quite small boroughs snapped and he found his candidates defeated and Tories returned. So long as power could come to the Tories — and it could and did for most of Queen Anne's reign, the factors which made for political stability — bribery and influence combined with open voting — were kept in check. Politics remained a game for two players.

Issues therefore counted; the gentry, who were very numerous, were divided sharply on questions of war and peace, on toleration of dissent and the succession to the Crown, matters which Elizabeth I thought should be reserved for Princes. In Queen Anne's reign they were questions for the electorate, a remarkable development in a hundred years. But, of course, they were not the only questions. Politics have always been more than a question of issues: they imply the pursuit of power. By 1700, politicians were well aware that the freedom of the electorate could be a stumbling-block in their quest for power. Already determined and successful efforts had been made to eradicate party strife in the constituencies and to reduce them to subordination. Every art was used to secure control. Of course, there was much variety. Sometimes the personal, patriarchal and traditional authority of a great family, not necessarily very rich or very generous, was sufficient to dominate the small parliamentary borough that nestled against its estate: such was the authority of the Rashleighs at Fowey, the Burrards of Lymington or the Leighs of Lyme. But such corporations were getting rare by 1700. Most voters, no matter how loyal to a person or a party, knew that they possessed, in their parliamentary franchise, negotiable currency. Many of them liked to turn it into hard cash.

There has been too much evasion of the question of bribery: money played its part throughout the eighteenth century. Indeed, expenses steadily grew, particularly after the Septennial Act of 1716, which gave a seven years instead of a three years return on the investment. At

Weobley in Herefordshire voters expected a minimum of £5 and often secured £20. And, as ever with bribery, they sometimes took money from both sides, but this was a dangerous practice when voting was open and gentlemen could break a mere tradesman's head with impunity. But bribery, like rich and lavish entertainment, seems to have been endemic in certain boroughs. Weobley, until most of the vote-houses were bought up, had a very bad name; so had Stockbridge and Great Bedwyn, where the poor weavers got what they could whilst the going was good. At Coventry, however, it was all drink, food and riot, usually organised by the innkeepers, that made its elections some of the most lurid of the eighteenth century. But it is as well to remember Coventry, along with Westminster, Middlesex and elsewhere, for they demonstate that eighteenth-century politics could be savage and brutal with mobs roaring and rioting through the streets. Nor, as we shall see, was this violence necessarily confined to election times: political crisis too could unleash violence, and permit the individual to assuage his hatred of a system that more and more excluded him from power.[10]

But the political world of the Augustans did not consist merely in venal or riotous boroughs. Half the members of Parliament came from boroughs with moderate or small electorates. Until the total defeat of the Tory Party in 1715 and its obliteration from the serious world of politics, these boroughs were often very difficult to manage. Even small electorates, such as that of Buckingham, which only numbered thirteen, could be touchy. They expected entertainment; that was the *sine qua non* of politics throughout the century: a voter looked forward to gigantic binges at the candidates' or patrons' expense, not only at elections but also on other corporate occasions, such as the election of a mayor. They required more solid pledges: plate to adorn their guildhalls, schools and charities for their sons, water supplies to save themselves the expense, but, above all, jobs. The letter-bag of every MP with the slightest pretensions to influence was stuffed with pleas and demands from voters for themselves, their relations or their dependants. Places in the Customs and Excise, in the Army and Navy, in the Church, in the East India, Africa and Levant Companies, in all the departments of state from doorkeepers to clerks: jobs at Court for the real gentry or sinecures in Ireland, the diplomatic corps, or anywhere else where duties were light and salaries steady. These were the true coin of politics, the solvent that diminished or obliterated principle. And they worked faster once the Tory Party had no hope of power. This was apparent to the meanest intelligence by the 1730s when Bolingbroke finally threw in his hand and retired to France.[11]

Naturally with places comparatively scarce there were always more applicants than jobs, and this led the political managers to attempt to get rid of the electorate when they could, or discipline it when they could not. At first this may not have been a conscious process, but it rapidly became one.

In the small corporations the elimination of unwanted voters became a process of steady attrition: freemen, if they had the vote, ceased to be made, or the fee for admission to the freehold was pushed beyond the pocket of the small tradesman. In others, honorary freemen, usually reliable gentry from the surrounding countryside, were made in order to swing the electorate at the appropriate moment. More often than not, in an election disputed on petition, the House of Commons came down heavily on the side of the narrower franchise. To make the question of franchise more certain and therefore more manageable, the House passed in 1729 the Last Determinations Act, by which franchises were frozen to the last decision of the House on the question. Where votes went with property, it was bought up, at excessive cost maybe at the time, but future expensive contests could be eliminated. At Weobley in Herefordshire the electorate was quickly reduced from about 150 to 45 by such means.

Corporations with large electorates and the county constituencies posed different problems. Some voters in both types of constituency were controllable. It was rare, although not unknown, for a tenant to disobey his landlord and vote against his wishes; mostly they did as they were told. Nor could craftsmen be expected to disoblige rich and powerful merchant aldermen living in their wards. Voting was open, and in these large constituencies it became common after 1700 for votes to be printed after the election in order that they could be analysed.[12] And, of course, there were loyalties – familial, territorial and political. Then, as now, men were born into the politics which they professed. All of this gave cohesion – at least to parties – but they did not diminish the enmity between them, whether these parties were political or factional or a mixture of both, particularly at a time when the gentry were both numerous and sharply divided. But contests in large constituencies became ruinously expensive, particularly after the Septennial Act of 1716.[13] In large counties such as Yorkshire with a numerous gentry, subscriptions could make even an expensive fight feasible, but, in smaller counties, the cost grew too high, so in county after county a treaty was made. Men sank their differences – the aristocracy sometimes taking one seat for a Whig, the gentry the other for a Tory: occasionally the gentry got both: in other counties the representation was divided geographically. After 1734 county contests became exceptionally infrequent. Twelve counties were not contested between 1754 and 1790, fifteen only once, so that it was a rare freeholder who exercised a vote more than once in his life-time, and thousands never had even that one chance.[14] A marked contrast with the period between 1688 and 1725 when county elections were exceptionally common, and freeholders voted time and time again.

Hence, by the middle decades of the eighteenth century, a diminished electorate functioned only intermittently – with regularity at all elections only in about fifteen constituencies of which three, oddly enough, were in Kent.[15] Elsewhere contests were uncommon, often twenty years or more elapsing without a contest. Hence, the individual who possessed a political franchise very rarely had the opportunity to exercise it. Political power, both local and national, had been absorbed by groups of political managers whose ambitions, of course, varied as much as their own natures, but self-interest loomed larger than political principle. Indeed, principles might have died a total death but for the fact that the parliamentary system never became completely closed or the public without influence.

Politics, fortunately, are more than a matter of elections and the exercise of a franchise. Men were touched in their daily lives; often indeed knocked down by them. Although the volume of eighteenth-century legislation, in a public sense, was small; its private legislation was immense: and the eighteenth-century gentleman set about making a world to his own liking. Commercialisation of agriculture had begun centuries before, but the pace became headlong in the eighteenth century, which witnessed the near-elimination of the peasantry as a class. Enclosure Bills rattled through the Commons. They were hated: throughout the country, the peasantry rioted against them. In 1710 the villagers rose at Bedingfield and the Norfolk Militia had to be called out to put them down.[16] Turnpikes were no better loved but they proliferated. The birds of the air, the rabbits of the heath, the fish in the streams were ferociously protected for the sport and sustenance of gentlemen. property acquired the sanctity of life and theft meant death. Benefit of clergy was abolished and hanging as a punishment for crime increased.[17] Trivial crimes might mean transportation for life, first to America and then, after the Revolution, to Australia. The gentlemen merchants who ran the towns did not neglect themselves. In the 1760s and 1770s Enabling Acts permitted them to charge rates for many public services – paving, lighting, even police – which they supplied, although without notable efficiency. Politics was power, not only for individuals who manned the pumps and sluices of the parliamentary system, but also for the class which had come to dominate British life – commercially minded landowners with a sharp eye for profit.

In the earlier decades of the century the strains of the agrarian revolution had caused divisions within the landowning class; indeed this is the social basis of the cleavage between Whig and Tory, but the plight of the smaller gentry, still subject to vicissitude, had gradually eased and by the middle of the century a golden era was opening for them. This too helped to give solidity to the political system, which by 1750 had acquired a seemingly adamantine strength. What was increasingly obvious to the world at large was the development of a self-gratifying oligarchy that held power for its own profit.

The political nation, however, was always greater than those involved in the parliamentary system. It was growing throughout the eighteenth century both in size and in economic and social importance, and this aspect of politics was not affected by the setback of the Tory Party. The seventeenth century, particularly its three periods of violent political struggle – the Civil War and Protectorate, the Exclusion Crisis and the Revolution of 1688 – had accustomed literate Englishmen to controversy: pamphlets, ballads, books were all used to influence political passion or to convince by argument. And the spread of the coffee house – viewed with alarm by Charles II and his ministers – had created, along with bookshops, not only centres for the dissemination of literature but also meeting grounds for men passionately interested in politics. Political literature spread to the provinces, to the country houses, to the taverns and inns of large country towns: provincial bookshops were more common than historians have allowed (after all, think of Johnson's father): the citizens of London were not the only clubbable Englishmen: King's Lynn had a flourishing Whig dining club by Queen Anne's reign, if not before. By the time of Swift's first political pamphlet, there was a wide literate public, willing to spend its sixpence on a good piece of invective and to spread the copy around amongst like-minded neighbours.

Nor did this public diminish after 1715; indeed it grew; the public grew as the electorate diminished. The success of the *Craftsman* was due entirely to its existence. True, the usual edition of the *Craftsman* was only about 3000, and not infrequently below that figure; but issues which caught the public's attention soared to 6000 and may have reached, on one or two occasions, 10,000.[18] And each copy was read by far more people than would read a present-day weekly. We know that the *Craftsman* was in great demand in the provinces.[19] But the *Craftsman* was but one paper, and there were many others from *Fog's Weekly* to the *London Evening Post* that were equally concerned with politics. And the newspaper was not the only means of propaganda. Pantomine, harlequinades, burlesques, Punch and Judy shows were given political twists. The London stage has never been more dominated by politics than it was between 1725 and 1737 when, slandered beyond endurance, Walpole instituted a censorship of the theatre.[20] Whether he had a chance to vote or not, the literate and semi-literate Englishman had plenty of opportunity to jeer and scoff at his rulers. And at a more serious level he was exceptionally well informed.

Furthermore there was something of a cultural explosion in the middle decades of the eighteenth century, when literacy increased by leaps and bounds. Because of the decay of Oxford and Cambridge and some of the old-established grammar schools, there has been too ready an acceptance of the view that these years witnessed not only stagnation but retrogression in education. But schools were sprouting like mushrooms. Primarily they were started to provide elementary commercial training for boys, a veneer of middle-class polish for girls, and of course a fortune for the schoolmaster. As so frequently in eighteenth-century life, the fee was often more important than the service and schools could vanish overnight.[21] Nevertheless, many were good and stable. Something of the extent of this development may be assessed from the fact that 100 schools, most of them newly established, advertised in the *Northampton Mercury* between 1720 and 1760, and, even more impressive, the *Norwich Mercury* advertised 63 schools between 1749 and 1750.[22] And, a point which requires very little labouring, there was now a provincial press to advertise in. By 1760 there were 40 provincial newspapers established in all the major towns of England. And, of course, the papers were not confined to the towns they were printed in – an elaborate system of itinerant pedlars, who often travelled 40 or 50 miles in a day, disseminated them throughout the land. The *Northampton Mercury* was on sale in Sheffield, Cambridge, Warwick and Oxford – indeed throughout the East and West Midlands. Similarly the *Stamford Mercury* travelled up and down the Great North Road with the stage coaches.[23]

This new and growing literate public was also politically active. One has only to turn over the pages of Cowburne's *Liverpool Chronicle* for 1768 to discover that it is alive with political debate – letters urging freeholders how to vote in the coming general election, political information from Ireland and America, and curiously enough Wilkes' fortunes in the Middlesex election were avidly followed, the sympathies of the paper being entirely with Wilkes. Fifty or sixty years previously there had been no such politically minded public in Liverpool: indeed there was not a public sufficient to run a newspaper, let alone two. There had been politicians, Whigs and Tories, a corporation well aware of political issues and a few hundred freeholders of varying political independence who were not unaware of the great issues at stake at Westminster, but now politics in Liverpool had moved into a different dimension. There were now thousands, not hundreds, of men and women alive to political issues and keen to debate them, even though they had no vote.[24]

The same was true not only of large and growing towns such as

Liverpool, Bristol, Newcastle or Hull, but also of a new class of men and their skilled workers who were beginning to plant industry not in towns, but in the English countryside. Josiah Wedgwood at Etruria followed politics as keenly as his partner Thomas Bentley followed fashion in London.[25] And Jedediah Strutt over at Belper kept his eye on the political scene in London.[26] And, when the supporters in Middlesex of Wilkes are analysed, what do we find? The bulk of them are middling people – traders, craftsmen, petty manufacturers, men of small property.[27] Here was the public for whom Tom Paine was to write. His *Rights of Man* entranced Wedgwood. Here, indeed, is a political nation whom Namier and his followers have almost entirely ignored: as essential a part of the structure of politics at the accession of George III as the Cornish boroughs or the Shropshire gentlemen. Evidence of the political nation's size and vigour everywhere abounds. These are the people who roared for Chatham and hissed George III, who subscribed for comforts for American prisoners of British forces, who read and studied Paine, Priestley, Price and Cartwright. Were there then two worlds of politics in the eighteenth century – a tight political establishment, linked to small groups of powerful political managers in the provinces, who controlled Parliament, the executive and all that was effective in the nation, and outside this an amorphous mass of political sentiment that found expression in occasional hysteria and impotent polemic, but whose effective voice in the nation was negligible?

Actually the political nation and the political establishment had never been completely divorced. Their relations certainly were strained and their contacts intermittent, but they existed. For one thing contests in the populous boroughs and counties sometimes took place and when they did more than the actual voters took part: mobs, processions, addresses and the like made those active at the hustings conscious of the popular will on political issues and those free from the straitjacket of direct influence could be swayed by a sense of what they felt the nation wanted. Undoubtedly the enormous popular sympathy for Wilkes amongst the lower and middling classes affected those freeholders of the eastern and urban districts of Middlesex that were less prone to the influence of a landlord.

And there were Addresses. The right of a county or a corporation to address Parliament was age-old. Although in the middle decades of the century the Commons was dominated by a single party, it was factionalised, and in the 1760s the factions were often at loggerheads on political issues of importance – America and Wilkes: later there were even more issues – reform of Parliament, slave trade, Ireland, even commerce with France. Issues, *pace* Namier, abounded. And they divided counties and corporations. The Excise Bills even in 1733 had set the

country aflame and Addresses rained on Parliament.[28] During the War
of American Independence the situation was equally intense. Again from
the letters of Josiah Wedgwood we see how sharply Staffordshire was
divided: some willing to support George III and Lord North in their
intransigence, others driven frantic by it, and both sides addressing
Parliament from totally opposite standpoints in the name of the county
as a whole. Such Addresses were usually initiated at a so-called meeting
of the county – gentlemen, substantial freeholders, office holders and
Church dignitaries, that is men who belonged to the official political
establishment. But they needed the political nation to back them, so
Addresses required signatures and we know that copies were left in local
taverns where men were solicited to sign. Such solicitations could only
lead to argument and discussion and to a widening of political horizons.
At Westminster, Addresses, except loyal ones, had very little effect, but
they helped, perhaps, to moderate political passion. In the provinces
they brought like-minded men into greater cohesion, and made them
realise something of their own importance.

So by the 1760s there existed, in effect, two political nations in
England, one growing, the other shrinking, with little contact between
them. Had there been more, the grosser follies of handling both Wilkes
and America could scarcely have taken place. The formal electorate was
dwindling and called to execute its judgement less and less. Those who
by education and interest might reasonably expect a political voice but
were denied it, were steadily increasing. There were other factors, too,
at work to help widen this cleavage: the dissenters. For decades their
leaders had hoped against hope that their civic disabilities would be
removed. Many, but by no means all, now felt that only a radical reform
of political institutions could bring this about. Much of the aggressive
criticism of Parliament in the second half of the century came from
dissent.[29]

Again in 1763, over twenty years of war came to an end. That war
had been commercially aggressive: 'Commerce', in the words of Burke,
'had been made to flourish through war': both patriotism and profit had
helped to still the voice of criticism. The dislocations of peace, however,
combined with what seemed to many merchants a wanton return to
France of commercial privileges seized during the war, helped to breed
discontent. That is why they received George III at the Guildhall in stony
silence. Demobilisation and unemployment added yeast to the dough.
And, for once, the professional politicians were in need of public issues.
George III was young and there were no prospects of succession. Hence
there were no 'futures' for them to dabble in. Some, like the Duke of
Newcastle, had played the 'in game' for so long that rousing the public
had no charms for them, but Chatham possessed no inhibitions, and

even Burke saw the necessity of exploiting the American grievances on behalf of the Rockinghams. Public protest, so long as it was skilfully handled, acquired a certain attraction for the Venetian oligarchy: they could now find a personal use for public discontent. It was the fusion of these circumstances which helped to create some of the great political debates of the 1760s and 1770s and provided Chatham, Wilkes and Junius with their opportunities. The political establishment might ignore Wilkes and only give America a modicum of its attention, but it could not remain absolutely impervious to the criticisms and claims of the wider political nation. After all, John Wilkes did win his battle with Parliament. Nor could the oligarchy remain deaf to threats to itself.

The demand for parliamentary reform in the 1770s and 1780s developed primarily in the towns. Even in the 1760s the Liverpool Debating Society was arguing whether politics could ever be purified without the introduction of the ballot box. It was the exclusion from the political power which they felt was rightly theirs because of their social and economic activity that led men such as Josiah Wedgwood to support annual parliaments, universal suffrage and the control of a member's actions by his constituents. The growing criticism of Parliament as an institution swelled to a gale in the late seventies as disaster after disaster dogged North's American policies. It was not only the unrepresentative nature of Parliament which came in for the fury of attack, but also the graft which the political establishment lavished on itself. This new radicalism covered numerous shades of opinion from republican to Tory. Historians, I feel, never give sufficient emphasis to the prevalence of bitter anti-monarchical, pro-republican sentiment of the 1760s and 1770s. Sylas Neville's diary and papers demonstrate clearly enough that in the provinces, as well as in London, there were many men and women who were enthusiastic supporters of republican ideas, with strong sympathies towards America, men and women who possessed as much hatred of George III as the most dedicated Boston radicals. After all, Neville never had the slightest difficulty in collecting a few cronies on 30 January to toast the execution of Charles I.[30] And Tom Paine's books, it must be remembered, sold in far greater quantities than those of any other political commentator. Indeed Paine and his readership cry aloud for further investigation.

This powerful radicalism was strongest in London, the big seaport towns and the growing manufacturing districts of Lancashire, the West Midlands and the West Riding of Yorkshire, but it combined with, and indeed was itself infused with, the ideas of the Tory radicalism of the earlier decades of the century which had called, not for fundamental reform, but for the purification of political institutions. The country-squire's old panacea of annual Parliaments and the exclusion of placemen from Parliament acquired in the hands of the Reverend Christopher Wyvill and the Yorkshire Association fresh vigour. Even their suggestion that the number of Knights of the Shire should be increased in order to strengthen the independent element in Parliament was no novelty. It had been adumbrated in the first year of the century.[31]

There is no need here to trace the course of the first strong movement for parliamentary reform or even to discuss whether or not this brought England to the very edge of revolution. For my purpose it is enough to indicate the width of political interest and to underline the conflict which existed between the political establishment and the political nation: a conflict which did not begin with Junius or end with the failure of the Association movement. Its origins lie in the seventeenth-century emergence of the electorate and the division was not healed until the late nineteenth century, for the growth of the political nation was always far faster than the spread of representative government. What are of interest, in the context of this paper, in the last two decades of the eighteenth century are two developments. One is the even more rapid growth of the political nation which began to acquire new leadership and a more sophisticated organisation, and the effect of patriotism in helping the establishment defeat its aspirations. Nor were these two factors dissociated. Fears for property proved a strong stimulant to loyalty.

Interest in politics penetrated deeper into society during the last two decades of the eighteenth century, although in London, at least, political interest amongst the working classes may have been more extensive than historians have allowed. A Swiss traveller, César de Saussure, was highly amused in 1726 to see shoe-blacks reading newspapers for the foreign news.[32] And craftsmen were well aware that Parliament's legislation affected their interests – usually adversely.[33] By 1750 what was essentially a lower-middle-class debating society – the Robin Hood (well named) – had achieved notoriety. There were a number of deist and political clubs operating in a twilight world of mechanics and intellectuals. The part played by the humbler freemasons in starting and maintaining such clubs, which were partly educational as well as political, needs investigating, but the connection may be close. After all, Thomas Hardy was an active member of the pseudo-masonic organisation called the Gregorians.[34] Lower middle-class radicalism grew during the 1780s and 1790s and received further impetus from the early phases of the French Revolution. Tom Paine's *Rights of Man* is reputed to have sold 400,000 copies, a prodigious figure, even allowing for a considerable margin of error.[35] And contemporaries were quick to notice who was reading it. 'Our peasantry now read the *Rights of Man* on mountains and moors and by the wayside' wrote T. J. Mathias in 1797.[36]

Radicalism was getting out of hand. The expensive books and pamphlets of Priestley and Price, the dilettante leadership of Horne Tooke, Major Cartwright, Earl Stanhope and the like could be tolerated, but Thomas Hardy's organisation was beginning to take on the unwelcome air of a revolutionary movement of *sansculottes*. And the example of France was not beguiling. The solid bourgeois wing of the political nation read its Burke and drew far closer to the political establishment in sentiment. It did not want revolution; nevertheless it still desired power. So it entered into a more direct competition with the oligarchy over seats in Parliament. After 1790 contested elections begin to increase rapidly again, and the cost of elections soared to new heights. There was a definite push by the richer commercial and manufacturing interests to buy their way into political power. Few such men as Beckford, Townsend or Sawbridge, city millionaires who supported Wilkes, were to be found consorting with the aggressive radical movement that took Paine for its hero. The French Revolution did not only close the ranks of the professional politicians. It did more than this. It drove deep fissures into the political nation itself. Whereas in the 1770s reform had not seemed to threaten property or status, it now reeked of revolution. As politics became national, they sharpened class division. And the terrible spectacle of a literate, politically minded, working class began to stalk the land. But it is not only the French Revolution that added a fresh dimension to the complexities of politics, divided as they were into this twofold world of political establishment and political nation. Patriotism became an issue as well as property.[37]

Of course patriotism is a highly complex matter, involving self-interest, aggressive economic appetites, xenophobia and a host of disreputable and semi-disreputable motives; it is a singularly powerful emotion. However, I am concerned not with causes, but with effects. We can see patriotism influencing radicalism in the later stages of the American War of Independence. Support for America had been very widespread in both London and the provinces, but, as soon as the American war became a general war, involving France and Spain, that support began to wither. Bristol, from being pro-American, became pro Lord North.[38] Even that ardent supporter of all things American, Josiah Wedgwood, began to have his doubts. If victory for America meant defeat of Britain by France and Spain, he was not at all sure that he could face such an outcome and he felt that he might have to support North. Although his radicalism remained firm, he was confused and baffled by the issues which *patriotism in the time of war* raised.[39] And, of course, the long wars against Revolutionary France and Napoleon in which armies were lost, invasion threatened and hundreds of ships sunk, posed a graver threat. It enabled Pitt and his supporters to denigrate radicalism as Jacobin, alien, antipatriotic. In other countries – America, Russia, China – radical attitudes to society have joined with patriotism and been immensely strengthened by it. In England radicalism was seriously weakened first by the American War of Independence and afterwards by the wars against France.

By the end of the eighteenth century, the political nation had grown until it had begun to embrace some of the lowest classes of society. The true working class, however, that is the unskilled labourers in town and countryside, were, in spite of Tom Paine, still largely outside politics. They were stirring: increasingly they were beginning to realise that their condition in life depended on the political institutions by which they were governed and the men who ran them. The threat of a possible fusion between the lower middle classes and the working population, inspired by revolutionary ideas of political and social justice, spurred the richer leaders of the political nation and the political establishment to find a *modus vivendi*.

The division between the two, which had steadily grown during the eighteenth century, was, however, still deep in 1800. Provincial bankers and merchants, men such as Pares and Biggs of Leicester, felt that they lacked power both locally and nationally commensurate with their social and economic status. So long as such men did so, there was always a danger of a revolutionary situation. But they were as terrified as Hannah More of a politically conscious proletariat, and between 1800 and 1832 they fought their way into power through the old methods of the establishment – money and the unreformed system of parliamentary representation.[40] By the 1820s, some of the old-established conservative forces were losing the battle and running short of cash: for example, Leicester corporation, a bulwark of traditional oligarchy, had to mortgage its estates in 1826 to fight off the radical threat to its parliamentary representation. By 1831 it could not afford the money necessary to outbid the Leicester manufacturers who clubbed together to get their reform candidates in.[41] This was a far safer method of prising open the gates of political power than manning the barricades. The Reform Bill of 1832 marks the realignment of political forces: the powerful and rich leaders of the political nation, men who had used public issues and public agitation, forced the old political oligarchy to accommodate them – at a price. The old landowning and farming interests were strengthened by the large increase in the county membership. Politics remained, as it had been since the middle of the eighteenth century, an affair of two nations. But, as in the eighteenth century, they were not divorced: those who controlled the political machinery were susceptible to opinion. Europe was to give them lesson after lesson of the folly of ignoring the political hopes and aspirations of the mass of the people: and Britain's increasing riches permitted the extension of franchise without undue fear for the traditional institutions. So a process begun in the seventeenth century, and only temporarily checked in the eighteenth, was brought to fruition in the nineteenth. The process was the spread of politics to embrace the entire population. It was done with such skill that the conservative forces continued to dominate English life in spite of universal suffrage. Not until 1945 did Britain have a really radical government.

The eighteenth century opened with a large parliamentary electorate accustomed to exercising its powers; it was divided and organised into parties that were separated by sharp political issues. The total collapse of the Tories after 1715 permitted the development of oligarchy which both diminished and disciplined this electorate, although never to the point of extinction. This process was counterbalanced by a steady growth in the political consciousness of the nation at large, and by the development of strong economic and social interests that demanded political power. And the conflicts and struggles that ensued gave a life and vitality to eighteenth-century politics which steadily engulfed larger sections of the population. Political life in the eighteenth century was therefore always richer, freer, more open than the oligarchical nature of its institutions might lead one to believe. And this gave Englishmen in this century a political experience that was unique. The richness and variety of that experience has received recently all too little attention. As far as the eighteenth century is concerned, political decisions and the turmoil they aroused are the heart of politics, not elections. It is time we returned to their study.

PART TWO

HISTORY AND HISTORIANS

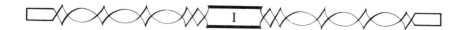

Finding a Purpose

Just as painters are interested in painters of all periods often copying, mimicking or developing not only their methods and technique but also painting varieties of particular pictures, so do historians have a life-long preoccupation for the writers of their craft. Even as a small boy I had been fascinated by Clarendon – not only to read but to compare with S. R. Gardiner. I kept an elaborate notebook, which consisted of their views on Charles I, Laud, Cromwell, Pym, Hampden, etc., and of other historians whom I read – Firth, for example, and even Wakeman. No one told me to do this or knew about it. It was a private hobby, mainly practised in the vacations at the Leicester Public Reference Library. I stumbled on the idea and enjoyed the results, noting particularly how bits and pieces of Clarendon, especially his views of human character, infused all their judgements. Mostly, I think, I enjoyed reading Clarendon for his sonorous prose and the convincing authority with which he wrote about men and events. The first Old Master which I bought decades later was Hanneman's portrait of him.

When I moved into the professional world I was struck by the widely differing nature of historians' reputations – between M. M. Postan, for example, and G. M. Trevelyan. To the general public in the 1930s, Postan was totally unknown, yet his reputation was exceptionally high amongst undergraduates and graduates, higher than any member of the Faculty, whereas Trevelyan whose books sold in their tens of thousands decade after decade, was intellectually despised by most dons and undergraduates. Lip-service was paid to his great-uncle Macaulay and, of course, Edward Gibbon; even to popular Victorian historians such as Froude. There were one or two professional historians, such as Eileen Power who wrote with grace or R. H. Tawney whose prose glowed with ideological passion, who managed to create bridges between public regard and professional approval. In my very early days two young historians did so too – A. L. Rowse and Veronica Wedgwood – both of whom were highly regarded by Trevelyan. He called them 'Real historians. Write well!' Both became members of the British Academy, Rowse early, Wedgwood late. (Her candidature was once dismissed by the formidable Dame Lucy Sutherland on the grounds that she wrote so well that it brought a kind of superficiality to her work!) Both would find it impossibly difficult to get in today for the breach between academic historians and the writers of history has become a yawning chasm.

One of the odder features of my lifetime has been the vast increase in the number of professional historians on the one hand and their growing incapacity to fulfil a valuable social purpose on the other. In the 1920s and 1930s, let alone before, the Faculties and Schools of History at the universities were not designed to produce academic, professional research historians. They were there primarily to educate, to exercise the mind, promote judgement, and to inculcate a balanced view of the value of Britain's historical institutions — Parliament, Law, Church and Monarchy — and to promote a sound knowledge of the course of European history since the Fall of Rome, and of the way men of intelligence and integrity had thought about the nature of politics and of political institutions. An historian would have his own private field of research, but that might only have a modest connection with what he taught and what he lectured on.

Of the great figures of Cambridge of my early memories — Trevelyan, Clapham, Temperley, Butterfield, Oakeshott, Knowles, Postan — not one had taken a PhD or had any formal training in research; most of today's professors have, yet no one could for one moment believe that they have the quality of their predecessors. Research has acquired a charisma, ceasing to be a mere tool to become an end in itself. Philosophic history has been buried by a plague of antiquarianism. This development that grew over the years fascinated as well as horrified me for its dangers were glaring and large. In consequence I have written a considerable number of essays on what might be loosely described as history as a profession.

One of the greatest dangers brought about by professional historians' increasing myopia was their total indifference to the social purpose of their work. The Marxists had no such doubts; for them history had a powerful social purpose — it was a vital part of revolutionary ideology, so vital that it had to be moulded, rewritten where need be, preached with sophistry from highly selective material, manipulated with all the methods and dodges which the academic historians rightly deplored. The distortions might be obvious, but much of the analysis by Marxist historians could not be lightly dismissed. If one believed like Butterfield that all historic acts were acts of Providence, then refutation might be easy, but for those of us who thought social change to be due to acts of human beings and not of the Almighty it was a more challenging and a more difficult task to cope with Marxist history. One had to think hard and deep not only about such matters as the Industrial or French and English Revolutions, but also about more difficult problems still, of how political or religious ideas could suddenly become social attitudes. Marxist countries' use of history, as well as the strict Marxist interpretation attempted by historians of capitalist countries, present an immense challenge to western historians. Too often they are ignored, more dangerously, praised for the wrong reasons and rarely, if ever, is a sound alternative presented by the West or taught in western schools, where the same fragmentation of the teaching of history has taken place as in the professional writing of it. When the problems of history, its writing and teaching began to press heavily on me in the late 1950s and early 1960s, I realised that Marxists were not only imposing an ideological interpretation but also fulfilling an important human need, as potent in capitalist countries as in Marxist ones. The intelligent public hungered for answers to the *why* of human history. In the West they were fed largely with pulp, laced by the occasional vitamin. The Fundamentalists clung to their Bible, the Catholics asserted the accumulated wisdom of the Church, fortified by the miracles of the Saints and the theology of the Fathers.

The choice for optimists was H. G. Wells, for pessimists Oswald Spengler, and for the highly intelligent but totally uncritical (often civil servants and lawyers) Arnold Toynbee.

It was because I felt so passionately the need to give a broad interpretation of the human story yet retain a proper professional and scholarly base that in 1959 I began to explore with Alfred Knopf in New York and Robert Lusty in London the possibility of publishing a thirty-volume work on the *History of Human Society*, each volume written by a distinguished professional scholar. The scheme was grandiose and, of course, vulnerable to criticism; far more space was to be given to advanced societies and their history (including, of course, China and India) but little to the undeveloped Third World, one volume for Africa and Latin America, none for Indonesia. It was a bold concept for which I had the strong backing of two very fine publishers, and I possessed, I thought, sufficient reputation to secure the service and support of eminent scholars. As a preface to each volume I printed a kind of manifesto which I was to develop later. The individual volumes had great success – the concept none at all. I was regarded as rather old-fashioned and flat-minded because the very word progress closed my colleagues' or my critics' minds. Of course I was not using 'progress' in the sense of the Enlightenment, implying moral progress, but a much more literal sense of progress, arguing that the betterment of the material side of human life had taken place.

Also I wanted the West to have an historically justifiable account of its achievement, one which challenged the Marxist interpretation, yet not relying on Providence or other outmoded concepts, but on the realities of human existence. For the following decades I elaborated this theme as often and as frequently as I could, finding a more sympathetic audience in America, and in Europe and in Japan than in my own country. My first opportunity to write about the problems of history arose through discussions with Anthony Godwin, the brilliant young editor at Penguin. We agreed that the problems which beset history also affected the humanities in general and in 1964 I published *Crisis in the Humanities*. It was rumoured that it cost me the Chair of Modern History at Cambridge. That is as may be, but certainly (and I found it difficult to understand why) it upset a number of established professional historians, not only conservative and Christian historians but also most Marxists. Perhaps it was not entirely surprising that it should irritate – it struck the Right as old-fashioned radicalism – a revival of Buckle in modern dress – and the Left as a sell-out to wishy-washy liberalism. It took a long time for people to realise that, in essentials, it was speaking for some elements in the suburban Conservatism which was to carry, decades later, Mrs Thatcher to power. As a child I had seen acute deprivation among men, women and children of material things – like shoes, food, shelter. I had seen long lines of miners in 1926 queuing for a bowl of soup. I was shocked and bewildered. I was fourteen, from a comfortable, suburban lower middle-class home. I had never seen a mine or a miner before, or a child without shoes. I was cycling to North Wales to visit all of Edward I's castles and my route took me through Cannock Chase. That shock gave me a sense of the importance of *things* to those who do not have them. It was an unsophisticated reaction, maybe, but the vision of those queues in the General Strike has always been with me. It took me many years to discover by what historical processes the material life of men had been improved and how unbelievably complex they were. History began, albeit slowly, to be more than fun with Clarendon and the Civil War. I began tentatively the long journey that was to take me back to prehistory and to Sumer, Akkad and Egypt, across the world to China and Japan, and so to the Aztecs and Mayans. With my belly firmly glued to the eighteenth century, I reached out like an intelligent octopus as far as I could in the hope of fresh material. The *History of Human Society* might have flopped but my passion for the history of all peoples and all epochs has never ceased. And, I suppose, it created a kind of faith that the present world for all its faults – its tyrannies, holocausts, genocides, bombs, wars, horrors, brutalities and repressions – was still a better place for the majority of human beings to be alive in than at any previous moment in history. That faith has strengthened, not weakened, and if it seems simplistic to some of my quirkier colleagues like Maurice Cowling, so be it.

It is best to begin this long section on History and Historians with some of the essays I have written about history and progress or, put more grandiosely, the need for a 'philosophic history' for the West.

The Introduction to the History of Human Society

I

Over the last fifty to a hundred years, man's belief that the historical process proved that he was acquiring a greater mastery over Nature has received a brutal buffeting. In his early youth H. G. Wells, a man of vast creative energy, of rich delight in the human spirit, and of all-pervading optimism, viewed the future with confidence; science, born of reason, was to be humanity's panacea. When, in the years of his maturity, he came to write his *Outline of History*, his vision was darker, although still sustained with hope. World War I, with its senseless and stupid slaughter of millions of men, brought the sickening realisation that man was capable of provoking human catastrophes on a global scale. The loss of human liberty, the degradations and brutalities imposed by fascism and communism during the 1920s and 1930s, followed in 1939 by the renewed world struggle, these events finally shattered Wells' eupeptic vision, and in sad and disillusioned old-age he wrote *Mind at the End of its Tether*. His hope of mankind had almost vanished. Almost, but not quite: for Wells' lifetime witnessed what, as a young writer, he had prophesied – technical invention not only on a prodigious scale but in those realms of human activity that affected the very core of society. And this extraordinary capacity of man to probe the complexities of Nature and to invent machinery capable of exploiting his knowledge remained for Wells the only basis for hope, no matter how slender that might be.

Growing disillusion with interpretations of man's destiny rendering it almost impossible for a professional historian to venture with confidence beyond his immediate province. And that can be very tiny – the Arkansas and Missouri Railway Strike of 1921; the place-names of Rutland: seventeenth-century Rouen; the oral history of the Barotse; the philosophy of Hincmar of Rheims. And so it becomes ever more difficult for the professional historian to reach across to ordinary intelligent men and women or make his subject a part of human culture. The historical landscape is blurred by the ceaseless activity of its millions of professional ants. Of course, attempts at synthesis have to be made. The need to train young professional historians, or the need to impart some knowledge of history to students of other disciplines, has brought about competent digests of lengthy periods that summarise both facts and analysis. Occasionally such books have been written with such skill and wisdom that they have become a part of the West's cultural heritage. A few historians, driven by money or fame or creative need, have tried to share their knowledge and understanding of the past with the public at large.

But the gap between professional knowledge and history for the masses gets steadily wider: professional history becomes more accurate, more profound, whilst public history remains tentative and shallow.

The theme of *The History of Human Society* is the most obvious and the most neglected; obvious because everyone is aware of it from the solitary villagers of Easter Island to the teeming cities of the Western World; neglected because it has been fashionable for professional and Western historians to concern themselves either with detailed professional history that cannot have a broad theme or with the spiritual and metaphysical aspects of man's destiny that are not his proper province. What, therefore, is the theme of *The History of Human Society?* It is this: that the condition of man now is superior to what it was. That two great revolutions – the Neolithic and the Industrial – have enabled men to establish vast societies of exceptional complexity in which the material well-being of generations of mankind has made remarkable advances; that the second, and most important, revolution has been achieved by the Western World; that we are witnessing its most intensive phase now, one in which ancient patterns of living are crumbling before the demands of industrial society; that life in the suburbs of London, Lagos, Jakarta, Rio de Janeiro and Vladivostok will soon have more in common than they have in difference: that this, therefore, is a moment to take stock, to unfold how this came about, to evoke the societies of the past whilst we are still close enough to many of them to feel intuitively the compulsion and needs of their patterns of living.

The range and variety of human societies is almost as great as the range and variety of human temperaments, and the selection for this series is in some ways as personal as an anthology. A Chinaman, a Russian, an Indian or an African would select a different series; but we are western men writing for western men. The westernisation of the world by industrial technology is one of the main themes of the series. Each society selected has been in the mainstream of this development or belongs to that vast primitive ocean whence all history is derived. Some societies are neglected because they would only illustrate in a duller way societies which appear in the series; some because their history is not well enough known to a sufficient depth of scholarship to be synthesised in this way; some because they are too insignificant.

There are, of course, very important social forces – feudalism, technological change or religion, for example – which have moulded a variety of human societies at the same time. Much can be learnt from the comparative study of their influence. I have, however, rejected this approach, once recorded history is reached. My reason for rejecting this method is because human beings experience these forces in communities, and it is the experience of men in society with which this series is primarily concerned.

Lastly, it need hardly be said that society is not always synonymous with the state. At times, as with the Jews, it lacks even territorial stability; yet the Jews provide a fascinating study of symbiotic social groupings, and to have left them out would be unthinkable, for they represent, in its best form, a wide human experience – a social group embedded in an alien society.

As well as a theme, which is the growth of man's control over his environment, this series may also fulfil a need. That is to restore a little confidence in man's capacity not only to endure the frequent catastrophes of human existence but also in his intellectual abilities. That many of his habits, both of mind and heart, are bestial, needs scarcely to be said. His continuing capacity for evil need not be stressed. His greed remains almost as strong as it was when he first shuffled on the ground. And yet the miracles created by his cunning are so much a part of our daily lives that we take their wonder for granted. Man's ingenuity – based securely on his capacity to reason – has won astonishing victories over the physical world – and in an amazingly brief span of time. Such triumphs, so frequently overlooked and even more frequently belittled, should breed a cautious optimism. Sooner or later, painfully perhaps and slowly, the same intellectual skill may be directed to the more difficult and intransigent problems of human living – man's social and personal relations – not only directed, but perhaps accepted, as the proper way of ordering human life. The story of man's progress over the centuries, studded with pitfalls and streaked with disaster as it is, ought to strengthen both hope and will

Yet a note of warning must be sounded. The history of human society, when viewed in detail, is far more often darkened with tragedy than it is lightened with hope. As these books show, life for the nameless millions of mankind who have already lived and died has been wretched, short, hungry and brutal. Few societies have secured peace; none stability for more than a few centuries; prosperity, until very recent times, was the lucky chance of a small minority. Consolations of gratified desire, the soothing narcotic of ritual, and the hope of future blessedness have

often eased but rarely obliterated the misery which has been the lot of
all but a handful of men since the beginning of history. At long last that
handful is growing to a significant proportion in a few favoured societies.
But throughout human history most men have derived pitifully little
from their existence. A belief in human progress is not incompatible
with a sharp realisation of the tragedy not only of the lives of individual
men but also of epochs, cultures and societies. Loss and defeat, too, are
themes of this series, as well as progress and hope.

Progress Fifteen Years Later

Although the first volume of the *History of Human Society* was not
published until 1965 (it had been first discussed in 1958) the preface
was written early (1960) to show to the authors whom I approached
what the thrust of the series would be. I knew enough about my
colleagues' attitudes to history to refrain from sending it to many whom
I admired, but for whom the underlying philosophy would be an
anathema. What did surprise me was how few responded wholeheartedly
to my approach. And for many, of course, the prospect was too daunting.
Twenty years later I had a golden opportunity to expand my views on
the idea of progress when Robert Nisbet, a gifted member of the neo-
conservative group in America that included Irving Kristol and Gertrude
Himmelfarb, published *The History of the Idea of Progress*.

Robert Nisbet, The History of the Idea of Progress

Like justice, freedom, liberty or even property, progress is an extremely
versatile word, chameleon-like in its capacity to camouflage. After all we
speak of a sick person making progress, even of someone who has been
mutilated in an accident, although the end result may be in marked contrast
with what went before – a weakened or a crippled person contrasted
with a healthy one. A child may make progress at school and yet a teacher
might be most reluctant to forecast a life of steady progress in a chosen
career. An athlete may make progress but reach quickly a barrier which
he cannot break. The devoutly religious may make moral progress yet
fall into mortal sin. These concepts – obvious and common-place as they
are – have considerable relevance for this new book of Robert Nisbet's

His concern is to trace the idea that history is progressive, that the
story of mankind is one of betterment. He believes that a great deal of
the accepted wisdom about this idea is wrong – i.e. that the ancient
philosophers believed in the cyclical nature of human life; that death
and decay and destruction were as inherent in society's as in a person's

life. On the contrary, his view is that many philosophers believed the opposite. He would argue, too, that the idea was not foreign to the middle ages in the Western world. For Robert Nisbet the idea of progress is an inherent part of the western tradition which stretches back to Hesiod.

Robert Nisbet is a scholar of very wide and precise scholarship; he is a political philosopher with a most acute analytical mind. He has never been hoodwinked by conventional ideas either of scholars or philosophers. Hence his work must be taken very seriously – it can also be taken with pleasure for Robert Nisbet's pen is as lively as his mind. And he has certainly written one of the most stimulating books, *History of the Idea of Progress*, since J. B. Bury's great book of the same title.

Robert Nisbet, of course, realises the complex nature of the idea of progress but he defines it succinctly as 'the idea of progress holds that mankind has advanced in the past – from some aboriginal condition of primitiveness, barbarism or even nullity – is now advancing and will continue to advance through the foreseeable future'. From this derive two propositions – one that there has been a steady and cumulative improvement in knowledge as embodied in the arts and sciences and the other that there has been a spiritual and moral improvement – an ever greater perfection of human nature. He, of course, realises that the first proposition is both easier to prove and to accept and that the latter has been more subject to criticism and less universally believed.

After defining his ideas, he proceeds to his history from Hesiod to the volcanic rhetoric of George Steiner, and all the great philosophers are there – Protagoras, Plato, Aristotle, Lucretius, Seneca, St Augustine, Otto of Freising, Joachim of Flora. The Renaissance, indeed, provides an ebb tide, but the concept is given redoubled impetus by Jean Bodin, and Nisbet then moves quickly into the Scientific Revolution, the Enlightenment and the nineteenth century, the traditional epochs for the flowering of the idea of human progress – although some of the flowers were definitely evil such as Gobineau's belief in racial progress which gave the palm to the German race. However British and American philosophers and historians were doing much the same for their own societies with their concepts of Manifest Destiny but with less *éclat*.

In so vast a discussion it would be more than possible to cross swords with Nisbet in the hope of winning a point or two – for example, the fact that the Fifth Monarchy Men were millenarianists, that they expected society to be changed suddenly for the better and for eternity, scarcely makes them firm believers in the idea of progress – if it does the concept becomes a ragbag of an idea. It could embrace the concept of conversion: Saul of Tansus made progress en route for Damascus. The coming of the millennium, religious conversions, are acts of God not of man. Although there are a number of places where one could pick at Nisbet's narrative of philosophy, it is pointless to do so. Most of his exposition is admirable and extremely enriching. There are, however, criticisms which are more fundamental towards which the first paragraph of this review pointed.

There is no doubt that Hesiod, Protagoras, Plato and other great philosophers realised that there had been social development in Greece from more barbaric and primitive societies. Yet the major leaps forward – the control of fire, the discovery of arts and crafts, particularly metal-working – were due not to man but to intervention of the gods or Titans – Prometheus and Hephaestus – and so it was argued the gods might intervene in the betterment of mankind. However progress for some Greek writers, it seems, required a *deux ex machina*. Secondly, Nisbet's treatment of St Augustine loses, I think, a certain candour in order to make this fit into the projected history of this idea from the Greeks to the nineteenth century. Certainly St Augustine believed in the developmental nature of human society but the image that he used, as indeed Nisbet points out, was physiological from *infantia* to not only *seniors aetas* but also to *senectus*: hence decay and enfeeblement were an essential part of human society, the ages of mankind depended also not on man but upon God. Indeed God is the prime motive force of St Augustine's concept of human destiny in time – his will in all things is final, not man's intelligence or capacities. The danger of Nisbet's approach is to extrapolate remarks of St Augustine on history and the process of time from the matrix of his theology. His historical concepts, his view of man's past, present and future destiny are components of that theology. That some men were capable of betterment in a secular as well as a spiritual sense should also be offset by St Augustine's firm belief that some societies and multitudes of men and women were not and were doomed to destruction and everlasting hell-fire. It is not only with St Augustine that by tearing some concepts from their ideological frame-work a distortion is created: it occurs elsewhere in the book. It is, of course, a pitfall almost impossible to avoid in a book that covers so many centuries, so many different worlds of thought and feeling.

There is, I think, a larger criticism. Voices were raised against slavery from the ancient times onwards with little or no social effect. Suddenly in the second half of the eighteenth century in England, they began to acquire an unstoppable social force that finally ended with the abolition of slavery. Why that happened is much more important than the narra-tive history of anti-slavery ideas of philosophers and theologians. Simi-larly the idea of progress acquired little or no social force (if you exclude millenarianism, as I certainly would) until the eighteenth and nineteenth centuries. And why it did so is not discussed by Nisbet. Why ideas become social attitudes is one of the great problems for historians of thought and culture. And so is the negative of that statement. Why do ideas cease to remain social attitudes? Nisbet stresses that the advanced, industrial western world (non-Marxist) is turning, indeed has almost turned, away from the idea of progress as a historical force; but he offers little explanation. Of course it is a complex subject but one factor is important – material progress. The idea of progress was at its most powerful when the vast material progress of man appeared to be achieveable in the foreseeable future – but the advanced industrial societies of the West have achieved that material progress. There are great inequalities but the mass of western mankind has almost all it wants and needs – particularly in America where history as a subject is dying as quickly as the idea of unstoppable and unending progress. Of course, there are many other factors but I suspect that this is central – belief in progress is more of a social attitude in Cuba, Brazil or West Africa and the world's depressed nations.

It is the exploration of the social context of ideas which I find the weakest part of this exceptionally stimulating book. In spite of two major faults – the almost alarming elasticity of the concept in Nisbet's hands and his lack of interest in the varying social reactions to the idea – it remains a very impressive book. In it there is material for endless seminars, endless discussions. It seems churlish to criticise so admirable an achievement.

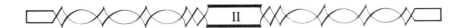

The Sense of Crisis

During the 1950s a new kind of atmosphere began to develop in the Faculty at Cambridge. Kitson Clark, conservative, Christian, rich, became (to use one of his own favourite metaphors) the midwife to radical reform. He began moderately enough towards the end of World War II, pleading for the reform of the Tripos as soon as peace was achieved and undergraduates had returned to Cambridge. He envisaged a wider range of papers (a little of this had been agreed before the end of the war), and a greater choice of the kind of history an undergraduate might wish to study: for instance, in a paper entitled *Constitutional and Economic History* the student could choose to do three-quarters of his questions on either constitutional or economic history. By an odd coincidence I was elected to the Faculty Board in 1947 – the appointment had been earmarked for Ralph Bennett of Magdalene, F. R. Salter's young protégé, for Salter worked closely with Kitson Clark; furthermore Bennett, having been elected to a Faculty post just before the war was the oldest 'junior historian'. It was expected that the other junior historians, namely those of us who had been appointed to temporary posts, would be solidly behind Bennett, but much to my surprise I became their candidate for reasons I have never been able to fathom. Naturally I was overwhelmed to sit with G. N. Clark, Herbert Butterfield, David Knowles and other well-known historians to direct faculty policy and administration. Kitson Clark had succeeded in getting the idea of Tripos reform accepted by the Faculty Board and G. N. Clark who was Chairman at that time adroitly proposed a small committee. Both Butterfield and Oakeshott were elected to it and I was proposed by G. N. Clark to represent junior opinion. When it met, I quickly joined forces with Butterfield and Oakeshott as my views on the teaching of history were much closer to theirs than to Kitson Clark's. I saw no need for radical change in the Tripos, fought hard for the retention of papers on the whole of English and European history and for a compulsory theoretical paper. What little expansion of papers took place was limited to Part I, and Part II remained virtually unchanged. This, of course, took one or two academic years to achieve. The committee itself had not been in any great hurry to report back to the Faculty. This committee brought me into contact with Michael Oakeshott for the first time – an evasive, intriguing and disturbing scholar with a quicksilver mind who had a passion for women and for racing – one would have thought an unlikely friend for the teetotal, Methodist lay preacher, Butterfield. Not a bit, Butterfield worshipped Oakeshott with almost an adolescent's intensity. Their views of men and affairs usually chimed melodically. They were very chuff with their victory in limiting reform. Kitson Clark, however, was not easily defeated; he was a man of elephantine tenacity. He was prepared to waste hundreds of hours lobbying, cajoling, enticing the younger historians to support him with prospects of more jobs if there were more papers. He was just as conservative in politics as Oakeshott and as deeply Christian as Butterfield. But Kitson Clark could not see, as they did quickly and realistically, that his proposed changes would create opportunities for the expansion of the radical Left. And so remorselessly Kitson went on with reform, wearing down opposition and getting his supporters elected to the Board. Curiously enough the conservative and mainly Christian Right have always maintained power in the History Faculty at Cambridge and have largely appointed men of their own kind, often men of very modest attainments. Yet strangely enough their passion of Tripos reform has never ceased – only paused to take breath. The result has had a most deleterious effect on the teaching of history in Cambridge. They have abetted an almost lunatic professionalism by which lecturers have been allowed to lecture only on subjects upon which they are doing research, which has, on occasion, resulted in a class of one or two pupils or even none at all. The Kitson Clark policy destroyed an excellent Tripos that gave a sound historical education to men and women with no intention of becoming professional historians. At the same time periods of history have given way to historical themes, some not without merit or educational value but adding another dimension to the fragmentation of historical teaching. This process was recently attacked by my young colleague Dr D. N. Cannadine with fervour and panache but, I suspect, with the same ultimate lack of impact that my attack, on almost identical lines, had in 1965. (See David Cannadine, 'British History, Past, Present and Future', *Past and Present* (1986), No. 113.) Criticism was swept aside and the process did not end; although lecture rooms continue to empty because of the narrowness of the subjects offered as well as the incompetence and indifference of many lecturers; until the situation borders on scandal no serious attempt will be made to stop the rot. But shortage of money will probably accomplish what critics could not. A lecturer with a minuscule or non-existent audience needs to be backed by a fat budget and a complacent administration. Those days are past. And this development will be strengthened by the increasing reluctance of schools to teach history seriously or the lack of interest of young people studying it. All of one's forebodings have come to pass.

The Historian's Dilemma

One of the greatest successes on Broadway during the early 1960s was Edward Albee's *Who's Afraid of Virginia Woolf*, an appealing title for a savage, grim, searing, three-hour dialogue between an historian and his wife. The personal situation, dominated by a screeching American version of the Earth Mother (the historian's wife), provided the hypnotic focus of the play's power, but its magnetism, the disquiet it bred, derived from its deeper implications. The historian is sterile and impotent. He talks endlessly of an imagined child (the future) and babbles bewilderingly about his past. Did he or did he not kill his parents? There is a conflict of evidence, and great uncertainty. No one including himself can ever know. His wife, who possesses all the force, the violence, the passion of an instinctively living woman, hates his failure, his verbosity, his confusion, his inadequacy, but hate him as she does, her desire is also strong and she cannot disentangle herself from his needs. History and life are doomed to live it out in hate, in distrust, in mutual failure. They are lost in timeless falsehood; bound by dreams of the past that may not have existed, and enslaved by their own lies about the future. And this as the audience streamed out into the flashing neon lights of Broadway seemed to have the force of truth. History is without meaning, without power, without hope. Is it?

Just over a hundred years ago, the great English historian Macaulay, visited the Great Exhibition of 1851. He experienced, he said, the same feeling of awe as he had first felt on entering St Peter's in Rome. This was not meant satirically: it was not meant to be derogatory either to the Great Exhibition or St Peter's. Macaulay was a matter of fact man who told the truth. He was moved, he goes on to relate, by the same sense of wonder when confronted by two marvellous triumphs of the human spirit – St Peter's and the Crystal Palace. They justified human history. They spoke of man's progress – material and spiritual. And Macaulay believed loudly, emphatically, in progress. He expresses his faith in a trumpeting breathless passage in his *Essay on Bacon*:

It has lengthened life; it has mitigated pain; it has extinguished diseases; it has increased the fertility of the soil; it has given new securities to the mariner; it has furnished new arms to the warrior; it has spanned great rivers and estuaries with bridges of form unknown to our fathers; it has guided the thunderbolt innocuously from heaven to earth; it has lighted up the night with the splendour of the day; it has extended the range of the human vision; it has multiplied the power of the human muscles; it has accelerated motion; it has annihilated distance; it has facilitated intercourse, correspondence, all friendly offices, all despatch of business; it has enabled man to descend to the depths of the sea, to soar into the air, to penetrate securely into the noxious recesses of the earth, to traverse the land in cars which whirl along without horses, and the ocean in ships which run ten knots an hour against the wind. These are but a part of its fruits, and of its first fruits. For it is a philosophy which never rests, which has never attained, which is never perfect. Its law is progress. A point which yesterday was invisible is its goal today, and will be its starting-post tomorrow.

Progress – the results of the application of reason to observation – was for Macaulay the unifying theme of human history: its core; its meaning. In the hundred years that have elapsed since Macaulay's death, his view of history which was then commonly held, has been so completely rejected that neither prophets of history, nor philosophers of history, nor even practitioners of history, consider it seriously. Among professional historians the idea of progress is out. Ninety per cent, perhaps, prefer Albee's view, that the subject they practise is meaningless in any ultimate sense. And there is a further tragic paradox. This century has witnessed 'the brilliant conquest of the most distant frontiers of historical knowledge'[1] yet fewer and fewer historians believe that their art has any social purpose: any function as a coordinator of human endeavour, or human thought.

Then what do historians believe? To understand the present crisis in history one needs to go back to Macaulay and a little beyond. Macaulay was not essentially a Victorian, he was the child of the Enlightenment, nearer to Voltaire than to Darwin. Contemporaneously with the rise of science in the seventeenth century, a belief had grown up in the idea of historical progress; indeed, like science it was regarded as an almost certain consequence of the triumph of reason. Man's history was wrenched out of the hands of the theologians, to become an autonomous field of study, to be explained, in human not providential terms. Yet a great deal of the old theological attitude reappeared in rationalist guise. History still had its ultimate goal, whether it was Rousseau's return to a state of blissful nature (a sort of Garden of Eden in reverse), or Marx's classless society, or Acton's growth of liberty, or in our own day the existentialist's leap into freedom. Few historians, certainly not Macaulay himself, have ever been content with the mere fact of material progress.

The idea of progress was inextricably entangled with social, ethical and political concepts of a highly debatable nature.

By the middle of the nineteenth century, except in some instances to which I shall return, the best historians had turned away from the rationalist approach of Voltaire, Macaulay, and the Enlightenment. The eclipse of rationalism and the destruction of the idea of progress were due to two major developments – the growth of scientific historiography and the development of 'historicism'.

The rise of natural science deeply influenced historians. They admired the exactitude of science, the clarity of its arguments, even more than the certainty of its conclusions. Such methods should they felt be applied to history. At the same time the fashionable success of positivist philosophy enabled them to concentrate their attention on scientific method rather than attempt to formulate theories. Although Leopold Ranke, the greatest and most influential historian of Macaulay's day, was not a positivist, his work and his constant reiteration that facts, and facts alone, are important, established the historical positivist as archetype of academic historians. Get the facts right, theories will then follow: alas, historical facts are as numberless as the grains of sand. That did not stop them. Ranke believed that all facts were equally important and that 'the strict presentation of the facts is the supreme law of historiography'.

To understand the compulsion, the fascination of the fact itself for Ranke and his disciples, one must remember the state of history at that time – encrusted with fable, devoid of critical methods, starved of archival material and the ancillary sciences which we all take so much for granted – paleography, archaeology, numismatics etc. – were then almost non-existent. As Ranke and others forced open the doors of the secret archives out came tumbling startling discoveries – facts and lies galore, but all needing great technical skill in their handling. Technique became supremely important and historians inevitably became increasingly professional. The contribution of the scientific attitude to history has been monumental. It has given the subject an intellectual discipline which it had never previously possessed and it has multiplied the material of history a millionfold. Fortunately, the facts of history are limitless so the search for fresh facts, new material, can go on and on and on. Ranke was bold enough to consider a *Universal History*, his scholarly descendants prefer a five hundred page study of Wigston Magna or a hefty thesis on the Missouri and Northern Arkansas Railroad Strike of 1921. Yet in the welter of monographs that have deluged the world since Ranke's day there has been not only the recovery of fascinating detail but also fresh light on the causal connections in human society. The trained professional historian now has at his disposal an extraordinarily rich material, which can and does illuminate almost every aspect of the past. But each study is largely an end in itself, a pursuit by professionals for professionals. History is now strictly organised, powerfully disciplined, but it possesses only a modest educational value and even less conscious, social purpose. Occasionally in this arid desert of monographs, one spies a small oasis – a work of superlative professional *vulgarisation* such as Marc Bloch's *Feudal Society*, Garrett Mattingly's *Defeat of the Spanish Armada* or Arthur Schlesinger Jr's *Age of Jackson*. Here and there, but isolated and lonely, there are a few professional historians who still believe that history should be more than a professional or educational activity and should reach out to inform, instruct, enliven and ennoble and render more profound the common heritage of man. In spite of the myriads of monographs, the positivist dilemma is still with us – generalisations must, it would seem, be put off until the buried facts, billions of them, are brought back into academic light.[2] Historians appear to be dedicated to the theory of total recall. The reason for this lies very deep, primarily in the lack of faith in the ultimate value of historical enquiry. Placed against the obvious power and effectiveness of scientific enquiry or even economic analysis, historical generalisations must seem hopelessly tentative and jejeune. And this natural inferiority has been strengthened not only by the anarchy of professional activity but also by the spiritual nihilism which pervades the subject. This is due, almost entirely, to the second major development in historical studies during the nineteenth century – the growth of historicism.

Historicism started as an attack on the confidence of the Enlightenment and it found the concept of human history as a steady triumph of reason, an inevitable progress towards the heavenly city of the philosophers, an easy target both for argument and satire.[3] Marx, Comte, Pareto, Freud, to mention only the greater names, showed how men and nations were at the mercy of irrational forces, and how frequently rational ideas were merely rationalisations.

Severely conditioned by irrational forces of which he was largely unaware, how could any historian achieve an unbiased, impersonal view of history? Most philosophers answered, never: many practising historians thought it not only impossible but undesirable. The historian's task was a matter of empathy, he was to project himself into the past, in order to recreate it for his own age. Each age would take from the past what it wanted in order to deepen its own experience of the present. Here is Burkhardt, one of the greatest of nineteenth century historians, whose rejection of the scientific historiography of Ranke was so final that he refused to succeed Ranke at Berlin: he writes in his introduction to the *Civilisation of the Renaissance* as follows:

To each eye, perhaps, the outlines of a given civilisation present a different picture; and in treating of a civilisation which is the mother of our own, and whose influence is still at work among us, it is unavoidable that individual judgement and feeling should tell every moment both on the writer and on the reader. In the wide ocean upon which we venture the possible ways and directions are many; and the same studies which have served for this work might easily, in other hands, not only receive a different treatment and application, but lead also to essentially different conclusions.

All historical interpretation and presentation is personal to the historian. There is no escape from self. Since Burkhardt's day philosophers have accepted and refined his attitude. For such thinkers as Collingwood in Britain, Croce in Italy, Becker and Beard in America, Aron in France, 'The world of History', to quote one of these, Becker, 'is an intangible world, recreated imaginatively, and present in our minds.' All history must be contemporary history, and so constantly rewritten:[4] 'the greatest historians', according to Aron may 'comprehend different perspectives even when they seem contradictory and see in their multiplicy a sign not of defeat but of the richness of life'. The distance between Aron and Albee is small, but both are nearly a light-year away from Macaulay.

Obviously for the relativist, or the historicist, call them what you will, the idea of progress is hopelessly naïve. An idea that was quite, quite impossible, said Collingwood, and no philosopher has bothered to disagree with him. His argument was simple. As we could not divest ourselves of ourselves, so we could not enter totally into the past, in consequence we could not know its satisfactions, for what may be disagreeable to us may have been delightful to those who experienced it. What may seem to be progress to us could be retrogression to others and as goals in history cannot exist, there is no objective standard by which judgements about progress may be formulated. The idea that history justifies a belief in human progress is, therefore, a logical absurdity; at most a useful delusion. So the modern historian is crucified by this dilemma: he must act like a scientist although historical objectivity cannot exist. His work can have no validity except for himself, and, perhaps, for fellow historians playing the same game by the same rules or perhaps for those men of his age who think and feel like himself. For them his work may deepen their experience as a novel might, or a poem, or even a play like Albee's. The philosophers of history will allow history to be a profession: even admit to its having educational and literary value: what they will not tolerate is the idea that it has a social purpose, that by analysing the past one may learn to control the future, that historically motivated governments will be more efficient than those ignorant of or indifferent to, historical causation. Above all, they will not allow any objective, universal validity to the human story. History, they say, is a present world, it can never be the past. It is a dream world made up of actual events.

In Albee's language it invents the past, and projects lies about the future.

Now that may be a satisfactory diet for philosophers, playwrights, historians, perhaps even teachers; it is useless to common humanity. Men believe, accept that the past existed: any other attitude for men in action is impossible. And because it exists, for them it must have a meaning. Hence the success, in publishing terms, of Spengler, Toynbee; of those historians who have sought to find the pattern of history and its repetitive logic. And yet by rejecting the idea of progress these pattern makers too have given little hope. But pattern-makers have not been the only diet for the common reader hungry to unravel the mystery of the past. He has also been served by what academic historians usually describe, somewhat disparagingly, as literary historians. (Croce calls them poetical historians but he used poetical in a derogatory sense.) True, most literary historians are largely unconcerned with analysis. Their aim is to evoke the past, and as with literature to deepen men's understanding of himself and his environment by processes of imaginative identification: to do, indeed, what Croce and Becker tell them it is possible to do. The majority of literary historians deliberately eschew historical analysis and avoid much discussion of causation. They use narrative structure and are usually happier with wars, plagues, and people than the less easily presented problems of political, cultural, economic or social history. Nevertheless many of the books of the leading figures of this genre – Barbara Tuchman, Elizabeth Longford, Alistair Horne, Christopher Hibbert and many others are vivid, informative and far more enjoyable to read than most monographs of professional historians.

So there we have them. The idealists insisting that history is merely a present world, ever-changing, never static, the academic positivists burrowing like boll-weevils in the thickets of facts, mindless, deliberately of purpose and meaning outside the orbit of their own activity. The public prophets using pseudo-science to justify a repetitive, cyclical interpretation of history, and the litterateurs preoccupied with evocation and exercise of the imagination. The result is nihilistic and socially impotent.

All are equally guilty I think of wilfully rejecting the one certain judgement of value that can be made about history and that is *the idea of progress*. If this great human truth were once more to be frankly accepted, reasons for it, and the consequences of it, consistently and imaginatively explored and taught, history would not only be an infinitely richer education but also play a much more effective part in the culture of western society.

Now one of the most astonishing facts about the idea of progress is that it arose very late indeed, in human history. It is a purely western idea; neither Islam nor classical China nor India possessed any similar concept. It began to emerge in the sixteenth century: and the writers who began to formulate it – Bodin, Bacon and their followers – gave their reasons quite simply: the discovery of the New World, the mariners' compass, the invention of printing and gun-powder – to their minds these represented a triumph over all previous ages and presaged future victories. And as might be expected, the idea of progress developed as the scientific revolution got under way. It is no accident that its complete formulation was made by L'Abbé St Pierre and Fontenelle, contemporaries of Newton, Boyle and Leibnitz. By then, the idea of progress had come to embrace not only the idea of man securing control over his material environment through the application of his reason, but also predicated moral and social progress. The golden age no longer belonged to the past, it was projected into the future.[5]

By the end of the eighteenth century, the idea was an unquestioned truth of most reasonably cultured men. When Lord Macartney conducted an embassy to China in 1793, he took a number of scientific and technical gadgets with him which the Chinese emperor refused to see. 'It is vain', Macartney wrote in his Journal 'to attempt resisting the progress of human knowledge. He thought, and rightly, that all the power and authority of the Chinese emperor and government would be incapable of arresting the inevitable infiltration of western knowledge.

Although by the middle of the nineteenth century the idea was, as we have seen, still held by historians such as Buckle who are no longer fashionable and by many political scientists and sociologists, from Tylor to Spencer, its acceptance by intellectuals, however, became increasingly hesitant.

The loss of faith in the idea of progress was quickest in Europe, slower in Britain – and slowest of all in America, excluding, of course, New England, where Henry Adams and other patrician historians were seeing degeneration in the spread of industrialisation. In Great Britain few historians believed as explicitly in progress as Macaulay: others such as Stubbs, Acton and Maitland discarded as almost irrelevant the materialist concept, and concerned themselves with the progressive development of institutions, liberty or law, looking there for evidence of man's moral progress. (Perhaps it is not without ironic significance that Acton's great history of liberty never got written.) But, even as intellectual and historical circles were rejecting the idea of progress, men active in affairs – politicians, administrators, above all manufacturers – started to act as if it were axiomatic. Many of them began consciously to search for means by which they could obtain greater intellectual control over their environment in order to improve it; the penetration of science, or of scientific methods and assumptions, into their conception of the past gathered momentum.

So now in our society we have a curiously schizophrenic attitude towards history. Large sections of western society act as if the idea of progress was a part of the built-in mechanism of modern history yet the historians, philosophers and popular prophets of history avoid the idea like the plague. In our social fabric they act like death-watch beetles, sapping the strength and confidence that history should give to leaders of society.

Now why has the idea of progress, material as well as moral, been rejected, or ignored or regarded as irrelevant? For this is a profoundly important problem, because there can be no doubt that a total lack of belief in human progress weakens the dynamic force of any society.

The reasons it seems to me are three-fold. First, the idea of progress is essentially secular, based on science and reason; secondly, it has come to be regarded as not only socially radical, which it is, but also politically radical, which it may not necessarily be. And thirdly, the revolutionary socialists have appropriated the idea so vociferously that the taint of Marxism, which would seem to be attached to it, has rendered it intellectually suspect.

At last let us turn to the idea itself. By progress in history, I mean nothing more than that man's increasing control over his environment is historically verifiable, as are its consequential results, namely, that this increasing control has rendered more and more of men's lives longer, healthier, more secure and more leisured, and that the species itself has be come more numerous, more firmly established, more in control of the physical world. And, as a consequence, there has been − and here I move to slightly more debatable ground − an increase in *civility*. This progress which was never regular or uniform, or without retrogression, has accelerated as man applied his intellectual powers, by the inductive method, to the material world. The more scientific his approach to the problems of his environment, the more speedily he has solved them. Neither prayer nor exorcism can stop smallpox; vaccination will. The idea of progress is essentially materialist and must, therefore, be inimicable to Providential explanations of history as science is to the mystical explanations of phenomena. Doubtless, that is why Pius ixth anathematised the idea in 1864 in his *Syllabus of Errors*. That is why the idea of progress has been rejected by historians as diverse as Sir Lewis Namier and Professor Butterfield.[6] If the most important fact of history is revelation, then progress is irrelevant and meaningless. The soul's progress becomes the central feature of existence and, obviously, the soul can make progress anywhere, at any time, in any conditions. It is just as possible for the soul to make progress towards the realisation of God among the bestial conditions of a medieval village as in a New York skyscraper. Obviously, therefore, the idea of progress must make an uneasy bed-fellow for religion. They may not be ultimately incompatible, but they must seem, superficially speaking, to be antagonistic to each other.[7]

However, the implied radicalism of the idea of progress has probably been a greater enemy to it than its secularising aspects. This is in no way logical. The fact that the expectation of life in London in the Stuart times was probably 17½, of Liverpool in 1846 26 and in Boston, Massachusetts 66·7, are historical facts that are neither radical nor reactionary, although they establish quite clearly enough what I mean by the idea of progress. How it has been brought about brings us nearer to disputed territory. Industry, technology, science are the immediate and obvious answers and these again are politically neutral. It is when we move from this broad generalisation to the social involvement implied by these developing processes, and the intellectual attitude which they demand, that leads one to see why the idea of progress has in most European countries at least developed such a pink glow.

Much of the obvious success of industry has been due to the growth of education, greater economic and social security for the working class, improved health and housing, which has only been made possible by a larger slice of the profitable industrial cake being offered to the working class, either by industries, industrialists or governments. The idea, however, that productivity and profit are directly or closely associated with such processes was never readily accepted, except by the most enlightened industrialists. Some of the ameliorations of social life were forced on the possessors of property and further industrial expansion rendered possible only by social change; particularly in those countries in Europe where the traditional patterns of society were deeply entrenched and where the weight of power lay in the hands of the landowners great and small. Indeed, in some countries intense industrial development was only released by violent social revolution. In Britain that never took place, largely because by the nineteenth century the proud possessors of landed wealth had been partially involved in the new sources of industrial and commerical money making. Yet the immense social distaste for industry is clear to anyone who reads the literature of the twentieth let alone the nineteenth century: and that certainly is true of New England, and perhaps of America as a whole. Even if itself not radical the idea of progress implied, or seemed allied to, a radical attitude towards the structure of society.

Also this assumption – that progress was radical – was strengthened by the dogmatic assertions of the Marxists that progress was inevitable but could only take place through their kind of revolution. Then, and then only, could the material condition of society take a great leap forward. This as we all know has forced the Marxists into very odd historical attitudes. Almost by definition workers cannot benefit from capitalist industry, or why should anyone want to revolt? They have to be proletarianised, exploited, victimised. Hence every incident of brutality and poverty in the nineteenth century industrialisation of Britain is stressed in an attempt to deny the fact that the conditions of life of the majority of the working class have improved.[8] Marxist historians *must* maintain the fiction that the age of Dickens continued to exist for 100 years after it had vanished. Of course, some of their better theoreticians were more subtle and shifted England's proletariat to the colonies and India as they did America's to Central and South America. But even there their prognostications proved nearly as fallacious. Dogmatic Marxists seem to be intellectually incapable of separating the effects of industrialisation from a criticism of the means by which it is achieved. However, there can be no doubt that constant iteration by Marxists of the inevitablity of dialectical materialism has given a bad smell to the idea of progress. It is because of this that the justifications for Western Society – its world image – have been looked for in more immaterial ideas – freedom, toleration, etc. We have turned away from what is simple, obvious and true to moral and ethical propositions which mean so very little in the slums of Bombay, that are pretty meaningless against the hard facts of food, health and shelter, which ironically, the West have produced far quicker and far more impressively than any other society: certainly far better and far quicker than Marxist societies.

Yet neither its essentially secular bias, nor its radical implications, nor Marxist overtones are entirely responsible for the present rejection of the idea of progress, or for its lack of acceptance as the organising thesis in historical research and teaching. Ideas are usually imbedded in social attitudes, and neither its secularism nor its radicalism would have been so inimicable to its acceptance, but for the structure of western society and in that I include New England.

What is true for the structure of British society is also very largely true of western Europe and a great deal, if not all, of America.

Now between 1380 and 1640 Heralds and the College of Arms in England flourished as never before and the courts of chivalry became intensely active. Many *nouveaux riches*, farmers, landowners or merchants bought their genealogy and coat of arms, along with their lordship of the manor and their right to hold courts baron. Rich men, will buy the insignias of affluence that already exist. No matter how bastardised feudalism might have become, its trappings were good enough for a Tudor yeoman. New wealth in an old society will rarely create its own social mores, it will adopt those of the ancient rich. So, too, in the nineteenth and twentieth centuries, the sons of Manchester manufacturers were sent off to Rugby to acquire a classical education. Their fathers bought estates, their sisters hunted. The College of Heralds was as busy as ever, as Sir George Bellew, Garter King of Arms recently said, commerce is not necessarily inimical to heraldry.

As it was in Britain so it was in Eastern America. The late nineteenth century witnessed a hunt for ancestors on a gigantic scale. In the 1890s a number of newspapers established genealogical departments; New York Public Library became the proud possessor of one of the largest genealogical collections in the world. There was a vast hunger to establish roots, to create a personal right to a share in the past. The reason was that the rising tide of industrialism seemed about to obliterate all of the old social distinctions that the patrician families has assumed to be theirs by natural right. So men of established position came to hate the present and taught the new men to hate it as well. But what has this to do with history and the idea of progress? This much. Industry, science, technology until recently have been at a moral discount and the ethos in which the successful moved was confused, backward-looking, concerned with preservation, not change. Also many of its most vocal members were depressed by the violations that industrial society wrought, rather than impressed with the benefits which it conferred. Industry rips up the countryside, vulgarises cities, renders sea-coasts hideous and plays hell with social relations. Its irresistible needs break down the barriers of privilege quicker than the successful can be absorbed within them. Now, obviously idealists and positivists could teach very happily in a social climate of mild despair and confusion, such as the Adamses, Lodges and Cabots created in Boston. History became a personal game, a poetic effusion, unpredictable, irresponsible: providentially controlled or biologically doomed; all these views carried, in this atmosphere, the force of truth. Many a successful industrialist sloughed off his social hope for traditional nostalgia as he worked his way into patrician society. They exchanged Macaulay, first for Henry Adams, and then for Toynbee. Gentle evocations of the past – nostalgic, sad, all in fancy dress – became much more welcome than rugged explanations of history that pointed with red arrows towards the future: better Mont St Michel than Middletown. Along with the feudal heraldic trappings, the successful progeny of the Industrial Revolution absorbed the ethos, with its sense of increasing loss, of the older possessing classes, the patricians and planters. Nor was the sense of violation and of loss confined to the possessing classes alone. The Industrial Revolution was often much rougher to traditional modes of work than of ownership. Crafts were destroyed, ancient patterns of living broken up and the urbanisation of the country-side and the industrialisation of agriculture galloped ahead. It seemed to many that a second dimension of horror, akin to the vileness of the slums, was to be added to the bleak vista of the industrial scene. And it is not surprising that sensitive men and women with little or no sense of the past and with little or no instruction from those who had, should have come to deplore what it thought to be the destructive nature of the industrial world. Parkman took refuge in the romanticism of the plains and Charles Frank Adams believed that the future of America lay with the scattered agricultural communities of the north-west. 'In their hand', he wrote 'will rest the ark of the Covenant.' The cult of Thoreau in America, and of Hudson in England, taught the young to hate the city, the dynamo of progress. Indeed, revulsion from industrialism has been one of the great stimulants of twentieth-century literature, and of course not only literature, it pervades intellectual enquiry as well as artistic expression. It runs like dry rot through literary criticism.

The atmosphere intellectual, moral and social was exceedingly inimic-able to the idea of progress as the synthesising idea of human history. In this atmosphere it would probably have withered and died anyway. But events too gave it hammer blows. World War I, the Somme, Verdun, Passchendale, millions of slaughtered men and World War II with millions more and the interval made macabre by Hitler and his maniac persecution of the Jews and the monomania of Stalin and his purges, and the horror of Hiroshima and Nagasaki. These events have made it doubly hard to cling to the idea of progress in human affairs. In addition we have the constant example of the prejudice, the greed, the hatred that runs through all contemporary life. Without any further searching, these events themselves, many felt, ought to be enough to destroy any belief in human progress. And this, of course, the publicists of the idealists and positivists, as well as those who believe in Providence, have been quick to seize on. But, of course, such an attitude is intellectually shallow. These things are horrible: they ought to be stopped. But they can only be stopped if humanity expands the bounds of its progress and applies its rational powers to a greater area of its activity. That is, that it learns its lessons of history; and even, if, as is possible, mankind should finally destroy itself, it would be just as absurd to say that mankind had made no progress, as absurd indeed as to maintain that a man who had fallen off the north face of the Matterhorn had not started to climb it. For any historian, it seems to me, who can bring himself to believe that the past exists outside his own head, the fact of human progress remains undeniable. The material and intellectual progress in the last 7000 years is staggering, not only in its complexity but in its increasing rapidity. Put a flint knife by a computer or a handloom by a sputnik. And surely it ought to be the prime duty of the historians to investigate this process, to describe it, to attempt an explanation of how it came about, and for this theme to be their social purpose. It ought to be the historian's duty to lay bare these processes by which social progress has taken place, in the hope that knowledge and understanding may lead to their acceleration and development. So, too, should they concern themselves with those factors in society which have inhibited growth and change and, even at times, led to retrogression, so that these might, in the future, be avoided. Such preoccupations would not mean as Geyl would have us believe that history would become unimaginative, blinkered and insensitive and concerned entirely with success.[9] Because one believes that the most important feature of human history is the story of man's progressive control over his environment, this does not mean that one throws overboard all one's imagination, insight, and judgement or one's sympathy for what fails and what is destroyed. But to ignore the implication of the concept of progress seems to me to lead to disintegration, nihilism, and to the proliferation of meaningless investigations. In so doing historians turn their back on their social function. His investigations of the past should lead to an explanation of it for his time and generation, so that, by explaining, man's control over his future may be increased.

Now, the failure to do this, exists not so much in our historical work as in our historical teaching. Much historical work in progress is deeply concerned with historical change or with the major forces that have moulded society. Nor is the failure so complete in the teaching of history to historians, although this is often terribly disorganised, at times superficial and, frequently, concerned with tertiary issues. Nevertheless anyone with imagination and some scholarship can deepen his experience about the nature of man in society and the historical processes of change. The young historian will not, of course, in my own University, Cambridge, be led directly to such considerations. He will, for example, be expected to know far more about Tudor Chamber finance or the Anglican Settlement than the impact of the geographical discoveries, or the scientific revolution. Instead of being central to his education, the idea of progress will be incidental to it. What we can be certain about is that the social purpose of history will neither mould his studies, nor help him to form his attitude to the past. He will be taught inexorably to distrust wide discussions and broad generalisations, to eschew any attempt to draw conclusions or lessons from history. He will be encouraged to read history and treat history as an intellectual pastime, with little rhyme and less reason. Those who go off to teach in schools go to instruct and not to educate. And worse still history fails to fulfil its social function, in government, in administration, in all the manifold affairs of men.

Rarely has history been so socially impotent. And some responsibility must lie on its own shoulders, on the reticence of historians, their ambiguities, their reluctance to accept the social responsibilities that their subject imposes on them, and their adamantive conservatism towards the teaching of history. Yet, as humanity crawls up the face of the Eiger, hesitates, slips and then miraculously scrambles back, it seems a little hard that those who plot its course should give no encouragement.

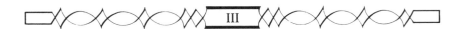

Historians, Great and Smaller

I suppose that when I decided to write in 1946 *The History of England in the Eighteenth Century*, I had cast my lot with that ever-diminishing band of professional historians who wanted to keep the writing of history as a part of our literary culture. Certainly I had strong advice from several friends, including C. P. Snow, not to write it, as it might be professionally harmful. He, like the others, thought that I ought to go back to my PhD thesis, revise and extend it; in fact become a mainstream professional. I could not. I realised that I had thrown in my lot with G. M. Trevelyan and all that he stood for. Just after I had published *England in the Eighteenth Century* in 1950, I was approached by the British Council to write a supplement to their *Book News* on Trevelyan.[1] I accepted with alacrity and read all of his books which I had not read before such as *Meredith*, *Grey of Fallodon*, *England in the Age of Wycliffe* and *Scenes from Italy's War* during my free time in the winter of 1950–1. I then took myself and my notes to Brighton at Easter, settled in the Old Ship Hotel and wrote 10,000 or so words on Trevelyan in ten days – a nice steady pace which gave me time to absorb Brighton, the Pavilion and the great Georgian terraces along the sea front. They stimulated my interest in George IV to great advantage, indeed that singular monarch became a minor obsession for some years. Before that visit to Brighton my views on George IV were entirely conventional, his monstrosities accepted, his qualities ignored. It was to take me several decades to get the full measure of the man. On the way I made a speech – one of the best I have ever made – at a dinner in the Pavilion at which the American ambassador, David Bruce, was present which brought me friendship with the Bruces. I had decided to go to Brighton on the spur of the moment. It might easily have been the Imperial Hotel at Torquay. Thank God it wasn't, for later in the year I was asked by Batsford to write on *The First Four Georges*. I might have declined, although there were new things to say about the early Georges, but it was George IV who beckoned and what a splendid tragi-comic ending he made.

There were also long walks to Hove, for I like to think about what I am to write and then the writing comes very quickly. As I brooded about Trevelyan I realised he was a more complex man than I had thought when I was his research student; I found it difficult to make up my mind about the most decisive act of his life when he resigned his Fellowship at Trinity, and foresook the academic world for twenty-five years, living on his private means and what he earned by his pen. He, himself, said that he found the atmosphere of Cambridge too hypercritical for a creative man. Half a century later it was no better. The years between had not helped his professional reputation amongst Cambridge academics. He wrote great books which sold not for a year or two but for decades. He even sold more than his great-uncle, Lord Macaulay. Yet they brought him no professional respect. Most historians in 1950 preferred to think of history as a social science not as a part of a nation's culture and literature. So a critical assessment of Trevelyan presented me with a kind of dilemma which had been implicit in his decision to quit. He gained creative time and freedom; he lost, and it showed in his work, contact with new material, new ideas, new approaches to the problems of history – the yeast so very necessary to enliven the imagination as well as the intellect. I, too, was at the crossroads of my career. I could dedicate my life to the politics of Britain between 1689 and 1715 for ever and a day. The fact of my acceptance to write a critique of Trevelyan showed that I had instinctively made up my mind not to do so. I was not, am not, given to biting the hands that feed me. Also I had no doubt that Trevelyan was a great man and thirty years later when I reassessed his work, I still had no doubt. He possessed a natural nobility of character. Not that he was without his self-indulgent foibles. At Hallington, his beautiful house in Northumberland, one got into an iron-bed with a wooden mattress from a linoleum-covered floor and no heat. His cook Emma's potato pie put Trevelyan into ecstasy; his joy was a mystery to his guests. Wine was unknown and the cider commonplace and rather sour. He loved walking ten miles in the biting rain along the Roman Wall until he was thoroughly soaked. I found it an ordeal. His eyes might fill with tears as he read in his high croaking voice some of the dimmer verse of Browning and Meredith but it never occurred to him that his guest might be bored to distraction as he went on for an hour. He taught me that the ascetic liberals of Victorian England enjoyed their ascetism with a kind of gluttony. And yet even at his most self-indulgent times he never seemed gross. When raspberries were in season he ate a very large bowlful four times a day; or at every breakfast he wolfed down Frank Cooper's marmalade piled on thick brown bread and butter as precariously as a pyramid of Chinese gymnasts. It was all performed with a kind of noble indifference. Only poetry-reading was done with emotion when he might become so consumed by it that he sobbed. Of course he was not without fault: overwhelmed by the death of his first son, Theo, at the age of five he was, as indeed his wife was, somewhat indifferent to his children. On hearing that his brother had had a bastard at the sprightly age of eighty, he refused to speak to him or see him for some years, indeed until his desire to show me the great family house at Wallington where his brother lived grew the better of him. He took me over and gruffly greeted his brother whom he had not spoken to for so long. Sexual matters disturbed him. He refused to allow the incestuous-seeming letters of Thomas Macaulay to his sister, Hannah (Trevelyan's grandmother), to be published until he was dead, thereby shutting off an historical source of great value. He was not faultless, he could live greedily with an air of dedicated austerity; but his faults were all venal. He was without envy, magnanimous not only to friends but to enemies. He believed in honesty and practised it. His loyalty was boundless and he possessed reverence for the English past, the English countryside and for the English culture; but his deepest reverence was for the anonymous men and women of history, caught and lost in time.

G. M. Trevelyan

George Macaulay Trevelyan is the heir of a great tradition. His great-uncle was Lord Macaulay who, with Gibbon, is the chief glory of English historical writing; his father, Sir George Otto Trevelyan, was also a historian of great distinction, a most important figure in the development of Anglo-American understanding; for his great work on the American Revolution did much to dispel ancient prejudice. With this inheritance it is not surprising that G. M. Trevelyan has a high sense of the duty of a historian. For him the writing of history, like the writing of poetry, is a part of English culture, a culture not limited to the few but available to all men so that it might deepen their understanding. History, then, for him, has a literary and moral purpose. His inheritance made this attitude clear enough to himself but it required an obstinate courage to maintain it, for the view was no longer fashionable amongst academic historians. They preferred to treat history as a science; to concentrate on evidence, techniques, statistics, and if the public found the results unreadable that did not matter, for history was a specialised study by professionals for professionals. In the face of such opposition Trevelyan had to define, and defend, his attitude, and this he did in his volumes of essays, *Clio: a Muse* (1913), and *An Autobiography and other Essays*

(1949). For anyone wishing to study the whole of Trevelyan's works, these books should come first and be followed by the *Memoir* of his father (1932), the book on Meredith (1912), the *Life of Grey of Fallodon* (1937), for these make clear his personal inheritance, the background of tradition which fed that rare poetic imagination, perhaps his greatest gift.

I

In his *Autobiography*, written in the evening of his life, he writes:

> More generally, I take delight in history, even its most prosaic details, because they become poetical as they recede into the past. The poetry of history lies in the quasi-miraculous fact that once, on this earth, once, on this familiar spot of ground, walked other men and women, as actual as we are today, thinking their own thoughts, swayed by their own passions, but now all gone, one generation vanishing after another, gone as utterly as we ourselves shall shortly be gone like ghosts at cock-crow.

He made the same moving affirmation when he became Regius Professor of Modern History at Cambridge in 1926:

> The appeal of history to us all is in the last analysis poetic. But the poetry of history does not consist of imagination roaming at large, but of imagination pursuing the fact and fastening upon it. That which compels the historian to 'scorn delights and live laborious days' is the ardour of his own curiosity to know what really happened long ago in that land of mystery which we call the past. To peer into that magic mirror and see fresh figures there every day is a burning desire that consumes and satisfies him all his life, that carries him each morning, eager as a lover, to the library and the muniment room. It haunts him like a passion of almost terrible potency, because it is poetic. The dead were and are not. Their place knows them no more and is ours today. Yet they were once as real as we, and we shall tomorrow be shadows like them.

There is one beautiful example of 'imagination pursuing the fact and fastening upon it' in his own early work, *Clio: a Muse*, which illustrates how much his poetic imagination, blended with such wide ranging human sympathy, is stirred by the visible memorials of a past time.

> The garden front of St John's, Oxford, is beautiful to everyone; but for the lover of history its outward charm is blent with the intimate feelings of his own mind, with images of the same College as it was during the great Civil War. Given over to the use of a Court where days of royalty were numbered, its walks and quadrangles were filled, as the end came near, with men and women learning to accept sorrow as their lot through life, the ambitious abandoning hope of power, the wealthy hardening themselves to embrace poverty, those who loved England prepared to sail for foreign shores, and lovers to be parted for ever.

There they strolled through the garden, as the hopeless evenings fell, listening, at the end of all, while the siege guns broke the silence with ominous
iteration. Behind the cannon on those low hills to northward were ranked the
inexorable men who came to lay their hands on all this beauty, hoping to
change it to strength and sterner virtue. . . . The sound of the Roundhead
cannon has long ago died away, but still the silence of the garden is heavy
with unalterable fate, brooding over besiegers and besieged. . . .

This has an incomparable beauty of tone: having read such words as
these, who could doubt that here was a great artist at work; at work in
a medium – the writing of history – in which scholars have been plentiful
and artists rare. But why did Trevelyan choose to use his gifts of imagination in history rather than in poetry? The answer to this question is
manifold, but one overwhelming reason cries aloud in the three
quotations given above; this is his preoccupation with Time. Many
artists – Wordsworth and Proust immediately spring to mind – have been
deeply moved, one might almost say that their art has been controlled, by
the sense of the loss involved in the nature of Time. But nowhere more
than in the study of history is the artist so acutely aware of the tragedy
of man caught inexorably in the temporal world of flesh. Each historical
fact is implicit with our doom: as the long story of man's achievement
is our one straw of hope. And this is made keener for a historian unable
to accept the fact of personal immortality, as he looks back over the
countless lives, as numberless as the sands of the sea, that go to make our
history. Those wide Border lands in which Trevelyan grew to manhood –
there were the lasting physical memorials of unknown men which
haunted him with their sense of destiny – the walls and forts of the
Romans, the villages of Saxon and of Dane, the ruined abbeys and pele-
towers, the battlefields with their forgotten dead: those to Trevelyan are
what the lakes and the woods and the trees were to Wordsworth – the
symbols of man's tragedy and hope.[1]

The circumstances of Trevelyan's life have done much to strengthen
this feeling for the passing of time, just as the social and cultural interests
of his family have had their say in directing his historical interests.
Trevelyan was born in 1876; his family background was both aristocratic and upper middle-class. His father's family could trace their
ancestry back through the centuries, from Northumberland to Somerset,
from Somerset to Cornwall, a long line of typical English gentry, never
of national distinction but playing their part in the local affairs of
their day. His grandfather, a successful Indian civil servant, married
Macaulay's sister who introduced the atmosphere of middle-class culture
with its piety and its liberal views on politics and society. Trevelyan's
father knew intimately the great figures of Victorian civilisation; at the
same time he was accepted as a member of aristocratic society.[2] His

marriage with Caroline Philips, the daughter of a Manchester merchant, free-trader, Unitarian, friend of Cobden and of Gladstone, strengthened the family ties both with liberalism and the middle class. And so Trevelyan grew up amidst all that was best in the late Victorian world of art and politics, imbibing its liberalism, its free-thinking and its culture to which his own nature was so responsive. The background to his life was the country houses of an earlier age, particularly Wallington, the great house in Northumberland, which his father inherited in 1886. Here, he was able to savour that stable, English country-life which had endured for centuries.

Time has not been kind to this early world of Trevelyan's. Of the great houses in which he lived as a boy, Welcombe, his mother's house near Stratford-on-Avon, is a British Railways hotel, and Wallington in Northumberland has been given to the National Trust, of which he himself has been an ardent supporter and a munificent benefactor. For the Trust has helped to preserve many of the great houses of England and much of the loveliness of the wilder countryside of cliff and fell which have meant so much to him. But far more has been lost, and now the pace has accelerated; in another generation the civilisation which Trevelyan knew as a young man will have passed and then his occasional works, his essays, memoirs and the biographies of his friends will not only help readers to understand his own works but also have great value as historical documents in their own right. Yet one cannot doubt that the passing of this world, of which he is intensely aware, has given a keener edge to his preoccupations with history, particularly with those aspects of nineteenth-century English history which are linked with his own and his parents' past.

Trevelyan's education was the same as any rich young man of his day: preparatory school in Berkshire, Harrow and then Trinity College, Cambridge; but of course with him it was more formative. His interest in history had developed very early, particularly in military history. At Harrow he was exceptionally fortunate in his history masters, Robert Somervell and George Townsend Warner. Somervell had a rare gift of teaching boys to write well and Townsend Warner was a scholar of distinction.[3] As a freshman at Cambridge he fell under the spell of Maitland, the great English medieval and legal historian, of Cunningham, who was founding the study of economic history, and of Lord Acton, the greatest Catholic historian of modern times, whose learning and wisdom were unrivalled. But he fell foul of Seeley, Acton's predecessor in the Regius Chair of History: Seeley was an ardent champion of scientific history and loved to denounce Macaulay and Carlyle; to one Trevelyan had his family loyalty and the other had illuminated his first year's work at Cambridge. Ever since he had been a devoted admirer of the superb imaginative quality of Carlyle's work, especially the *Cromwell* and the *French Revolution*.

Naturally, with his background, Trevelyan was drawn to the liberal intelligentsia and he became a friend of Bertrand Russell, Desmond MacCarthy and G. E. Moore. Many young men at the university reject the beliefs in which they were nurtured, but the circles in which Trevelyan mixed at Trinity helped to strengthen the liberal attitude to life which he had derived from his family. This attitude was essentially Protestant, infused as it was with a strong scepticism of all doctrinaire beliefs either in religion or politics. When Trevelyan came to start historical research it was natural that his interest should be aroused in a historical movement deeply concerned with the belief in individual freedom. His imagination was caught by the Lollards, by the Peasants' Revolt, by the first stirrings of national consciousness in England. It was this work which won for him the Fellowship at Trinity: it was published in 1899 with the title *England in the Age of Wycliffe*, and in the same year he issued with Powell a collection of documents which he had used as evidence, and which he thought deserved a wider currency.

England in the Age of Wycliffe achieved immediate success, and it has enjoyed a continuing popularity, having been reprinted fourteen times. It was an astonishing achievement for so young a man. Many of the views, especially on economic and legal matters, would now require modification; about the whole work there is a slight but definite archaic air, derived very probably from its militant anti-Romanism. It is well written — even as early as this Trevelyan's style was completely under his control, and what a marvellously flexible instrument it is! The narrative moves with exceptional speed; his descriptive passages evoke the dark and the light of Chaucer's England; the analysis of social causes and human motives is crisp and clear. The book has a pace and *élan* which will carry it on through many editions yet to come. Although there is a marked bias towards Lollardy, Trevelyan's historical judgement is never darkened by prejudice, and the facts, truly ascertained, are made to give their own evidence. Even more remarkable is the skill with which Trevelyan uses narrative and descriptive writing; so, too, is his capacity to reveal motive by description of events. In this way the reader is made aware of why these conflicts and battles took place without the tedium of detailed analysis. Remarkable, too, the certainty both of the writing and the convictions of the author. In his work there is the steady affirmation of a faith that would last a lifetime, whatever Time brought forth, for it was a faith begot by inheritance and by tradition, and it is made explicit in the closing words of the book:

In England we have slowly but surely won the right of the individual to form and express a private judgement on speculative questions. During the last three centuries the battle of liberty has been fought against the state or against public opinion. But before the changes effected by Henry VIII, the struggle was against a power more impervious to reason and less subject to change – the power of the medieval Church in all the prestige of a thousand years' prescriptive right over man's mind. The martyrs who bore the first brunt of that terrific combat may be lightly esteemed today by priestly censure. But those who still believe that liberty of thought has proved not a curse but a blessing to England and to the peoples that have sprung from her, will regard with thankfulness and pride the work which the speculations of Wycliffe set on foot and the valour of his devoted successors accomplished.

II

For his work on the age of Wycliffe, Trevelyan had been awarded a Fellowship at Trinity in 1898, and a straightforward career as a professional academic historian was open to him. He began to teach for his college: he started to lecture. He had accepted the offer of Methuen to write a textbook on Stuart history, as one of their series on the *History of England*. These were all easily recognised stages in the making of a don. Then suddenly he left Cambridge. The reason he gives in his *Autobiography* is that he knew that he wanted to write literary history and that 'I should do so in more spiritual freedom away from the critical atmosphere of Cambridge scholarship.' The artist in him had dominated, and instinctively bolted from an uncongenial world, although to the outsider it must have seemed a curiously wilful gesture for a young professional historian to desert the citadel of his profession. Of course, Trevelyan has been fully justified. His output has been far greater than the majority of his generation because he was able to avoid the time-consuming hack work of academic life – the endless supervisions and lectures and examinations. But more importantly he escaped from the withering atmosphere of hypercritical scholasticism which has grown stronger and more powerful in Cambridge during the twentieth century. The fine points of argumentative scholarship exercised with equal zest on the important and the trivial have had no fascination for Trevelyan, and he has an even stronger distaste for the shifting quicksand of historical abstraction. Again, the fields of history upon which Cambridge historians were concentrating – economic, diplomatic, constitutional – were fields which offered little attraction to Trevelyan. They lacked story; they lacked drama; they lacked the warmth of human life. Because of these things, the artist insisted on escape.[4]

Away from the inhibiting influence of Cambridge, Trevelyan produced a book of outstanding quality. His *England under the Stuarts* (1904) was far and away the most impressive volume in this series published by Methuen. When the others have been forgotten, it will still be read, for it may be generations before the most dramatic century in English history is so finely portrayed between the covers of a single book. The advance on his first book is obvious but remarkable. The nineteenth century had been profoundly interested in the struggle between Crown and Parliament, for they felt that the triumph of Parliament had made their own democratic world possible. Nor were the Victorians dismayed by the intensely biblical language of Puritan thought and action, for the middle classes of the nineteenth century were equally capable of testing political issues by religious principles and expressing themselves with equal force in Old Testament terms. Nevertheless, the old Whig attitude of seeing Charles and his cavaliers as dissolute despots and Cromwell and the Roundheads as apostles of liberty had mellowed by Trevelyan's day. It was fashionable to be more than scrupulously fair to opponents in debate, and in consequence, although Trevelyan is, in his final reckoning, on the side of the Roundheads, his sympathies do not at any point in his book inhibit his imaginative insight. In many ways it has remained the least biased summary of the seventeenth century, for the last twenty years has witnessed the development of a concealed apologia for the Stuarts under the cloak of a more exact scholarship. The same movement has sought to denigrate Cromwell as the prototype of a fascist dictator because of his grave failure to secure constitutional government and his resort to force – for neither of which is he spared by Trevelyan. These Tory historians – as dangerous as their Whig counterparts – should read and re-read Trevelyan's magnificent paragraphs on the execution of Charles I, which must be quoted in full, for they demonstrate one of his greatest virtues as a historian:

> If there was any chance that the establishment of a more democratic form of government could gradually win the support of the people at large, that chance was thrown away by the execution of the King. The deed was done against the wish of many even of the Independents and Republicans; it outraged beyond hope of reconciliation the two parties in the State who were strong in numbers and in conservative tradition, the Presbyterians and the Cavaliers; and it alienated the great mass of men who had no party at all. Thus the Republicans, at the outset of their career, made it impossible for themselves ever to appeal in free election to the people whom they had called to sovereignty. Their own fall, involving the fall of democracy and of religious toleration, became therefore necessary to the re-establishment of Parliamentary rule. The worship of birth, of pageantry, of title; the aristocratic claim to administrative power; the excessive influence of the large land-owner and of inherited wealth; the mean admiration of mean things, which became so powerful in English society after the Restoration – all these gained a fresh life and popularity by the deed that was meant to strike them dead for ever.
>
> It is much easier to show that the execution was a mistake than to show what else should have been done. Any other course, if considered in the light of the actual circumstances, seems open to the gravest objection. It is not

possible to say with certainty that if Charles's life had been spared Cromwell
could have succeeded in averting anarchy and the disruption of the empire
until opinion was again ripe for government by consent:

> 'This was that memorable hour
> Which first assured the forced power'

– that was the verdict on the King's execution privately passed by Cromwell's
secretary, Andrew Marvell, a man of the world if a poet ever was such, who
in the same poem wrote the lines we all still quote in praise of Charles's
conduct on the scaffold. The situation at the end of 1648 was this – that any
sort of government by consent had been rendered impossible for years to
come, mainly by the untrustworthy character of the King, and by the intolerant
action of Parliament after the victory won for it by the Army. Cromwell, in
the Heads of the Proposals, had advocated a real settlement by consent, only
to have it rejected by King, Parliament and Army alike. The situation had
thereby been rendered impossible, through no fault of his. But he was not the
man therefore to return to his private gardens and let the world go to ruin.
He took upon his massive shoulders the load of obloquy inherent in a situation
created chiefly by the faults of others. Those Herculean shoulders are broad
enough to bear also the blame for a deed pre-eminently his own, inscribed
like a gigantic note of interrogation across the page of English history.

This is a complete realisation of all that is important in an historical
incident of profound significance, beautifully and confidently expressed.
And the book abounds in similar passages.

Along with a deepening historical judgement, there was a growth in
craftsmanship. In his earlier book, Trevelyan had been most humanly
tempted to spend many pages on those aspects of his subject which
contained a deeply personal interest, but *England under the Stuarts*
witnesses a more rigorous personal discipline. Military and social history
are kept firmly, at times almost too firmly,[5] in their place and never
allowed to clog the narrative, which moves at a furious pace – surely
no textbook has ever before or since been written with such a gusto.
Although the general reading public gave the book an ardent reception,
the professional historians received it rather coldly. It was considered
only worthy of a short notice in the *English Historical Review* and the
space was largely devoted to a consideration of Sir Charles Oman's
preface – only ten lines being given to the book itself. The reviewer,
Professor C. Sandford Terry – whoever he may have been – thought the
chapter mottoes platitudinous and the success of the book questionable.[6]
So great had become the gulf between professional and literary history!
But Trevelyan had no cause to complain, for this book fully justified his
decision to break with academic life.

In the same year as the publication of *England under the Stuarts* there
took place what he has described as 'the most important and fortunate
event of my life' – his marriage to Janet Penrose, a daughter of Mrs

Humphry Ward, the novelist and social worker. Amongst the wedding presents was a collection of books on Italian history, including Garibaldi's *Memoirs* and Belluzzi's *Ritirata di Garibaldi nel 1849*.

Immediately the creative artist in Trevelyan saw that in the story of Garibaldi was a subject which exactly fitted his genius. It touched some of the deepest springs of his nature, and the work and study necessary for the undertaking could be woven into the fabric of his personal life, for his wife had a passion for things Italian perhaps even keener than her husband's. From a public point of view the choice could not have been more judicious, had it been made by a sophisticated journalist in search of a best-seller. The year in which Trevelyan wrote *Garibaldi's Defence of the Roman Republic* was 1906, and it was published in 1907. These were the years of the greatest liberal victory in English politics for a generation. The intellectual world responded to the optimism of the politicians. Here was the manifest triumph of that long nineteenth-century tradition of liberal humanism; the final defeat of obscurantism was at hand. It was one of those rare moments in history in which the atmosphere of life is lyrical and charged with hope, when man seems his own master, and his destiny secure. Trevelyan's personal life was completely in tune with the world at large. Newly married, the father of a son and heir,[7] an established success in his chosen career in which risks had been taken and justified – this for him, too, was a time of hope.

The Garibaldi story fitted these moods. The struggles, defeats and ultimate success of Italian liberalism in the nineteenth century had seemed to many Victorians a demonstration by Providence of the justice of their attitude to life, and of its capacity to save other nations from spiritual and political obscurantism. Again, it was heroic, and personally heroic. It did not seem to be the long culmination of an anonymous historical process but the dramatic act of individual men, and of those Garibaldi was the greatest. Hence a consideration of the story of his achievement did not appear to disturb historical truth. For Trevelyan personally it touched perhaps deeper springs – not only of his mind but of his heart, for within the Garibaldi story there was one of the world's greatest love stories – the passionate and tragic love of Anita.

As with many great historians, Trevelyan has a very strongly developed topographical sense. The very act of standing on the battlefield of Blenheim or on the heights of the Janiculum, where Garibaldi conducted his defence, released the springs of his historical imagination. It would be impossible for him to write well about any historical events of whose setting he was ignorant. It is necessary for him to walk over and to see, to experience with all of his senses, the locality of history. And this he had already done for Italy as he tells us in his *Autobiography*:

But eight years went by before I ever thought of writing on any Italian theme, although during those years my chief walking-grounds were the Tuscan and Umbrian hills, and the Alban and Sabine heights that look down on the Campagna of Rome. I kept the high ground as much as I could, with the help of ordnance maps and compass. I used to prolong my walks till late into the charmed Italian night, under those brilliant stars, known and named so long ago; at the right time of year I could walk after dark, mile after mile, to the continuous song of innumerable nightingales.

So that the topographical setting for his Garibaldi was, when he came to write it, as well known to him as the wide border lands of Northumberland. All was prepared – his love of nature, his personal romance, his beliefs and attitude to life – all were pointing to Italy and to Garibaldi, but it needed that chance wedding-present to release the springs of imagination.

I began one day to turn over their pages [he writes], and was suddenly enthralled by the story of the retreat from Rome to the Adriatic, over mountains which I had traversed in my solitary walks; the scene and spirit of that desperate venture, led by that unique man, flashed upon my mind's eye. Here was a subject made to my hand, if ever I could write 'literary history', this was the golden chance.

Just as he had been unconsciously prepared to write it, so the public had been unconsciously prepared to receive it.[8] It established Trevelyan, and rightly so, as the foremost historian of his generation. It is a wonderful book, and it is a miracle that all the detailed work and the writing could have been accomplished in twelve months, yet the pace with which it was done adds undoubtedly to its quality. Had the writing been prolonged it is unlikely that the note of intense lyricism could have been sustained, for in many ways it is the most poetic of Trevelyan's longer works, certainly the most completely so. Apart from the beauty of the writing, its greatest strength lies in the handling of the narrative. This dramatic and exciting story has enthralled, and will continue to enthral, generations of readers, yet never once is historical accuracy satisfied for the sake of literary effect. In his characters, too, Trevelyan was fortunate; both Garibaldi and Anita were simple, direct, lacking in psychological subtlety and complication; a man and a woman of epic quality. Their thought was action and their action thought. Their words expressed, and never attempted to conceal, their response to life. With them Trevelyan seems to have felt a kinship of spirit, and he was able to re-create not only the history of their deeds but also the warm human reality of their lives.

The reception of *Garibaldi's Defence of the Roman Republic* was so enthusiastic that it was impossible for Trevelyan to leave the rest of the story of the *Risorgimento* untold even if he ever wished to do so. *Garibaldi and the Thousand* was published in 1909 and, two years later, he completed the trilogy with *Garibaldi and the Making of Italy*. He had not, however, finished with Italy, for he spent the years of the 1914–18 war as the Commandant of the British Red Cross Ambulance Unit and worked with the Italian army on the Isonzo and Piava fronts from 1915 to the end of the war. He summarized his experiences of these years in *Scenes from Italy's War*, published in 1919, which proves one thing – if nothing else – that great as Trevelyan is as an historian he would have found it difficult to earn a living as a journalist. The book is fascinating to read because of its singular lack of merit: history-in-the-making failed to quicken his imagination. Finally, he wrote his last book on Italian history in 1922, *Manin and the Venetian Revolution of 1848* (published 1923); the result of many visits to Venice and of contacts with Venetian intellectuals during his war service. It gave him great pleasure to write but the public received it with less enthusiasm, and, I think, rightly so, for the intricacy of Venetian politics and society, twisted and encrusted with traditional and personal attitudes, and, moreover, a society as far gone in decay as it was developed in sophistication, was not a world for the great simplicities of Trevelyan's heart and mind.

But to return to the Garibaldi books, a theme which was peculiarly suited to his genius. They have weathered the years remarkably well, and they have achieved a permanent position in historical literature. In my estimation, they rank with the works of Prescott or Parkman – in fact with the world's best narrative histories. They have, of course, their weaknesses: the motivation of nationalism is largely unexplored, especially the economic and social causes; the Papacy and papal policy, the motives of Louis Napoleon and the French, are judged too harshly; the self-interest of British policy too consistently ignored. Yet it remains the best, and the least biased, account of the *Risorgimento* in any language, and acclaimed so by a generation of Italian scholars for whom the movement for Italian liberation was too recent and too *political* to allow such an objective attitude as Trevelyan maintained. In many ways, these three books are the highest achievement of Trevelyan: never again were his theme and his imagination so completely fused. But these works will remain as long as English literature is read, a contribution of outstanding worth to historical scholarship.

III

Trevelyan was now established as the foremost literary historian of his time, and naturally as soon as the war was over he was eager to return to his study; but it was less easy to find a theme which matched his gifts so absolutely as the Italian books. Like many writers of great natural creative power he was always very wary of themes which failed to touch the deepest springs of his own experience. Through his mother's family he was connected with the great movement for free trade, associated with Manchester, of the mid-nineteenth century, and before the 1914–18 war he had written a *Life of John Bright* (1913). It was not favourably received, and nowadays it comes in for little notice and less reading. The weaknesses are obvious and Trevelyan himself is very conscious of them; he did less than justice to the opponents of Bright, and the complexity of the political difficulties which faced Peel are simplified to his disadvantage. Yet the book has a very real and positive value which far outweighs these shortcomings. His grandfather had been a friend of Cobden and Bright, and he had acquired from him and his mother an understanding of the rugged moral power of the great nineteenth-century liberals. In the recreation of the past it is essential for the historian to recapture the conscious aspirations of men, and to do full justice to their ideals as well as lay bare whatever unconscious grasp they may have had of the purpose and destiny of the social class to which they happened to belong. And this Trevelyan achieves. It should never be ignored by anyone wishing to understand the power and force of the Manchester School.

His next choice was less happy: *Lord Grey of the Reform Bill* (1920).

> The theme of glorious summer (in this case the summer of Reform) coming after a long winter of discontent and repression, is, as I have said, congenial to my artistic sense. And then the background of Grey's life was my own – Northumberland.

But here his local, political and personal loyalties, his instinctively Whig attitude to life and history, got in his way; made him visualise too clearly and too simply issues which were dark and involved. The intricate interplay of social dynamics and political activity of which, at times, politicians are the ignorant marionettes is not a field for the exercise of his talents. He was too consciously aware of the final achievement of Victorian constitutional development to appreciate fully the desperate insecurity and the sharp revolutionary edge of these years; and it prevented him from seeing the Reform Bill for what it was, a rapid and instinctively cunning readjustment to new conditions by those self-same social classes which had dominated eighteenth-century politics, and were to dominate English political life until the introduction of the ballot box. The real difficulty lay in this – that neither personalities nor the detailed narrative story were the crux of the historical situation – its reality lay outside formal politics and within the strained structure of society. Because of this *Lord Grey of the Reform Bill* has become outmoded: a fate which has not overtaken many other of Trevelyan's books.

The early 1920s must have been a difficult period for Trevelyan. His last three books, judged by the high standard of success of his Garibaldi trilogy, or even of *England under the Stuarts*, had been failures. No theme had captured his imagination in the same way. Much of his creative energy was being absorbed in public work – he was a member of the Royal Commission on Oxford and Cambridge, and a strenuously active supporter of the National Trust. The writing of the *Bright* before the Great War and the *Grey* after it had entailed a great deal of work and thought on the whole range of nineteenth-century history which, no doubt, like all good artists, Trevelyan thought that it was a pity to waste. Whatever the reason may have been, *British History in the Nineteenth Century* appeared in 1922. It was avowedly a textbook – in many ways far more of a textbook than *England under the Stuarts* – but its success was great. A well-balanced, well-constructed, comprehensive book, even in texture, beautifully written, it became the staff of life for generations of adolescent historians, bent on examination success. For the general reader as well as for the student it remains the best introduction to nineteenth-century British history, weak though it certainly is on the economic side, to which very little space is devoted. Yet the importance of the book lay not entirely in itself but rather for the idea it gave to both Trevelyan and his publishers. Its success showed that it filled a real need; there was a greater: no comprehensive, single volume *History of England* of any merit had been published for over fifty years, since J. R. Green had written his *History of the English People* (1874).

This venture entailed an immense amount of work, intensive reading in fields with which he had little acquaintance and the book took three years to write. Trevelyan's own comment in his *Autobiography* on this really great achievement is almost absurdly modest:

> In April 1926 my *History of England* came out. It has been, as regards sales, the most successful of my books, except the *Social History*, because it treated so necessary a subject as the history of England at the length, and to some extent in the manner, which suited a large public, including schools and Univerisites. Some day, very soon perhaps, it will be replaced, but it will have served its generation.

Not only has it served its generation, there is no doubt that it will outlast it, and many more, taking its place by the side of J. R. Green's masterpiece. Let us admit its faults at once. Too little space was devoted to the development of industry, trade and finance; it has – although one might almost say 'Thank God!' – a bias: it is frankly liberal and protestant; the archaeologists might grumble a little at the brevity of its prehistory; specialists can no doubt attack it on point of detail. Yet what a massive achievement remains! Within 700 pages the story of the

English people is told with an unmatched verve; rarely has narrative been so brilliantly sustained. Its judgements on men and affairs glitter with wisdom. Once more the deepest springs of his creative imagination had been released by the story of the race to which he belonged and of the countryside which he has so deeply loved, and in which, and this is important, he had faith. For this book could only have been written by a liberal and a humanist. Conscious though he is of the disastrous weakness of men confronted by the problem of their own destiny yet he has never been without hope.[9] This enabled him to give full and true value to the positive contributions of Englishmen to civilisation and to do full justice to the aspirational side of their endeavours. His book glows with human warmth, and some of the best chapters are those in which he re-creates the world of ordinary men and women, the medieval peasants, the Tudor yeomen, the Hanoverian squires, the working men of Victorian England, all nameless now and forgotten.

But the *History of England* had a social as well as an intrinsic worth. Millions of Englishmen have derived from his book the little history that they will ever know.[10] Hence the importance of Trevelyan's attitude and beliefs.

> In answer to the instincts and temperament of her people [he writes in his Introduction to the book], she evolved in the course of centuries a system which reconciled three things that other nations have often found incompatible – executive efficiency, popular control and personal freedom.

It is his stress on these qualities, as well as on the material and spiritual contribution of Englishmen, that has given the book such enduring worth. He has laid bare the common grounds of tradition, possessed by rich and poor alike, and fortified their belief in their way of life, now so desperately challenged. And it is well that this should be liberal and humanist, stressing the genius of our race for compromise, for tolerance, for social justice, and freedom of the spirit. Yet he does not gloss the lapses; the brutality of our Irish policy is not ignored, nor the human suffering entailed in the Industrial Revolution left undescribed. This wise, just book would by itself have secured Trevelyan's place in the great tradition of English historical writing.

IV

After the publication of the *History of England*, the circumstances of Trevelyan's life once more changed course. In 1928, his parents died; he inherited Hallington Hall in Northumberland from a distant relative; and Stanley Baldwin offered him the Regius Professorship of Modern History at Cambridge, which he accepted. Many honours quickly followed, but none gave him greater pleasure than the conferment of

the Order of Merit in 1930, a distinction which his father had held
before him. The return of Trevelyan to academic life did not mean,
however, a return to the academic chores from which he had escaped a
quarter of a century before, for the duties of administration and lecturing
of a professor are not onerous and rightly allow plenty of time for
creative work, and, although there was still a powerful atmosphere of
destructive criticism abroad in Cambridge his confidence in his own
abilities was now unassailable. And the third phase of Trevelyan's
historical writing begins – his great three-volume book on *The Reign of
Queen Anne*. But before dealing with this major contribution to English
historical studies, there are three other books of this period which are
too frequently neglected. He published a charming *Memoir* of his father,
Sir George Otto Trevelyan, in 1930, which in many ways is a document
of great worth for the social and cultural history of late nineteenth-
century England, and invaluable for understanding the compulsion in
Trevelyan's own nature which made him a historian. In the same *genre*
was his *Life of Lord Grey of Fallodon* (1937), a labour of love for his
distinguished Northumbrian neighbour, and this book is pervaded with
nostalgia for the way of life which Grey represented and which Trevelyan
knew to be passing. In both of these works one is made keenly aware
of Trevelyan's preoccupation with the poetry of Time and of Nature.
Then, in 1934, there was a masterpiece in miniature, *The English Revolution, 1688–89*, published in the Home University Library. The social
analysis of politics has never been Trevelyan's *forte* but in this book his
descriptions of the social forces which brought about the Revolution are
profoundly stimulating, and his realistic intuitions have been fully justified by subsequent research.

The motivation for writing the chief historical work of his life, *England
under Queen Anne*, is best described in his own words:

> The idea of taking up the tale where my great-uncle's history [i.e. Lord
> Macaulay's *History of England*] had broken off, was perhaps a fancy at the
> back of my consciousness. But I was more seriously attracted by the dramatic
> unity and separateness of the period from 1702–14, lying between the Stuart
> and Hanoverian eras with a special ethos of its own; the interplay and mutual
> dependence of foreign and domestic, religious and political, English and
> Scottish, civil and military affairs; the economic background and the social
> scene and their political outcome; the series of dramatic changes of issue,
> like a five-act drama, leading up to a climax of trumpets proclaiming King
> George. . . . In Anne's reign, it seemed to me, Britain attained by sea and land
> to her modern place in the world, having settled her free constitution and
> composed by compromise and toleration the feuds that had torn her in Stuart
> times.

It was planned, therefore, on the most considerable scale and intended to be his greatest contribution to the study of English history. But what of the achievement? Personally, I feel that in the choice of subject Trevelyan's intuition for once failed him. The Reign of Anne, unlike the Italy of Garibaldi or England of the Stuarts, was not an heroic age, and even Marlborough, who most nearly approximates to the hero, has none of the hero's simplicity and emotional force, that direct response in action to emotional need, which marks a Garibaldi or a Cromwell. The other chief characters in this part of our history – Harley, Bolingbroke, Godolphin – were men of exceptional psychological complexity, tortuous in thought, feeling and deed, whose words often bore little relation to intention, and intention none to avowed aspiration. Backstairs politics, the worldliness and cynicism of men seeking power at all costs, twisting and debauching institutions to get it, is not a world in which Trevelyan moves with instinctive ease. Furthermore, his traditional outlook on English politics distorted his vision of the Augustan age. He is a firm believer in the historical continuity of the two-party English political system.[11] In the reign of Anne, party politicians, it is true, used party clichés, exploited for their own purposes social animosities which lie concealed under party names, and they were prepared to enforce legislation of a party nature; but this is only the surface story, concealing the real drive for power and for the fruits of office. In this struggle, family and territorial connections were always, in the last resort, as strong as a party. The failure of the Whigs to obtain any clear-cut and detailed definition of the Constitution in 1689 led to the disintegration of politics, making the growth of oligarchy easy, desirable and certain. The system of Walpole was based on the system of Harley, sometimes using the same men and their connexions, which had been fostered by the 'Tories', but which were easily adaptable to 'Whig' purposes. The straightforward conception of a two-party system does not forward the analysis of this intricate and involved period of our political history; such analysis must come from the detailed study of factions and connexions, as yet largely undescribed. Nor was the unity of the period so actual as Trevelyan would have us believe; in all aspects of English history – social, economic, political, religious, constitutional and diplomatic – the play had got well and truly into its second act by 1702. In consequence, the structure of these books is to some extent artificial, and the construction does not arise so naturally from the historical situation as it does in the Garibaldi trilogy.

But it is, of course, a work of tremendous quality; the opening chapters which draw a picture of England at the opening of the eighteenth century are outstanding for their imaginative insight, and for the warm spirit that breathes through them. Actual and vivid, they compel belief even though he lays major stress on the ease, virtue and sweetness of life of the possessing classes and glosses somewhat the brutality and suffering which were the lot of the common man. Apart from the social background the best part of the work is that which deals with the naval and military history; certainly, too, by far the best character study is of Marlborough whom Macaulay had detested and to whom Trevelyan, conscious of a major family blunder, was determined to do full justice. Full justice is, indeed, done both to his capacity as a general and to the persistence of his will in diplomacy. As in all of Trevelyan's work the narrative is treated very cunningly: the pace of the book is intense, especially in *Blenheim* (1931), the first of the three, for the battle gives a natural and dramatic climax to the book. In his second two parts, *Ramillies and the Union with Scotland* (1932) and *Peace and the Protestant Succession* (1934), there is no such natural climax, and inevitably the story is more broken up, with a consequent loss of intensity. Stylistically, these are the most beautiful of Trevelyan's books. In his earlier works there are strong traces, especially in the descriptive passages, of Ruskin and Carlyle, which to our modern taste impart a sense of straining after effect. It is possible that the writing of the *History of England*, in which every word had to count, helped to simplify his style without weakening his gift for a memorable phrase. Whatever may have been the cause, words in these books are used with absolute mastery; passage after passage stir the heart and mind with their elegant clarity and evocative beauty. *England under Queen Anne* is a great work and a great achievement, but one cannot help regretting that, in the fullness of his powers, he had not been drawn to a subject more apt to his genius.

The Mastership of Trinity College, Cambridge, is a Crown appointment, and it must have given Winston Churchill great pleasure to confer it on Trevelyan, when the vacancy was created by the death of J. J. Thomson in 1940, for they were contemporaries at school and, in a sense, rival historians, for Churchill's *Life of Marlborough* had been published about the same time as *England under Queen Anne*. This last and greatest distinction of his academic life has, as he has written, 'made my life as happy as anyone's can be during the fall of European civilisation'. The depth of his feeling for his College, great in men and history, and for the beauty of the stone and buildings in which it lives its corporate life, may be seen in the pages of the little book, *Trinity College*, which he published in 1943. It will continue to give pleasure to generations, not only of Trinity men, but to all whom Cambridge has enriched.

But the most outstanding success was yet to come. Before the war Trevelyan had been working on a social history of England, as a companion volume to his *History of England* which had been mainly concerned with politics and war. In 1940, he decided to drop the early part of the work and begin with Chaucer.[12] From that point onwards the book was already written, but owing to war shortages it was not published until 1944 in this country, when it appeared under the title of *English Social History: a Survey of Six Centuries*. By 1949, it had sold 392,000 copies and has by now far exceeded this large total. This book must have reached thousands who do not normally read history. I was told by a friend who did his military service in the Suez Canal Zone that he saw it being read by soldiers who had left school at fourteen and who had probably never held a stiff-covered book in their hands since the day they had left. And my friend tells me that they lay in their bunks for hours, reading with all the keen and eager enjoyment which they might have derived from an adventure story. In many homes it must be the one and only history book. This work is not only a social history but a social phenomenon.

Once more, as with the Garibaldi books, Trevelyan was exceptionally fortunate in the moment of his publication – 1944. The war, which we were bringing to a successful end, had jeopardised the traditional pattern of English life, and in some ways destroyed it for ever. This created amongst all classes a deep nostalgia for the ways of life which we were losing. Then, again, the war had made conscious to millions that our national attitude to life was historically based, the result of centuries of slow growth, and that it was for the old, tried ways of life for which we were fighting. Winston Churchill in his great war speeches made us all conscious of our past, as never before. And in this war, too, there were far more highly educated men and women in all ranks of all of the services. The 1920s and 1930s of this century had witnessed a great extension of secondary school education, producing a vast public capable of reading and enjoying a book of profound historical imagination, once the dilemma of their time stirred them to do so. Trevelyan's book was a beautifully timed response to the need which so many were unconsciously feeling and its nature widened its appeal, for it was the story of how the ordinary men and women of England had lived out their lives, enduring their times as best they might, and it was read by just ordinary men and women who were enduring times as hard as the English people had ever faced, and perhaps with far less hope for their future; in such tribulation it was natural to read with avid longing of ages more gracious and more secure, and to draw strength from our chequered past.

Intrinsically the book deserved its fame, its glory, its continued and continuing success. Throughout his life the poet in Trevelyan had been drawn to a contemplation of the ordinary nameless man, caught up inexorably in Time. In volume after volume which he published on

English history there were chapters which evoke the past life and lost countryside of our island. It is usually in these chapters that his writing acquires its most lyrical note. The subject, therefore, of the *Social History* touched the deepest springs of his temperament and was one which he had long contemplated. By and large, during the centuries about which Trevelyan wrote, the great contributions to our civilisation were made by the aristocrats and squires and yeomen, by merchants and craftsmen, by owners of wealth, great or small; in fact by those classes with which he was instinctively familiar, and from which he derived his own ancestry. Their world is dead, their opportunity past, and it is as well that their elegy should be pronounced by one who loved their ways of life so well, and by one who could respond to their apsirations and to the beauty of the material civilisation which they created, and who could accept, if uneasily, the poverty and suffering upon which it was, of necessity, based. This attitude gives a sunset glow to the whole work, softening the edges, obscuring some of the harshness, bitterness and conflict which have, at times, distracted our country, but in the main fulfilling the great purpose which he set himself:

> Each one, gentle and simple, in his commonest goings and comings, was ruled by a complicated and ever-shifting fabric of custom and law, society and politics, events at home and abroad, some of them little known by him and less understood. Our effort is not only to get what glimpses we can of his intimate personality, but to reconstruct the whole fabric of each passing age, and see how it affected him; to get to know more in some respects than the dweller in the past himself knew about the conditions that enveloped and controlled his life.
>
> There is nothing that more divides civilised from semi-savage man than to be conscious of our forefathers as they really were, and bit by bit to reconstruct the mosaic of the long-forgotten past. To weigh the stars, or to make ships sail in the air or below the sea, is not a more astonishing and ennobling performance on the part of the human race in these latter days, than to know the course of events that had been long forgotten, and the true nature of men and women who were here before us.

Few books have responded so nobly to the demands of their age.

V

Such are the many triumphs and the few failures of Trevelyan's contribution to English historical literature, and it remains to access his achievement. What perhaps is most frequently forgotten, or ignored, is the skill of his literary craftsmanship. Trevelyan is a born writer, and a natural story-teller; and this, amongst historians, is a rare gift; only Prescott, amongst the great historians, has this facility in equal or greater measure. In consequence, those episodes of history which were full of dramatic action, with a firm beginning and obvious end, have brought forth some of his best writing – the *Garibaldi* books, *England under the Stuarts*, much of the *History of England*, and perhaps *Blenheim*. As a stylist he cannot be compared with Gibbon, Macaulay or even Clarendon, and amongst his own generation he would have to concede the first place to R. H. Tawney, but he has written passages of greater lyrical beauty than any of them, when the heart of the poet has been stirred. A poet at large in history is a unique phenomenon of our literature and will create for Trevelyan a special place in the history of English letters. Certainly, I think, it will secure a permanent niche for *Garibaldi's Defence of the Roman Republic*, which, were it fiction, would live as one of the greatest love-stories, told with exquisite feeling and poetic power. The same poetic temperament has been responsible for some of the best evocations of times past that have been written in our language. They are scattered throughout his works but brought together and continuously sustained in the pages of the *Social History*. If one quality is to be singled out, it should be this, for, of all historians, he is the poet of English history.

His work has one other great and enduring merit – the tradition within which it was written. The Victorian liberals and their Edwardian successors have made one of the greatest contributions to science and to culture ever made by a ruling class. To these by birth and by instinct Trevelyan belonged. Therefore, as time passes, his work will acquire fresh significance and become the material of history itself, for these books of his will show how these liberal humanists considered their past, from whence they derived their tradition, by what they would like themselves judged. And because he has written from such a standpoint, he has helped to inculcate into the hearts of men and women, born in more desperate times, a regard for human justice and personal freedom.

A Final Word on Trevelyan

In 1981 Trevelyan's daughter wrote a memoir of her father, not good but not wholly bad, and a useful peg for me to reconsider him some twenty years after his death. And naturally my mind also turned to Namier, that other colossus of my youth. He, too, had been dead for twenty years, his 'school' long dispersed either by death or obscurity, only John Brooke showing any real stamina to keep going along the old paths and write and edit books of some significance. So probably it was my last opportunity to take stock of both of them. No British historians of my generation had matched either of them in reputation. Now Namier's books are not much read, except by specialists, and it is sad that a man so near to genius failed to maximise his immense talents. Trevelyan is still read, still in print, still enjoyed, and he can still enrich the informed, as well as the uninformed. Many of his gifts were inferior to Namier's but he maximised every bit of talent which he possessed. Namier had too many selves to be true to; Trevelyan only one. His life was integrated not fissured. There were times when I thought that Trevelyan ought to have been a poet, a sadder modern Wordsworth, but only recently has it occurred to me that Namier's demons could only have found a true creative outlet in the novel. Probably his superb critical intelligence would always have inhibited him, but what a novel might be written about his life, all darkness and light, an amalgam of sin, guilt and terror, a situation ripe for a Dostoievsky. Trevelyan's life was always so much duller than his books; only, I think, Jane Austen could have dealt with so narrow a compass, so guarded a heart.

The True Voice of Clio

G. M. Trevelyan left instructions in his will that no biography of him should be written. This was a response to a deep strain of stoical melancholy that threaded his nature but it was not a very realistic gesture – his life will be written not once but many times. His daughter has sidestepped the issue by calling her book a memoir although she deals, briefly it is true, with parts of Trevelyan's life about which she can have no memories – his days at Harrow, his time at Trinity as an undergraduate and fellow.

Both as a life and as a memoir it is a curiously unbalanced book, for the core of it deals with Trevelyan's service in Italy during the First World War – the material for this period of his life is quite rich as he was then a most active correspondent and his letters have been preserved. However the period subsequent to the First World War – the years of Trevelyan's fame as Britain's leading historian – is dealt with very peremptorily; presumably because the material is less rich. Trevelyan did what he could to make a biographer's life difficult by destroying most of his own records.

Nevertheless I am sure a great deal remains, some of it buried in the archives of the History Faculty in Cambridge and the archives at Trinity and at the National Trust. It is a pity that no oral history project was based on him whilst the fellows of Trinity who knew him as a young man were still alive. But when the time comes there will be enough. And much, of course, is revealed in Trevelyan's own works.

The biographer will, however, turn to this memoir. It is an act of piety and the most attractive sides of Trevelyan's personality (and they were many) are shown to advantage – his deep concern for his country and his friends; his passionate loyalty; his unstinting work for the countryside; the love that he had for literature and history; his utter dedication to his talent.

During my lifetime as an historian I have only met two colleagues who impressed me as very great men – Trevelyan and Namier; as the years have passed, Trevelyan's greatness endures, Namier's diminishes. Namier had a towering personality, a capacity for concentration denied to the majority of even very clever men, a sharp analytical mind of great dialectical skill but he was – and this has become increasingly apparent as the years have passed – lacking in a sense of human realism.

Such a criticism would have hurt him deeply as he took pride in what he thought to be his knowledge of character, cutting through the humbug and laying bare the corruption and weaknesses of men in pursuit of power. The pursuit of power, the pursuit of place and profit, these subjects brought that harsh, almost sadistic, gleam to his eye: but he was too clever to be satisfied with a shallow cynicism, he was aware of the ways men could console themselves from being either failures or merely losers. The victors and the defeated had need of ideas to clothe their nakedness but he could hardly allow that men might pursue ideas for their intrinsic value. Hence Namier was at his best with characters such as the Duke of Newcastle or Lord North: at his worst with complex intellectuals such as Edmund Burke and totally baffled by a John Wilkes whom he could only see as a licentious exhibitionist. Namier could never have been moved by the thought of Garibaldi and the Thousand. Thus he could never grasp or give proper weight to the public politics of the 1760s or to the divisive effects on Britain of America's fight for independence. And he had a very grave weakness as an historian, he never wrote a book. He lacked the capacity to construct a narrative; all of his work consisted – like J. H. Round whom he much resembled – of analytical essays. Nor was he gifted as a stylist. He was capable of an epigram: a terse and telling sentence but paragraphs and chapters were beyond him – he quoted too much; he flogged his concepts not only nearly to death but almost to eternity. Yet through Namier's immense and unflagging industry, we know more about day-to-day actions in the House of Commons in the 1760s than anyone before his day would have thought it possible to know. And yet there were immense limitations to Namier's work judged as research activity.

Trevelyan was not very interested in Namier's type of work. He well realised its value. He was prepared, cautiously, to use its results. Trevelyan wanted to do two things in writing history: to tell for his time the story of great events and to reach through these events to human character – its heroism, its endurance, its follies and its weaknesses. He was searching like a poet for human truth in time and attempting to make us feel it. That is why he thought that history must always be a part of literature. The historian had to have empathy, a writer's empathy, as well as a scientist's love of fact.

Like most richly creative men, Trevelyan wrote very fast. The *History of England* took him only just over two years. His output over a long and busy life (although interrupted for five years by the war during his most creative period) was very large, as indeed was Macaulay's or Gibbon's before him. Creative men usually write a lot not a little. And it is with Macaulay and Gibbon that he has to be compared. He could write with greater poetic beauty than either of them yet never with so sharp or so confident an intelligence as they. Indeed Trevelyan wrote the most beautiful historical prose of any British historian: but there is a lack of intellectual bite.

He is now probably at the nadir of his reputation – some of his books, although far from all, have gone out of print although the major works are still available, still bought and still read. His revival will come when he is seen more strongly in the context of his age and then, I suspect, he will loom over the twentieth century as Macaulay looms over the early nineteenth. He has, alas, few rivals. History, even before Trevelyan's day, was beginning to draw more and more men and women of high intelligence and little creativity. They were concerned with problems or with fact collection, the former often insoluble, the latter unreadable. At the same time the social function of history steadily weakened during this century. as history grew more academically professional, it became more socially useless and ineffective – at least in intellectual circles and in education – though not with the public at large. They still want history as literature; and still see it as Trevelyan did as one of the great creative activities of man. That is why they buy Clarendon, Gibbon, Macaulay and will buy Trevelyan. Trevelyan's was a far lonelier voice than it need have been but it was the one true voice of Clio.

Not, I think, that Trevelyan's greatness lay totally in his work – it lay also in his personal qualities. Absolute integrity and total honesty – personality, beliefs and creative statement – combined to make him one of the greatest men I have ever met. That man is brought vividly alive in Mrs Moorman's highly personal memoir.

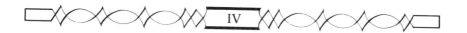

The Good, the Bad, the Indifferent

Robert Nisbet Again

Of course, I was not the only professional to be concerned with the necessity of trying to give some sort of meaning to the course of human history. The success of Toynbee to a world-wide audience, the continuing sale of H. G. Wells' *Outline of History*, and constant references to Spengler showed that his ghost was still haunting the minds of some intellectuals. In Toynbee and in Wells there was much to admire. I was able to express my opinion of Toynbee and Spengler, and for once my opinion did little harm, may be even a little good for myself. And I was alert to all attempts to make sense of the past over the millennia.

Most Cambridge historians disdained such efforts: particularly Maurice Cowling, the neo-conservative pundit, whose temperament, so very much more agreeable than his intellect, is wayward, comic, wry, and unpredictable. His capacity to understand what he reads, however, seems as capricious as the man himself. He has always quaintly lumped me with the advanced Left – Christopher Hill, E. P. Thompson or Eric Hobsbawm. Naturally he failed to notice my admiration for Robert Nisbet who has so often attempted to cover the centuries with a wise and critical, yet conservative, eye. The need to explain human history has always appeared as simplistic to Cowling, as well as impossible: as impossible as a theologian attempting to explain the mind of God and His intentions, and also politically dangerous, smacking of Marxism. It is a view that in some conservative circles has become popular, but it is profoundly dangerous, for what is neglected will be cultivated by others. Fortunately these quirky views of the Cowling school of history are highly parochial and so limited to a narrow Cambridge cult which carries little or no weight in America or in Europe. Hence the name Robert Nisbet is virtually unknown in Cambridge although he is one of the subtlest and most profound of conservative scholars contemplating *la longue durée,* to use Fernand Braudel's splendid phrase for the seismic aspects of the human story, a phrase which not surprisingly renders Cowling choleric. Nisbet published in 1969 a brave attempt in his book *Aspects of the Western Theory of Development* to survey social change from the Greek historians to contemporary sociologists. It was an exceptionally stimulating and original book, one that ran counter to most of his colleagues' preoccupations. My review may have been of some value to him in America where such surveys were not despised, but in Britain few took any notice either of his book or my review.

Robert Nisbet, Aspects of the Western Theory of Development

To cover two and a half millennia in 300 pages takes a brave man. Historians of ideas who used to range with such confidence over the history of natural law, social contract, liberty, despotism, freedom and democracy, leaping from century to century, have taken to their cabbage patches, often indeed to their own carefully nurtured cabbage, even at times restricting their gaze to one leaf and its myriad veins or to the strange curlicues of its outline. Nowadays to study the whole of Aristotle, to cover all of Rousseau's works, to devote oneself to a life of Marx is almost brash: to cover a larger period still – the Renaissance or the Enlightenment – is to offer oneself like St Sebastian as a target for a hail of scholarly arrows, mostly poisoned.

What then of Robert A. Nisbet, who discusses the Greeks, St Augustine, the Christian epic, the Enlightenment, social evolution, the comparative method en route for Spengler, Toynbee, Niebuhr, Chardin, Talcott Parsons, Neil Smelser *et al.*, and, as if that is not enough, spends a few pages on Marx, Engels and the twists and turns of their theories in the hands of their Russian commentators. In 300 pages he covers two and a half millennia! A brave, brave man, Mr Nisbet, and he must be already wincing with anticipated pain. At least from me he will get a bouquet, and without many thorns.

This is a tough book for the general reader; the historian and social scientist will find it exciting and stimulating. Everyone, however, will need to read it with close attention; no skipping, for the argument is closely knit. But it is worth every hour spent on it and it would be a great pity if this fine book were to find its way only to the shelves of sociologists, anthropologists and historians. It possesses a great deal of illumination for all who brood about the way destiny has haunted men's thoughts.

In simplicity or in sophistication man tends to think in metaphors, intuitively drawn from his social and personal experience. One of the most profound and enduring of these metaphors is the concept of growth. The life cycle which man observes around him he applies not only to his own institutions, but also to human societies and to civilisations. The very nature of things leads through birth, adolescence, maturity, old age to death. This interpretation of man's history and destiny has underlain all interpretations from Aristotle to Toynbee. The same concept of growth underlies both the Christian epic and the linear concepts of progress developed in the eighteenth century.

Development that is purposeful, destined and necessary, underlies all the social thinking of the nineteenth century, whether it be of Darwin, Herbert Spencer or Karl Marx. The social scientists of today attempt to impose similar concepts of growth in relation to social change. So Mr Nisbet sees this metaphor of growth as one of the most fundamental concepts in European thought from the days of Hesiod to modern sociologists. The danger of Nisbet's method is that in less scholarly and sensitive hands it might lead to banality. He is aware that societies have twisted the basic metaphor to suit their needs, and he approaches a distinction which should be made, but which he never quite makes — the difference between a 'past' and history itself.

All societies manufacture pasts for a variety of social needs, and they vary from the simple to the complex. Indeed Nisbet's book would have been far richer, and much longer, had he indicated more clearly the relationship between the various stages of growth theory and the societies that produced them. He does this admirably with the comparative theory of social evolution in the nineteenth century, and the book quickens into ever more vigorous life at that point.

Curiously enough, I wish Nisbet would have ranged a little further. He would have found variations on his metaphor of growth and decay long before the Greeks, in ancient Egypt. China, both classical and imperial, India in Vedic or Buddhist days could have provided him with more. Indeed, there is one aspect of his theme that he never explores — the metaphor of growth and decay as a social anodyne. All things grow, wither and die. Ancient Egyptian poets, Old Testament prophets and Chinese Mandarins contemplated the ruins of ancient times, saw that noble and commoner were united in death by total loss. Hence they sang of the vanity of human wishes, advised the gathering of rosebuds before they withered, a philosophy which soothed the sensitive, calmed the unsuccessful intellectuals, and eased all those, who had failed or not competed in the harsh jungles of political life. The metaphor of growth contains immense nostalgia for living things and their fate as well as a sense of purposeful development. It pervades literature, painting, music as well as political and social theory. Nor is this in any way surprising:

we have been living for the last 8½ thousand years in a dominantly agrarian society; varying in complexity and overlaid at different depths with craft, commerce and industry.

It is, therefore, to be expected that there should be resonances, echoes, common chords and even similar symphonic themes in the ideas that men have developed about their destiny. Nor is it surprising that the most fundamental should be the metaphor of growth and decay which, to stress a banality, is his own experience of life.

The end of this metaphor may be nearer than Nisbet thinks, for, as we begin to move into a full scientific and technological world, a process that historically speaking has only just begun, it is possible that man's concepts of his destiny will change fundamentally and that old metaphors will die, just as there are signs that the power of socially manufactured pasts with their sanctions for morality and institutions are also dying.

These profound questions loom like spectres over Mr Nisbet's book, which is as stimulating as it is satisfying. His arguments are convincing and his conclusions wholly admirable. This is a fine book for the intelligent layman as well as the professional.

Arnold Toynbee

That the intellectual climate in America was more favourable to broad surveys was clear long before Nisbet wrote – Arnold Toynbee had become immensely popular, selling large quantities of his interminable volumes and lurching from campus to campus lecturing for succulent fees with the air of an obsessed prophet. In Britain he was the subject of savage scholarly attacks, some written with sparkling wit and elegance, like Hugh Trevor Roper's rightly famous essay; others just clobbered him for his clumsy capacity for factual error or poured withering scorn on the blithe way he could dismiss or forget whole epochs of human existence which might prove difficult for his theories. He was easy to demolish but more difficult to explain away, and quite impossible to write off. Whether one likes it or not he became an intellectual force in the post-war world, given (unlike in Britain) great critical and academic welcome not only in America but also in West Germany. There was something heroic, they felt, in his attempts to make some sense of the huge panorama of human history. And there were thousands of his readers who thought that he had discovered the answer to Marxism. However, Toynbee's fame was truly meteoric: it collapsed as quickly, more quickly, than it rose. The reputation of the sage of the fifties and sixties burnt out in the seventies. He has become a name, a label, like Spengler. Criticism triumphed: faith lost.

Toynbee: Prophet rather than historian

There is in the western world no historian whose name is more widely known than Arnold Toynbee's, yet there is scarcely one professional historian in Europe or America who would accept either Toynbee's theories or his scholarship without considerable reserve. For many, including myself, his huge *A Study of History*, which is supposed to demonstrate the immutable laws of history, is as meaningless as the mumbo-jumbo of the alchemist.

True, some scholars pay lip-service to the impressive range of Toynbee's scholarship, which seems equally profound whether he is dealing with the Greeks or the Eskimos, the Egyptians or the Polynesians. There are philosophers who say that they enjoy the mental agility with which Toynbee sustains his complex argument that stretches over twelve volumes and covers millions of words. There are some critics who profess to see beauty in his style with its endless quotations from the classics and the Bible. There are even said to be one or two academics who actually believe that he has found the key to mankind's strange and complex story.

The majority of historians, however, regard his book with contemptuous hostility.

Yet his sales go on and on; his views are sought on every problem – past, present, and future – and foundations send him careering around the world to inspect those rare societies on which he has hitherto refrained from comment. He himself has courteously considered the criticism of his theories and rejected most in a volume that treats his theories with the respect that might be given to Einstein's.

Toynbee doubtless believes his work is here to stay. The savage attacks of the professional historians have battered his public image but not destroyed it. His name carries authority and his theories conviction with millions of readers. Why?

To understand Toynbee's success, one must pinpoint him in his class and generation. He belongs to the upper middle-class English intellectual society that was bred to govern, preach, or inform at a time when the sun was setting rapidly on the British Empire. By birth and upbringing, therefore, Toynbee belonged to a country and a class that had lost, and was to go on losing, power. Although a Christian, he had like so many scholars of his day a respect for science, particularly Darwinianism. His education, however, was entirely classical and humanist, and his belief in scientific method was as much an act of faith as his religion.

Naturally concepts of growth and decay and of the mutability of human destiny appealed to his imagination. Equally naturally he was convinced of the superiority of spiritual experience to material well-being. (Once the latter is secure, preoccupation with it may be regarded as vulgar.) Toynbee came to judge civilisations according to the refinement and vigour of their religious experience rather than by their economic resilience or the stability of their social structures.

It was because the centre of Toynbee's creed lies in his own peculiar interpretation of religion that he could dismiss the last 400 years of the history of the Western World as an uninterrupted disaster. Yet these are the centuries which saw the birth of science and industrial technology and their dissemination to the four quarters of the globe. This era witnessed the beginning of the end of poverty for the people of Europe and North America and the germination of a like hope in the rest of the world. Toynbee's panacea, however, is not more material progress but a fresh conversion to Christianity. Otherwise, he feels the disintegration of western civilisation will end in total decay. And to bolster up that prophesy, for Toynbee is a prophet rather than historian, is the purpose of *A Study of History*.

This huge work deals, in what Toynbee believes to be an empirical method, with the nature of civilisations, the reasons for their birth, the conditions of their growth, the prerequisites of their success or failure. The first three volumes deal with the genesis of civilisations (21 of them according to Toynbee) and they contain the famous thesis that all civilisations are a response to a challenge.

The factual range of these books, their wealth of quotation from ancient and classical literature and the high-pointing of the text with a plethora of biblical texts has been praised even by critics as ferocious as Professor Geyl. He, like many others, has expressed his admiration of Toynbee's intellectual agility.

He is too generous. The depth of Toynbee's scholarship is illusory. If one analyses his references to the Eskimos, or the Incas, or the Polynesians, one finds a very modest handful of books or papers selected, one feels, almost by the chance of what happened to be present in the library in which Toynbee happened to be working. All scholars who have considered what Toynbee has to say on their own fields have remarked not only on the paucity of his sources, his ignorance of recent research and his factual inaccuracy, but also on his wilful interpretation or suppression of evidence.

Few more subjective books have been written than this, and certainly none which made such a parade of being objective and scientific.

And yet in spite of the professional hostility which these books have aroused, Toynbee goes on being read. The reasons for this are manifold, but one is of great significance.

The majority of his readers go to him because the professional historians have failed in their social purpose, which should be to explain to humanity the nature of its experiences from the beginning of time. Scarcely an historian of ability has attempted an outline of history that is meaningful to the world at large. Yet all people hunger to know where they stand in the complex and baffling history of man. At least Toynbee gives them answers; bogus and absurd they may be, but at least they attempt to explain.

The tragedy is that Toynbee belongs to a dangerous and dying section of western culture which has led him to ignore the one aspect of the human story which both makes sense of it and also gives ground for the hopes of men – that is, the material progress of mankind which has gone on from civilisation to civilisation, from society to society and from place to place, but so far has only paused and never ceased.

It is one of the ironies of history that the Western World, which has made such great contributions to the happiness and well-being of millions of men, should treat material progress with such scant respect, should despise its historical prophet, Macaulay, and take such pessimistic and inaccurate historical illusionists, as Spengler and Toynbee, to its heart.

However, there is no better way of purging oneself of belief in Toynbee than by reading him.

Oswald Spengler

Perhaps the fate of Oswald Spengler should have given Toynbee food for thought before he embarked on his *Study of History*. When I was trying to become an historian in the late 1920s and early 1930s Spengler was still held in high esteem amongst conservative intellectuals, American as well as British. Spengler's acceptance of the crude biological images – the life and death of societies comparable to that of men and women – youth, age, decay, death – struck many with the force of truth. He was seen to substantiate a tougher realism which rejected betterment and accepted the inevitability of evil in men, combined with the indifference of their nature. When I was given an opportunity to write an essay for a series on Great Blunders, I seized with some joy on Oswald Spengler.

For a thousand people who know the title of Spengler's book, (*The Decline of the West*) perhaps half a dozen have read in it; I doubt whether even one of these persisted with it from cover to cover. Yet because of its title, and because of its reputation, it holds a most important place in the attitude of contemporary men and women towards the past. Unread, it is known to contain the truth. Even before World War I, this obscure German, Oswald Spengler, had discovered the way the world was going. And he knew the way it was going, because he had solved some of the major problems of man's history. He demonstrated that the history of mankind is a collection of cultures, or rather

> the drama of a number of mighty Cultures, each springing with primitive strength from the soil of a mother region to which it remains firmly bound throughout its whole life-cycle; each stamping its material, mankind, with *its own* image; each having *its own* idea, *its own* passions, *its own* life, will and feeling, *its own death*. . . . Each Culture has its own new possibilities of self-expression which arise, ripen, decay, and never return.

Societies of men are subject, like men themselves, to the same biological cycle of birth, growth, senility and death. And this, according to Spengler, hits the broad truths of human history. Sumer, Akkad, Egypt, Athens, Rome blossomed, withered, and all but disappeared. Nor was this a European phenomenon only – the Incas and Aztecs, Easter Island, Ankor Vat; lost worlds everywhere abounded. How could Spengler be wrong? And if he was not wrong, then surely the end of Western Europe culture, as he saw it, must be at hand. His interpretation of history foretold this. He prognosticated in 1928 that there would be the rise of a new Caesarism (with Mussolini on the stage, Hitler in the wings and Stalin conducting his own overture, this was not too difficult to discern). This new Caesarism would smash capitalism, and its lackey democracy and there would be triumph of 'race – quality, the triumph of the will to power – and not the victory of truths, discoveries, of money that signifies. And so the drama of a high culture . . . closes with the return of the pristine facts of the blood eternal that is one and the same as the ever circling cosmic flow. The Western World, therefore, whose highest cultural achievements had been reached in the eighteenth century was to end in tryanny and violence; capitalism, democracy were to vanish and their allied culture in science and art would stop.

Few philosophers of history have blundered more monstrously than this. And time has underscored his blunder. Capitalism flourishes as never before in Western Europe, and even the lackey, democracy, bruised in places as it is, is still the dominant political institution of the West. And as for the blood and race nonsense whose triumph Spengler foresaw, that, fortunately, has been destroyed.

Spengler's crass mistakes are too obvious for a prolonged refutation.

The West, the old capitalist West of Spengler has shown remarkable resilience, not only economically but also culturally, particularly in those aspects of culture which Spengler thought were played out – science and mathematics. 'It remains now', he wrote, 'to sketch the last stage of western science. From our standpoint of today [1917], the gently-sloping truth of decline is clearly visible.' Spengler's book is full of spectacular infelicities of this kind. Perhaps, the most glaring arises from Spengler's investigation of the Russian soul, the form of which has been revealed, of course, by Russia's history. Spengler decided that the key to the Russian soul was the fact that 'the Russian looks horizontally into the broad plain'. And so the Russian becomes identical with it; his spirit, his culture is horizontal. And so Spengler exclaims 'The idea of a Russian's being an astronomer! He does not see the stars at all, he sees only the horizon.' Well, well!

As well as infelicities, there were, of course, monstrous howlers, of the type that we have grown more used to since Toynbee became an historical prophet; at least it is charitable to call them howlers. Spengler ignored, suppressed or distorted evidence that did not fit his emotion-haunted attempt at logic. His rhetoric washed away professional difficulties and flowed over and around all awkward facts. Impossible almost to read, he was nevertheless wonderfully apt for a quotation and, of course, the implications of his title fitted the mood of the western intelligentsia, many of whom hated the world in which they lived. So Spengler was discussed in the 1920s and 1930s, argued about and considered very seriously. His name occurs in all discussions of history and its philosophy. Unread, his ideas were absorbed into the West's consciousness of itself; his enormous blunder became for many an unconscious assumption. The thousands who had never read him believed that he proved the decay of the world in which they lived and of the culture of which they enjoyed.

About the same time H. G. Wells published his *Outline of History* (1920). It sold so fabulously that Wells was paid a larger cheque than had ever previously been paid to an author – $1,000,000. For thirty years, in one form or another, The *Outline of History* has sold hundreds of thousands of copies and thousands read it. No one however discusses it; philosophers of history do not refute it; academics ignore it. Spengler has a place in historiography; Wells none. Yet Wells told the truth, Spengler preached error. Of course, there are mistakes in Wells, errors of fact, misinterpretations, etc. but the broad sweep of his outline is the true story of mankind and because it is true, his prognostications carry the stamp of truth too. Wells preached not decline but a qualified hope for further progress. He knew there would be further tyranny, slaughter and hatred but he also knew that science and education would persist.

As he himself said, 'Human history becomes more and more a race between education and catastrophe.' And he realised well enough that the race would be long, hard and frequently subjected to setbacks. 'Yet, clumsily or smoothly, the world, it seems, progresses and will progress.' That is the one true lesson that he felt he could derive from his narrative of the human story and it is a valid one. Wells was right, Spengler wrong. But, if Wells had many readers he has had few disciples; whereas Spengler can claim a multitude of converts — politicians, philosophers, sociologists, literary critics, historians, publicists of all kinds — to his title at least, if not to his historical theses. Spengler's blunder — one of the greatest of the twentieth century — persists, and dangerously persists. It has undermined hope: it has strengthened the fear of change.

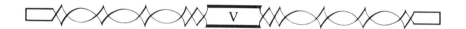

History by Committee

The need for a world-view of the history of mankind naturally enough became a burning ambition for UNESCO. It was, of course, to be free from bias, to be 'scientific history' and certainly not Eurocentric and, equally naturally, it required committees to bring about its birth — committees to choose authors, committees for the grand design, committees for each volume and such committees, too, required to be balanced between East and West, Marxist and Capitalist, Christian and non-Christian, Catholic and Protestant etc. A lot of meetings, a lot of travel, endless heat in discussion ending in wishy-washy compromise. Budgets were no problem. UNESCO budgets were ample enough to fly, feed, house the historians here, there and everywhere. So the years passed until finally the first volume, UNESCO's *History of Mankind* (873 pp.) was published in 1963, at least a decade overdue. Volume II (1048 pp.) appeared two years later. If professional historians wished for a proof that world history could not be written, then here it is. It is almost impossible to conceive how bad this committee history is. There is no sense of proportion; the rare good chapters drown in the plethora of bad. The editor of the second volume, Luigi Pareti, seems to have been a scholar of monumental incompetence and a mind of startling silliness. This volume was a sharp decline on the standards of the first which, if not high, at least commanded respect.

Even had all six projected volumes appeared, they would have been useless to the general reader, impossible for the student and patchily inadequate as works of reference. They certainly did not fulfill what many academic historians in America felt to be a growing need.

Opinion amongst academic men for a decade or so had been divided about the role of the paper 'The History of Western Civilisation' which before World War II had played a central role in the first year courses of most American universities. Often it had been shunted off to poor lecturers; it was subjected to sharp criticism for its vague generalisation,

clichéd explanations and its Eurocentricity and yet there were the strong
remnants of faith (amongst students as well as staff) for its broad
educative value. Some universities considered replacing it by a course of
world history. The Faculty of Columbia University attempted with its
own resources to create the essential text book. The result was *The
Columbia History of the World* which my friends John Garraty and
Peter Gay edited. It was a remarkably brave attempt, but it failed.
Basically it remained a textbook for the Western Civilisation paper with
chapters on the wider world stitched on. And it lacked, as all composite
books must, a steady vision of what the important processes were in
man's struggle to dominate his world.

   However, the total failure of committee history did not deter attempts
on the seemingly unassailable peaks of world history and the best
attempts have been by British scholars. The strangest, perhaps, is that
by Veronica Wedgwood, an historian of brilliant talents, who devoted
years of her creative life to producing a history up to the sixteenth
century – a short book, having plain narrative, of what happened. Not
simple, for accurate and balanced narrative is very difficult if you are
covering the world in a few hundred pages. Yet the absence of ideas, of
a vision, gives a strange flatness to the book and sad thought it is
to admit it, the book must be regarded as a failure. Better, far more
idiosyncratic, is Hugh Thomas's *An Unfinished History of the World*
(1979); often distended, at times inaccurate, it is immensely readable
and its underlying theme carries conviction. Yet better still is John
Roberts' remarkable book, *History of the World* (1976), extraordinary
in its balanced coverage of global history, which time and time again
convinces in its analysis of why times were as they were. It was turned
into a good, if not brilliant, television series (both direction and camera
were weak); I suspect that it has done more than any book since H. G.
Wells' *Outline of History* to educate millions of people in the history of
their species. It is more accurate in detail than Wells, superior in analysis;
it lacks Wells's large-hearted passion and his rhetoric. But like Wells,
too, it has been ignored when it has not been envied, and met largely
with silence by academic society and professional historians. That it did
not prevent John Roberts from being elected the Warden of Merton is
one of the minor miracles of our time – due, I think, to the secret
hunger of all academics to appear on television. They hunger for it like
adolescents for their first girl.

UNESCO's History of Mankind, Volume I

Two hundred years ago scarcely a fact in this almost 900-page book was known to man. Then his history was much simpler, more super-natural, but as various as the races, nations and tribes of mankind. Now uniformity has replaced diversity, flint sequences have displaced the descent from the gods, and, except for a few fundamentalists and the relics of primitive peoples, the framework of man's early history is accepted from Omsk to Omaha.

The story that has been uncovered by archaeology and anthropology is breath-taking. Odder, more miraculous, it is a greater stimulant to compassion and endeavour than the old myths by which man's course on earth was formerly explained. Yet how little of this gets across to the ordinary man and woman. Only H. G. Wells managed, in the compass of one volume, to convey to millions the whole exciting story of mankind. Inaccurate and old-fashioned as his work is, it remains the best in the field, and this huge cooperative work of international scholars, even when abridged, will not replace it.

Of course, this book is valuable; it has been written with clarity, if little *élan*, by two scholars of distinction. Factual detail and tentative generalisation achieve a remarkable degree of accuracy, greater in Jacquetta Hawkes' section than in Sir Leonard Woolley's, who stuck manfully to his own idiosyncratic theories and interpretation.

The organisation of the book, doubtless the compromise of a UNESCO committee, which is sponsoring and financing the six-volume study, is bewildering: Neanderthals pop in and out of four chapters; *homo sapiens* is equally elusive, and the story never gets going. Even when the course gets straighter with the Neolithic revolution, the book becomes so dense with detail the common reader will be tempted to give up. That would be a pity for, embodied in this complex and difficult book, is the epic story of man: a remarkable revelation of his endurance, his courage, his infinite capacity; an epic, too, that displays the tragedy of his passions as well as the miracle of his intellect.

The one constant theme in man's history from the first faint view of the small-brained men who may have been our ancestors to the fully-developed, luxurious, hunting societies of western France is the powerful, innate desire, almost compulsive, to control his environment – a desire curiously mixed with a capacity to tolerate an existence giving only the minimum satisfaction to his instincts. Curiosity, capacity for intuitive ideas, drive him constantly towards technological change, yet his easy tolerance of circumstances creates an immense inertia that just as constantly thwarts his ingenuity.

For tens of thousands of years, generations of men that must have contained their Newtons, Einsteins, Faradays and Edisons, were preoccupied with the slow refinement of tools for hunting and with the complex lore of food gathering. The ingenuity with which they manipulated flint and bone and wood required the same skillful combination of eye, muscle and intelligence that is needed in a good mechanic. And as the Lascaux paintings demonstrate, these ancestors of ours possessed imaginations just as vivid as our own.

One feels that this society might have gone on, refining methods a little, reaching great heights of pictorial art if favourable times, to the world's end; as the pygmies and Bushmen have gone on to our own day. The control of food production might never have happened. As it was, it came incredibly late in the history of man, tens upon tens of thousands of years after his full intellectual and physical evolution.

Yet once the control of crops and animals had been achieved the Neolithic revolution spread not only rapidly and extensively but also in complexity. Social organisation, and all the ancillary arts it required, accelerated with a speed that may seem slow to us but was dynamic by the standard of what had gone before. Within a thousand years the prospects of man had been transformed. Yet men once again settled to the burden of their days and accepted the poverty, the tyranny, the brutality, the ravages of war and the harsh rituals that their priest-kings, preoccupied with the return of the seasons, imposed upon them.

What the Neolithic Revolution lacked in contrast with our present Scientific Revolution, was consciousness of itself. The dramatic changes which men had brought about by their own observation and cunning were buried deep in myth and magic. A process was reduced to an event. Self-consciousness was only made possible by the greatest, and perhaps most singular of the achievements of the urban societies that grew out of the Neolithic revolution, the art of writing.

Once achieved, writing gave man his first step toward immortality. The ability to store complex information and ideas released him from the slow and limited confines of physical evolution and gave him the chance to master not only the world but also the universe. Against this potent weapon nature was doomed to subservience.

Now it all seems so commonplace, so elementary a part of man's equipment, that the wonder and the miracle of the invention of writing is hard to grasp. That is why, perhaps, the chapter, 'Music and Literature', is the most moving in the book; the poems of Sumer, Babylon and Egypt with their love, hatred, compassion, acceptance of fate and hope of future bliss, and replete with all the tyrannies and sorrows of life, speak directly to us; these men, at least, were our brothers.

Reading these poems, one realises how little our characters have changed: then as now, there were rare moments of bliss, many of resignation, and sorrow everywhere abounded. They underline, as indeed does the whole book, the vast need for man to study himself and his relations with other men – as intensely and as exactly as he has studied the world about him. The very rapidity of our social evolution over the last nine thousand years may easily delude us, and so prevent us recognising the immense distance we must travel, at least in the control of ourselves, as well as our environment. In our heart, if not in our heads, we are still close to the Neanderthals.

UNESCO's History of Mankind, Volume II

I don't often wish I were as rich as Paul Getty. Today I do. I want to buy time on every commercial radio and TV from Patagonia to the North Cape, to hire sky-writing planes in all the world's capitals, to take pages of advertising in all the world's press, just to say how awful, how idiotic is this second volume of UNESCO's projected six-volume 'History of Mankind'.

The venture is directed by UNESCO's International Commission for a History of the Scientific and Cultural Development of Mankind – and one can scarcely conceive the time and the money that have been wasted on it. Ancient and learned men have tottered, at the world's expense, to Mexico City or New Delhi to sit in solemn conclave in proliferating committees to plan the unplannable or comment on the unreadable. Who chose them? Each other, it would seem.

The British corresponding members, according to this volume, are an odd lot. Joseph Needham, the learned Marxist historian of Chinese science, seems explicable enough, but Bertrand Russell, a nonagenerian not remarkable for his historical gifts, seems a trifle quaint. Sir Ernest Barker, the only other member listed, has been dead for nearly ten years. And certainly I did not realise that the quality of historical scholarship in Spain was so great that it deserves equal representation with the USSR (eight corresponding members from each country). But, at least, I am comforted by the thought of coolies struggling over the Himalayan passes to get the proofs to Professor Gokal Chand in Nepal.

Here and there, especially among the fourteen members for the United States, a name indicates a reputation of distinction. In general, the names are just names. Not that it matters: a committee of Thucydides, Gibbon, Ranke and Macaulay would have been hard-pressed to turn these 1,000 pages into a readable history of the ancient world.

'The present work', writes René Maheu, the Director-General of UNESCO, belongs to that noble line of great syntheses which seek to present to man the sum total of his memories as a coherent whole. It has the same two-fold ambition, to embrace the past in its entirety and to sum up all that we know about the past. And it adopts the same intellectual approach — that of the interpretative as opposed to the descriptive historian — reducing events to their significance in a universal frame of reference, explicit or implicitly.

Noble words, noble intention, but totally ignored.

Take the evolution of writing systems, which has half a chapter devoted to it. There is not one single interpretative idea, but page after page of short paragraphs devoted to one alphabet — of which this rigmarole is a typical example:

> Later, when the Phocaeans became Ionicized, they changed their system, but the original arrangement had its results in the appearance of the Red alphabet in districts with which Phocaea had relations. These included Lemnos and Phrygia, and the stations along their Western voyages — namely Elea, Neapolis, Corsica, Tartessus in Spain, and the neighbourhood of their colony Kybos in Numidia.

And, apart from the profound statement that the Phocaeans came from Phocis, that's that.

One might think perhaps that each section was a detailed, comprehensive, encyclopedic catalogue. One would be wrong. In the section dealing with irrigation, trade, artisans, light industry and markets, China is totally ingored except for a brief reference to the lateen sail. Of geographical knowledge, only the Greeks and Carthaginians are noticed, but two paragraphs are devoted to Chinese astronomy. The civilisations of Central and South America (although not really existing in the chronological confines of these volumes, 1200 BC to 500 AD) play will-'o'-the-wisp through these chapters. Ignored in astronomy but not in alphabets, they get a brief reference in mathematics. But the splendid road systems of the Incas find no mention in transport, and so on.

Anomalies of this kind everywhere abound. The impression grows that — when the grand plan had been settled by committee — Professor Luigi Pareti of the University of Naples (who is listed on the title-page as the chief author) worked within the chapters so decreed by a process of free association. The total effect is of an encyclopedia gone berserk, or resorted by a deficient computer.

Nor is this welter of information particularly valuable. Each chapter is encrusted with a list of comments by other scholars in which the views of Professor Pareti are frequently and sharply contradicted and his errors exposed. Professor Pareti died in 1962 — and this work has since been edited and re-edited. It seems most peculiar that his mistakes, either of fact or judgement, could not have been corrected in the text.

To be fair, however, there are one or two sections of this book that are of value and, indeed, are quite readable. The chapters on public administration in Greece and Rome are less a catalogue of facts than the rest of the book and give a reasonably coherent picture of their government. Even here, however, there is a lack of awareness of the social and economic forces that were moulding political institutions. Indeed, Professor Pareti showed a quite remarkable indifference to such interrelations. Most of what he has to say on socio-economic matters is both cursory and trivial, as may be seen from his treatment of slavery.

The illustrations are as bad as the book; ill-chosen, ill-arranged and ill-produced, they would have been shameful 50 years ago. Sometimes there are attributions to museums, sometimes not. The nadir is reached with No. 65, a lacquered basket of the Han dynasty, a faint, meaningless illustration, if ever there was one.

What is so infuriating is not the vast waste of money and time which these volumes represent but that such a signal failure should be possible in a history of one of the most exciting, dramatic and important epochs in the life of man. This was the time when the Middle East, India and China became densely peopled; when urban life became not only possible but commonplace; and when, most significantly of all, men through writing and mathematics created an artificial memory which could transmit knowledge and ideas from place to place and from generation to generation. This was the great step forward, a leap in evolution, yet one deliberately fashioned, and one, too, which made our world possible.

Without literate administrative systems the great iron age empires of China, Persia and Rome could never have existed. Perhaps, however, the most vital aspect of this epoch lay in the growth of the human population – plus the diversification of opportunity which the new complexities of living created for men. Not that humanity gained all and lost nothing. The mass of mankind were subjected to a life of endless labour; new class and caste divisions imprisoned generations of men and women in frustration and poverty; war, pestilence, famine achieved fresh dimensions of horror.

One might have hoped that – in a work professing to be interpretative of the history of mankind – such matters should have found extensive discussion and illumination. Instead, we are presented with three-quarters of a million words of a jumbled, factual catalogue and one searches in vain for historical analysis, wide-ranging interpretation or the evocation of what life was like. If UNESCO wished to produce an encyclopedia, it should have done so. At least that would have been of value. This is neither history nor encyclopedia, but an incoherent stream of detritus, hacked out of a score of pedestrian textbooks.

Most History in 500,000 Words

This surely must be the most improbable book for a decade – a history of the world written by the faculty of *one* university – Columbia. Since the book was conceived, organised, and the chapters allotted, the faculty of Columbia has suffered sad blows – not only the death of Richard Hofstadter but a minor diaspora of historians following the campus riots. Any composite history produces almost insoluble problems: most authors are quick to accept, slow to produce, and the labours of the editors must have been herculean. Even more amazing is the quality of the book. No history faculty, indeed no campus, is a nest of geniuses or even talented writers, let alone talented historians. But this book is immensely readable. Anyone with a modicum of historical knowledge and a real appetite for understanding man's history can sit down with this large, fat volume and read it from cover to cover without boredom. It is reasonably comprehensive; it is, by and large, accurate in judgement as well as fact; it is, more often than not, a pleasure to read. Amazingly, it is all brought within the compass of half a million words. Its success on the campus will be immediate and it deserves a wide public success as well. Yet excellent as it is, I think that it could have been better or, should I say, different and therefore better. But first its excellences, which, because praise is forgotten sooner than criticism, need to be strongly emphasised.

After a judicious survey of man's evolution to the Neolithic revolution, the book gets off to an exceptionally brilliant start; indeed, the first 21 chapters, apart from three which deal all too cursorily with the East, are written with such *élan*, interlaced with sardonic and amusing wit, that one is almost impelled through the rest of the book. These cover the history of the ancient world and that of Greece and Rome to the beginning of the Middle Ages and are written by Professors Morton Smith and Elias Bickerman in brilliant tandem, a quite remarkable *tour de force*, which at some time should be detached and published as a paperback. Here one sees two really acute and original minds at work, synthesising boldly, drawing on an exceptional range of scholarly learning with masterly skill, and expressing themselves pithily and at times with refreshing acidity.

No other section of the book is, unfortunately, as sustained as this, although there are splendid chapters from acknowledged masters of their trade. Indeed, one is soon plunged into the factual swamps that all too often litter books of this kind – a moderately interesting chapter on Islamic civilisation ends lamely in a meaningless list of Sufi orders; the chapter on the Mongols – fabulously interesting, one would have thought – becomes as arid as the Gobi Desert, gritty with personal and place names that no one wants to know, and the book could easily have died in medieval Byzantium had the chapters not been mercifully short and embedded in a truly excellent section by John Mundy, who recaptures the brilliance and tone of the writing on the Ancient World.

Once we arrive at Renaissance Europe, the book again takes wing and there are few weak or boring chapters – astonishingly few for so complex an authorship – in the rest of the book, which ends with a perceptive and sensitive statement by Jacques Barzun on the state of culture today. It is invidious, perhaps, to select chapters from this part of the book, which is so sustained in the quality of writing and of historical judgement. In the chapter on Darwin and Freud, Richard Hofstadter deals splendidly with Darwin and we are made to feel again the tragic loss that we have suffered by Hofstadter's death. Peter Gay on Freud is at his very best – perhaps one should say his provocative best – giving us, one hopes, a foretaste of his next major book.

Taking each chapter, there is much to praise and little to blame, but I could not help feeling that the book wasted opportunities and in places seriously lacked balance owing perhaps to the editors' and publishers' eyes being too determinedly fixed on the university course, still very widely taught in American universities, known as the Rise of Western Civilisation. Almost three-quarters of this book is built around this theme, with the result that the chapters on Eastern history, particularly Chinese history, are absurdly short. The whole of Imperial Chinese history, from the rise of the T'ang to the fall of the Ming, fits into two short chapters; Japan, from the Meiji Restoration to the present day, goes into a few pages; the twentieth-century history of China likewise; and the few paragraphs on Red China are concerned almost entirely with its international relations. On the other hand, Western Europe is fully served, its thought, and to some extent its artistic culture, explained, and explained to a degree that allows nuance and subtlety. Eastern culture, apart from its earlier manifestations, appears in tiny but indigestible capsules.

And, for me, there was one further disappointment. In spite of Joseph Needham's massive work, there is scarcely more than a sentence or two on Chinese science and technology and the debt which the western world has owed to it. Indeed, there is little or no comparative history, no discussion of the enormous social consequences of the differences in writing Chinse and writing European languages; and even leaving cross-comparisons of great cultures on one side, there are some oddities in the editorial arrangements of the mainstream. Slavery in America is discussed almost entirely in terms of the struggle for its abolition; slavery elsewhere might hardly have existed. Considering the development of comparative history is the last decade one would have wished to see more of it here. Basically this is a history of western civilisation with additions, not a world history. Almost any such book is open to criticism. Every historian would have a different way of structuring such a book, and it would be churlish not to stress again its quite exceptional excellences: it is the best world history available, certainly the most readable, and, when dealing with western culture, the most intellectually stimulating. In a sense, is that not enough?

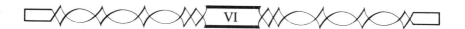

VI

Churchill

There was one public figure for whom Trevelyan had an almost uncritical admiration throughout his life – Winston Churchill. Like Churchill, Trevelyan had been a liberal in Edward VII's reign, an uneasy Conservative after World War I: uneasy because he hated fascism in Italy and the Nazis in Germany. Although inclined to pacifism in World War I (he volunteered for medical service in Italy), he disliked appeasement in the 1930s, and was drawn towards the policy advocated by Churchill, Eden and Duff Cooper. And there was also the strong Harrovian connection. Both men loved their old school, both had been greatly influenced by two excellent masters there – Somervell and Townsend Warner. Their love for history had been developed and nurtured by them. It is false to think that Churchill was a dunce at school; he excelled in history like Trevelyan, and it was this common experience and natural delight in history that made them life-long friends. It gave Churchill the greatest pleasure to nominate Trevelyan as Master of Trinity, as it had Stanley Baldwin, another Harrovian, to make him Regius Professor in 1928.

The real bond between them, however, was belief; they both saw the history of England as a great unfolding, leading to the achievement of liberty and freedom, hammered out over the centuries, through conflict between the Crown and Parliament. Thus we established the rule of law. To both men, the British heritage was not only unique but also the best. Both as they grew very old felt that Britain had lost its sense of destiny. As one might expect on this issue, the writer was gloomier than the statesman, but then statesmen are usually more optimistic men than writers. Unlike Trevelyan who wrote magnificent prose, there was, at times, a crudity, a *Boys' Own Paper* quality in Churchill's writing that jarred. When Churchill was 90 a coffee-table book was created out of Churchill's four-volume *History of the English Speaking Peoples*; its title was *The Island Race* and it certainly encapsulated Churchill's basic historical vision. As I wrote in my review of it in *The Spectator* in 1964:

225

They are all there, the Kings and Queens, the Generals and the Admirals, the battles on land and sea, the statesmen great and mean who, to Sir Winston's thinking, have made this kingdom what it is. How these beautifully printed pages dazzle one with great ships, blazing guns, charging cavalry and the brave, stern-faced men who ordered death so easily.

War, politics, violence, these are the stuff of Churchill's history: but glorious not nasty, no burst heads, no unravelled guts, no split livers rotting in the sun, no anguish, just fame. Men die for greatness, suffer for liberty, withstand tyranny, defeat the perfidy of France, never lose their lives for other men's greed and lust for power. The evil is lost in the blaze of triumph.

And so with history in general. The millions who made it do not signify: one tiny picture of a slum, one of a pretty mill; eighty-six words on the intellectual and artistic achievements of the seventeenth century, not many more on the Industrial Revolution. The minds and hands which built the power of Britain which gave it what distinction it possesses in the creative life of mankind, are scarcely mentioned. It is pointless to turn to this history to learn of Shakespeare, Bacon, Milton, Newton, Boyle, Faraday, Wordsworth, Tennyson and the rest. How strange this island race must seen to our children – a saga world of killer patricians, entangled by tradition and events in a few human decencies.

The History of the English Speaking Peoples had deliberately been written as a pot-boiler to sustain the way of life that Churchill enjoyed in the 1930s. War delayed its publication but made certain of its world-wide success for Churchill had led his country to victory. It became the most famous of Churchill's books on history, but it is perhaps his worst, for Churchill as an historian was a multidimensional creature. He wrote general history, family history (ancient and modern), and vast histories of the history in which he himself had been a leading figure. Only Clarendon amongst British historians had combined the roles of statesman and historian. No one could claim that Churchill was in any way superior as an historian to Clarendon, far from it, yet he has great significance: his energy and his output is astonishing: his experience unique amongst historians. Naturally so Promethean a figure preoccupied me. Also, like Trevelyan, he was one of the last great exponents of and believer in the Whig tradition. Indeed, he made it a component of his rhetoric of war.

Churchill: The Historian

I

The Baroque chimney stacks of Blenheim flaunt their grandeur against the sky, the final dramatic gesture of a palace that was always a monument and rarely a home. Achievements riotously carved in stone, obelisks of victory, sweeping columns, vista piled on vista create a sense of drama, of battle, of victory. There is no house like it in the western world; and certainly not one in England that is dedicated so emphatically to one man – John Churchill, Duke of Marlborough, who decisively defeated the French armies of Louis XIV with a motley crew of Dutch, Germans, Danes, Scots, and a few regiments of the English. This great palace lies, therefore, at the heart of the Whig legend of that past which the English had manufactured in order to underpin their Imperial ambitions and in which Winston Churchill had implicit belief. Born at Blenheim, educated amongst the descendants of the great Whig aristocracy of Stuart and Georgian England, his life was spent as a politician, strategist, and historian in the service of that curious ideology of the Whigs, half-truth, half-fiction; half-noble, half-base. Many of its principles possessed for Churchill the quality of absolute truth, indeed as absolute as any religious dogma. Somewhat sceptical in religion, towards which at times he could permit himself a caustic yet felicitous epigram, he was totally unhumourous and solemnly reverent when it came to the great institutions of government – monarchy and Parliament – or even to 'freedom' and 'liberty' as interpreted by the English governing class. Such unthinking acceptance of the traditional beliefs of his class was to temper his strength as a statesman and, indeed, was to enable him to lead his country through its darkest and most desperate hours, but it fissured his history and rendered must of it obsolete as soon as it was written. This is particularly true of his formal historical works, although, perhaps, less so with his autobiographical works of contemporary history, whether it be the *Malakand Field Force* or the massive volumes on the two world wars. To understand Churchill the historian, one must look closer at his inheritance; particularly the historical assumptions of his class.

For Churchill, English history was a progression, a development of inherent national characteristics, a process whereby the Englishman's love of liberty, freedom, and justice gradually, by trial and error, discovered those institutions of government which were apt to his nature. Churchill, like all good Whigs before him, discovered the seed of this momentous historical process in the dark Saxon days.

> After the shapeless confusion of darker centuries, obscure to history and meaningless to almost all who lived through them, we now see a purpose steadily forming. England, with an independent character and personality, might scarcely yet be a part of a world civilisation as in Roman times, but there was a new England, closer than ever before to national unity, and with a native genius of her own. Henceforward an immortal spirit stood forth for all to see.

This genius absorbed the Danes and the Normans, triumphed over the ravages of the former and the conquest of the latter. The barons,

the great landowners, checked the tyrant-kings, particularly John, calling
in the people of substance to help them keep a balance in the Constitution. And so Parliament, sometimes weak, sometimes strong, rooted
itself in English life, becoming the bulwark of freedom and liberty.
Justice, from time to time corrupt and perverse, grew in stature and in
independence as century followed century. The break with Rome,
followed as it quickly was by England's first victories overseas, under-
lined England's special destiny and confirmed her powerful individuality.
England, at last, found her full identity in the reign of Elizabeth I. All
was put in peril by the Stuarts, and England was unhappily plunged
in fratricidal strife. But again this proved providential. The taste of
republicanism proved too bitter and Englishmen returned to their natural
allegiance, monarchy. True, at first there were faltering steps and a
peculiarly stupid monarch in James II. But the Glorious Revolution of
1688 – the most venerable of all events in Whig mythology – brought
the perfect relationship: a permanent Parliament and a docile monarchy.
Under the aegis of the great Whig magnates, the freedom-loving English
battled against the tyrant French, first Louis XIV, then Napoleon, and
defeated both. And, of course, marched forward to her Imperial Destiny.
Difficulties there were and faults. The loss of America could be, and
was, blamed on George III and his sycophantic friends. Industrialisation
threatened the cherished institutions, yet brought such wealth that it had
to be fostered. Both Empire and the people were problems which taxed
English genius to its utmost, but it solved both. The British Empire was
the most just the world had seen, and its people enjoyed the richest
and freest democracy history had ever known. The English and their
institutions were the result of time working on natural genius. And the
centuries-old leaders of this miraculous historical development were
those 'great Oaks', as Edmund Burke called them – the great landed
aristocratic families who were the guardians of England's destiny and
its natural rulers.

This, of course, was not history; it was a past which generations of
Englishmen – workers, politicians, poets, even novelists – had created
to give a sense of meaning and purpose to the events in which they were
involved. It was a past which always confirmed the present. It was
intensely usable and Churchill used it constantly. It helped him formulate
his political ideas. It governed his attitude to India, to Ireland, to Europe.
It invaded his strategy and his tactics. It inflamed his rhetoric with a
measured and unforgettable passion. It regulated his political decisions.
It imbued everything that he wrote. One of his motives as a historian
was to demonsrate the truths of these beliefs which he had inherited.

Time and time again these sentiments crop up in his books and speeches like a favourite chord in music. His very first book, *The Story of the Malakand Field Force*, ends with these sentences:

> The year 1897, in the annals of the British people, was marked by a declaration to the whole world of their faith in the higher destinies of their race. If a strong man, when the wine sparkles at the feast and the lights are bright, boasts of his prowess, it is well he should have an opportunity of showing in the cold and grey of the morning that he is no idle braggart. And unborn arbiters, with a wider knowledge, and more developed brains, may trace in recent events the influence of that mysterious Power which, directing the progress of our species and regulating the rise and fall of empires, has afforded that opportunity to a people of whom at least it may be said that they have added to the happiness, the learning and the liberties of mankind.

Forty years later, in his *Marlborough, His Life and Times*, the same theme was being played but with more mature and complex variations.

> No dreamer, however romantic, however remote his dreams from reason, could have foreseen a surely approaching day when, by the formation of mighty coalitions and across the struggles of a generation, the noble colossus of France would lie prostrate in the dust, while the small island, beginning to gather to itself the empires of India and America, stripping France and Holland of their colonial possessions, would emerge victorious, mistress of the Mediterranean, the Narrow Seas, and the oceans. Aye, and carry forward with her, intact and enshrined, all that peculiar structure of law and liberty, all her own inheritance of learning and letters, which are to-day the treasure of the most powerful family in the human race.
>
> This prodigy was achieved by conflicting yet contributory forces and by a succession of great islanders and their noble foreign comrades or guides. We owe our salvation to the sturdy independence of the House of Commons and to its creators, the aristocracy and country gentlemen. We owe it to our hardy tars and bold sea-captains, and to the quality of a British Army as yet unborn. We owe it to the inherent sanity and vigour of the political conceptions sprung from the genius of the English race.

For Churchill, the past confirmed the peculiar genius of the English race and proved its right to be rich, Imperial, and the guardian of human freedoms. He was not alone. He imbibed this attitude from all that he read or saw. His views were the commonplace of the classroom and the themes of the historical best-sellers throughout his long life – J. R. Green, G. M. Trevelyan, Sir Arthur Bryant. And this mythology, basically aristocratic, or at least landed and genteel, had been accepted unthinkingly by the industrial middle class and by vast sections of the literate labouring population too. They needed no further proof than a map of the world splashed all over with red. Churchill and the governing classes of the English nation shared a common sense of the past. To grasp this is most important, for history was not, for Churchill, like painting, something one turned to for relaxation or merely to turn an honest guinea to meet his mountainous expenses. History was the heart of his faith; it permeated everything which he touched, and it was the mainspring of his politics and the secret of his immense mastery. Just as in a sense De Gaulle has been engaged in a historical dialogue with his nation, so Churchill was with his. His violent disagreement with Neville Chamberlain did not spring solely from thwarted ambition or personal dislike. Such motives may have sharpened the phrases and honed his epigrams, but the long policy of appeasement, the weakening of Britain's world role, the acceptance of oppression and racialism were to Churchill a denial of English's historical destiny and, because a denial, bound to end in disaster. And, on the verge of war, he advised Hitler to study English history so that he might ponder what would very likely be his fate. And when the final challenge came, it was the strength of the past to which Churchill turned again and again. For he well realised that he was leading a nation more deeply conscious of, and committed to, its sense of the past than any the world has known since Imperial China. Churchill the historian is far more than Churchill the writer of history books. He is, perhaps, the last great practitioner of the historic theme of England's providential destiny. The past in which he intensely believed has been shattered by the 1950s and 1960s. It no longer holds credence either for the governing élite or the nation at large. There are pockets of believers who comfort themselves with the works of Sir Arthur Bryant, but they know in their bones that their past is dead. What gave Churchill his confidence, his courage, his burning faith in the rightness of his cause – his deep sense of the miraculous English past – has been lost. It no longer explains our role or our purpose. The role of history is vanishing from politics, but because it is, it is so very necessary to stress how deep the roots of history penetrated Churchill's world and how in tune this attitude was with the feelings of the nation he served. In consequence, therefore, it is not surprising that when he composed his historical works they should enjoy from first to last the most exemplary success. Yet before turning to their consideration, there remains a further stand to be explored in the making of Churchill the historian.

II

Historians are formed not only by the age in which they live and the class into which they are born, bur also by their own personal characters and the interplay of them with their environment and education. And in this Churchill was no exception. Professional historians are forced by their training to develop an acute sense of awareness of their conditioning and of the response of their own personalities to the subjects which they may be investigating. Churchill, however, had no professional training as an historian at all. To him, historical criticism was an almost unknown art, hence the effect of his personality, of his prejudices, and of his enthusiasms on his historical writing was very direct.

Churchill had a difficult childhood in the ordinary circumstances of his class. His father, Lord Randolph, was gifted, flamboyant, reckless, an orator who could hold the Victorian House of Commons spellbound and yet behave with outstanding pettiness and pomposity towards his own sons. Unpredictable, he seized the young Winston's imagination in a vice-like grip and at the same time totally overawed him. Lord Randolph died early, a failure: crushed and defeated by the inexorable men of small mind who are the bone and sinew of politics. And his father's fate bit deeply into Churchill's heart, drawing him to the odd, the flamboyant, the reckless, and nurturing a bud of hatred for the complacent, the controlled, the cautious men of self-confirmed moral rectitude. One has only to turn to *Great Contemporaries*, one of Churchill's most valuable contributions to the understanding of English political personalities of the twentieth century, to see how deep was his attachment to his image of Lord Randolph, and how the bitterness that he felt in regard to his father worked itself out in his relationship with other men. His delight in Birkenhead, in Rosebery, in Joseph Chamberlain, in Lloyd George and, above all, in Charles Parnell had its origins in his father's character. And it is not surprising that the first formal piece of historical writing which Churchill attempted was the life of his father. Churchill's mother – gay, pleasure-loving, self-preoccupied, affectionate and indifferent by fits and starts – played a less important emotional role in Churchill's life. Her effects were more practical. She encouraged an extravagant husband to expenses they could not afford. Accustomed, as the daughter of an American millionaire, to riches, she squandered her inheritance with insouciant eagerness. In personal relations, much as she loved social life, she always remained a little apart. She created no warm home life for her sons. And although they enjoyed the solid trappings of aristocractic life – governesses, expensive preparatory and public schools, houses in Grosvenor Square and weekends at Blenheim or Althorp – Churchill early realised that he was poor. He was poor at Sandhurst, and poorer as a subaltern in the 4th Hussars. Yet the only life that he knew was aristocratic and rich. His education was as fissured as his social background. Backward at Harrow, he learned little. He struggled with Latin prose, plodded dutifully through the abridgement of Hume's *History of England*, and enjoyed odd bits and pieces of literature, Macaulay's *Lays of Ancient Rome*, and Robert Louis Stevenson's tales. At Sandhurst, he did better. He loved the military life – strategy and tactics fascinated him: he rode and shot with pleasure. He got into scrapes. His cheques bounced, and he became a leader of a clique of high-spirited, horseplay-addicted subalterns. And then the change came. His father's death, the loss of his old nurse whom he loved like a mother, a turn of duty in India – suddenly the springs of his creative nature were released. He wanted fame, he wanted power: to acquire both required knowledge. So, during the long, hot Indian afternoons at Bangalore he lay on his bed and read Gibbon, Macaulay, Adam Smith, and Hallam. He had a score of volumes of the *Annual Register* sent out to him, and he carefully worked his way through the Parliamentary debates, reliving the issues which had streaked his father's life with controversy, making elaborate notes as he went. Both Gibbon and Macaulay entranced him. Here he found history entirely to his liking – forceful, decisive, Olympian in the grandeur of its prose. Afterwards, when he learned more of the age of William III and Queen Anne, he came to detest Macaulay, whom he considered to be something of an intellectual fraud, yet Macaulay's influence and that of Gibbon remained paramount. They caught his imagination at the moment of his intellectual adolescence, and they left an indelible mark on all that he wrote. They were in harmony with his own nature, which was rich but not complex, decisive rather than devious; basically happy, eupeptic, outward-going, even though furrowed by shadows, by intimations of the tragedy of human life. At the roots of his personality Churchill was a simple man as, I suspect, most great statesmen are likely to be, no matter how subtle and complex they may appear on the surface. Churchill's private life was always straightforward and easy. He married late and very happily. There was no complexity, no unmentionable passionate drives as in Lloyd George. Yet friendship did not come easily to him. Most men, particularly the safe and the mediocre, distrusted him. They were disturbed by his burning thirst for power, his vivid imagination, and his natural assertiveness. He was drawn to colourful, unusual men like himself – Birkenhead, Beaverbrook, Brendan Bracken, and even the weird Cherwell: his relationships with these men were marked by an obstinate loyalty. Many thought Churchill rash because he made decisions easily – not only about actions, but about people and about principles. Once made they were difficult to change. He enjoyed being obstinate, being demonstrably right, even though he alone did the demonstration. And it was this compulsive desire for decisive action which led him to prefer military and political history, to delight in the forceful delineation of character, and to make lively, almost immoderately pungent historical judgements. Although simple and somewhat inflexible, Churchill's character bubbled with passion. He obviously enjoyed anger and ferocity, yet he was also warm-hearted, quickly moved to tears, and could indulge in generosity that is rare in political life.

He responded directly to a sense of occasion with something of the unawareness of a child. This is as true of his histories as of his life. And here again one is reminded of Macaulay, another man of straightforward feeling and judgement, quick to praise, quick to condemn, resolute, forthright, blinkered to subtlety: ebullient, self-centred, yet magnanimous. Certainty, warm feeling, a restless love of action – these are all qualities which, when transformed into the language of literature, make for a mastery of narrative, a clarity of exposition which most historians can never hope to possess. And, like Macaulay too, Churchill possessed one other inestimable virtue as a writer – elephantine stamina, an essential necessity for a narrative historian who must go on and on without losing zest, without checking his pace, through hundreds of thousands of words. And Churchill's histories are immensely long, far, far longer than most professional historians': probably among these only Ranke rivals him in output. These advantageous gifts, however, had their corollary of weakness. Unlike Macaulay, Churchill was not technically a clever man: his intellectual machinery was adequate rather than distinguished. This, of course, saved him from self-criticism, from that gnawing intellectual doubt which may haunt the creative faculties of gifted men. In Churchill the historian, however, it created serious limitation. A self-indulgent man, he could not drive himself where he did not wish to go; hence, the history of ideas, of science, of complex intellectual issues remained an almost closed book to him. He never mastered the giant intellectual figures of his youth and early middle age – Marx and Freud. He never turned hungrily to the works of philosophers, economists, social scientists. His intellectual tastes were as simple as his taste for literature. The devious subtleties of human nature, as explored by Proust or Dostoievsky, possessed no charm for him. There was and is, in his work, a touch of the philistine. His culture, such as it was, was the simple culture of his class – the Bible, Shakespeare, Milton, Scott, Dickens, and a little Trollope, topped off with Rudyard Kipling.

Social background and temperament mould the historian, and so does experience. Churchill first became ebulliently, passionately, creatively alive when he experienced the frontier skirmish which he described in *The Story of the Malakand Field Force*. Indeed, the taste was so heady that he plunged into a welter of military activity – Egypt and the Boer War. No one can read any of the accounts of these adventures without realising that through them Churchill fulfilled his nature in an exceptionally deep sense. So, too, did his first essays in politics. His success at Oldham intoxicated him. He spoke night after night for hours on end to audiences ranging from hundreds to thousands. The wonder and power of rhetoric gripped him in a thrall from which he was never to escape. War and politics, these were the grand themes of his life, the

springs of his creative imagination, and the muscle of his immense
stamina. They led him to greatness, to world stature, to immortality.
But, and this should be remembered, he was a writer first, an apprentice
historian even before he was first defeated at Oldham. Hence he was a
rare and singular hybrid: a writer-statesman and a statesman-writer.

Few historians have experienced the drama of history so closely, so
intimately as Churchill; among English historians only Clarendon, to
whom he must be compared – and, alas, to his disadvantage. They had
much in common: both their careers were outstandingly successful yet
marked by defeat and rejection, although Clarendon's was personally
the more tragic experience. Both in their political worlds were rather
lonely men, somewhat out of tune with the less sensitive, politically
committed men of their times. Both changed their parties early in their
political careers and were never, in consequence, uncritically accepted
by the party which they joined. Clarendon, however, was a sadder man,
sadder in his temperament as well as in consequence of his experience
(after all, he died in exile). He was less ebulliently creative than Churchill,
but he penetrated further. He sensed the deeper tides in men and affairs:
the forces that would break long-established institutions, those which
might topple the most securely held power. Many a Marxist historian
had gone to the old royalist to condemn only to be amazed by Clarendon's grasp of economic and social issues. Clarendon stood a little aside
from life, somewhat suspicious of men and events. He lacked the deeper
convictions and certainties which were as natural a part of Churchill as
his red hair and pink skin. Churchill never saw so far nor so deeply into
human character as Clarendon. In perception, the balance tips towards
Clarendon, and for me still tilts that way when their styles are compared.
Churchill could write magnificently about the events of his time: no
statesman, other than Clarendon, can compare with him for splendid
and majestic set pieces; but, good as Churchill's prose is, it remains all
too frequently rhetoric, oral rather than written literature, and his style
is something of a confection, a hybrid by Macaulay out of Gibbon, a
style which by the 1940s, let alone the 1950s, was curiously oldfashioned
and somewhat out of place, like St Patrick's Cathedral on Fifth Avenue:
a building perfect in its faithfulness to the Gothic and splendidly designed
and built, but distinctly odd in the context of Rockefeller Center. Clarendon, however, was the natural master of the prose of his age. His
sentences unfurl their coils with the smoothness of an arabesque by Inigo
Jones, yet carry the weight, the richness, the fruitfulness of a Grinling
Gibbons carving. Clarendon never achieved the brutal and pungent
epigram which Churchill could produce with explosive effect, but he
achieved dignity and precision and sensitivity in page after satisfying

page. Intellect and style both subtly make Clarendon the more satisfying a historian – at least to me.

In narrative, the balance tips slightly Churchill's way. His forceful, impatient character bullies the narrative along and the reader with it – an admirable quality in a historian who writes works in six volumes. Whereas Clarendon was leisurely – given to quite gigantic asides – even though he never lost his grasp on the overall structure of his history. And finally, what gives merit to both their works, shared by few other historians, English or foreign, is the wonderful sense of reality and truth which they create when writing of their contemporaries in *political action*. And this, of course, derived from their involvement in the great events of their age. The fact that they were both figures of the greatest significance in their time adds a dimension to their histories which is denied to other historians. Their histories are also the living material of history. And how rare this is!

III

Churchill's histories fall into two categories – those in a formal, professional sense and those which deal with contemporary events in which he himself was involved. The second type evolved from the quasi-autobiographical *The Story of the Malakand Field Force* to the multi-volume *History of the Second World War*, in which Churchill attempted not an autobiography, nor quite a general history, but a mixture of both. Churchill's contemporary histories are more numerous and much more interesting than his formal histories, which consist of two acts of piety and a bid, wildly successful, to make a heap of money. As they throw light on his character as a statesman and contemporary historian, it is easier to deal with them first of all. The acts of piety were his life of his father, Lord Randolph Churchill, whom he felt to have been wronged by the Conservative Party, above all by Lord Salisbury (the Prime Minister), and his vast biography of his ancestor John, Duke of Marlborough, the greatest of English generals, whose reputation he felt had been blackened by Macaulay. The bid for cash was his four-volume *History of the English-Speaking Peoples*, conceived when his career was in the doldrums during the 1930s, completed but not proof-read by 1939 when, naturally, it had to be laid aside for many years: much revised it began to appear in 1956, by which time Churchill himself was almost too tired to appreciate its staggering success with the general public. In many ways the most satisfying of these works is the life of his father.

Churchill published this biography in 1906. His experience of politics, although not profound, was already sufficiently deep not only to weigh professionally the decisive moments of his father's career, but also to sense the changes in the national life which made that career possible. Furthermore, he had come to know many of Lord Randloph's allies and a few of his enemies. He knew them both as men and as politicians. He had also become acquainted with Lord Salisbury, Arthur Balfour, Lord Rosebery, and Joseph Chamberlain, and several of Lord Randolph's great Liberal opponents – particularly Lord Morley. He was as familiar with the political issues as his father's enemies, for in India Churchill had steadily worked through the Parliamentary debates of his father's lifetime, including the petty, as well as the major, matters of state. And, of course, he possessed his father's papers. He was also able to draw very considerably on Lord Rosebery's archives; a generous gesture, since Rosebery was himself writing an essay about Lord Randloph. Even so, much was denied Churchill. He does not, however, seem to have made very strenuous efforts to get at documents in the possession of others which would have helped him. Some papers, among those which he had, he quietly suppressed – not only the Duchess of Marlborough's outburst to Salisbury on Lord Randolph's death, which is understandable, but much of the sharp and savage invective which Lord Randolph showered on his contemporaries. Where he could, he smoothed Lord Randolph's prose, adding a little in stateliness and dignity even though he could not, and probably did not wish to, eradicate entirely the ferocity, the arrogance, the vituperation embedded in Lord Randolph's character and reflected in all that he wrote. The detachment of the professional historian is not present in this book. It was a justification of a life, an act of piety, not an historical assessment. The major characters were polished for presentation. Yet Churchill grasped forcibly enough the central success of Lord Randolph's life – the rallying of the newly enfranchised working class to the Tory standard. And he stresses, very rightly, how miraculous this seemed to men of that time. The incredulity of the Tory leaders led them to indifference, and it took all the determined energy of Lord Randolph and a few friends to make them realise the extraordinary future which was opened for them, but which they scarcely deserved. Churchill makes us realise that what often seems so obvious, so inevitable, was almost unbelievable in 1880. Only a man of the political genius of his father was able to perceive the opportunities offered for the slogan of 'Tory democracy' among the newly enfranchised masses. Here we see at work Churchill's strong grasp of political realities, and his description of Lord Randolph's dialogue with the electorate and its effects on the leadership of the party is, in many ways, the best part of this book, the liveliest and the most convincing. And yet, even here, he asks no questions that a natural or a trained historian would ask. What was the reason for this paradox? Why did millions of men, working-class men on the edge of poverty, vote for a party of aristocrats, landowners and bankers? Why was it that Toryism steadily grew in radical Birmingham? Here is a suggestive problem calling for the conceptual powers of a historian and his knowledge of social processes. But into these matters Churchill does not delve. Lord Randolph won the labouring classes for Toryism by his own efforts and those of a few supporters. 'To rally the people round the Throne,' cried Lord Randolph. 'to unite the Throne with the people, a loyal Throne and a patriotic people – that is our policy and that is our faith.' According to Churchill, Lord Randolph did just that by convincing them of the rightness of his ideas, but why the sense of the past of the upper classes or their traditional institutions appealed to a new industrial proletariat is a historical problem of the greatest significance, but one upon which Churchill throws no light.

His life of Lord Randolph was acclaimed as one of the great political biographies of the age, which is a gross over-assessment. It is highly readable: it gives a good, if biased and doctored, account of Lord Randolph's life. It evokes some of the clash of personalities and ideas, and that is all. Had it been written by a man of less significance, it would have long since grown dusty on the library shelves. It lacks historical penetration into the nature of the society which made Lord Randolph's political career possible, but a greater deficiency is a lack of psychological insight into his father's character which, even when the history had become dated, might have kept the book alive. Lord Randolph, as a human being and a politician, still awaits his biographer, his character was so very complex, and his capacity for self-destructive action so curiously compulsive; his bitterness went down to the very roots of his character, and his relations with even his friends were so very spiky that the man remains an enigma. The difficulties of his character Churchill describes, but the causes for them he discovers in the superficial events of his life, explaining that Randolph's quarrel with the Prince of Wales drove him into Tory radicalism. What eludes Churchill is that in the bitter invective, in the outrageous violence of language, and in the wild response this evoked, Lord Randolph found his own nature.

As with Lord Randolph, so with John, Duke of Marlborough. The main motive for Winston's huge biography of his ancestor, apart from turning an honest penny, which he never despised, and of which in the 1930s he was always in need, was to repolish and render refulgent the image of his ancestor which he felt Macaulay had tarnished. Macaulay's Marlborough loved power and loved money: in his youth he exploited his handsome good looks amid the courtesans of Charles II's court; in his middle age he laid his hands on whatever gold was going; fearful of a fall from power, he was quite prepared to correspond with James II at St Germains while he served William III at Kensington. He went, according to Macaulay, even as far as jeopardising an English expedition sent to attack France in the famous case of Camaret Bay. That this last accusation was false was well known, for it had been exposed by John Paget as early as 1874. The other charges proved more difficult for Churchill to refute, but he tried hard enough.

For his life of Marlborough Churchill had inestimable advantages, some of which he exploited and some of which he ignored. He was rich enough to be able to employ first-class research students to do many of the grinding chores of historical research – the long tedious hours copying and searching in muniment rooms. And he had the disposal of the vast archives at Blenheim. These were closed for many years to other scholars, even to G. M. Trevelyan, so that whatever they might reveal could be reserved for Churchill's benefit. This last advantage, however, was useful rather than great. The indefatigable Archdeacon Coxe, whose monumental *Memoirs of the Duke of Marlborough* (1820) provides not only the foundations but much of the structure of Churchill's biography, had printed fully, and reasonably accurately, the core of the Blenheim archives.* And so the new material that emerged when the volumes were published did not add up to much. Nevertheless, Churchill's transcripts are far more accurate in detail than Coxe's and somewhat fuller in extent, and the most valuable part of Churchill's volumes lies in these extensive quotations. They are the one aspect of the book that a professional historian might still consult. Churchill also sent his assistants to the obvious sources – the diplomatic correspondence and state papers at the Hague, Vienna, Paris, and, of course, London. These were the obvious sources. Churchill used few others; and those that he did were dealt with most superficially.

Every country house in England would have opened its archives at Churchill's request. But the request was rarely made. Apart from Blenheim and Althorp, the Duke of Portland's archive at Welbeck was the only substantial private archive in England that is listed in Churchill's bibliography. But the use was superficial. This archive contains huge quantities of letters and memoranda which belonged to Robert Harley, a major figure in Marlborough's career in Queen Anne's reign. Virtually no use is made of any of these papers. Further correspondence of Harley, and well known to scholars, is to be found at Longleat, a short drive from Blenheim. Not a paper was looked at. This was typical, and one could list a score of houses that Churchill should have ransacked and did not. The Brydges papers, which belonged to Marlborough's paymaster, were over in America at the Huntington Library. They

---

* And what he had not published was largely to be found in his voluminous transcripts in the British Museum. These Trevelyan used.

presented difficulties because they were scarcely catalogued. In consequence, their surface was skimmed in the lightest possible way. The
archival research for these volumes was superficial, exceptionally superficial. Valuable material was missed even in the Blenheim archives – a
large block of the Cabinet memoranda of Marlborough's son-in-law,
Sunderland, remained unopened: indeed, the treatment of Sunderland's
papers as against Marlborough's was somewhat cavalier. The consequence is that the political side of this biography adds next to nothing
to our knowledge of the period, which has since been vastly enriched
by the archives which Sir Winston skimmed or ignored. The opportunity
was there; it was not taken. The biography, huge as it is, remains
deficient in sources.

The best parts of the book are the set battle-pieces. Almost equally
well handled are the complicated diplomatic manoeuvres which secured
the grand alliance against Louis XIV, but even here there are many errors
of detail and emphasis.

And the book is also splendidly constructed. The problem which
confronted Churchill was a difficult one, the type of problem, indeed,
which a professional historian tends to shy away from. There were many
distant battles and several wars – and these were always far from the
centre of control, which, in London at least, depended on the fortunes
of an intricate political structure and violent party warfare: in Holland
the problem was almost as involved: in Paris, Turin, Vienna and the
German states it was less so, but even in these places Churchill faced
the necessity of dealing with internal pressures as well as foreign policy
and military activity. Hence the narrative problem was very complicated,
with the distant theatres of war having repercussions on Marlborough's
strategy. Furthermore, there was the struggle at sea, or rather on the
Seven Seas. In addition, England and France were also fighting each
other in Canada, in America, in the West Indies, and in the Far East.
Add to this the richness of personalities and their conflicts in all armies,
navies and governments. To orchestrate so many instruments and to
develop so many themes required Wagnerian genius, but Churchill
achieved it. His long book is eminently readable and so pellucid that the
complexity of so many interlocking themes is very easy to grasp. The
qualities which gave Churchill his massive mastery of detail in time of
war are present in the biography of Marlborough. Although open to
criticism as history, it remains a splendid work of literary art.

Does it succeed as biography? The answer is no. There is far too much
piety in the treatment of Marlborough and his virago duchess, that
impossible termagant. Marlborough loved money, loved fame, and loved
Sarah. These sentiments might be shuffled into a different sequence, but
their truth persists. The Marlboroughs became immensely rich, as rich

as a sovereign prince of Germany, which Marlborough longed to be, and for this honour he intrigued with relentless assiduity. And the riches were acquired by all the dubious methods of this age. But Churchill did not bother to probe. That Marlborough loved money Churchill could not deny, but he used all his oratorical skill to gloss the fact, writing 'this though was not without a certain grandeur' etc. even maintaining that in William's reign Marlborough was the most impecunious Earl in England, a ridiculous statement that a trivial amount of research would have quickly destroyed. Marlborough was a large-scale investor in the Bank of England, in the East India Company, and, probably, other companies. This may be trivial, but it is typical; Marlborough, a complex, arrogant, princely character, who cultivated his personality with the care of a skilled stage director, emerges from Churchill's biography glowing with virtue, skill, and grandeur, a paragon among men *sans peur et sans reproche*.

The book's faults, therefore, were the lack of archival work, a generous sprinkling of historical errors of fact and interpretation, and a gross misjudgement of the major characters; its strengths lie in the splendid clarity of a complex narrative and the brilliant descriptions of battle.

A graver fault remains. Churchill was unable to disentangle himself from his belief in the traditional interpretations of the English past: this is all implicit in the book – the freedom-loving English, Parliament the watchdog of liberty, the tyranny of France – the old Whig claptrap echoes in chapter after chapter. The confusion of purpose, the haphazard nature of men's intentions, the totally different nature of institutions in Queen Anne's reign to those which bore the same name in Queen Victoria's – these were never perceived. What dominated Churchill's writing was a sense of the past that was interlocked with history only to distort it.

This was even more obvious in the *History of the English-Speaking Peoples*. Although Churchill, under the general guidance of Alan Hodge, the editor of *History Today*, employed a small army of professional scholars to vet his proofs, the effect on the book was very small. Errors of fact were changed with courteous alacrity; subject to strong pressure, an adjective might or might not be pruned, but the grand design proved immutable. Likewise the interpretation. By 1950 Churchill was too old, too tired to undertake the detailed work necessary to bring himself up to date with the previous forty years of English historical scholarship, even had he had the inclination. And it is doubtful whether he ever enjoyed professional historical work or read much of it. Judging from Lord Moran's invaluable diaries, it is obvious that he still read a great deal, but the books which he chose were largely the old biographical authorities of his youth and early manhood, Moneypenny and Buckle on Disraeli, Morley on Gladstone, the giants of his father's day. His greatest pleasure, which Lord Moran also reveals, as he worked over his proofs, was to savour the sentences, to change an epithet here and there, or reverse the order of phrases, break up sentences and sharpen them, to enjoy indeed the creative delights of writing. But, as with his statesmanship at that time, detailed application was too burdensome for him. He was too tired, too old. So when the *History of the English-Speaking Peoples* appeared, it was like an apparition from the nineteenth or early twentieth century, as if Henry Hallam, Bishop Stubbs, J. R. Green or the young G. M. Trevelyan were still the accepted authorities in English historical scholarship. Yet it was a remarkable book and its publication a remarkable event, remarkable, very largely, because Churchill had written it. (What would we not give for Roosevelt's *History of America*, or Stalin's *History of Russia*, or, for that matter, Mao's *History of China?*) In it he laid bare the core of his national faith, displaying on what foundations his beliefs in the singular destiny of the English peoples were based. To comprehend fully Churchill's statesmanship, or even his strategy, let alone his relations with the working class, or India, or the monarchy, one must study this book. It contains his secular faith. As history, it fails, hopelessly fails; as a monument to a great Englishman's sense of the past, it is a brilliant success.

As might be expected, the military and political history is well told: the narrative rattles along, the comments are pungent, and human achievements in war, especially endurance and courage, are expressed in eloquent and moving prose. But it is descriptive history: the motives, the reasons for conflicts largely those which contemporaries themselves felt to be the causes of their actions. And the judgements of men and events are conventional and Victorian – one has only to read the section on the Civil War and the Commonwealth to see the banality of Churchill's interpretation, beautifully phrased as it often is. There is no real grasp either of Charles I's or Cromwell's character or intentions. Every opportunity of mockery of the Puritans is eagerly seized – their destructions of maypoles, the savage laws against adultery, their opposition to racing and cock-fighting; sneer follows well-directed sneer. No understanding whatsoever is shown of the Commonwealth Government's remarkable attempts to reorganise on a far more rational basis the institutional machinery of law and of government. Churchill's aristocratic blinkers are right down. Vigorous and lively as the prose is, sharp and strong as the delineation of men and events may be, there is an absence of historical imagination and also of human warmth, not for individuals – there is pity for Charles I, even compassion for James II – but for the mass of mankind. Take even the military history – it is the glory, the courage, the triumph, the valour of British arms which draw forth the majestic phrases, not the terrible horrors of the soldiers' and sailors' lot – we are never regaled with the broken heads, the spilled entrails, the burning and reeking flesh, the wild hysterical cries of men shattered to death, driven to their desperate trade by poverty, by social injustice, and the curse of fate. As with war, so with society – this is a gentleman's history and, therefore, contains little or no discussion of the labouring masses, or even of the reaction of the governing classes to them. It is politics and men seen through the eyes of generals, admirals, and statesmen.

One looks in vain for so much that has conferred distinction on the English-speaking peoples – their literature, their science, their philosophy, and their industrial technology. There is scarcely a word on Shakespeare or Hobbes or Locke, hardly anything on Newton, Boyle, Davy, Faraday, Clerk Maxwell or Rutherford. The Industrial Revolution and all the political and social changes which it produced are brushed aside in a few pages. In fact the major part of England's contribution to world civilisation is blankly ignored. And these serious omissions are indicative of Churchill's major fault both as a historian and as a statesman: he lacked a sense of the deeper motives that control human society and make it change, just as he lacked an interest in the deeper human motives. The past is only comprehensible in the terms of its future, but Churchill's mind was immersed in tradition. This made him a splendid symbol for a nation in torment, but inhibited his vision when he came to survey the broad sweep of English history. The influence of England's exceptionally intricate class structure and the problems created by an even more remarkable tenacity of its feudal continuum in an industrial society eluded him. The pageantry of a coronation superimposed on the steelworks of Sheffield or the sprawling suburbia of Manchester never struck him as odd; for him the right things were in the right places; embattled they might be, threatened perhaps by the future, but so long as the Island people rallied round their monarch and their Parliament, the world might be defied. In spite of his generosity and the warmth of his devotion to the British soil and its people, he could not see its future; so his vision of the past was clouded, limited to the past of his ancestors, of Lord Randolph, of Marlborough, of Blenheim. Here was the true heart of England. For Churchill, the core of English history lay in the struggle of its gentlemen against the Crown for their liberties, and then, when these had been won, in the harmony with it on their forward march to wealth and Empire. Churchill's old-fashioned, deeply patriotic book is the elegy for the generous view of English history and institutions, but one which lay at the core of the beliefs of the class in which he was nurtured. Faulted and criticised it may easily be, but this tradition is not all nonsense: it possesses some grains of truth. The English acquired and maintained political liberty, not for the reasons Churchill would have given, but acquire it and maintain it they did. And the history of Europe, or the world for that matter, shows that this is no easy thing even for an affluent and dominant society. And the Whig aristocracy played some part in England's unique achievement. It should not be forgotten. As we shall see, when Churchill combined his historical beliefs with statecraft, his dream acquired reality.

In those fields where his work challenges comparison with professional history, Churchill remains, at the most generous assessment, a gifted amateur. His abilities are clear – narrative power, grasp of structure, and a rich, full-blown style. His weaknesses are equally glaring – paucity of historical knowledge, lack of analytical power, and an ignorance of economic, social, and intellectual history of staggering proportions. The major significance of these works will lie in the fact that Churchill was the author. They illuminate his mind far more than they do the subjects about which he wrote.

IV

The formal historical works are, however, only a part, and a lesser part, of Churchill's output of historical writing. From the earliest days in India to 1950, Churchill was actively engaged in writing accounts of the great historical events in which he himself was involved. They range from the slight but exciting *The Story of the Malakand Field Force* and *The River War* to the vast, multi-volumed accounts of World Wars I and II. Yet among these books a further distinction can be made between the tales of adventure of Churchill's youth and the great war books, or the assessment of his friends and colleagues in *Great Contemporaries*. The early adventure books provided Churchill's apprenticeship in narrative history, for which he possessed a natural gift that he exercised, pruned, and sharpened. And, indeed, this application was necessary, for his capacity was overlaid with glaring faults. Fortunately for Churchill, his personality and social position gave his books a flying start which would have been denied to an unknown writer. Even though his temperament disturbed many of the leaders of opinion, he was a member of the Establishment, and the Establishment worked for him. The Prince of Wales wrote him a letter of congratulation on his first book, society talked about his book, even read it and pushed it. The space given in reviews was generous in the extreme. The book is verbose, uncertain in style, plummeting from Gibbonian phrases to the crooked complexities of a schoolboy in search of a style, and yet throughout shines a most definite personality – decisive, pungent, generous, alive. Even now, when subject and style are as outdated as Kipling's *If*, it retains a curious vitality – that vitality in writing which can only come from a deeply creative writer whose personality has been absorbed, totally absorbed, in his task. And Churchill's own response to his first book was typical of the committeed writer's: despair at the proofs, fury at the obvious errors and misprints, a sinking sense of opportunity missed. He need not have worried, for the book sold and the fame came. And Churchill realised what he could do. With his connections, with the success of this first book, he could launch himself into the world that he wanted. And that emphatically was not Bangalore and the Indian Army. Wherever great events were taking place, there he wanted to be – both participating in them and writing about them. Journalism, politics, books – the life of action, decision, and creation. These beckoned. But he was, for his social rank, poor and extravagant, with a younger brother, and a mother whose self-indulgence soared beyond his own; indeed she raped his inheritance and reduced his own slender resources. So although the future beckoned, and in his heart of hearts the decision was taken, he hesitated and tried to make the best of both worlds, retaining his commission as a soldier but seeking material for his pen. And he got it. By sheer persistence and by tugging every wire persistently, he got himself seconded to Kitchener's army in the Sudan. The result was *The River War*, which confirmed his qualities as a writer and plunged him into the controversies that he enjoyed. But before that book was published, he had quitted the army. A juicy contract with the *Morning Post* and the prospect of financial success with *The River War* confirmed a decision already half made. Furthermore, even though he toned down his criticisms of Kitchener, he well realised that his military career was bound to be frustrated by his journalism, especially as his temperament was frank, critical, and not easily controlled. His hopes of his book were very high, and he was assiduous in collecting information from Lord Cromer in Egypt as well as from Kitchener's staff officers; he attempted far more in this book than in his first. He wanted to see *The River War* in its historical context, to trace England's involvement in Egypt, the rise of the Dervishes, the failure of Gordon, and then on to his climax at Omdurman. The result is a long, uneven book: the professional historical part poor, the personal experience vivid and absorbing. Churchill simply did not know enough, and had not read enough, to give an adequately balanced account of the complex Egyptian problem. He felt a lack of mastery, and, as is usual in such cases, his style labours and verbosity echoed the uncertainty of touch. But when Churchill reached the dramatic events – the Battle of Omdurman, in which he himself took part – the book flares into life. The sentences are short, economic, sparse in adjective, and the Gibbonian echoes are used only to give an occasional solemnity. And in handling this battle, Churchill shows great advance on his first book, not only in control and narrative power, but also in rendering with extreme clarity the battle's complexity. The tactics, the terrain, the deployment of forces, the effects of gun-power are all made obvious *within* the excitement of the story. And any reader can feel the confidence of Churchill in these pages, the confidence that derived from the mastery of creative powers. That he possessed this confidence and was aware of it is further borne out by the type of books which he was considering writing at this time – either a life of Garibaldi or a history of the American Civil War. *The River War* obtained excellent reviews but far fewer sales than Churchill's first book; and yet it was a finer one, more ambitious, more important in theme, better written, and it has secured a permanent niche in historical literature. There is no better, no more vivid account of Kitchener's final campaign against the Dervishes, for what that may be worth.

Fortunately for Churchill, no sooner was *The River War* at the printers than the thunder clouds loomed up in South Africa. Churchill scented war, did a splendid deal with the *Morning Post*, packed six dozen bottles and collected field glasses and telescope, and careered off to the Veldt. The upshot was two more books, and the more dramatic material for his most satisfactory book of all, his autobiography *My Early Life*. The two South African books, *From London to Ladysmith* and *Ian Hamilton's March*, both sold splendidly, 14,000 and 8000, even though they were largely the *Morning Post* articles refurbished. They have never been republished, partly because their materials are used again in *My Early Life*. They are not of great importance in Churchill's development as a historian – they exercised further the powers of which he was already aware: his capacity to tell a story well, his direct and shrewd observation, his growing capacity for a phrase that stabbed the reader. There is, however, no development.

These early books of adventure would, probably, have fallen into oblivion had they not been written by a man who became a world statesman. Perhaps they would have been discovered by a historian of India, Egypt or the Boer War and plundered for a phrase or two, or used to illuminate a historical setting with first-hand experience. As it is, they are of enormous biographical value, historical documents within the context of Churchill's life, and because they are so vividly alive they will continue to present the image of the young politician at the outset of his career. As he was to continue to do throughout his life, Churchill began his career writing his own history.

Read alongside his vast works on the First and Second World Wars, they cast a curious and revealing light. These great dramas are approached in the same way that Churchill approached Omdurman or the attack on Chakdara. The story is Churchill's major concern: and it is the surface drama upon which he lavishes his rich prose which now has a strong rhetorical cast and, even if one did not know, one would have suspected that these books were dictated rather than written. *The World Crisis*, together with *The Unknown War: Eastern Front* and *The Aftermath*, make up a six-volume study of the First World War, and are far patchier books than his great effort on the Second World War. For one thing, he commanded, in his own possession, far fewer archives. After all, he was out of power after the failure of his Dardanelles campaign, and the offices which he held did not give him the same comprehensive sweep which was naturally his as Prime Minister. Hence, for much of his account he had to rely on external, published sources, and he was further constricted by the need to maintain a certain secrecy. Naturally all statesmen-writers are generous to themselves and to each other in the interpretation of the Official Secrets Act; nevertheless it constrains them, and in these books Churchill glides over matters of paramount importance not only in diplomacy, but also in subjects such as Intelligence, which had a direct bearing on strategy. Often the books give the appearance of overwhelming documentation, when in fact the amount used is, from a professional historian's point of view, quite slight. Churchill prints fully his own memoranda and letters and, naturally enough, those from others which he received or which had been officially received, but always this material is within the context drawn by Churchill himself. The documents never, as they so often do in professional history, create the context because they are drawn from diverse sources and not used merely to substantiate or enrich an argument.

Other archives, of course, existed, and some have since appeared, but at the time Churchill wrote, either they were not available, or Churchill did not make serious efforts to get at them. Hence these books, constructed in the methods of formal history, are really personal accounts, based on personal papers of a uniquely placed observer. And none of these works can ever be regarded as a reliable account either of the war or its direction; this is more particularly true of *The World Crisis*, which now wears a dated air. The major virtue of this book lies in its sharp perception of the statesmen, admirals, and generals at work: Churchill's vignette of Lloyd George in 1917 summarises brilliantly the Prime Minister's achievement, and underlines his effectiveness and mastery better than anything that I know.

> Mr Lloyd George possessed two characteristics which were in harmony with this period of convulsion. First, a power of living in the present, without taking short views. Every day for him was filled with the hope and the impulse of a fresh beginning. He surveyed the problems of each morning with an eye

unobstructed by preconceived opinions, past utterances, or previous disap-
pointments and defeats. In times of peace such a mood is not always admirable,
nor often successful for long. But in the intense crisis when the world was a
kaleidoscope, when every month all the values and relations were changed by
some prodigious event and its measureless reactions, this inexhaustible mental
agility, guided by the main purpose of Victory, was a rare advantage. His
intuition fitted the crisis better than the logical reasoning of more rigid minds.

The quality of living in the present and starting afresh each day led directly
to a second and invaluable aptitude. Mr Lloyd George in this period seemed
to have a peculiar power of drawing from misfortune itself the means of future
success. From the U-boat depredations he obtained the convoy system: out of
the disaster of Caporetto he extracted the Supreme War Council: from the
catastrophe of 21 March (1918) he drew the Unified Command and the
immense American reinforcement.

His ascendancy in the high circles of British Government and in the councils
of the Allies grew in the teeth of calamities. He did not sit waiting upon events
to give a wiseacre judgement. He grappled with the giant events and strove
to compel them, undismayed by mistakes and their consequences. Tradition
and convention troubled him little. He never sought to erect some military or
naval figure into a fetish behind whose reputation he could take refuge. The
military and naval hierarchies were roughly handled and forced to adjust
themselves to the imperious need. Men of vigour and capacity from outside
the Parliamentary sphere became the ministerial heads of great departments.
He neglected nothing that he perceived. All parts of the task of government
claimed his attention and interest. He lived solely for his work and was never
oppressed by it. He gave every decision when it was required. He scarcely
ever seemed to bend under the burden. To his native adroitness in managing
men and committees he now added a high sense of proportion in war policy
and a power of delving to the root of unfamiliar things. Under his Administration both the Island and the Empire were effectually organised for war. He
formed the Imperial War Cabinet which centred in a single executive the
world-spread resources of the British Monarchy. The convoy system, which
broke the U-boat attack at sea: the forward impulsion in Palestine, which
overwhelmed the Turks, and the unified command which inaugurated the
victories in France, belonged in their main stress and resolve as acts of policy
to no one so much as to the First Minister of the Crown.

This is a fascinating passage displaying Churchill's strength and weaknesses as a contemporary historian. Firstly it summarises the creativity
and effectiveness of Lloyd George as a statesman: one can immediately
sense why he dominated those years and why it was right that power was
given to him. Churchill carries conviction; a true professional assessing
generously another professional and analysing his success. But it stops
there. We know from Beaverbrook and a host of other writers that
Lloyd George's methods were as devious as they were subtle, that he
was vindictive, that he personally relished power. To the darker side of
motive Churchill shuts his eye; perhaps he could never open it. And this
is responsible for a certain naïveté in the total picture. It is a vivid
summary of action, not a portrait. Similarly, the style is a compound of

good and bad. Obviously this passage was dictated: the cadences are those of speech, and echo with Churchill's mature and measured rhetoric, yet, from time to time it is repetitious, some phrases are clumsy, and the whole passage is mildly verbose. It could do with more Tacitus and less Gibbon. Whatever its shortcomings, it illustrates Churchill at his best and most valuable. In *The World Crisis*, his dramatic battles may be more brilliant set pieces (Jutland is a fine example), but they do not add much to history, even though they are great contributions to entertainment. But this passage expresses effectively what we might easily miss: the technique of Lloyd George's statesmanship in action. If, however, we wish to see Churchill at his rhetorical worst, one has only to turn, in the same book, to his chapter on the Russian Revolution and, in particular, to his paragraphs on the abdication of the Tsar. Here is overblown rhetorical prose combined with a naïveté of insight that borders on the ridiculous, especially in one who, for a short time, controlled so effectively the destiny of the British people. *The World Crisis*, therefore, is a very uneven book: much of it is naïve, dated and opaque. It is largely story-telling, eschewing analysis in depth and devoid of penetrating studies of personality, but it handles the *executive* capacities of men with rare and masterly skill. It deals convincingly, as few books do, with men operating power ; ignoring why they sought it and, very largely, even the means by which they gained it. The same excellent quality runs through his book *Great Contemporaries*. When he writes of men with whom he had sat in the Cabinet or mixed with in active politics, as with Birkenhead, Joseph Chamberlain, or even Philip Snowden, he has always something penetrating to say; he always, as it were, adds a dimension which other historians rarely perceive – the quality of men as rulers. When he tries to assess great men whom he scarcely knew or actively disliked, such as Lenin or George Bernard Shaw, the lack of insight and imagination, the dominance of simple but vice-like prejudice is quite depressing in so great a man. Both these books, *The World Crisis* and *Great Contemporaries*, need to be handled with care, but they will remain an invaluable source for that age.

The Second World War 1939–45 is in a different category. Churchill was the only statesman, caught up in the huge complexity of a world war fought on a scale that man had never endured before, who realised, even as he toiled, that he might one day write the history of the events in which he was involved. Knowing this, he took the necessary measures not only to acquire the materials but to arrange them. Events and their planned history marched hand in hand. Hence, these six huge volumes on World War II require the most careful assessment, and one not yet made: soon, however, the scholars must get to work, and what a task they will have! By 1940, Churchill had been writing and living history for well over forty years, and no one was more anxious than he that all that he did and all that he said would be judged by the historians of the future. This must have influenced him, both consciously and unconsciously, particularly when he set out his arguments in memoranda which he knew would become historical documents. All this not only led to a certain inflation, but also to an emphasis on what Churchill himself thought to be of major significance for the future. To assess the effects of this interplay of forces, character, and sense of future time will require an exceptionally sensitive scholar. But the historian in Churchill was responsible for deeper issues than this, which is a problem of intricacy rather than depth. He came to World War II with the memory and knowledge, not only of the First World War, but also of the whole panorama of European military history stretching back over a thousand years. To him, Germany was not only the Germany of Hitler but of Bismarck and of Frederick the Great; Russia was not Stalin's Russia but also the Russia of Nicholas II and Alexander I and of Peter the Great. Above all, France was not merely the France of Pétain, but of Clemenceau, of Napoleon, of Louis XIV. His sense of the European past was as acute as that of General De Gaulle, and it informed and, at times, moulded his strategy and his forward-thinking of the European future. A less historically based statesman might easily have been unnerved by the collapse of France and the deep penetration of the German armies into Russia; but Churchill well knew that an encircling alliance had only temporarily failed in the previous three hundred years of European history and, short of a qualitative change in the balance of weapons, was unlikely to fail in 1941 or 1942. At times his sense of historical strategy may have clouded his judgement – it is arguable that he placed too strong an emphasis on the Mediterranean and the Balkans, too little on a frontal assault on Europe. In this book, such strategic concepts as the projected thrust of Alexander's forces into the Danubian basin are argued historically as well as justified by the subsequent course of events. Yet one cannot fail to realise how deeply his sense of history enriched his strategic thinking if one turns from Europe to the East. There his knowledge of history helped him not at all, and he constantly played with dangerous ideas such as landing in Sumatra or Java. He knew the historical geography and military history of Europe supremely well; of the Orient and the Pacific he was as innocent as Roosevelt was of Europe. A fruitful comparison could be made between the great leaders as to the effect history had upon their concepts both of war and peace. Certainly Roosevelt would emerge as the booby. But to analyse all these matters with the care that they deserve would prolong this essay into a book.

When Churchill came to write his history of World War II, he had the materials organised, the concepts at hand, the structure ready. Backed up by a massive organisation, he was the first in the field (a fact of which he realised the importance). With his huge resources he was able to cast his work into an almost official mould, and often it rises to a degree of objectivity rare in the memoirs of great statesmen. Nevertheless it is Churchill's book, in which he himself looms larger than life and his role in the drama, great as it was, magnified. More important is the fact that the war, its narrative and its structure, is organised in a deliberate way by Churchill. The phases of the war are the phases into which he divided it. And this will deeply influence, indeed has already deeply influenced, subsequent historians. They move down the broad avenues which he drove through war's confusion and complexity. Hence, Churchill the historian lies at the very heart of all historiography of World War II, and will always remain there. And the book itself will continue to be read. It is too verbose, at times it is too heavy with self-justification, and, quite understandably, its orientation is often too British. Nor is Churchill always fair to those, such as Wavell, who fell foul of him during the course of the war: of others, especially the Navy, he is too uncritical. The work has the faults that one expects, but it also possesses majestic passages, and throughout it is pervaded by a generous and magnanimous spirit. Furthermore, Churchill's sense of the past brought him a modest measure of hope for the future of mankind. It is, in spite of its theme – war and destruction – a heartening book.

History served Churchill best in his dialogue with his nation. He of all the leaders could give a sense of hopeful destiny even in the hours of darkest trial, and he was able to do this because he had faith in what history taught him about men and women. He was aware of evil, of corruption, of self-seeking and self-indulgence, but when he looked at the great panorama of the past from Blenheim, he saw not only the dark valleys but the broad uplands which he felt humanity might reach. And this hope, this faith, call it what you will, was historically based, and nationally based. England's history was a long struggle for liberty, for freedom and the decencies of human life. In spite of poverty, of greed, of exploitation, the movement had been towards greater civility, towards a greater and more general prosperity. The economic side, of course, was much less significant to him than the political liberties, of which he felt his nation to be the proud guardian – this gave Britain the right to act as a moral bulwark of mankind's decencies. There is, of course, immense simplicity in this attitude. Its historical justification lies in the power of a manufactured past. Yet it is not entire nonsense. The British people have been freer to speak their minds, to dissent from their governments, to go their own wayward way in politics and religion than almost any other community in the Western world; and certainly none so powerful, with so vast an empire, has had so long a history of political and intellectual freedom for its governing classes or made the transition to full democracy with such ease. And this was not only Churchill's source of strength, his constant refreshment in times of tribulation and disaster, but also the nation's which he led. They, too, were historically oriented in a way which few other nations were in 1939. Their national symbols were all historically based. Historical memories were cultivated with extravagant care. Their historical heritage – in cathedrals, castles, manor houses – littered the land but spoke not, as in France or Russia, of revolution; nor, as in Germany, of fragmentation, but of a continuous past, a continuous growth in liberty and in power. And so, throughout the war years, particularly in his great speeches to the people, there was a constant dialogue between Churchill and the nation, in which the past was constantly invoked to fortify the present. And I venture to think that only a statesman steeped in history could have roused and strengthened the nation in the way in which Churchill did during those years. And yet he was using a past which died with the war: indeed, the remarkable thing about Churchill was that this past which he used was still so living, so dynamic, so dynamic a reality for him.

His attitude to the past had been shared by most of his class, and by the historians who belonged to it. G. M. Trevelyan, particularly, thought and felt about the past in much the same way that Churchill did. He, too, was concerned with the story of freedom, of liberty, of the right to dissent, of the decencies between men and classes of men that marked English history over the last two hundred years or more. But in his works there is a strong elegiac note, a sense of despair that is not purely personal, a deep regret for a world that is fading – the world of manor houses, country pursuits, the rule of liberal and tolerant gentlemen – these things, Trevelyan knew, were being destroyed by the accelerating Industrial Revolution. And he realised, too, that the Empire had gone as well as the old values. His view of the past brought nostalgia, a surge of love, but also hopelessness; above all, he wished to turn away from the future.

And Trevelyan's mood was, I suspect, much more in tune with that of the governing class than Churchill's. In 1939, the ruling circles in Britain did not give the impression of being full of eupeptic optimism , but the mood of the upper classes was not necessarily the mood of those who had to fight the war. Their lives, in spite of depression and unemployment, had become decisively better in the twenties and thirties. They were enjoying leisure and mild affluence and a liberty that their grandparents had never known, and they possessed just enough sense of the past for Churchill to draw from them the response that was needed. He painted for them a sense of heroic destiny, and for a time, stimulated by the Blitz, they accepted it. And so Churchill imposed on his nation an essentially aristocratic sense of the past, and so effectively, that the nation responded to his rhetoric.

Once the dangers were over, that sense of the past, so close to myth, did not last: reality broke in. The past which held Churchill in so powerful a grip can no longer move men and women in the way that it did: some of the middle classes may be nostalgically moved, but to the emerging world of scientists, technologists, or affluent suburbia, it is a pasteboard pageantry that indicates nothing and certainly does not sign-post the future. Above all, it dictates neither action nor belief.

The past which Churchill served died with him. In many ways he is the last historic symbol of the Whig tradition – a tradition that was dying and only sprang into renewed vitality through the stress of war. And yet, no one can deny that Churchill was deeply conditioned by his ideological inheritance; that history was not an activity to which he turned for solace or for profit, but a living reality which imbued all that he did or said. History for Churchill provided the dogmas of his faith, the dynamic force which kept him going through the long years of waste and the frightful burdens of power.

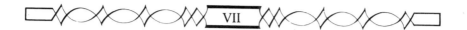

Lord Macaulay

His great-uncle lay at the heart of G. M. Trevelyan's interest in history as much, perhaps, as his own father George Otto Trevelyan whose *Life and Letters of Lord Macaulay* is one of the classic biographies in the English language. Every time (and that when Trevelyan was an undergraduate at Trinity meant every day) he entered the college chapel, he saw the dominating sculptured figure of his uncle. He, himself, came to possess large sections of his great-uncle's library (the margins scored with annotations in Macaulay's hand). Furthermore a great deal of Macaulay's archive came into his possession. I always felt that for Trevelyan Macaulay was a living presence, a man of genius whose reputation was a most sensitive issue for him. It was always Trevelyan's intention to attempt the continuation of Macaulay's *History of England*, at least as far as 1715 – hence his volumes on the reign of Queen Anne, written at the time that Winston Churchill was working on his life of Marlborough. Perhaps one of the most astonishing gestures of Trevelyan's life was that he refused to ask permission of the Duke of Marlborough to consult the Blenheim archives even though they were one of the principal sources for Anne's reign. It is true that Archdeacon Coxe had printed large extracts from these documents in his *Memoirs of John Duke of Marlborough* (3 vols, 1818–19) but Coxe missed much, as did Churchill and his research assistants (for example the cabinet memoranda of the Earl of Sunderland, see p. 82). When I knew Trevelyan well I asked him why he had denied himself the Blenheim archives and he replied, 'I thought that they should be Winston's: after all, they belonged to his family.'

Neither Trevelyan's volumes nor Churchill's reach anywhere near the heights attained by Macaulay, surely, after Gibbon, Britain's greatest historian. In the twentieth century Macaulay has not been in fashion. Although his vigour and his rhetoric may win a little praise he has been dismissed as having a coarse mind and a very simplistic view of the past.

To be consumed with success, to see history as a clear road to progress is regarded as totally insensitive as well as unrealistic; all historical periods are swamps with waterways leading seemingly nowhere, and often it is backwaters rather than the mainstreams that fertilise the future.

Perhaps the most successful attack on the Macaulay–Churchill–Trevelyan view of history was published in 1931, by Herbert Butterfield. Butterfield was the outstanding protégé of Sir Harold Temperley, a pompous, magisterial figure, well-known in Whitehall, as he was heavily engaged in Diplomatic History, then occupying in official esteem the *piano nobile* of the house of history but now packed off to one of the smaller attics. With his connections and his growing volumes of diplomatic papers, Temperley had confidently expected to be nominated to the Regius Chair in 1928. Stanley Baldwin preferred Trevelyan. Butterfield's *The Whig Interpretation of History* (1931) was, although Butterfield refrained from saying so openly, an attack on Trevelyan's historical beliefs. It was a beautifully chosen title, slyly misleading, for that good Tory Sir Arthur Bryant was an even more ardent exponent than Trevelyan, so was Churchill who could only be regarded as a Whig historian by twisting the facts. Patrician history certainly, but the common belief of Tory statesmen as of Whig. *The Whig Interpretation* was also a very short book – short enough to hold the attention of a moderately industrious sixth-former and its views quickly began to appear in the examinable papers of scholarship candidates for Cambridge and Oxford. It should have been subtitled 'Temperley's revenge'.

It also coincided with the publication of Namier's second book and a revived interest in his first which had demolished, for example, the work of Sir George Otto Trevelyan who was a strong link in the descent of 'Whig' theory. It is ironic to think of two such bitter enemies as Namier and Butterfield pursuing, without acknowledging it, the same end.

Macaulay naturally had been a central part of my own work. No one can write about the reign of William III or the Revolution of 1688 without reading him. And no reasonable, educated man could miss reading either his essays or his nephew's life of him. Macaulay's shortcomings were as obvious as his gifts, but his gifts could not be lightly discarded.

In the 1950s a slight revival of interest in Macaulay took place that strengthened steadily in the following decades and led to the great biography by John Clive, *The Young Macaulay* (1973) and the excellent Pinney edition of Macaulay's *Letters* (1982). And Butterfield's book, as time passed, was also brought into sharper focus. It is now regarded as a mere polemic pamphlet which distorted history, if not quite so badly as the distortion which it attacked.

In fact 1955 saw the last great blistering attack on Macaulay's mechanistic and materialistic attitude in Pieter Geyl's *Debates with Historians* (The Hague, 1955) and it was partly in response to this that I published an essay about him. As it appeared in a fairly obscure Canadian journal, *The Toronto Quarterly*, it hardly made a stir. I had previously written an extended review of a selection of his prose and poetry when I had outlined my views of his work and his character. On the latter I made a vital mistake. Trevelyan would not allow me to see Macaulay's letters to his sister Hannah, and that ought to have alerted my suspicions, and in consequence I assumed that Macaulay's emotions were simple and less passionate than they were. However I still hold to the basic concept. Yes, Macaulay loved his sister deeply but that love was never clouded by guilt. Only an uncomplicated man could accept such a relationship as utterly natural, so after the Toronto article, I am printing a review of Macaulay's letters, written twenty years later in which I consider the new evidence. And finally there is a little *jeu d'esprit* on the 'Whig' interpretation and what might replace it. The replacement, I thought, utterly ludicrous; I am now reliably informed it is the passionate belief of a Tory historian at All Souls. Quaint.

Thomas Babington Macaulay

I

On the day in November 1848 when the first volume of Macaulay's *History of England* appeared, Ludgate Hill was jammed with carriages struggling to get to Messrs Longman in Paternoster Row. Three thousand copies were sold in ten days and the pace began to increase rather than slacken. The time came when Robert Longman pressed a cheque for £20,000 on Macaulay on the grounds that he had too much money in his own account. At a guinea a volume this was a prodigious achievement for Victorian times. Although Macaulay naturally thought well of his work, its public reception astonished even him. The reviews were almost uniformly as eulogistic as they were lengthy, but the book was far more than a success of metropolitan literary society:

> At Dukinfield, near Manchester, a gentleman who thought that there would be a certain selfishness in keeping so great a pleasure to himself, invited his poorer neighbours to attend every evening after their work was finished, and read the History aloud to them from beginning to end. At the close of the last meeting, one of the audience rose, and moved, in north country fashion,

a vote of thanks to Mr Macaulay 'for having written a history which working men can understand'.[1]

His success at Windsor was as great as at Manchester. The Prince Consort was so deeply impressed by his book that he immediately offered Macaulay the vacant Chair of Modern History at Cambridge, which Macaulay immediately declined on the grounds that if he were to lecture well he would be forced to give up his *History*. And if he were to write the *History*, his lectures would be bad. Some years later, Queen Victoria recognised Macaulay's unique position in English life and letters by making him a peer – the first writer to achieve such a distinction.

It is obvious from the great financial rewards and public honours which Macaulay's literary works brought him that he wrote very much what his time and generation wished to read. Certainly his own sympathy with his age was greater than that commonly found amongst the great historians. Gibbon who, alone of English historians, can be compared with Macaulay to the latter's disadvantage, offended a considerable section of his reading public by his ironic treatment of the mysteries of the Christian religion. Although perfectly in harmony with the philosophic attitude of the Enlightenment, Gibbon displayed a complete detachment from the aspirations and ideals of the active part of the nation to which he belonged. Macaulay, however, was totally involved in his age – in it he found an echoing response to his own boundless energy and eupeptic confidence. Indeed, it is remarkable how closely Macaulay's character mirrors the strength and weakness of the early Victorian period. And his success must partly lie in the fact that the men and women who read him so eagerly, felt as he felt and believed as he believed: his truth was their truth. That this was so is also borne out by the fact that Macaulay now seems not only far below Gibbon in quality and achievement, but also below Michelet, below Burkhardt, and well below Ranke. He lacked the range of Gibbon, the imagination of Michelet, the penetration of Burkhardt and the wisdom of Ranke. Nor has his scholarship worn so well as theirs.[2] Even so, his qualities still claim for him a place amongst the great historians of the nineteenth century. It is likely that he will always maintain that place, and always be quite widely read. For this reason: in temperament he was very close to a fairly common variety of human personality. To make this clear, Macaulay and his time need to be described in a little more detail.

II

He was born 25 October 1800, the son of Zachary Macaulay who had recently returned from West Africa where he had been in charge of the settlement of freed slaves at Freetown.

Zachary was an evangelical, a member of the Clapham Sect, one of the Saints, a man of formidable and relentless piety. Equally formidable and equally relentless was his industry. The only holiday which he ever took was at Rothley in Leicestershire at the time of his son's birth. Not that this holiday was due to his pleasure in acquiring an heir; it was due entirely to ineluctable circumstance. Zachary had fallen from his horse and broken both arms. Naturally such a father was not slow to inculcate those virtues which he believed to be the only sure guides in a world full of sin. Like Wesley, he believed that industry was the best antidote to temptation. He insisted, of course, on absolute honesty and upon a deep respect for those institutions by which society was governed – the King, the Church, Parliament and the Family. Although Zachary Macaulay was an ardent supporter of the abolition of slavery, he was no reformer. He accepted government as God-given and his desire for reform was limited to the individual conscience. Macaulay's father was, therefore, a man of certainties, one who never hesitated to judge men or events by his own rigid standards. Macaulay's mother held very much the same views as her husband but they were tempered with more obvious affection and, not surprisingly, more obvious ambition for her child. But both parents believed ardently in will-power and in the effectiveness of ratiocination – and from his earliest years Macaulay was encouraged to act like an adult. Childish behaviour or wilful attitudes were thoroughly deplored. He was expected to devote himself actively to a boy's principal task – learning.

Few parents have had a child so apt to their purpose, so willing or so eager to tread in the paths marked for him.

Macaulay possessed a formidable mental equipment in which the most outstanding and remarkable gift was his photographic memory. After having read *Paradise Lost* twice, he could recite without fault the bulk of the poem. He himself said that if Shakespeare's works were to have been destroyed, he could have reproduced them entirely from memory. A memory of such proportions naturally strengthened Macaulay's self-confidence: on questions of fact he was always right; time and time again he triumphed over less exact men. Such a faculty fed his self-assertiveness, and, as he believed that his judgement was based on knowledge, he had few doubts about the validity of his attitudes. A powerful sense of certainty pervades all that Macaulay wrote and there can be little doubt that this was strengthened by the absolute accuracy of the facts which he could recollect.

Yet essentially Macaulay's was a selective memory controlled and exercised by those preconceptions which were the very fibres of his personality. The facts were fitted into his pattern of judgement. They demonstrated the virtues of liberty and progress or they could be used to show the iniquity of those men who tried to oppose their development. Facts never became the object of imaginative exercise. Macaulay never tried to feel through them, irrespective of judgement, to the reality of times alien to his own world. He remembered what was useful to his own sharp, confident vision. The irrelevant was, however, meaningless to him. His memory was neither the stimulator of curiosity nor its servant; it was a weapon of didacticism.

A fabulous memory was not the only outstanding quality of Macaulay's intellectual make-up. He possessed an immense appetite for learning. As soon as he could read, he was wolfing down universal histories, plays, sermons, poems, classics. He mastered languages with ease and delighted in mathematical exercises – throughout his life he had a passion for doing long arithmetical calculations in his head. To memory and appetite was added order. There was nothing ragged or diffuse about Macaulay's interests. He quickly reduced his knowledge to a system. His earliest essays, even his earliest letters, are remarkable for the lucidity of their arrangement and the aptness of the facts and quotations used to illustrate his arguments. And finally to this impressive list of intellectual qualities must be added a sense of style as personal as it was powerful. At the age of five, a servant of Lady Waldegrave's scalded his legs with hot coffee, and when asked some minutes later how he did, he replied, 'Thank you, Madam, the agony has somewhat abated.' And for the rest of his life his style remained formal, balanced and frequently pompous. His public performances, either in essays or in speeches, were also loaded with erudition, yet he was never dull. All that he had to say was too pungent, too vigorous and too decided to allow a reader's interest to decay.

Macaulay was, therefore, extravagantly well endowed. He possessed a mind of exceptional range and almost incredible accuracy. His intellectual energy displayed volcanic force, but the rapid, almost torrential, flow of his thought was confined by a strict sense of form and order. Few men have been equipped with Macaulay's ability to reduce a complex mass of fact and argument to clear and lucid exposition. And yet these qualities were matched by weaknesses which have grown more apparent with time.

III

Macaulay's emotional make-up was exceedingly simple; as simple as his mind was complex. Although in his journal he left a detailed record of his daily feelings, it is almost devoid of those emotional experiences which provide the structure of most men's lives. Macaulay was never in love. His strongest attachment was to his family. When his sister, Hannah, decided to marry, he was surprised, pained and then resigned to the separation realising his own obtuse folly in never having considered such a possibility. That blow was the most grievous personal loss that he ever experienced and he buried the pain it caused him very quickly. Time and time again in his diary he refers with pleasure to the sustained happiness of his life. On his fiftieth birthday he wrote:

> Well, I have had a happy life. I do not know that anybody whom I have seen close, has had a happier. Some things I regret; but, on the whole, who is better off? I have no children of my own, it is true: but I have children whom I love as if they were my own, and who, I believe, love me. I wish that the next ten years may be as happy as the last ten. But I rather wish it than hope it.

His last sentence refers to his fear of death, one of his only terrors throughout his early life. He could, however, have 'hoped it', for this fear weakened as death itself approached and he met it with the same serenity with which he lived so much of his life.

Yet, although there was an inner core of tranquility, based on successful repression, Macaulay was not devoid of strong feeling. He was insatiably ambitious and when writing his *History* he was constantly preoccupied with speculations as to how it would be regarded in the year 2000 or 3000. He thoroughly savoured and enjoyed the great fame which came to him, and felt that it was a proper reward for his unflagging industry and his concentration of purpose. Furthermore his feelings about public affairs or individuals could be intense: the reform of Parliament, the abolition of slavery, the duties of Englishmen in India, or Byron, Boswell or Horace Walpole – all aroused in him strong feelings. Heredity, education and temperament gave him a bias towards decided moral attitudes in which powerful feeling was blended with absolute certainty of right or wrong. This moral passion in Macaulay, so much in tune with the atmosphere of his age, sprang to some extent from the directness of his own feelings. The lack of any real sympathy with the strong, surging animal passions which could destroy and ruin men, was a serious defect in a man who aspired to be a historian of genius. Yet the fault lay deeper than this. It was not the moral weaknesses of men such as Boswell or Shaftesbury that disturbed Macaulay so profoundly. There was a deeper jealousy at work.

Both in character and in intellect Macaulay was in the last analysis a simple man – simple and lucid – no matter how intricate the surface machinery might appear to be. On occasion he could be hot and choleric yet always about surface matters. He lacked the roots of life, sexual passion, and the sense of tragedy that it arouses – the biting, painful sense of the transience of living and loving men. Oddly enough the cool-tempered Gibbon, so much more detached from life than Macaulay, felt these things much more strongly. At the heart of Macaulay's being there was immaturity, an inhibition of passion, or an inability to face where it might lead him, which made him distrust it in other men. But unfortunately for Macaulay creative energy is usually fertilised by the chaos of passionate life – not always, but frequently. Consequently, Macaulay never penetrates to the heart of human existence. His attempts at poetry are dreadfully banal – the metrical exercises of a clever boy in which the emotional situations have been taken from literature and not from life.[3] The same sterility, the same artificiality of feeling, is present in most of the great descriptive passages of his *History*. Although his account of the siege of Londonderry is *a tour de force* of narrative skill, the human figures are two-dimensional, conventional characters, lacking the convincing reality which a more imaginative and creative writer would have given them.

The limitation of Macaulay's emotional range was one of the grave faults of character which weakened his powers as a writer, but it was not the only one. Creative thinking often works very mysteriously, one might almost say in darkness. Suddenly there is a moment of illumination; inconsistencies are resolved, interrelations discovered, and a new vision of reality perceived. In Macaulay's mind, however, there was no darkness, no obscurity, no inconsistency, nothing unrelated. Everything was lucid and certain. Macaulay lacked doubt; lacked the confused, groping, searching mind which is often so much more creative, except perhaps in mathematics, than a mind of absolute clarity. And paradoxically enough, though Macaulay loved facts, he did not possess a really inquiring mind. At first sight that may seem a fantastic statement, yet it is true. Macaulay took pleasure in being accurate, yet he did not love facts for their own sake, but merely to arrange them in patterns to his own satisfaction. The patterns were those of a conventional and accepting mind. He viewed the Revolution of 1688 as did the average Whig reader of his day. His vast learning became merely a brilliant illustration of commonplace ideas, for his ideas were rarely formed by his knowledge. His knowledge decorated his convictions. He saw the seventeenth century in terms of his own political beliefs, and in terms of his own morality; and he was quite content to do so. This, of course, was a crippling handicap to a historian for it produced satisfaction and decision too quickly. Lacking curiosity and suspicion, Macaulay had little or no interest in ferreting out facts for their own sake. The hope of a new or startling revealation never sent him searching in strange places for new sources. Compared with other great nineteenth-century historians he added remarkably little that was new to our knowledge of the past. Accepting too easily facts which suited his didactic argument, Macaulay committed grave errors of scholarship. Forster, Paget and

Spedding had little difficulty in marshalling convincing evidence against judgements that Macaulay had made with too great confidence on too little evidence.

This severe limitation of curiosity to the accumulation of the knowledge which Macaulay wanted was responsible for his weakness as an historian: his lack of grasp of the intricacy of human character and his over-confident judgement of it. True, his own emotional deficiencies had severely restricted his experience of the dark, passionate, tumultuous side of life, yet often creative men have lived lives as quiet as Macaulay's. They, however, have been haunted by imagination, or known the jungles buried in their own hearts, so that they were able to appreciate the difficulties and confusions of more active men. But for Macaulay the precepts of morality were as clear as those of politics and as simple. The complexity of character was lost on him and he depicted the men and women of his *History* and *Essays* in simple terms of good and bad. He never sought beyond the obvious. In consequence, Macaulay was far more successful in describing action or political debate than he was in portraying human beings.

Macaulay was, therefore, a man of formidable learning, fluent, confident, decisive in his judgements. But beneath a powerful intellect there lay a simple, rather childlike heart. Although he was a thrusting, ambitious man, with a muscular, forceful mind, yet in certain fields of human experience he was curiously opaque. His lack of subtlety or of real creative depth proved to be no obstacle to his success. The men and women of his time loved to hear certainties; confidence was a part of the air they breathed.

IV

Although as a child Macaulay had spent hours writing vast verse dramas and world histories, it proved quite impossible for him as a young man to follow a literary career. Indeed, though he wrote a good deal, he probably did not in his early youth desire such a career. Precise scholarship did not appeal to him; and he was drawn irresistibly to politics where his intellectual capacities and immoderate fluency were bound to make him famous as well as redoubtable. His success was immediate, and within a short time he could fill the House of Commons as no other speaker could. He was no debater, no orator in the usual sense. He spoke in a loud, clear, unmodulated voice without a gesture. One of the parliamentary reporters of the time described his manner in these terms:

> Vehemence of thought, vehemence of language, vehemence of manner were his chief characteristics. The listener might almost fancy he heard ideas and words gurgling in the speaker's throat for priority of utterance. There was

nothing graduated, or undulating, about him. He plunged at once into the
heart of the matter, and continued his loud resounding pace from beginning
to end, without halt or pause. This vehemence and volume made Macaulay
outside their ordinary experience, they were fairly nonplussed by the display
of names and dates, and titles. He was not a long-winded speaker. In fact,
his earnestness was so great that it would have failed under a very long effort.[4]

Although he become one of the great speakers of the Commons, he
was not, considering his abilities, a successful politician. He quickly lost
his Tory principles, much to his father's regret, and became an ardent
disciple of moderate Whig reform. He had no use for Brougham whom
he considered to be an immoral, as well as a dangerous, radical. He
strongly disapproved of socialist or Jacobin sentiments – indeed, he
detested Wordsworth's *Prelude* because he thought its political implications too revolutionary. He believed passionately in orderly progress,
gradual reform and in the ultimate triumph of technology through liberal
education. He was convinced that it was England's singular destiny to
disseminate these virtues through the world. For Macaulay the 1851
exhibition was the crowning glory of human achievement. He wrote in
his diary of his visit to the Crystal Palace:

> I made my way into the building; a most gorgeous sight; vast; graceful;
> beyond the dream of the Arabian romances. I cannot think that the Caesars
> ever exhibited a more splendid spectacle. I was quite dazzled, and I felt as I
> did on entering St Peter's.

This was the demonstration of England's industrial majesty, the final
justification of the long struggle for civil and religious liberty. 'The
history of England', declared Macaulay, 'is emphatically the history of
progress' and by progress he meant what he saw about him in the Great
Exhibition – material progress – for he believed that the amelioration
of the conditions in which man lived made him more virtuous. Macaulay
saw in Francis Bacon the first great exponent of this empirical philosophy
and he realised that many would mock him for this materialist outlook.
'Some people', he wrote, 'may take the object of the Baconian philosophy
a low object but they cannot deny that, high or low, it has been attained.'
And after dismissing ancient philosophy as sterile and useless, he
hammers home in a passionate, breathless passage the victories of
empirical philosophy:

> It has lengthened life; it has mitigated pain; it has extinguished diseases; it
> has increased the fertility of the soil; it has given new securities to the mariner;
> it has furnished new arms to the warrior; it has spanned great rivers and
> estuaries with bridges of form unknown to our fathers; it has guided the
> thunderbolt innocuously from heaven to earth; it has lighted up the night

with the splendour of the day; it has extended the range of the human vision; it has multiplied the power of the human muscles; it has accelerated motion; it has annihilated distance; it has facilitated intercourse, correspondence, all friendly offices, all dispatch of business; it has enabled man to descend to the depths of the sea, to soar into the air, to penetrate securely into the noxious recesses of the earth, to traverse the land in cars which whirl along without horses, and the ocean in ships which run ten knots an hour against the wind. These are but a part of its fruits, and of its first fruits. For it is a philosophy which never rests, which has never attained, which is never perfect. Its law is progress. A point which yesterday was invisible is its goal today, and will be its starting-post tomorrow.[5]

This outlook has been criticised as philistine, blinkered, nerveless, unimaginative. At the time that Macaulay was trumpeting his praise, Carlyle, Disraeli and others were brooding over the suffering and poverty which the Industrial Revolution had brought into being – a fact which many observers were quick to seize on. Aesthetes and philosophers deplored the frank materialism of Macaulay's outlook and modern commentators have not been much more sympathetic. Professor Geyl, Macaulay's most perceptive critic, maintains that this 'religion of progress' prevented Macaulay from being a really great historian. 'That feeling', he writes 'of absolute certainty about the superiority of the present and about the unqualified beneficence of the gradual increase of the technical and scientific knowledge at the disposal of mankind . . . must lead the historian to view the past in terms which may be entirely irrelevant and result in a picture lacking in the truth of intimacy . . . to my way of thinking, however stimulating and instructive and powerfully intelligent I may find Macaulay's work, this mental attitude towards the past is in the deepest sense unhistoric.'[6] Since Macaulay wrote, the prevalent mood of European society has been one of doubt if not of despair – at least in literary and philosophical circles – and it is a mood that naturally enough is deeply antipathetic to Macaulay's own.

And yet in that way was Macaulay wrong? The material progress of mankind is the one certain, glorious triumph which no one can deny. Treating history polemically, and it can be treated polemically, Macaulay was quite right, incontrovertibly right, and in no way unhistorical except in so far as he attributed a conscious and deliberate purpose to man's evolution. But history can be more than polemics: it is also a quest for reality in which suffering, ignorance, folly, decay and failure are as valid as happiness, knowledge, wisdom, growth and success. These are the realms which more imaginative and sensitive historians, such as Ranke or Burkhardt, have made their own, and because their works have recreated a more complex and accurate reality, their scholarship is both more profound and more durable. Yet unsubtle, dogmatic and philistine as Macaulay was, he still has the best of the argument. Man's prime reason for self-congratulation is his triumph over the material universe.

For Macaulay life and history were all of a piece, the unfolding pattern of virtue, justice, progress. A gigantic, if naïve, faith infused his attitude to present politics as well as to the historic past. The same direct, materialistic common sense made him very effective on specific political issues, but it rendered him too unyielding, too unsupple for the shifty world of high politics, where more imagination and more sense of reality would have served him better. Although he reached cabinet rank before he was forty (as Secretary at War), his greatest achievement in public life was not in politics but in administration during his residence in India as a member of the Supreme Council, particularly the time that he spent as President of the Commission of Public Instruction and afterwards as President of the Law Commission.

The tasks which Macaulay tackled while he held these posts in India were completely commensurate with his abilities. His minute on Indian Education is a masterly summary of the complexity of native languages, customs and educational methods, and the difficulties which would face India unless a common language were found to meet the needs of a more uniform and complex administration and of the growth of technology. He then planned a scheme of education, primary, secondary and technical, including the production of qualified teachers; as might be expected his attention to detail was absolute and reached down to textbooks and grammars. As President of the Law Commission he set about reducing the wild chaos of Indian customary law and argued strongly for the introduction of the principles of British justice, with the consequence that one of the greatest benefits conferred by the British on India has been a reasonably unified, coherent and wise system of law. The brilliance of Macaulay's administrative ability is thus partly responsible for the excellence of Indian education and justice. On these questions the strength of his mind and character had full play; his weaknesses were of no importance. A comprehensive factual knowledge and a sense of relevance were more apt than creative imagination or a knowledge of fellow men and women. And his empirical philosophy was fully justified.

V

Politics and administration provided large opportunities for the exercise of Macaulay's singular talents; the majority of men might have been content with his achievements and the rewards which they brought. Undeniably they gave Macaulay deep satisfaction, but curiously enough they proved in the end inadequate. He had never ceased to be drawn to literature; he had started to scribble as a child and he could not stop.

From the age of twenty-four he wrote regularly for the *Edinburgh Review*, and what he contributed was so novel, so exciting, that his reputation was quickly made. Macaulay in his very first essay used the pretext of a review to write a short biography of the subject of the book under discussion – in this case, Milton.

Biography had not, in Macaulay's day, become an important, regular part of the yearly output of books. Apart from Boswell's *Johnson* it was still largely a matter of short memorial sermons or pamphlets or huge and tedious compilations of ill-edited letters and memoirs.[7] In his essays Macaulay provided something fresh and exciting. Usually after a few paragraphs displaying the profound ignorance of the author's knowledge of his subject, and of course the superiority of Macaulay's, he settled down to give a short biographical sketch in which his judgements were as rapid, authoritative and final as the style was flamboyant and pungent. As Macaulay could compress a massive quantity of material into a short space and without the least confusion or congestion, he was able to give a remarkably comprehensive account not only of a man, but of the time in which he lived. Macaulay in these essays set out deliberately to startle the mind and he sought paradox rather than avoided it. He wrote them too with magnificent journalistic verve – once read, never forgotten. To give some idea of their flavour here is a passage on Horace Walpole:

The conformation of his mind was such that whatever was little seemed to him great, and whatever was great seemed to him little. To chat with blue-stockings, to write little copies of complimentary verses on little occasions, to superintend a private press, to preserve from natural decay the perishable topics of Ranelagh and White's, to record divorces and bets, Miss Chudleigh's absurdities and George Selwyn's good sayings, to decorate a grotesque house with pie-crust battlements, to procure rare engravings and antique chimney-boards, to match odd gauntlets, to lay out a maze of walks within five acres of ground, these were the grave employments of his long life. From these he turned to politics as to an amusement. After the labours of the print-shop and the auction-room, he unbent his mind in the House of Commons. And, having indulged in the recreation of making laws and voting millions, he returned to more important pursuits, to researches after Queen Mary's comb, Wolsey's red hat, the pipe which Van Tromp smoked during his last sea-fight, and the spur which King William struck into the flank of Sorrel.

In everything in which Walpole busied himself, in the fine arts, in literature, in public affairs, he was drawn by some strange attraction from the great to the little, and from the useful to the odd. The politics in which he took the keenest interest were politics scarcely deserving of the name. The growlings of George the Second, the flirtations of Princess Emily with the Duke of Grafton, the amours of Prince Frederic and Lady Middlesex, the squabbles between Gold Stick in waiting and the Master of the Buckhounds, the disagreements between the tutors of Prince George, these matters engaged almost all the attention which Walpole could spare from matters more important still, from bidding for Zinckes and Petitots, from cheapening fragments of tapestry and handles of old lances, from joining bits of painted glass, and from setting up memorials of departed cats and dogs. While he was fetching and carrying the gossip of Kensington Palace and Carlton House, he fancied that he was writing history.[8]

Rarely before had the public been regaled with such language or treated to the opinions of a scholar so absolutely confident of the morality and wisdom of his judgements. Naturally his essays brought him great popularity and his literary fame grew as he made his way in the world of politics. Macaulay himself, however, did not set great store by these essays: he did not realise that he was helping to create a new taste for short, vivid biographical studies and he himself thought of his work as being merely ephemeral. Yet he drew a deeper satisfaction from these brief excursions into literature than he did from most of his public activities and the fortunate combination of a valuable legacy with his defeat at the General Election of 1847 brought about his decision to retire from politics and devote himself entirely to history. The last twelve years of his life were spent in writing a *History of England* from 1688 to the nineteenth century. It was planned on a monumental scale to challenge comparison with the world's greatest historians – Thucydides, Herodotus and the rest – for Macaulay's ambition was as grandiose as his conception;

He failed even to complete the reign of William III and he was honest enough to admit that his work fell short of the highest achievements in the writing of history. Nevertheless, it remains one of the great historical works in the English language, second only to Gibbon's. And probably at no time in his life could Macaulay have written a better one, for by the time he settled down to write his history his mind was formed, his style perfected and his experience completed. His beliefs were straightforward yet unshakeable. He put his trust in those same virtues which his evangelical father and mother had bred in him: honesty, loyalty, charity, industry and absolute respect for the Christian ideals of marriage and family life. If a man lied, took bribes, dabbled in treason, or fornicated, he was a bad man, so Shaftesbury and Marlborough were bad men: an occasional peccadillo, especially if discreet, could be forgiven as William III was forgiven for having a mistress, but the combination of immorality and chicanery to be found in Shaftesbury was too much for Macaulay. These simple black and white judgements are couched in absolute terms: the *need* in a Shaftesbury or a James II for the life that they led is never explored.

Macaulay's characters, however, had to pass more than moral tests. They were required to have discovered the right side in politics. Macaulay believed that the prosperity, liberty and political freedom of his own time were the result of those seventeenth-century struggles between King and Parliament, between Church and Puritan, and between Tory and Whig. Prosperity and imperial greatness marched with liberty, toleration and Whig doctrine. William, Prince of Orange, became the embodiment of the good – the hero of the Victorian world and a maker of the nation. Although this estimate contains more truth, perhaps, than many modern critics of Macaulay would allow, it is altogther too simple, too *determined* to carry conviction. It leaves out the muddled, chaotic, stumbling nature of human activity, and in doing so distracts rather than clarifies the reality which Macaulay hoped to depict. And of course he is baffled, totally baffled, by a character as complex as the second Earl of Sunderland who, after acting as James ɪɪ's confidant almost to the Revolution, reappears shortly after it as the trusted adviser of William ɪɪɪ himself.

To some extent historical events, too, had to be forced into the same mechanical pattern and they are judged by Macaulay as men are judged, according to whether they aided or thwarted the Whig cause. It was quite impossible for him to see that the Tories were largely responsible for the Revolution of 1688 although the facts stared him in the face. Indeed for a modern scholar his history of political management is naïve and jejeune, weak in analysis, and unscholarly in detail. He attempted the impossible task of forcing the politics of William's reign into a rigid dichotomy of Whig versus Tory. Once more his love of clarity bedevilled the truth. He would have men and events clear cut and therefore got them wrong. The rigidity of his intellect and the simplicity of his heart are implicit in almost every page that he wrote.

Glaring as these faults are, the *History* remains a great book. By the time Macaulay was 47 he was naturally fully aware of his literary abilities. He knew that he possessed admirable skill in narrative, for his fabulous and accurate memory and his disciplined schematic mind could hold the complete, detailed story that he wished to tell, ready for his pen. His great set pieces, like the Siege of Londonderry or the Massacre of Glencoe, were written straight out of his head, once he had digested and memorised his materials. This, of course, gave them a wonderful fluency and unity. And although he frequently altered his words and rewrote considerably, he never had to verify the detail which he knew with such absolute certainty.

Furthermore, he had developed his style to the point where it was a complete reflection of his thought and feeling so that the full flavour of his truculent, virile personality could be savoured in every paragraph. Few historians have been so easy to read or so easy to remember once read. The authority with which he wrote induced a ready acceptance of his vision of history in the mind of his reader. Also his great intellectual powers and his personal experience of politics enabled him to recreate the political debates of William's reign in a way which can, perhaps, never be bettered. He gives the excitement of a battle to the struggles in the Commons. In some aspects of his history, too, Macaulay showed great originality. He realised from his knowledge of his own times that the political structure of a country is deeply influenced by its economic interests and by the pattern of its society, so he devoted considerable space to depicting the social habits of the late Stuart times and gave many pages, and very admirable ones, to the foundation of the Bank of England and the Recoinage.

In spite of all the criticism which can be levelled against it, the *History* remains a great work of literature and scholarship. And so do Macaulay's essays. In a hundred years England has not produced a historian of his stature. He was an intellectual giant and although he lacked the imagination, the poetry, the sense of tragedy which is present in the very greatest writers, these were almost all that he lacked. Every other quality that a great writer needs he possessed in abundance: he was able to project his mind and personality into words so forcibly that his history has become a part of our common heritage. And what some choose to regard as his prejudices command both admiration and respect. He believed in liberal virtues and faith in man's capacity to control and order not only history but the world about him. Although this led him to many false and intolerant judgements, they should not blind critics to the basic truth of Macaulay's conviction. In the material world in which he took such optimistic delight, man has made undeniable progress by the use of those qualities that Macaulay possessed in such abundance – memory, order, intelligence.

The Letters of Thomas Babington Macaulay

When I used to stay with Macaulay's great-nephew, G. M. Trevelyan, in the evening of his life, he did, from time to time, express his concern about what critics and biographers might make of some of the expressions used by Macaulay in his letters to his grandmother, Macaulay's favourite sister, Hannah. After his death, the full Macaulay archive became available to scholars.

The first in the field was John Clive with his masterly biography of *The Young Macaulay*, and a perceptive essay by Peter Gay in *Style in History* which would seem to justify Trevelyan's fears. Thomas Pinney, who has edited superbly these first two volumes of what will be the definitive edition of Macaulay's correspondence, has no doubt that Hannah's imminent departure to India with her husband, Charles

Trevelyan, in 1859, destroyed Macaulay's will to live and 'therefore contributed directly to his death in that year, shortly before her departure'. Peter Gay states quite bluntly that Macaulay's feelings for his two young sisters were erotic, and that his passion for Hannah was a gratifying, if ungratified incest. Some twenty years ago I took the opposite view, that Macaulay was not a sexually complicated man. Where lies the truth, and do these letters give us new insights into the wells of Macaulay's creativity and ambition? So far, the letters only reach 1833, but these were the formative years of Macaulay's formidable talent, and they contain a very large number of letters indeed of Macaulay's adolescence and early manhood. From the middle of 1831 Hannah becomes his major correspondent. So the material is fully available, at last, to formulate a considered judgement.

The evidence of these letters is, I think, incontrovertible about one aspect of Macaulay's nature. He was a much more deeply affectionate, one might say passionately affectionate, man, certainly than I allowed, or indeed most of his critics have so far allowed. Also one must agree with John Clive and Peter Gay that his Jehovah-like father, Zachary, played a crucial role in both the formation of his character and in the making of his ambition. Zachary, whose letters to Macaulay have sometimes to be read indirectly through his son's replies, obviously offered a disturbing mixture of love, approbation, suspicion, and sharp criticism. He was capable of playing the moral heavy-weight and often condemned the light-hearted gaieties of Macaulay's letters with a ponderous authority. Macaulay begged his father to allow him to write without weighing the moral, political, or social implications of every sentence. He wanted to write, he said, as he might talk at home. This plea had no effect on Zachary, who went on remorselessly criticising and condemning, although, to be fair, from time to time he did express immense pride and satisfaction in his son's achievements. Few could now doubt from the evidence of these letters that Zachary knotted his son's emotions in a way that could never be untied. What young man would cease to write for a magazine at the age of 22 because his father disapproved of its other contributors with a passion that bordered on religious mania? Macaulay did. Macaulay's relationship with his father was deeply ambivalent, and the need for his father's approbation was a dynamic force in Macaulay's overwhelming ambition. However, one has only to read his schoolboy letters to realise that the strain and ambivalence towards his father intensified with the years, as Macaulay himself grew successful and independent; a time, alas, when his father began to fall, and this was the period when the knots in his relationship tightened. During Macaulay's childhood and adolescence, his relationship with his father had contained a great deal of sweetness and love. Also, by thirteen

Macaulay was powerfully ambitious, omnivorous for knowledge, and parched for approbation, and certainly not merely his father's. The full drive of Macaulay's life cannot be explained in relation to Zachary.

Almost all sons love their mothers, most, from the onset of adolescence, uneasily. This was not true of Macaulay. Indeed, it is the hallmark of the extreme candour of his nature, the simplicity and direct-ness of his emotions, and his capacity to accept them that, as a young man of twenty, he could write as follows to his mother:

> There is nothing I remember with such pleasure as the time when you nursed me at Aspenden. The other night, when I lay on my sofa very hypochondriac and sick with physic, I was thinking over that time. How sick and sleepless, and weak I was, lying in bed, when I was told that you were come! How well I remember with what an ecstasy of joy I saw that face approaching me, in the middle of people that did not care if I died that night. . . . The sound of your voice, the touch of your hand are present to me now, and will be, I trust to God, to my last hour . . . I must stop. I am not often sentimental, and I had no intention of pouring out what I am much more used to think than to express.

Measured against such feelings, all ambitions, all rewards faded into nothing. And, I think, the core of Macaulay's emotional life was his family. Sent away as a small boy to school for months and months on end, he felt banished from Eden. Doubtless he held his father partly responsible, possibly attributed to himself some indefinable guilt for his being cast away; but home and family retained the refulgent glow of love and warmth, of shared pleasures, excitements, hopes, ambitions. And when he finally got back to his family, the two young sisters were there: bright, loving, Hannah, with an intelligence almost comparable to his own. All of this was candidly, openly felt. But Macaulay wanted to triumph not only to win Zachary, but also to bathe in the approbation of his family.

At no point in these letters is there a sense of complexity, of a tortured spirit, of a man driven by deep sexual forces. A strongly affectionate man, certainly a man troubled by his father, but what is so impressive is the smooth development of Macaulay's intellectual strength and of his omnivorous appetite for learning that grows steadily, without check, from 5 to 25. And how very early developed that robust clarity of judgement, the downright common sense; no nonsense as a boy about the romanticism of Mary, Queen of Scots. And it is this very directness of response, not only to intellectual problems, but also to his own feelings for his mother, for his family, even for his father that makes me doubt too Freudian an interpretation of his attachment to his young sisters. After all, he was 30 before he became deeply attracted to Hannah, and by then he must have achieved some solution to his sexual needs, however strong or weak they were. That he needed Hannah, that she came to embody the forces of affection and creativity, no one can deny. All great writers are writing to someone. They need someone to convince about the truth of the world as they see it. Like limpets they seize on rocks that come to hand. Macaulay's rock was his family, and in the end the centre of the family was Hannah. To go beyond that, no matter how violent his statement when he learned of her certain departure, is to stray into speculation.

It should, however, be stressed that, apart from the light which these letters shed on Macaulay's inner life, and the drive of ambition, they also contain marvellous vignettes of the social and political world of the late 1820s and early 1830s — the great parties at Lansdowne House, the dinners with the Hollands, and an unforgettable description of Sidney Smith at home in his Yorkshire parsonage. Once Macaulay's quill touched the paper he was ebulliently alive. Loud-mouthed, bullying, a torrential talker he may have been: on paper he is all radiance.

The Good Old Cause

In spite of the battering at the hands of historiographers as diverse in their attitude to life as Herbert Butterfield and Peter Geyl, the Whig view of English history still dominates our conception of our past, and rightly so, for the narrative of English history is as Whiggish as that of America is democratic. This does not mean, of course, that English and American governments have always been imbued with a sense of liberty or democracy; or that they have pursued with missionary zeal the fulfilment in the world at large of those concepts which have found such nourishment within the growing structures of their own societies. But viewed as a story, there can be no convincing Tory history of modern England.

Clarendon could write Tory history because he could genuinely feel that Charles I should have won the Civil War or, rather, that it should never have taken place. Hume was still near enough to the seventeenth century to cast urbane Tory sympathy, like a miasma, over the events of his own immediate past. But, viewing the last three centuries, in what would a Tory have to take regret or delight? Delight in Cromwell's failure, but regret Exclusion; praise James II, yet condemn the Revolution of 1688; sorrow for the Pretender, but sneer at the Hanoverian succession; despise the Reform Bills and the spreading franchise of nineteenth-century England, yet take refuge in the hypocrisies of Tory democracy or the false pageantry of the Empire in India; gloat over the long delay of Ireland's freedom; connive at Carson's dabbling with treason;

grow purple at the thought of the Lords' reform; rail against the welfare state and the dissolution of Empire. It would be a weird society that read with avidity a history that regretted three centuries of its past. One need search no further for the continuing success of Macaulay and Trevelyan or why they are still read by tens of thousands of Englishmen. Nor, perhaps, as to why most Tory historians despise or evade narrative history or, if they should ever try to write it, as Churchill did, then proceed to write not like a Tory but like a Whig grandee of Holland House. And think of the galaxy of Tory heroes – mainly phonies or failures – Charles II, Danby, Anne, Bolingbroke, Eldon, Liverpool, Disraeli. What a fine, trumpeting, annihilating essay Macaulay could have written on this theme – biased, exaggerated, insensitive, evasive, yet polemically right.

That, as H. R. Trevor-Roper indicates, in a brilliant introductory essay to a new collection of Macaulay's essays, in the essence of Macaulay. His faults are brazen. He lacked insight into human character, could ignore motive, ride roughshod over facts that might trip up his interpretation, and belabour his antagonists with the vulgarity of an intellectual fishwife. His characterisation of Bacon is as ludicrous as his characterisation of Marlborough: unable to resist the dramatic antithesis of what he considered to be the two sides of Bacon's nature – the corrupt, sycophantic worshipper of absolute kingship with the progressive, scientific philosopher, he presents a travesty of interpretation, a wild exaggeration that distorts the truth except in its final equation, where the essence of truth remains. Bacon was prepared to back the authority of kingship to a point which would have endangered that extension of the political establishment which Macaulay regarded, perhaps rightly, as one of the great triumphs of seventeenth-century England. The same is true of so much of Macaulay: his greatness rests not only on the vigour of his narrative, nor on the immense readability of his prose, nor even in the quality of Olympic grandeur that infuses everything that he wrote. It goes deeper than that. He embodies an attitude which must seem true to the majority of those who read him: his belief in progress, not only material, but moral; and that belief chimes with an essential optimism that, in spite of the cloud of Jeremiahs that infest our intellectual life, is implicit in modern life. Such claims are too vast to be argued here, but they underlie the Whig interpretation of history, expressed in its broadest sense.

More narrowly, of course, the Whig interpretation is the history of how the British political structure, its political nation, has adapted and changed itself to meet new social conditions and so both evaded revolution or the loss of power. Whig and grandee are not entirely incompatible terms, and Whig history has never been radical history. Indeed, the most effective criticism of Whig history derives from the left rather than the right. Macaulay had no love for the masses, nor his great-nephew, Trevelyan, any delight in industrial society. Essentially Whig history is the story of success, or awareness of political reality, of capacity to adapt in order to survive; from which emerged a morality of liberalism capable, until very recently, of carrying the masses with it. This being so, it is easy to see why Macaulay judged character by the simplicity of events. William III brought about the Revolution of 1688, which succeeded, therefore he was praiseworthy. Milton opposed Charles I, supported Oliver Cromwell, *ergo*. In the flood-tide of early nineteenth-century confidence, it was easier to believe such simplicities than in the early twentieth, when G. M. Trevelyan was writing. The core of Trevelyan's beliefs about British society and British history differed little from Macaulay's, but the eupeptic confidence was gone; the world of the Whig aristocracy was too threatened for simple white and black: and in Trevelyan's pages black has become grey. Turn to anything that Macaulay found so easy to judge; for example, the execution of Charles I, in Trevelyan's pages, and the difference in tone is immediately apparent. Sympathy for Charles I, sympathy for the doomed cavaliers at Oxford, pervades his pages; a sense of tragic ineluctable destiny now replaces the brassy, triumphant note of justice meted out by Macaulay to those too stupid to comprehend the tide of history.

And so, in Trevelyan's work there is an extra dimension, an imaginative sympathy for the losers, stimulated doubtless by Trevelyan's profound conviction that the Whig world of benevolent grandeur was about to pass into oblivion, but this tenderness to the failures in history never submerges Trevelyan's fundamental belief that British society had been triumphant, glorious and wise and that the history of nineteenth-century England was, taken by and large, a moral as well as material triumph. A Whig attitude provides the anatomy of his work. Of course, there are personal differences, too, between these two historians. Macaulay's life was curiously overshadowed by personal pain, Trevelyan's was darkened by it; Macaulay's temperament was almost unbearably sunny, Trevelyan's bordered on the morose. Macaulay took immense delight in society, Trevelyan longed for solitude. But both were supreme craftsmen, both could write narrative history as no other historians of their generations could. They are still immensely readable; indeed, Trevelyan's *British History in the Nineteenth Century and After* is still unmatched: dated in some details of scholarship and interpretation, it nevertheless remains a great history, a great synthesis. Indeed, after re-reading it, and comparing his qualities of character and scholarship with Macaulay's, one is puzzled why he remains inferior to Macaulay, but he does. The answer lies partly in the fact that Macaulay always wrote at the maximum extension of his powers and with entire conviction: he can convey, right or wrong, an Olympian sense of grandeur. About political action he wrote with supreme virtuosity. His knowledge, insight and his deep practical sense ran deeper on this theme than any English historian who has ever written about it. Politics in action was Macaulay's chief concern not the motivation of a politician, that scarcely interested him; he focused on politicians at the moment of decision.

Trevelyan was a writer of great gifts, a man of deep conviction and natural poetic feelings but he was essentially a spectator; his temperament drew him away from the active battle of life. He was never a politician at any level, not even collegiate, and so the political history which he wrote in such quantities lacks a certain authority. There is greater power in his descriptive histories of English social life, a theme which engaged his whole temperament, for there a fading sense of greatness in British life mirrored his own tragic sense.

But Macaulay and Trevelyan are the great masters of the Whig tradition: in the hands of textbook expositors it became much cruder and much more distorted. It had never been strong on the interpretation of detail, of particular situations, or even capable of sharp insight into the growth of those institutions for which it felt a special responsibility. And so at the textbook level, the Whig interpretation jars intolerably on anyone with a wider professional knowledge of history; and nowhere is it more mistaken than when dealing with eighteenth-century political developments, so Derek Jarrett's, *Britain, 1688–1815* is particularly welcome. He has banished all the old Whig myths – cabinet government and the premiership coming in with George I because he could speak no English; the Tory intentions of George III go the same way. He has assimilated all the recent research on eighteenth-century politics and produced what is by far the most balanced account of this period; neither Whig nor Tory, but just good history. His literary gifts may not match Macaulay's or Trevelyan's, but his facts are more accurate and his interpretations (of detail at least) more reliable.

The Last Patricians

By the time of Churchill's death in January 1965, the great era of patrician history was drawing to a close. Its most successful practitioner was Sir Arthur Bryant who had caught Trevelyan's attention by writing what would now be called a 'revisionist' biography of Charles II, seeing in Charles a subtle, if seemingly languorous, politician who had successfully re-established hereditary monarchy and the Church as central institutions of the British Constitution and, equally successfully, cut Parliament down to size, destroying what was left of the radicalism generated by the Civil War. Charles II made possible, he thought, a Conservative Britain.

Of course, *pace* Butterfield, Trevelyan had never been locked into a doctrine of rigidly Whiggish interpretation and he found Bryant's book convincing and, equally exciting for Trevelyan, beautifully written. For some years the Cambridge University Press had been looking for someone to use the exceptionally well-ordered and voluminous notes of J. R. Tanner. Tanner, a don at St John's College, wrote one very good text book of its day, *The Constitutional Conflicts of the Seventeenth Century*, backed up by a fine collection of documents, but his *chef d'oeuvre*, a life of Pepys, never got written. Trevelyan thought Arthur Bryant ideal for the job (he quickly accepted the task) and the notes were handed over. The notes reached 1689 and so did Bryant's biography; the last decade of Pepys's life went unrecorded. The first three volumes were a great popular success; Bryant wrote with insight and panache, and Tanner's notes looked after the scholarship; Bryant's reputation soared.

And then came the war with Germany. The opportunity was golden. For Bryant Napoleon and the Revolution in France were as horrible as Hitler and Nazi Germany. Just as in the age of William Pitt, so once again would the heroic virtues of the British, with their undying, unquenchable love of freedom and liberty, defy the tyrant and would endure until victory was won. Three technicolour volumes came out

275

during the war years, heartening anyone who was ignorant of historical scholarship. There were canaries on cottage walls, roses round the doors, happy and contented peasants, willing to put up with near famine because of their patriotic zeal, and statesmen and generals larger in life than the gods on Mount Olympus. Even Churchill at his most sentimental might have found some of Bryant's paragraphs hard to take. It was the apotheosis of 'Whig' history, but written, of course, by a lifelong, dedicated Tory, for patrician history had never occupied party boundaries.

What Bryant longed for, his one abiding disappointment of life, was professional recognition. He would have given anything for an Hon. D.Litt at Cambridge, perhaps more for a Fellowship of the British Academy. He never had the slightest chance of either. And there was also a pleasing irony about Bryant's career. Both of his public honours, his Knighthood and his C.H., were given to him by Sir Harold Wilson, whose favourite historian he had long been.

Bryant, of course, had gifts. He wrote far better than nearly all professional historians. His books were carefully structured, his narrative skill was quite remarkable, his sense of timing, when to move from personality to action, elegant. He over-wrote certainly, and there was often a note of falsity, even of vulgarity, but largely his failure was of intellect.

I recognised his abilities in 1954 and most, if not all, of his faults. As I wrote in my covering letter to the editor of the *Times Educational Supplement*: 'I only wish that I had another couple of weeks to think about it for it is a very difficult book to review. One cannot help admiring its obvious virtues but, at the same time, I am sure the heart of it is utterly false and vulgar.' Like Churchill, but unlike Trevelyan, Bryant inflated patrician history so much that he destroyed it. Indeed, he vulgarised it to a degree that made it incredible.

Sir Arthur Bryant

After 1900 a deepening rift appeared between professional and popular historians, gallantly bridged by Dr Trevelyan, who insisted that history could and should be not only scholarly but also a joy to read. For many years he fought alone, but during the 1930s the tide began to turn and now it is lifting to the flood. Hundreds of thousands of Penguin histories, all by trained professional historians, have been sold in the last four years. The books of such scholars as J. E. Neale, A. L. Rowse and Veronica Wedgwood have become best-sellers. The public's appetite for history is vast, vaster probably than for any comparable academic subject. Admirable this may be, but it is not without its dangers.

The danger lies, of course, not in the popularity of history as literature but in this, that the historian himself may be tempted to respond too wholeheartedly to what he considers to be the emotional values of his subject. In his quite praiseworthy attempt to display the origins of what is good and noble in present society he may distort the values which men gave to their attitudes in the past or endow them with qualities of which they were ignorant. Of course, an historian who is concerned to tell the story of what he considers are the singular virtues of his own nation is more prone to these faults than one who considers the follies and nobilities of men to be a common heritage.

In the tragic circumstances in which man now finds himself it is harder than ever before to believe in the predestined greatness or moral superiority of any race or nation. Furthermore, the critical spirit thus fostered has been strengthened in the last three decades by the great growth in higher education. Aware and well informed of the complex difficulties of their own age, men do not expect times more remote to have been simpler. This is most probably why professional historians with a vigorously maintained scholarship have found themselves best sellers. The reading public is tougher-minded and better trained than ever before. Bold outline and simple colours are less necessary than they were; depth and complexity, so long as the historian has the literary skill to maintain interest and clarity, are now likely to be counted virtues in a popular historian.

Dr Bryant has for long enjoyed great popularity; his books on Charles II, Pepys and the Napoleonic Wars have reached as wide a public as any historical books of our time. It was only to be expected that sooner or later he would be tempted to tell the story of England. Few men writing have greater literary gifts and in this new book they are fully displayed. He is a master of narrative, interweaving with enviable skill the drama of events with the description of the circumstances which gave rise to them. The conflict of Henry II and St Thomas à Becket is a masterpiece in this respect. The constitutional conflicts implicit in the quarrel are set out in a way which would engage even the attention of a games-tired schoolboy sick of homework; while the clash of their temperaments and the story of their quarrel might even keep him from watching television. And, of course, Dr Bryant writes, when he is not consciously over-writing, with extraordinary felicity.

Yet, simple though the book may seem, both in outline and in texture, this is deceptive. He has been careful to give weight to difficult and intricate questions — feudalism, the organisation of law, the growth of towns and commerce. There is, also, one odd and surprising gain in Dr

Bryant's writing about the Middle Ages. For some readers his earlier works were marred by what seemed to them an unreasonable prejudice against radicals, liberals and reformers. But prior to the Reformation these creatures do not seem to make his hackles rise. And so this book is freer from political bias than his others.

Yet, in spite of its obvious and glaring virtues, the first volume of *The Story of England* is not an entirely satisfying work. In many ways it underrates the intelligence of the public to whom it is addressed, for it was Dr Bryant's avowed intention to write not only for boys but for men, for those who know some history as well as for those who know next to none. Although Dr Bryant is familiar with recent scholarship, assimilation does not seem to have taken place. This, at times, makes it easier for him to reject its conclusions than if he were immersed in his subject. King John remains the bad king; Simon de Montfort retains his role as the founder of Parliament; Richard is not deprived of his lion's heart. Here and there the vivid black and white of the ancient story is softened to a grey but the more complex human reality which modern scholars have laid bare is too frequently evaded. This is a grave weakness.

There is one more serious criticism. Not only does Dr Bryant render difficult problems too simply but he seems to falsify them by his basic assumptions. The assumption is that the highest-minded Englishmen were working semi-consciously towards an ideal national attitude.

'Loving private liberty, yet finding it could not exist without public order, the English devoted themselves to making the two compatible! Freedom within a framework of discipline became their ideal.'

This is the grand theme of English history which can be interpreted as a story with that conclusion. And so Dr Bryant has searched our medieval past for what he considers to be the virtues of this nation. Whether such virtues exist, or have existed long, or ever for a fleeting moment crossed the minds of Englishmen who grew up in a society as different almost from our own as that of Tibet, is open to argument. Furthermore, by this method it is so easy to assume a purely English virtue for habits of behaviour which were common in other societies and to diminish the ever-changing influence of European civilisation on our way of life. About the whole story there is a disquieting air of moral superiority – too much 'Englishry', a straining of truth and an evasion of the reality of life in the Middle Ages. In consequence, except in its literary skill, this book cannot compare with Lady Stenton's short masterpiece, *English Society in the Early Middle Ages*.

The weakness of this book lies in its author's intention, and illustrates admirably the dangers which beset an historian whose avowed intention is to write not only a popular history but also a popular history in which a pattern of belief is to be imposed on the past. Not even Dr Bryant's literary skill, nor his insight into individual human character, nor his concern for scholarship can prevent the result from seeming overwhelmingly false. Certainly, there is a need and a place for popular history, but the best and the most enduring will come from the pens of scholars who are concerned to re-create the past in terms of its own values. It is only to be hoped that they will write us vividly and as simply as Dr Bryant.

Trevelyan's Heirs-Apparent: i. A. L. Rowse

There was only one professional historian who might have taken, who, indeed, very nearly did take, Trevelyan's place in the 1950s and 1960s, and that was Dr A. L. Rowse whom Trevelyan himself selected to give the first 'Trevelyan Lectures', founded at Cambridge at the time of his eightieth birthday to honour him. (It was my first lesson in fund-raising, an activity which illuminates both the best and worst in human nature but never lacks its capacity to surprise.) By the time Dr A. L. Rowse gave these lectures in 1958, it was becoming harder for his friends to defend all that he wrote or said. The fissures in his character were becoming chasms. Great work still lay ahead. His life of Shakespeare, almost destroyed by his reckless arrogance and contempt, is, nevertheless, a book of great distinction. Readable and right, with uncommon insights into a man of towering genius who left little or no biographical facts about himself except those distorted by the necessities of art, it remains an extraordinary *tour de force*.

Rowse's best books were those when his defects were tiny cracks. His early books, particularly *Tudor Cornwall* and *The Structure of Elizabethan England* gave not only Trevelyan but also thousands of readers great pleasure. The scholarship was remarkable. Rowse possessed an exact and large memory and a strong visual sense; he had travelled every inch of Great Britain; his knowledge of any Elizabethan who had left a trace behind was phenomenal. Indeed, he wrote as if Elizabethan life were a part of his own world and experience. He was, like Trevelyan, infused with the poetry of life but unlike Trevelyan there were strict limits to his empathy. Puritans and radicals, destroyers of art and beauty, enraged him, and down came the portcullis with a crash. They were refused entry into his imagination and sympathy. Also he was increasingly soured by aspects of his own life, particularly its academic side. He was not honoured in Oxford; indeed often he was the subject of quite unnecessary churlishness and malice which galled him. Good at rage, not bad at malice, and superb in a contempt that gave as good as it received, the hostilities did neither party much honour.

His critics continued to scorn Rowse's books. This enlarged his faults and diminished their judgement.

Rowse's trouble was, I suppose, his immodesty, his lack of humility, and, to be fair to his critics, at times he was almost rabid. Now advanced in years, many of his best books are unread and forgotten; but his diatribes fall now like shrivelled leaves in an indifferent forest. Does he face oblivion? The answer to that is a resounding 'no'. He will be read. He is too enjoyable, too stimulating to the imaginative mind to fall into total neglect. And he possesses his own time bomb – a diary kept throughout a long life-time which in due course will explode on the world. Who will laugh then, or feel that their malice was well directed? It is extraordinary that people who employ the pen rarely think of what it might do to them.

I thought that his Trevelyan Lectures (regarded as 'superficial' by the professionals) were excellent for their purpose and a fitting valediction for Trevelyan himself who enjoyed them hugely. He came to every one, tottering down the lecture hall in a gown grown bottle-green with age, swathed in an overcoat which he told me had belonged to his father, brown muffler, grim moustache, steel spectacles, to a warm outburst of welcome, dominated by the heavy, self-congratulatory applause of Kitson Clark.

Owing to bad health, political ambitions and other distractions Rowse had not written a great deal before the war but after it his pen began to race – historical and biographical books, poetry, essays, literary criticism, books great, small and very small poured out, and naturally the quality of his work suffered, although Rowse's public estimation of himself reached new stratospheric heights. And contempt for the world, for people, for critics welled out of him like lava, scorching everything and everyone, making a desert around him.

He became a victim both of himself and his time. He wrote too much, grew careless and vituperative, giving his enemies overwhelming opportunities to destroy his reputation. And it seems sad that so gifted a writer, an historian of splendid talents, who has certainly enriched forever our knowledge of Elizabethan England and of Shakespeare should be so totally unhonoured: Bryant a Knight and a Companion of Honour, Rowse nothing. There are times when many of Rowse's diatribes about human nature do not seem entirely without merit.

The Elizabethans and America

This book is the first of what everyone hopes will be a most distinguished series. Dr Rowse was invited to give the first of the Trevelyan Lectures, founded at Cambridge to honour the greatest English historian of this century. Trevelyan has not only maintained the tradition of Gibbon,

Macaulay and the great nineteenth-century historical writers but also encouraged a younger generation of historians to pursue scholarship with art. Dr Rowse has proved himself a worthy pupil, and the Trevelyan Lectureship could not have got off to a more auspicious beginning: for this book is Rowse at his best, and Rowse at his best is very good indeed.

Of course, the intensely personal view of men and events is there – the snarling contempt for bigotry, the savage hatred of unreason, the romantic view of endeavour, the loving regard for the wayward man of genius. In these lectures, however, it is disciplined and never expressed in those sharp asides with which we have become familiar. Here everything, the hate as well as the admiration, is reasoned, argued, based on scholarship; even the Puritans who, naturally enough, get their knuckles rapped, are praised for their probity, public spirit, moral responsibility, humaneness as to punishment and mutual help in need.

A wise and tolerant spirit pervades this book, for the Elizabethan pioneers demand it, from that strange astrologer, Dr Dee, who convinced Elizabeth (she needed little argument) that she had a title to North America derived from King Arthur, to the flotsam and jetsam that found a gruesome death on Virginia's inhospitable shores; on the whole they were a tough, savage brood with a lunatic fringe.

By the time Englishmen began to search for fertile land and easy wealth across the Atlantic, Spain had already created an empire there and the Portuguese had netted the world in a web of trade. The English enterprises arose from a desire to plague the Spanish and to reap the riches of the New World. Nothing fortifies courage like cupidity combined with national sentiment, and Englishmen were soon dying in their hundreds and merchants back in London rued the loss of the ships and stores and guineas. The first settlements in Virginia failed abysmally, but they helped to stimulate that obsession with the New World which permeates the thought and literature of the late Elizabethan age.

Indeed, one of the best things in this book is the chapter which Dr Rowse devotes to this theme. America, for poets and philosophers as well as laymen, took on the quality of a dream world; a land of fertile soil, abundant in fish and food, alive with gold and adorned with savages that lived in a golden age of innocence – only rarely did reality with all its harshness break in. By Elizabeth's death rapacity, national pride, hatred of Spain, the lure of gold, the huge sums already sunk in American adventure, the expended lives, the courage and the adventure had entangled the North American seaboard into the structure of English life. It was only a matter of time before intelligence, sense and foresight prevailed to create the necessary conditions for permanent settlement.

Virginia was sustained in its tenuous beginning by the craze for tobacco (it is interesting that Harriot, its first advocate, died of cancer of the mouth) and fish and fishermen did as much as the iron courage of the Pilgrim Fathers to establish New England. Each colony rested on the experience and knowledge of those who failed: and Dr Rowse gives due weight to the immense contributions of such admirable Elizabethans as Sir Fernando Gorges, without whose earlier endeavours the Puritans would surely never have succeeded.

In this excellent book Dr Rowse has brought the whole story into accurate focus. His vast scholarship has enabled him to assess both men and events against the background not only of Elizabeth's England but also of Elizabeth's Europe. Indeed, these lectures are a brilliant *tour de force* and can be described in the words that Dr Rowse uses of Trevelyan's own work: 'A model of integrity in scholarship and accomplishment in art.'

ii. Dame Veronica Wedgwood

There was always a maverick quality about Dr Rowse which made him an ally rather than a central figure in the patrician view of history, whereas Veronica Wedgwood belonged to it in the same way as did Trevelyan himself. Her father, Sir Ralph Wedgwood, was a life-long friend of Trevelyan. He belonged to that great intellectual aristocracy which Noel Annan described so brilliantly in the *Festschrift*, which I edited for Trevelyan. His essay on the 'Intellectual Aristocracy' traces the complex web of family relationships – Darwins, Huxleys, Wedgwoods, Adrians, Hodgkins, Stracheys, and the rest, who dominated English intellectual life in the nineteenth and twentieth centuries, particularly in the Universities. So Wedgwood and Trevelyan shared a common heritage of ideas and of outlook, both regarded history as an essential part of high culture which needed to be written not for professionals but for the cultured classes: both shared the view that the English Civil War was central to the development of English liberty and the rule of law. And yet neither were in any sense radical; they might be, on balance, anti-Charles I but not anti-monarchical; pro-Cromwell but certainly neither Republican nor Puritan.

Again both enjoyed throughout their careers financial security, both largely avoided academic chores, although they had sailed through the early stages of a professional career with high distinction. Neither held a full-time academic teaching post that kept them living in an academic community, term after term, year after year. As with Trevelyan, most professional historians preferred to regard Wedgwood as an amateur.

Initially Wedgwood's success was immense. Every book was acclaimed in the popular press and sold splendidly. Biographies — *Strafford*, *William the Silent*, *Cromwell* (short and neat) — her narrative histories received even greater acclaim: *The Thirty Years War*, the best synthesis for its time now alas dated, and *The King's Peace* and *The King's War* which told the story of the English Civil War. Unfortunately these books were published at a time when professional historians, Marxist and non-Marxist, were battering away at the old accepted interpretations of the Civil War and so came in for almost remorseless criticism in the learned journals. Courteously, civilly and one might almost say with a kindly urbanity, Christopher Hill, the lively Marxist historian, naturally attacked her interpretation, but so did historians committed to other faiths or to none at all. These criticisms struck home — her great narrative history did not march forward to its destined goal of the Restoration. As a kind of coda, Dr Wedgwood produced in 1964 *A Coffin for a King*. It was, and remains, a small classic of narrative history, and nearly accomplishes Dr Wedgwood's belief that if the *How* of history is described truthfully and skilfully enough then the *Why?* of history would be apparent. As I had written in 1960:

> She has dedicated her creative life to this simple if frequently ignored idea: that history is a part of literature. And she sees history as similar in intention to novels or plays or poetry; it is simply a literary method by which human experience is explored. But there is this difference between history and literature: history must be true and facts riveted to words with all the precision that scholarship can give.
>
> Miss Wedgwood is well aware that historians are as self-saturated as novelists and therefore recognises that their sense of the past will be entangled in the sense, not only of themselves, but of their society and class. She regards this as dangerous, but in no way disastrous; it merely makes the historian's task much more difficult. Each generation, each society will wring from the past both the knowledge and the wisdom suitable to its needs. Naturally, such views lead Miss Wedgwood to recognise great virtues in narrative history. She believes historians should concentrate on the *How* rather than the *Why* of history, and 'the careful, thorough and accurate answer to the question *How* should take the historian a long way toward answering the question *Why*.'
>
> Of course, Miss Wedgwood is too wise and too subtle to leave it at that. She realises that depth is given to historical thinking by close scholarly study of 'the underlying mechanism of administration, the slow development of institutions, the intricate interlocking of economic and social facts. . . . All of these things,' she writes, 'are of the greatest importance in the study of history, but very few of them can be adequately or even honestly treated in an essentially literary manner.' She admits that the handling of such subjects can call forth, as in a Maitland or a Bloch, great art, but their history is not literary history. Hence between the professional scholar and the literary historian is a chasm, bridgeable perhaps, but profound — the scholar preoccupied with *Why*, the historian with *How*. Miss Wedgwood presents this view with persuasive charm and rare eloquence. No one is more skilful than she in the telling phrase, the apt illustration, yet I am only half persuaded that she is right.

Alas, when she applied this method decades later to a history of mankind, called *The Spoils of Time*, the result was a disaster. The facts were accurate, as one would expect, the book was beautifully written, but it meant nothing; it failed to illuminate anything because it lacked 'the Why' of history.

Trevelyan, in his last years, regarded both Wedgwood and Rowse as his natural heirs and few in the fifties would have disputed that they were. But history and high culture parted company in the sixties and history as literature became almost an impure thought. True Wedgwood received great honours and Rowse none, but their fate was essentially the same and tragic.

The Crisis of Authority

When Charles I was hurriedly taken by the Army in November 1648 to Hurst Castle, a grim fortress on a spit of shingle that runs out into the Solent, memories of Edward II, Richard II and Henry VI crowded in upon his close friends. Traditionally English Kings who failed were slaughtered in silence. And the profound sense of enormity that spread through Britain and Europe in January 1649 sprang as much from the King's trial as from his execution. There lay the innovation. The fundamental difference between the seventeenth century and the recent, or even mediaeval past, arose not so much from the acts of men as from their motives. The death of the King was no longer sufficient, for the nature of kingship itself was on trial.

Since the Romans the pattern of English history had been 'interwoven with rebellion, conspiracy, riot and murder: the block and the axe has blazoned the histories of most noble families and the aristocracy had always used the sanction of war against the monarchs they distrusted. Charles I appealed at his trial to the fundamental law and ancient constitution of his realm, maintaining that for one thousand years monarchy had been indivisible and hereditary, that no law could be law without his consent, and no authority exist which did not derive from him or his Parliaments which, for Charles, did not mean a Rump of the Commons, but himself with the Lords and all the Commons elected by ancient custom. Bradshaw, who presided at his trial, had been taught his history too and quoted back at Charles the example of those nobles who had wrung the Great Charter from King John, and whose descendants had been forced to accept its reaffirmation time and time again under the threat of violence. He also pointed forcibly to the repeated promises of Kings, on oath, to protect the liberties and freeholds of their subjects. Although the past brooded over that curiously muddled, ill-organised scene in Westminster Hall in January 1649, it was the novelty that shocked. A king was being done to death, not by his cousins nor by his power-thirsty barons: he was being arraigned in the name of his people and his judges were, by the standards of their age, common people. True, Cromwell and Ireton and their advisers had done their best to give an air of status and solidity to the Commissioners for the trial, and a few men of substance attended, but most were men of middle or lower- middle-class origins, men of that self-same class that was to give birth more than a century later to those who would sign America's Declaration of Independence and man the Revolutionary tribunals of France. But in 1649, that sons of tailors, brewers, and husbandmen should sit in judgement on their annointed king, condemn him for treason to his people, and execute him, seemed a violation of nature and God's law. Of course it was an act of desperate men, caught in intractable circumstances, fearful for the whole fabric of society and driven to a headlong decision because of what might follow. Indeed such was their haste that the execution itself was held up whilst Parliament rushed through a Bill to prevent Charles II being proclaimed after the deed was done. No provision for a Republic or for any new constitution had been made.

And here lies the key to the situation. The Grandees of the Army had been profoundly disturbed by the Levellers, as disturbed indeed as they were worried by what compromise the Presbyterian leaders were going to make with the King. Caught between left and right, they acted in order to maintain power not in order to reconstruct English society. They knew that reconstructions of a sort would have to follow the King's death, but their bewilderment, their lack of insight into the Revolutionary situation in which they were involved can be seen in their almost pathetic adherence to threadbare shreds of legality. After all it was they who maintained the absurd Rump and clung to traditional procedures in their Revolutionary Court, attempting to make their actions conform to past custom. They abdicated their revolutionary role almost before it had begun.

Yet momentous as the execution of Charles I was, this act like the whole Civil War itself, means less to us than it did to our fathers and grandfathers and will mean less to our own children and perhaps nothing at all to our grandchildren. And this brings us to the heart of the matter – Veronica Wedgwood's role as an historian. Her gifts are splendid and altogether exceptional. Had she lived in the nineteenth century or written in the early part of this, she would have been as revered amongst historians as George Eliot is amongst novelists. She is a great crafts-woman and a great writer. The structure of this book on the King's trial is wholly admirable, based firmly on comprehensive scholarship and written with compelling clarity and a sensitive insight into the nature of men and their motives. Charles, Cromwell, Bradshaw come vividly alive.

This, one feels, is the men they were, this is why they were driven along by their strange necessities. And Miss Wedgwood too, makes us aware of the deeper issues, the historic situation in which men were caught. And yet, in this book and in the first two volumes of her fine History of the Civil War, now reissued she is writing, in a sense, for an age that is passing. The army, and Cromwell, in 1649 acted on necessity and waited for Providence; they had little capacity for revolutionary thought or action. They might hate the acts of the Monarchy, long for a wider toleration of belief, but they were deeply suspicious of any realignment of social power. In the end the crisis of authority which shook England, was resolved in favour of its old not new masters. It was *their* political institutions, local and national, sanctified by time and made flexible by self-interest that survived. A class structure dominated by land onwership that absorbed economic and social change with the ease of a sponge lasted for more than two and a half centuries after the Civil War. Only for a very brief period from 1647–53 had this social power and these political institutions been seriously endangered. Then and then only was a bourgeois revolution possible. But the moment quickly passed, and Cromwell became the caretaker of the past not a midwife for the future. Hence for the English upper classes the Civil War and the trial and death of Charles I were traumatic. The time when they so nearly lost. Hence their continuing fascination!

In the nineteenth century, when the landowning classes were again threatened by the prospect of massive social change this historical epoch acquired a new hypnotic interest for them. Once again questions of freehold and liberty, of authority and democracy, of full religious toleration, and above all of the distribution of political and social power became issues charged with personal emotion. The small manufacturers or Yorkshire, excluded from authority by their religion as well as by their origins, could feel that Cromwell fought for them, that Marston Moor and Naseby were their victories. They were the heirs to the Roundheads. Likewise, for those who possessed estates, whose cousins were courtiers and brothers were bishops, they could revere the gallantry of their Cavalier ancestors and feel that their family had survived the worst of times and might do so again. But now who cares? For the laboratory assistant in Billingham, the mechanic in Croydon, the salesman in Walsall or the executive in Golders Green, Charles I is dead and Cromwell a bore: their society has different roots and they are hunting for a different sort of projection into the past. Caught in the greater crisis of fundamental social change, Roundhead and Cavalier lose their emotive force. And to their questions the beautifully written, scholarly narratives of Veronica Wedgwood do not, indeed are not intended to, give an answer. Nevertheless within the scholarly tradition in which she writes Veronica Wedgwood has few peers. Even though she may be a little unlucky to be writing when British culture is at the cross roads, she remains one of the outstanding historians of her time in English for more than a generation. And for those of us who still feel deeply embroiled in the seventeenth century, she is a peerless evocator of the past.

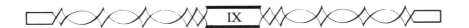

The Uses of History

During the mid-1960s I had become ever more preoccupied with the social function of history and the long, long roots of the institutions, social structures and habits not only of the West but of all developed societies. Also I was becoming acutely aware that the world – West and East, Capitalist and Communist – might be approaching a social revolution in which old habits, old attitudes, old institutions might undergo revolutionary change. Basically, the world in which I had grown up was the fully developed world of the Neolithic revolution. It was, however, studded with ominous portents, some technological – the combustion engine, aircraft, the mastery of electricity, complex chemicals, the micro-chip; some scientific – pure like relativity or the quantum theory, others applied, such as the splitting of the atom or the discovery of genetic structures. And these portents had been expanded by war: men reached the moon; the computer was followed by the micro-chip; genetic engineering became a reality; disease was being mastered; food supplies exceeded the world's need in the East as well as the West. By the later 1960s these great changes had begun to intensify social conflicts and also to undermine old institutions and attitudes. Yet few looked to history to understand the difficulties men and women now faced. They preferred to blame either themselves or the new styles of living that the scientific and technological evolutions imposed. I began to take a longer and longer view of the historical process, and I was delighted when in 1967 I was asked by City College, New York to give the Saposnekow Lectures.

For years I had read for pleasure the history of other societies – the Chinese, the Japanese, the Amerindian or of earlier epochs, particularly the history of the early Neolithic and Bronze Age civilisations. It struck me that not only were the political, economic and social structures basically the same but also that there were very strong cultural similarities in all of these civilisations and the use of the past was one. I

288

decided to call my lectures *The Death of the Past* and to explain how other civilisations as well as the West had used their knowledge of the past for social purposes. It quickly became clear that much of recorded history, until modern times, had been patrician history, used to confirm power and belief and to sanctify authority and custom. I realised that even the desire for factual accuracy and accurate documentation came very late in the history of mankind whilst the use of history to analyse the nature of economic, social, political or religious change much later still.

Much of my time in the late 1960s and early 1970s was taken up with similar questions, questions which had long roots, that reached back to Sumer, Akkad, Egypt or the early Han. It seemed to me that the knowledge of the modern world would be richer if there were a greater awareness of how the past was used. Of course I was not alone. A far greater historian than myself had been thinking for years at the Sorbonne on similar terms – Fernand Braudel, one of the greatest historians of the twentieth century. He and his colleagues, *The Annales School* as they came to be known, had put a new intellectual vitality into history to a remarkable degree and had made it a part of the modern high culture of France in the way that no other national school of historians had succeeded in doing. I felt myself therefore to be in excellent company. I had been in correspondence with Braudel since the 1940s when he agreed to supervise a quite exceptionally talented pupil of mine, Frank Spooner, and we met from time to time. He was a small round man of great modesty and charm. He professed to know no English or German, so once I had the agreeable sight of seeing Braudel and Elton conversing in dog Latin. I think that they could have done better in French and English with the enchanting Madame Braudel doing the interpreting. Actually Braudel read fluently in English, understood conversation well, but hated to speak the language. Braudel neither looked a great man nor behaved like one – he was too mischievous, too captivated by the moment of living and his tongue could never resist a phrase, especially if of contempt for a colleague. He had no use for Soboul, the great Marxist historian of the French Revolution, his opinion of Le Roy Ladurie (of *Montaillou* fame) was dismissive, Goubert and many others received short shrift. He was capable of admiration – Bloch and Febvre were his heroes. We English historians tended to regard The *Annales* School as a monolith of scholarship – as in all groups of scholars, the vitriol flowed and the battles were bitter.

Nevertheless Braudel's praise for *The Death of the Past* was encouraging. Like most of my books the reception of it was mixed; patchy in England, some very good reviews, but oddly ignored in a few important newspapers and journals. In America it was very well received, likewise in Germany and Sweden. It was translated into German, Japanese, Spanish and Italian, and in Spain it became a best-seller. In general I felt that what I wanted to say was finding a large and appreciative audience and for a writer that is what mainly matters.

For once I was in tune with my time for the late 1960s witnessed a great flowering of social history – women's history, black history, the histories of childhood and death, the history of madness and of sexual deviation, the social impact of railways, of leisure pursuits, of games, of racing and hunting, of dancing, of music, of circus, of theatre, all of these subjects have drawn to them a large number of young academic historians, tired and repelled by political, constitutional and economic history. The bibliography of such subjects has expanded at an unbeliev- able rate and many are taught now in schools as well as appearing in university curricula. This could not have taken place in the 1950s and early 1960s. It would have been regarded as outrageous. I found this at times exciting and stimulating; indeed, the last lectures that I gave as a Professor in Cambridge dealt with the commercialisation of leisure in eighteenth-century England. Yet I realised that there was grave danger in such developments. These themes of social history were rooted in the anxieties of our time; rooted perhaps in the young lower but ever more numerous middle class looking for a history and a culture. It had no ancestors who had sat in cabinets, won battles or ruled colonies, but they did have rebellious children, womenfolk longing for careers; they played games, went to concerts, sometimes they were living all too close to the mad and the deranged. Most of the historians who tackled these aspects of social history had emerged from the dark anonymity of history and not from families like the Wedgwoods and Trevelyans who had ruled or who enjoyed the culture which their ancestors had created. This kind of history spread most rapidly in the polytechnics, the teaching colleges, and the newer universities. The historian of eighteenth-century lesbianism would not have seemed out of place in a novel by Malcolm Bradbury.

And although social history is widely disparaged by the rigorous conservative historians such as Sir Geoffrey Elton, it is much more exciting and stimulating than most traditional research now being under- taken. Unfortunately, exciting as many articles are, or even the rare book, there is little coherence and practically no synthesis. Historians working on the growth of horticulture do not feel the need to know what was happening to music, and vice versa. And yet without synthesis, it is almost impossible to teach or to relate these historical processes to what, in the end, must be the dominant narrative history of any society – the politics, the wars, the inventions, the ideas, the *grand* history as against the history of the undergrowth. So what began as an exciting new direction in historical research and teaching ended up fragmenting professional history even more. New subjects require new teachers: the ranks of professional historians swelled to bursting point for there was little or no integration between the old practitioners and the new historian. Neither did the intrusion of social history lead to any new definition of the educational goals of the subject. Fresh colours were added to the kaleidoscope box but no one wanted to shake it to create new patterns. So when I was asked by the *Encyclopaedia Britannica* to take part in a symposium on tradition it seemed to me that the problems which had led me to write about the crisis in history as a young man still faced the profession.

*History and Tradition**

History is Janus-faced, but the faces are far from being identical. One is wrinkled with deep lines, as old as the distant ages of mankind; the other is youthful, vigorous, and in the full flood time of early maturity. These faces represent two very different types of history. The former is obviously riddled with traditional attitudes enshrined in works whose fame has lasted for millennia. The latter, too, is old enough to have established traditions of working and methods of expression, some of which, though not all, continue to be powerful. Two types, therefore, of history need to be considered. One is the way man has always looked at his past. He has turned to it to explain the roots of his society, to tell him its story; he searches it, as his forebears did, for examples of human behaviour, and often he scrutinises the past in the hope that it will enlighten him about the future. This is basically what Voltaire called philosophic history, whose truth may lie deeper than facts. And this for centuries on end was the totality of historical practice – sometimes simple, sometimes sophisticated and complex – not only in the West and throughout Islam but also in China and in Japan. As we shall see, this type of history persists, and rightly so, though the part tradition plays in it has grown at once more complex and weaker with time.

But the more youthful variety of history is easier to deal with and should be taken up first. When Chinese historians of the T'ang period looked back on the Han, or when Livy contemplated Roman history or Herodotus delved into the history of Egypt or of Persia, they were largely concerned to discover moral truths; although they had some concern for factual accuracy, it was not their prime concern. Herodotus, like Thucydides after him, thought nothing of inventing speeches and putting them in dead men's mouths. Similarly, the Chinese historians would deliberately switch the semi-miraculous happenings necessary for the birth of an emperor from father to son without any compunction, because they were necessary for moral emphasis, to demonstrate clearly that Heaven itself supported the new emperor, this being presumed in light of the fact that the emperor had successfully established a dynasty. And so, in the Middle Ages, the monastic chroniclers accepted, not incredulously but because of their belief in God's will and purpose, the miracles of founding abbots or of the saints who had embellished their orders. At the same time, all of these historians put into their works a great deal that was accurate – factual truths about the lives of men and women and events of their societies and communities. But the pursuit of factual truth was not their primary aim. They were illustrating the purpose of God, the truths of morality in which fables, miracles, or myths are as valuable as facts.

The development of critical history – the youthful face of Janus – was highly complex, with slow beginnings, and had, like all mighty rivers, many tributaries. And it is a purely western phenomenon. As I have written elsewhere, 'The Chinese pursued erudition, but they never developed the critical historiography which is the signal achievement of Western historians over the last 200 years. They never attempted, let alone succeeded, in treating history as objective understanding.'

Probably one of the basic reasons why Europe developed critical history was because its past had been badly fractured. There was a pagan past of Greece and Rome and the Christian past of the Bible that interlocked but did not properly fit, leaving for the critical mind a wealth of problems, chronological and technical as well as interpretative. Also, the half-obliterated pagan past was a wonderful hunting ground for antiquarians, those who were searching for categories of facts and so were discovering facts themselves. There was so much to collect and put in order: chronicles, literature, plays, poems, epigrams and epigraphs, medals, coins, wonderful fields of antiquarian specialisation that, from the fifteenth century onward, began to be ever more precise and accurate. The earliest traditions of exact historical scholarship began with the antiquarians and with the critical examination of texts – for example, Lorenzo Valla's famous proof that the Donation of Constantine was a forgery – in the fifteenth century. Valla belonged to a school of lawyers, a school that grew and strengthened over the next 100 years, and that was concerned to discover precisely what legal phrases, even words, meant at the time they became inscribed in law. These lawyers realised that time itself eroded and changed meanings, and that to understand legal concepts of Rome one needed to use historical criticism, to learn how to strip off the coruscations of time. Both processes encouraged the growth of erudition; the recovery and ordering or more facts about the past and the spread of critical methods of handling words and documents within their own special frameworks of time grew steadily throughout the sixteenth century, primarily in Italy and France but also, during the seventeenth century, in England. In France particularly this gave rise to the establishment of techniques – paleographic and diplomiatic – that have become a traditional part of scholarship. Similarly, some of the great works of scholarship – the *De Re Diplomatica* of Mabillon or the *Acta Sanctorum* of the Bollandists (still in course of publication after 300 years) – remain important books for the medieval historian. Here the tradition is firm; the growth of knowledge, through established techniques, steady.

Even so, there were rapid improvements in the eighteenth century, and the spearhead of critical history passed to Germany, particularly to the University of Göttingen. Elsewhere there was great improvement. Always historians had embedded charters, letters and documents in their histories and annals to help give veracity to their argument. But instead of being occasional embellishments, often now the volumes of the documents supporting a history were longer than the history itself. This was particularly true of a great but neglected English historian Archdeacon Coxe, whose exceptional documentation, accurately presented (at least for his age), not only has given his books enduring value but has also influenced generations of English historians. From Coxe's day, the editing and publishing of documents became an intense preoccupation of the growing number of professional historians of the nineteenth century. The *Monumenta Germaniae Historica*, whose first volume, edited by the great scholar G. H. Pertz, appeared in 1826, induced scholars in other countries to follow Pertz's lead (notably in the case of the Rolls series in Britain), and so was created a tradition of editing, and publication of fundamental sources, that is still assiduously followed. Indeed, one may say that a tradition of editing historical sources was established, if constantly refined, from 1826 until the present day. However, two factors have placed this tradition in jeopardy. One is the soaring costs of printing a text with elaborate critical appendices; the other is the ease with which nowadays any scholar can get a reproduction of almost any document that he may want. Even so, such editing, like its counterparts in historical erudition, the creation of historical dictionaries and collation of varied historical materials, remains a fundamental part of the historical profession; in essence, the rules laid down by Mabillon, and developed by the great German textual editors, are still followed. Here the traditional methods of scholarship endure.

*   *   *   *   *

The ambitions of the early professional historians were vast, however, and not confined to the editing of thousands of texts. The range of Leopold von Ranke was enormous; he planned a Universal History at the age of 90. His work still retains considerable value, through the care with which he used sources, the lucidity of his writing, and the sharp intelligence that he exercised, particularly in diplomatic history. Before Ranke, historians such as Gibbon – in a sense the first great critical and professional historian – had taken immense themes for their subjects, and historians continued to do so throughout the nineteenth century. In America (one has only to think of Bancroft, Prescott, and Motley) they all happily embraced great periods of time, rich with complex and multitudinous sources. Multi-volume narrative histories or biographies were a commonplace of historical literature by the mid-nineteenth century. Yet what seemed to be an established tradition by the 1870s had almost vanished by 1914.

The vast outpouring of archival material in the nineteenth century, combined with stronger professional standards of scholarly care and mastery of sources, naturally increased specialisation. This in turn was encouraged by the great national historical reviews that were established. Germany, not surprisingly, was the first in the field with the *Historische Zeitschrift* in 1859; France followed in 1876 with the *Revue historique*. Both England and America were much tardier. The *English Historical Review* was first published in 1886, and the *American Historical Review* in 1895. They were all symptoms of a development in the discipline of history that is now so deep-rooted as to be the most traditional aspect of academic or professional history. From 1900, journals for academic history of every kind proliferated rapidly and still continue to increase. In these journals a professional historian can treat of a small historical problem or throw new light on an aspect of a large one. It permits him to establish a reputation without the need to produce a book. And these journals have profoundly influenced the whole nature of historical investigation, for they are largely concerned with the 'whys' of history, concepts about how history happened, rather than a relation of events. This, too, is reflected in the books that great professional historians, bred in this new style of history, began to write at the turn of the century. They ceased to write great narrative histories on large historic themes and turned to more specialised concepts: the nature of feudalism, the origins of parliamentary government, the nature of the Renaissance, the causes of the Reformation, the influence of the frontier on American history. Indeed, Frederick Jackson Turner's famous essay on the frontier, published in 1894, was a turning point in American historiography. Then came the first light of the dawn of that 'new history' publicised and promoted by James Harvey Robinson and Charles A. Beard, who taught the methods, the techniques, and the attitudes toward the past that had been established in European historiography. From these and other points stems the great river of professional history, as wide and as long as the Mississippi, that flows through the universities and colleges of America. The influence of these men, and their pupils' influence, is still paramount.

The establishment of high professional standards bred specialisation, both vertical and horizontal; that is, aspects of human activity were easier to isolate and study than their complex relationships, so scholars devoted their lives to economic history, or ecclesiastical history, or the history of ideas, or the history of politics or law. And, of course, it was easier to deal with a short period such as that covered by the agrarian revolution in sixteenth-century England, or the role of the lawyers in seventeenth-century Toulouse, or the origins of the meat-packing industry in Chicago. This vertical and horizontal slicing of history has now hardened into a tradition, and is dominant in professional academic circles. Naturally, the strength of its hold varies from country to country. It dominates English academic life, where the work of Sir Lewis B. Namier, which was, in essentials, confined to a segment of political history of the 1760s, is regarded as one of the great achievements of professional history. His work on the history of Parliament has spawned a host of imitators. In America this tradition is also very powerful, as it is in France and the rest of Europe. However, among some of the most gifted historians writing today there is a growing disenchantment with specialisation that is too rigid in the orientation of the subject or too confined in time.

Many of the greatest academic historians of this century have always been deeply concerned by the limitations of high professional specialisation. Lord Acton, who believed this could be overcome by great cooperative enterprises, planned the *Cambridge Modern History*, by which he hoped to create a synthesis from the best specialists. The result was useful but dull, a fourteen-volume work of reference, of exceptionally varying quality; yet some chapters were brilliant, some volumes even admirable. And so the cooperative history of specialists established itself, whether dealing with all human history, such as the wholly admirable Columbia University's *History of the World* – perhaps the finest achievement of this tradition – or significant and large sections of the human story that the great Cambridge histories have covered. It is a method, however, that is less widely practised in Europe, and though now firmly established as a practice of the professional historians, and still dominated by the tradition established by Lord Acton, it has never proved wholly satisfactory, nor satisfied those historians who wish for closer contacts with the culture of their day.

Historians, since Gibbon's day, have been well aware of its Janus-faced nature. History has possessed since the earliest times of mankind a social purpose and yet, by its very nature, professional and highly specialised history can play only a very limited role. It is excellent for training the critical faculties; on occasion it can stimulate sympathy and understanding of societies and people different from ourselves; but most of it, perhaps 90 per cent of it, is uninteresting, even unreadable, except for those involved in its academic disciplines.

Fortunately, men and women since Homer's day and beyond have craved to know about the past. Who made the world? Why is there evil? How is good achieved? Questions as to how and why have always haunted generations of men and women whose curiosity about the past is insatiable, giving us works whose role has long endured – among them, and above all, the Bible, which in essence is a history. There is, indeed, a great constellation of epics – Homer, the Sagas, the Vedas, the early annals of China – that no amount of historical criticism can ever destroy, that remain to delight and to instruct the intelligent and curious reader. These epics merge in times closer to our own into the great traditional histories – Gibbon, Hume, Macaulay, Ranke, Michelet, Prescott, Motley – that so delighted out grandfathers and that are still read more by non-historians, perhaps, than by trained professionals. And so we have a curious anomaly, a traditional historical literature that is rarely read by the professional historian for its own sake. When the professional historian studies Herodotus or Gibbon, he does so historiographically, that is, to understand either what the author's vision of history was and why or the way he reflected the intellectual forces of his day. whereas the bulk of the readership of these works, which is non-professional, goes to them for entirely different reasons. These traditional works – particularly historians such as Prescott or Gibbon or Macaulay – are read because they are excellent narratives, telling, with excitement in pungent prose, what happened. The stories of the conquest of Mexico, or the decline and fall of Rome, or the English revolution are magnificent in themselves. And as well as stories, there are the historical characters – larger than life, who in their day dominated the human scene – from Alexander the Great to Napoleon. About all these books there is what the French call the 'odour of man,' the smell of life. We can, through these books, project ourselves into the lives of men who once walked this earth as we do and have now vanished, wereby we participate in what may be called the poetry of time, which is the poetry of history. It is because it affords us this opportunity that history is so enduring a part of literature, a part of the great tradition.

And that tradition still exists, but it has tragically weakened. Where today are the Michelets, the Prescotts, the Macaulays? Few remain, if any, even though history as literature, history to entertain, pours from the presses as never before. Much of it is effective, a delight to read. Sometimes a professionally trained historian wanders into the field of traditional historical writing, almost uniformly with excellent results. For example, Sir John Neale wrote a biography of Queen Elizabeth that is certainly open to technical criticism, as it idolises the Queen; but, nevertheless, it is a remarkable literary *tour de force* that millions of people have read with delight. Yet there are few professional historians at work in traditional history – studies of great events, biographies, and the like – and the reasons are not hard to find.

Traditional history, to be effective, requires great literary gifts – mastery of narrative structure, analytical insight into the vagaries of human behaviour, a capacity to evoke through the magic of words, landscape, the way life was lived – all of which are not in the least necessary for a professional historian engaged on precise and narrow issues. And traditional history cannot often be written within a small compass about a narrow issue, so the writer of traditional history has to take great risks. He can never master all of the sources; there will be too many documents, too many letters, too many monographs. No one now can read all that has been published about the conquest of Mexico or the rise of the Dutch Republic. Therefore, the professional historian is naturally shy of attempting to do what his whole training has conditioned him not to do: to use his imagination, his sense of human reality, to bet on his hunches without having full documentary proof.

The reluctance or inability of professional historians to write traditional history means that the writing of it is largely in the hands of amateur historians, working outside the universities and the professional bodies. The last great academic figure who insisted passionately on the premise that history was literature or nothing and indeed wrote great traditional histories throughout his long life was G. M. Trevelyan. But his influence within the professional faculties of history was almost negligible. Lacking professional training, somewhat daunted by the bibliographical and archival expertise that a professional would have entirely at his command, the traditional historian, almost always an amateur, moves insecurely and often disastrously. Never before have so many books of a traditional historical kind been written. Most of them are sitting targets for professional criticisms. Within a year or two they pass into oblivion.

So we have a sad situation: a public demand for traditional history, an extraordinarily large response in terms of books (indeed, not only books; historical television series also meet with vast acclaim in both America and England), and yet an almost complete decline in quality, scarcely a book worthy to sit on the same shelf as the great old masters.

To be fair, the decline is not in literary skill. Many recent books – Gene Smith's *Maximilian and Carlota*, Stanley Loomis's *Paris in the Terror*, or Robert Lacey on *Sir Walter Ralegh* – are beautifully constructed and written with the verve and panache worthy of a Prescott or Trevelyan. They fail to establish themselves permanently in the great tradition of historical writing.

One obvious reason for this is their lack of scholarship in depth. The great old masters – under less economic necessity, perhaps, as well as under less social pressure – tended to limit themselves to a few works on great themes. Gibbon spent his lifetime on the *Decline and Fall*, Macaulay, a man of monumental vigour, decades on his history, and even the output of a Motley or a Prescott was not large. In consequence, they had time to delve as deeply as any professional of their day into the sources of their work. Now, sources are more multitudinous than they were, yet the pressure on literary historians is to write quickly, to produce saleable one-volume works as frequently as they can. Hence, even to the untrained reader of history, there is often a sense of a lack of depth, of profound knowledge, no matter how skillful the literary craftsmanship.

There is, however, I think, a more subtle reason. There has been a sharp decline in the role that traditional history plays in modern society. History has been the great interpreter of the human destiny, the pantheon in which mankind has enshrined its heroes, the majestic story of the conflict of good and evil, or the more mundane tale of progress, both material and moral. And furthermore, in the nineteenth century, history became even more closely associated with national destiny – a national destiny, however, that was also providential. The great American historians saw America, freed from the corruptions of Europe, as the great torchbearer of freedom. And whether they were writing about the Dutch Republic or the Conquistadores, there is, in their works, a deep sense that the tidal forces of history led inevitably to the freedom, the maturity, and the intellectual life that nineteenth-century New England, at least, enjoyed. The same is true of the great English historians, who saw English history as a slow but successful struggle for political freedom and representative institutions. If we turn to France or Italy or Germany, we find the same deep chord of national destiny struck. Hence, when these historians were read by tens of thousands of their fellow countrymen, the response went far deeper than entertainment; they fortified belief in their nation's destiny, strengthened social confidence. And that, of course, is why historical studies spread so rapidly in schools and universities in the late nineteenth and early twentieth centuries, and why all governments felt that the history of their nation must be an essential part of education at every level. History had an immediate, an urgent social purpose.

That situation has ended. The time given to history in schools shrinks every year. The enrolment of students in universities for historical studies has ceased to grow, and in many countries has begun to decline sharply. If we turn to other social studies – from economics to sociology – there is far less concern with historical roots of problems than there was. Indeed, it is rare now for scholars, let alone the public at large, to look to history for an explanation of the problems of our time. And nothing is more in ruins than the tradition that the past explains the present, sanctifies its institutions, and indicates the future. That ordinary men and women still hunger for such explanations and such prognostications is apparent from the popularity of Arnold Toynbee's great work on *A Study of History*, and nothing indicates the decay of such an attitude better than the lack of any imitators or even rivals to that work.

And yet this is true only of the West. In the nineteenth century, Marx and Engels forged an interpretation of history – materialist, dialectic and inevitable – that, as developed by Lenin, has become a rigid tradition not only in the Communist countries of Eastern Europe and of China but also among Marxist scholars or politicians in the rest of the world. This interpretation is now as absolute, as revered, as the old Chinese historical interpretation of the Mandate of Heaven. Indeed, it is a curious paradox that as traditional history has begun to crumble, not only in democratic societies of Europe and America but also in Islam and in the less developed countries of Africa and the East, interpretations of history in Marxist countries have hardened into a steel-like dogma. At times this has odd consequences, for human events and indeed human beings have a Houdini-like capacity to escape the clutches of an inevitable historical interpretation; one needs only to recall the problems created by a rigid Christian interpretation of history not merely in the nineteenth century but even in the far distant days of Eusebius to see the point. And so, events – the denunciation of Stalin by Khruschev – create a constant need for revision of the accepted Marxist tradition, all creating cracks in the edifice, making for cynicism   perhaps the most powerful corroder of tradition of all.

History, therefore, and the practitioners of history are entangled in complexities and paradoxes. As the professional methods and attitudes to history harden into even stronger traditions, the old social purposes of history that stretch back to the very beginnings of written records lose their force. The traditional power of history weakens, even as curiosity about the people and the events of the past grows. This situation is, of course, dangerous – more dangerous than many professional historians realise – for no discipline can survive for very long or be the

recipient of vast funds, unless it fulfills an obvious social purpose. What is needed is what happened to history in the eighteenth century, when antiquarianism and philosophic history fused. The result of that fusion was the great historical literature of the nineteenth century. If only professional history could break with some of its traditional attitudes and take upon itself the burden of the history that society needs, the prospect for academic historians and for history in the service of mankind would be brighter than it is.

Fernand Braudel, The Mediterranean and the Mediterranean World in the Age of Philip II

French history has been the most exciting, the most original and the most satisfying history written over the last half-century. The great figures of the 1920s and 1930s whose first work had appeared before World War I – Marc Bloch, Georges Lefebvre, Lucien Febvre – are all dead: Bloch, let it never be forgotten, shot as a hostage in World War II, an enormity as monstrous as would have been the killing of a Beethoven or a Michaelangelo. These were the great figures in the founding of what became the most exciting of all historical publications in the 1920s, 1930s and 1940s, *Les Annales.* Lefebvre remained a lonely and independent figure, but both Bloch and particularly Lefebvre acquired devoted disciples; between the masters and the disciples loomed Fernand Braudel, Professor of History at La Collège de France, and now in the ripeness of years is the grand master of the *Annales* school, and the one who, more than the rest perhaps, has drawn to him more disciples, more *dévots.* As with any school, it has become more rigid and more exclusive with the years, taking on, *à la* Leavis, a touch of paranoia and often wandering into arid intellectual wastes, so that now *Les Annales* is a shadow of what it once was, with too many articles that are as unreadable as they are unimportant. But of that, anon. Let us first salute Fernand Braudel and his masterpiece, whose translation has long been overdue.

Before the 1940s every putative French historian had to take the combination *histoire et géographie* for his degree and this was at a time when French geography was both exacting and original, exploring the interplay of environment and community, revealing the influence of soil, marsh, forest, geological sub-structures and micro-climates on economic and social activity. This training is quite clearly apparent in the work of all the great masters from Bloch to Braudel. And indeed Braudel's book is geographically based – the huge Mediterranean basin with its mountains, deserts, alluvial plains, its forests and marshes, the problems of its boundaries, its routes and villages, its climates and weather are investigated and described in the historical context which Braudel has chosen – the age of Philip II.

But, like any great historian, he ranges with ease over the centuries, displaying an extraordinary erudition of all periods in all of Western Europe's major languages. The historical geography described in some 300 pages, Braudel proceeds to discuss population and economic activity, with particular concern for bullion and prices. This section, which completes Volume I, finishes with trade and transport. In each section he ranges from the Sahara to the Rhine Valley, from Syria to Gibraltar. As an intellectual and scholarly *tour de force* it is almost unequalled: each paragraph is not only erudite, but more often than not pierced with novel insights, at times of such daring that Braudel, who is personally present on every page rapidly warns the reader not to take them as anything but tentative suggestions – often a sensible if disarming caution, as it checks obvious criticism.

If any school of historians was open to new scholarly disciplines it was surely the French, and Braudel is alive to developments in sociology, folk-lore studies, psychology, particularly in its social aspects, as well as medicine, biology and sexology. There is nothing arid about his geographical and economic landscapes, they are alive with human beings, individuals as well as communities, and he is as concerned to distinguish the beliefs, superstitions, social attitudes as well as the economic activities of his mountain folk from those of the plain and cities. The great merit of the *Annales* school was that all human activity was considered the proper province of the historian – not merely political, diplomatic and economic but also panics, folk tales, taboos, sexual practices, diseases, weather – all that touches the life of man absorbed their interest.

This adds complex and fascinating dimensions to Braudel's work as it does to that of his disciples, often giving new insights, but almost always creating a sense of new frontiers, new horizons to be explored. Braudel time and time again points to exciting new regions of research. And this imparts to his book an excitement, a sense of expectation that his refusal to use narrative might so easily have destroyed. But this effect depends very much on Braudel's highly idiosyncratic method of writing history, which is largely lost in this translation.

The task, of course, was very difficult, and certainly this translation is readable and accurate, but the extraordinary flavour of Braudel's style has gone, rather as if a banquet at the *Tour d'Argent* had been frozen into a television dinner. But in the original French, Braudel's highly individual style crackles and sparkles, darts and twists in the most remarkable way, yet always so immediately personal that it is like listening to a brilliant rhetorician displaying his ideas and juggling with his facts for the first time in his study. Because of this the abrupt transitions are far easier to take in French than in English. Also Braudel, by brilliant if rare use of adjectives or adverbs or simile, can hone his thought to a fine razor's edge. Somewhere, somehow, these excitements are lost. In consequence, a few of Braudel's weaknesses, reflecting the weakness of the whole *Annales* school, become almost glaringly apparent.

Erudition always dazzles, and Braudel is formidably erudite, but it is not enough; erudition can easily befog, mislead and distort, and it must be admitted that there are pages of Braudel where statistics and facts are displayed to little purpose, which usually Braudel disarmingly admits, suggesting that although the facts prove nothing, there is a case for further monumental research – a mannerism which is made all too frequently nowadays in the pages of the *Annales*.

The great virtue of Braudel's method is twofold – the insistence on what he calls '*la longue durée*'; studying indeed the effects of geography, of economic activity, of climate even, on human communities, which can only be done over long periods of time and yet are essential if one is to comprehend the complexities of social life in any age. Also Braudel insists on full weight being given to what might be called the enduring social ideas, responses, and beliefs that infuse social groups. All of this has benefited history greatly, enriched it and given it depth, but in the hands of less able, over-devout disciples these preoccupations can lead to aridity and to wrong-headedness.

Braudel has always tried to give quantitative justification to his statements about the economic life of the Mediterranean – but, of course, even the best runs of statistics are both very local and usually deficient and, and like the good scholar he is, he is aware of it, and like the good artist he is, he uses his limited facts and figures decoratively; often they do no more than give a heightened sense of reality to the commonplace.

For example, Braudel uses great erudition and a lot of discussion on the average income of the poor and near poor, and the end product is what we all know – that a huge proportion of the population in the sixteenth century lived on the edge of destitution. How many ducats they had a year adds nothing: indeed, the margin of error is so great that the attempt to be precise is often more misleading than more literary evidence, because it seems more real. And this penchant for the decorative statistic has led a generation of capable historians into the arid wastes of price lists and port books, to an endless distinction of categories and commodities with which the pages of the *Annales* are now littered, adding little to history but statistical complexity.

The one great exception here is the work of Goubert and Le Roy Ladurie on family reconstruction – one field where complex statistical evidence of some reliability has been discovered and made to yield some secrets of social and family history hitherto unknown. But three-quarters of the statistical articles in the *Annales* are at their best boring and largely irrelevant, at their worst dangerous.

Again, the preoccupation of Braudel has rightly placed great emphasis on folk-lore, superstition, taboo, witchcraft, mass hysteria that played so vast a part in human living two or three centuries ago, and indeed is still rampant in more sophisticated forms today. And this again has enriched historical study. In the hands of a Mandrou or a Keith Thomas these preoccupations have resulted in extraordinarily brilliant monographs on sub-cultural history, but again, their less able followers think that if they describe folk beliefs in West Wratting or unearth a phallic cult in the Camargues that they are writing history. Of course, one must, one should, understand seismic movements of history; of course, one must be alert to what unconsciously influences societies and explore their buried fears and hopes. But the great weakness, indeed the overriding weakness of the *Annales* school, is their resolute indifference to anything else, particularly to narrative history and to those aspects of human thought and invention which led to success. They prefer to chase economic effects of unassessable complexity, or the sub-culture of those anonymous men and women who have vanished into the darkness of time.

History as well as moving seismically moves by the decisions of men. It is and must be narrative, 1000 pages on the historical-geography of Italy still leaves Caesar, Augustus, Pompey, Nero and the rest in the centre of the stage. And again, the life of Sir Isaac Newton is more important than a description of all the witch trials of seventeenth-century England.

Curiously enough, as the *Annales* becomes increasingly arid, its influence becomes more widespread amongst the younger historians. Now instead of the culture and tradition, it is the sub-culture that attracts – the squibs, the broadsheets, the folk-tales and pornography; historians are drawn to primitive rebels, bandits, highwaymen, arsonists rather than to the history of party or of trade unions; they busy themselves with sexual habits and mores of obscure village communities; if games and sports are within the context of a bucolic culture they are dealt with the reverence that used to be accorded to the development of cabinet government. Institutional history, constitutional and political history, even economic history in a narrative context no longer appeal; they lack manna. Failure and obscurity now powerfully attract the younger historians of Europe. The brightest young historians would now rather concern themselves with agrarian protest than the causes or development of the Industrial Revolution. And so willy-nilly the *Annales* school – so

wonderful, so creative, so productive in its early years, throwing new
illumination on the course of human history and lightening up for all
time some of its obscure corners has now put history in grave danger –
more so in Europe than in America.

History is more than the evocation of times past, more even than the
comprehension of a given society in time, valuable and moving though
such histories may be in the hands of a master. If it is to have any social
validity, history is also explanation, and explanation which links with
our own time and our own experiences, aiding our capacity for judgement. Now doubtless it is good for one to understand the mentality, the
cultural climate, that could do pathetic old ladies to death as witches;
it adds a little to our historical understanding to learn that English
peasants practised *coitus interruptus*. However, these things pale into
insignifiance against those major events in politics, in social and economic development which have made our world what it is. It is far more
important to try to lay bare the causes of Napoleon's rise to power and
assess his achievements, to understand how Lenin seized and exploited
his opportunities, or how England managed to hold on to and develop
her representational institutions. To comprehend the causes of the Industrial Revolution must be always more valuable than studying sporadic
agrarian protest. This is not to deny the value of such historical explo-
rations – but too frequently they are peripheral to the major and decisive
experiences of mankind that we need to understand.

Studies of the undergrowth of history, even of those seismic forces
which undoubtedly slowly push social growth into new channels can
only be of true historical value so long as they relate and help to explain
the narrative of history, and *pace* Braudel. History without events is no
history at all – and by events I do not mean the pitter-patter of everyday
life – but the wars, the catastrophes, the conflicts of institutions and
religions, class struggles and ideologies, political decisions at the centre,
and also the inventions, the ideas, the books that have moulded human
history. These things have made us what we are and what we may be.

Although the *Annales* school is wandering in a desert of arid scholarship, there are, of course, oases and at times the brilliance of the old
maîtres shows through. Certainly they – Bloch, Febvre, and Georges
Lefebvre – produced masterpieces of enduring worth, largely because
they never lost sight of history's true function. And, Braudel's great work
is worthy of the founders of what in its day was the most exciting
historical journal in the world. *Requiescat in pace.*

Capitalism and Material Life, 1400–1800

Fernand Braudel's two great volumes on *The Mediterranean in the Age of Philip II* have been acclaimed as one of the major historical works of this century. The majesty and scope of the book, the weight of its erudition, the brilliance of its style stilled most, if not all, criticisms. One or two of us, whilst admiring its brilliance and force, were troubled both by the method and the interpretation. The translation of *Civilisation Matérielle et Capitalisme 1400–1800*, again in two large volumes to be published separately (which, as with *The Mediterranean*, seems a pity) will meet with less adulation, for the weaknesses of this book which attempts to survey the material condition of mankind (not merely of the West) are, indeed glaring, so glaring that they may distract from its originality, its daring, and its educative value.

Braudel is a natural historian in the way W. G. Grace was a natural cricketer. He possesses the temperament and all the skills. He cannot look at a house, a chair, a banana, or a glass of calvados without asking when, how, why? His curiosity is omnivorous, yet never merely antiquarian. That is, he does not accumulate facts for the sake of facts. He is always searching for insights into social structures: and at times his urgent need to analyse and theorise transmogrifies fascinating information into bogus theory. Let us take Braudel's treatment of the chair and high table. These are European inventions; most of the world squats or sits on the floor and eats from low tables, or did so until the influence of Europe asserted itself in the last two centuries. Except for the very rich, chairs and high tables were rare in Europe until the end of the Middle Ages, becoming reasonably common only in the sixteenth century. However, they slowly crept into China, may be in the third century AD, known as 'barbarian beds'. The acquisition in China of chairs and the high tables that go with them corresponded to a new art of living; sitting and squatting existed side by side. But to see this according to Braudel 'merely as the story of the chair' is very simplistic. In fact a great surge of population took place in China, before the thirteenth century, when chairs became common, which created a social division, two types of behaviour – 'almost two different biologies' in the everyday life of the Chinese world between those who sat on chairs and those who did not. So far, almost so good – fascinating, illuminating, if sketchy and dogmatic. But then on he goes, back to the world that only squats and collapses into nonsense. 'Ultimately,' he says, 'a biological difference is involved . . . for "squatting" is impossible, or at best difficult, for a European.' In my boyhood, you could see rows of Welsh or Leicestershire miners sitting on their haunches quite comfortably for hours – playing cards, just gossiping, or taking the sun like a row of pigeons. Indeed, the chair has played a very complex social status role in Europe as well as China. But biology has nothing to do with it.

This long example is illustrative of the book. The information imparted is interesting, often informative, and on occasion gives piercing insight into western and Chinese societies, but when it is used to hint at social 'structures' of an unplumbable profundity incredulity sets it. Time and time again, the concept, the theoretical implication, is reached too fast on too little evidence. Behind it all lurks the baleful spirit of Lévi Strauss. This is a pity, for it makes it so easy to criticise and so it may detract from the book's splendid virtues.

The first and foremost of these is that Braudel deals impressively with subjects – food, fashion, furniture, clothes – that most historians ignore. Again and again he shows that their history provides insights into human society and human progress.

The book is obviously based on lectures. Would that lectures on subjects such as these were available in British universities, for Braudel is concerned with the deepest historical problems of human society – what makes it change? Why does change accelerate or lag? What inhibits growth or quickens it? Where, and why, does the grip of the past exert its greatest strength? The questions and the answers are not applied to an élite, or to a particular society, but range over the mass of mankind, an impressive variety of human societies. This is comparative and social history at its very best, flawed though the arguments are from time to time. And the lesson – and there is a lesson – that Braudel teaches is both stimulating and hopeful.

He never disguises the material misery in which the mass of mankind have lived their lives – the pitifully small food supply, the pathetic huts, the poverty of possessions; or how bleak were the comforts even of the handful of rich and powerful. Nor does he omit the plagues, famines and diseases which made life a lottery for everyone – rich or poor – until the most recent times. So many of the little comforts that we take for granted – well-heated rooms, soap, fresh bread – are for the majority of mankind in the West very recent gains, and still denied to the masses elsewhere. Material progress, even for the West up to 1800 has been slow and, moreover, given to very sharp recessions. At that time change and desire for change accelerated extravagantly in the West. The dynamics of this change are elusive and difficult to analyse, as Braudel well realises, but his eyes are wider open than so many of his colleagues. The rapidity of changes in the fashions of clothes, an odd peculiarity of the West, may, he realises, be as important an indication of acceleration as demographic graphs or price indices: the same is true of food patterns, and a score of other things which we accept without thinking about them historically. Time and time again he gives a new perception to the seeming commonplace of everyday living.

Most of the subjects that he touches in this volume – food, drink, houses, clothes, fashion and the like – have been ill-treated by historians. What Braudel writes is necessarily superficial in content if not in ideas. He indicates, however, vast areas for fruitful research. Again and again he strengthens the conviction that this is the way historical study will go, and must go. We shall understand the world in which we live – its complexities and contradictions, and the problems which we have both inherited and complicated only by this type of comparative social history. Such history ought to be the core of what is taught in schools and universities.

So long, however, as it is merely the core of historical study, and not the entire subject, for there are empty areas in Braudel's thesis – little or no discussion of institutions, war, art, law, education, social attitudes created by religion; the interplay between material civilisation and ideas that are socialised in institutions or create goals – these themes are never explored. He realises that Western Europe delighted in fashion more than any other civilisation, and that this had important repercussions, but the social reasons for this addiction to fashionable change get only a brief and jejeune treatment. About inventions he makes the obvious comment that 'the sanction of society was an invariable prerequisite of success', but never explains how that sanction was achieved. Indeed, any exploration of the causes of the acceleration of material progress in the eighteenth century which leaves out ideological change must fail. The change during the eighteenth century in attitude to the material world was as dramatic and as revolutionary as the acceleration in the production and distribution of goods and of far greater importance. Braudel often speaks of the 'languages' of material things, but he rarely stops to consider the language of ideas.

Also it is a pity that so fine a book is blemished by so many factual errors. Obviously Braudel depends too often on his memory, which is not a very precise instrument. Such howlers as 'William Peppys' for Samuel Pepys; the Duke of Oxford as builder of Houghton instead of Sir Robert Walpole; 'the barely covered sands of the Dogger Bank' – these are about 300 feet deep; and so on, should have been eliminated long before the book reached the public. And for an historian who is deeply concerned with quantification, there is a quite remarkable dependence not merely on eye-witnesses, but on a selected few, mainly French. This is particularly marked in Braudel's treatment of Chinese history. I suspect that factually and theoretically, this book will be faulted over and over again. That does not matter overmuch – what Braudel has done has been to indicate where the problems lie and where the work needs to be done. And in spite of the excess of factual errors, occasional dubious and portentous generalisations, a cloudy overall structure, and the omission of what for many historians are the critical agents of change, this, like all of Braudel's work, is a memorable achievement. Also it should be said that in Mirian Kochan he has found a translator worthy of his own vivid and exciting style.

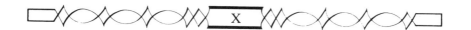

The Perspective of History

My work on the *Death of the Past* had stimulated my thinking about history to a degree which fundamentally changed my preoccupations as an historian and drew me back to my preoccupations of the late fifties when I was concerned to make some valid statements about world history. I came to feel that all the civilisations that stretched from Sumer to the United States of America were so many variations on possibilities which had been inherent in the Neolithic revolution, but the basic structures no matter how varied in outward expression were basically the same, a view which I expressed in an article for *Horizon* magazine, entitled *The End of an Epoch* which caused a stir in America.

I began about the same time to develop similar themes in a monthly column that I was contribution to *The Saturday Review*, called *Perspective*. They were directed at a large readership of some 600,000 mainly consisting of professional people dominated by academics and school-teachers – the middle-brows. The response was excellent if erratic – used loo paper arrived from Alabama when I wrote strongly on civil rights and against racism; a 900 stanza holograph poem proving Christ to be Satan and Satan, Christ came from Philadelphia *à propos* of nothing in particular; endless requests for a reading list and best of all letters of thanks. The column was extremely exciting to write – sometimes I could use a cluster of books, occasionally two or even one would do and once or twice no books at all arrived from America and so one could write a straight essay.

I tried to write on the widest variety of subjects I could think of, trying to give a dimension of time to the obscure as well as the obvious. I wanted to show that one of the greatest uses of history was to think historically about everything in life.

The *Perspectives* were so successful that I decided to run another series for *Horizon* magazine with whom I had become associated in 1960. More will be said about that wonderful journal in the next volume. As

309

ever, the editorial board gave the strongest backing and for some years I produced *In the Light of the Past* – articles double the length of the *Perspectives* and not, of course, pegged to a book review and therefore rather more enjoyable to write. Their success was as great, if not greater than the *Perspectives*, and the two series together proved, if proof were needed, that there is a deep and growing interest in historical interpretation. Historians did not have to limit themselves to superficial narrative or biographical history to entertain. The 'Why' of history had as much appeal as the 'How'.

There was no room for complacency in the 1970s, even less in the 1980s, for anyone who believed passionately in the value of history for society, for the old and the young and those between. There were signs of a growth in the interest and purpose of history but at the same time the professional world was not at all clear about its purpose. Students of academic history were getting fewer. Nevertheless, history as understanding, led by the French, seemed to be finding its way back into the cultural life of the West. The great structural changes of our time were having seismic effects on the historic inheritance of developed society, as well as its value and use and so I start this section with an essay on the main theme 'An epoch that started ten thousand years ago is ending'.

The End of an Epoch

An epoch that started 10,000 years ago is ending. We are involved in a revolution of society that is complete and as profound as the one that changed man from hunter and food gatherer to settled farmer and craftsman. Ten thousand years ago the Neolithic revolution closed an age that lasted for hundreds of thousands of years. The foundations of society created by that revolution have endured, no matter how sophisticated and elaborate the superstructure of civilisation has become; only within the last century have these foundations begun to crumble, as the new scientific and industrial revolutions spread with ever-increasing speed throughout the world.

But how few of us realise this is so! We rage against governments, rage against Churches, rage against cities, rage against schools, rage against marriage, rage against men; everywhere rage, criticism, disillusion. Nothing works, neither Lord nor government. Science, once the Great White Hope, is now the Hypocritical Polluter. Who, where there is freedom of expression, is thoroughly happy with present-day society? Or pitch expectation a lot lower. Who feels that this is the world that will endure, the one with which our children and grandchildren must live as best they might, that for better or worse this is the way that life will be organised for generations to come? Or have we in the advanced industrial nations lost all hope of stability? And are we at fault? Have we wrecked the great institutions that have moulded human life for so long – family, organised religion, government? Whatever our political commitment, there lies a burden of guilt on many of us, a feeling that somehow we have lost our way, that we are responsible for the break-down in social and private morality and in the discourse between the generations. What scarcely any of us realise is that we are all victims of an historical process. We are now involved in a second revolution of mankind and one probably more profound in its consequences than that which changed the destiny of man 10,000 years ago.

What did the Neolithic revolution do for mankind? First, it dramati-cally increased the food supply, so that millions of human beings replaced the scattered tens of thousands of the hunting and food-gath-ering era. True, at times famine swept millions away, but never for long, for peasant societies recover fast. Nature is capricious and the fertility of crops and animals became a focus of hope and fear that gave rise to elaborate rituals. At the earliest dawn of urban society organised religion is there; temples with estates to support the gods, both benign and evil, and their servants the priests. And sometimes combined with and sometimes distinct from the priesthood, we soon discover, a law-giver or a warrior who acts as King. The most magnificent relics of the earliest and most developed communities of the early millenia of the Neolithic revolution are the ziggurats of Sumer, Akkad and Babylon within their fortress cities; monuments to their gods and to their god-like kings. And in Egypt the Pharoahs were God and King: they created temple cities built for eternity. Naturally such complex societies made commerce more continuous and far-flung than it had been in the more primitive hunting days. And increased goods, whether from afar or provided locally for the temple or palace, required numeration. All early writing stems from the need to list and record goods. Some societies such as the Incas developed only a complicated knotting system, but Egypt, China, Sumer and the Mayans devised a complex pictorial shorthand that rapidly developed into a highly complex written language which, again, released new potentialities by creating a social memory, infinitely more reliable and exact than oral traditions could ever be. With written language the creative genius of men had an exceptional instrument. But this instru-ment was only available for a small elite. From the time writing was invented until the twentieth century only a tiny fragment of mankind has been able to read and write: the educated class that could be supported by societies based on agriculture and crafts was always small.

No matter where we turn, Imperial Rome, T'ang China, the France of Louis XIV, Mexico of Montezuma; these civilisations are all children of the Neolithic revolution, certainly with their own striking individualities and excellencies, but also with the same basic structures: the structures that we first discern in ancient Egypt and in the valley of the Tigris-Euphrates. In each of these civilisations, the bulk of mankind toiled on the land, struggling to wring a very modest living from the soil sufficient to pay taxes, to make offerings to their churches, indeed a sufficient surplus to sustain a social elite. In all of this economic activity the basic unit was the family: of course, some of the more sophisticated societies evolved more complex forms of economic organisation, but the family group – father, mother, children – remained the most effective social and economic group. As always in such societies only a minority lived in towns which were centres of government, of religion, of commerce and often of crafts and of learning.

The masses in all these societies were illiterate and poor and all societies of which we have knowledge through their written records regarded this as a part of the divine natural order. As the Sumerians bluntly put it, 'men are slaves of the Gods': their duty was to work. At times, as in all societies, the rage of the poor broke out in sporadic violence, but the remarkable fact is not the occasional rebellion, but the millenia of docility. Partly this was due to their terror of the mysterious forces of nature which dominated their lives and which could give them abundance or deny it. And so they needed gods, and priests and ritual, especially ritual to a degree we find hard to appreciate. Religion might be refined into theological speculation, reduced to simple human terms or slip into mere magical practices, but it touched the millions of mankind in their daily lives. Every village, every community, whether in sophisticated societies such as eighteenth-century England or simple ones like the farmers of Ghana, had its temple, its priest, its communication with the gods. For ten millennia men have been god-haunted through all the days of their lives.

Compared with religion the secular forms of government were less socially powerful, even though they could often dominate the structure of organised religion and indeed in Pharonic Egypt or Imperial China absorb many of its functions. Most societies possessed a warrior class from which the authority, the King, was selected. In most advanced societies the warrior class became a landed aristocracy, except in Imperial China where the scholar-gentry disdained the profession of arms, even though frequently enough it was the soldiers who called the tune. Elsewhere the great landowners together with successful merchants, lawyers, priests and government officials provided the governing elite, which tended to breed its own successors.

Theoretically, as in China, several societies provided a system by which the talented poor might rise to success: in practice, again as in China, this very rarely happened. In the epoch that is now closing, social mobility was rare. Schools and universities, like all forms of private culture, were produced by and directed towards the élite. Schools, often very rigorous and very austere, were designed to transmit the cultures of those who governed to the next generation of rulers. From Tibet to Ireland they were dominated by classical learning, for all of these societies reverenced the past as a storehouse of wisdom: and it was the past, too, that demonstrated the divine nature of authority as well as the truth of religion. Education was thus far more than learning a skill, it was the key to the understanding of life, of society, or universal truths. Although culture and the past largely belonged to the governing élite, particularly in advanced and complex societies, there remained a need for public art, mainly in the form of monumental architecture, statuary or descriptive pictures, which spoke of the majesty of kings or gods, and often complex rituals of music or drama in the more intimate service of the gods. A complex social matrix bound the governor and the governed together; a mixture of force, patriarchal protection, accepted natural authority and mythological sanction combined to create a sense of identity that in the favourable geographical and economic circumstances of Imperial Rome, Ancient Babylon and Pharaonical Egypt led to the establishment of highly developed and long-lasting societies. Civilisation, whether primitive or advanced, was highly ceremonial. The great public rituals of religion, whether a solemn *Te Deum* in Nôtre Dame or the dramatic human sacrifices in ancient Mexico, all forged a sense of identity between the ruler and the ruled and God.

No matter how complex these societies became, when analysed they bear a remarkable number of common features not only in the way the majority of men and women obtained their livelihoods, but also in the structure of their institutions. They were ruled by monarchs or priest-kings; there was organised religion supported by the state; there was an aristocracy of warriors and landowners. An élite of scholarly men were drawn from these classes to serve the state or its church and maintain the authority of the traditional past. Below them lay a class of merchants whose wealth commanded special privileges but who were often at risk. But the bulk of the population, however, lived in village communities, tightly bred in tradition both in work and belief. Towns were small, cities few and designed as centres of religion, government, crafts and trade, sometimes one function dominating, sometimes another, and occasionally as in the great cities – Rome, Peking, Paris, Mexico – combining all. Of course, exceptions may be found, but for over 10,000 years and all around the globe this has been the basic pattern of human living. One that began to crumble in any obvious way only a hundred years or so ago. Even then such changes as occurred were very small and their significance not understood. It was not until the twentieth century that it became obvious that this age-long social structure was breaking down, not until after World War II that it was incapable of survival. Only now are there a few historians, a few sociologists, a few perceptive thinkers who realise that we are – capitalist or communist – in the throes of a social revolution as profound as that which changed the destiny of mankind ten thousand years ago and that the ills of our society for which we so often take the blame, arise from the fact that the old basic institutions are less and less suitable for the modern world, and as yet we have failed to evolve institutions more suitable to our purpose. And naturally confusion and chaos is greatest where society is freest and experimentation permitted – in America and Western Europe rather than in Communist Russia or China where social institutions are held rigid, even though minor economic experimentation may be allowed to proceed.

Let us look more closely at the revolution in which we are involved and its consequences. It began haphazardly and, like the Neolithic revolution, went unnoticed by the world at large. A few men in Western Europe in the sixteenth and seventeenth centuries began to feel a new confidence, to believe that they or their descendants might outrank the ancients in knowledge and in achievement. Slowly, science captured more and more gifted men and secured greater and greater triumphs but, initially with little or no effect on society. But the idea gradually came to non-scientists that experimentation was admirable in itself and should be applied to economic life. Again this might have led nowhere, but Europe and particularly England had at this time a buoyant market for goods, a plentiful supply of money, an expanding population, a wide-ranging commerce and almost constant involvement in war – all of which stimulated production and helped to bring about in the early nineteenth century the first stages of the Industrial Revolution.

A hundred years later the Industrial Revolution had spread throughout Europe and America: the interaction of science and technology with the means of production had lifted mankind to a new level of civilisation. Men left the countryside and swarmed into the cities, until by the middle of the twentieth century the majority of people in Western Europe and America were living in cities. Crafts had ceased to be of much importance, production was now on a mass scale in complex factories.

A great revolution in living had taken place within the institutions of the pre-industrial world, but its culture, its intellectual and religious attitudes, were still derived from the past. But with every decade that passed, they were put at risk and called into question. Two epochs clashed as an ancient system of institutions and cultures struggled with a new system of production and a totally new economic life-style. The old institutions decayed and new, more appropriate ones did not at first arise to replace them.

Take monarchy, the most sacred of lay institutions, one which had emerged at the very dawn of recorded time: before 1900 only countries in America, apart from France and Switzerland in Europe, had managed to discard it. World War I shattered the world's monarchies, and World War II swept away the remains, apart from two or three counties where it was saved by obstinate tradition or lucky chance. Gone are the Tsars, the Kaisers, the Emperors, Kings, Serene Highnesses, Grand Dukes and Archdukes: they linger in pathetic little exiled courts huddled about Lausanne or Estoril.

Aristocracy, that ancient warrior class, whose strength in war had brought titles, riches, honours and land, found itself stripped of rights, deprived of power, often slaughtered or chased into exile to exist on a pittance – often forced indeed to work for a living. Even in England where political violence was rare and monarchical tradition strong, the legal and political powers of the peerage were sharply diminished. And no one now, not even the noblemen themselves, regard themselves as a race apart, set above all others by God to advise kings and rule men. But no society has evolved anything to provide the social cohesion or the dramatic ceremonial quality once given to life by the aristocracy and monarchy.

The new revolution has, however, attacked other human institutions more fundamental than monarchy and aristocracy, institutions which were given form and strength by traditional oligarchy. Let us take just four – the city, the school, organised religion, and the family – all of these institutions have for millennia been the matrix of society from China to Rome.

One of the first complex organisations to arise from the Neolithic revolution was the city – in no way essential to it certainly, but so frequent an occurrence that it can be regarded as one of the most efficient methods for mobilising the resources of modern communities. And those resources were mobilised for a number of social functions, one of extreme importance – the creation of a vast impressive centre for religion as at Thebes or Chichen Itaza, cities created purely for this purpose. In many other cities religion was combined with the sword: secular and spiritual authority might be combined in the same rule, though sometimes the two authorities remained distinct. There is no more impressive image of this duality which stretches back to the earliest cities of Ur and Lagash of Sumeria, than in the medieval cities of Western Europe where cathedral and castle sit side by side. But of course cities developed from these very origins more complex functions than religion, defence and worldly authority. Commerce fertilised them and made them grow, as did crafts and primitive industry, so that they became the economic centre of the surrounding countryside in which local produce could be exchanged and where foreign trade could be marketed. Market-places either within or just without were an integral part of city life. With religion in need of ritual, with secular authority in need of power, with commerce from afar providing exotic ideas as well as goods, cities early became centres of art and cultural exchange, the natural home for scholarly élites, the house of pleasure as well as of religion, the market for ideas as well as merchandise. They became the heart of society, a mirage that enticed the ambitious, the creative, the seeker of power or pleasure. Rarely has any human institution concentrated within itself so many functions or so much of the variety of life: and this is as true of Montezuma's Mexico, Socrates' Athens, Franklin's Philadelphia or Goncourt's Paris.

But what now? Look at the desolate centre of Detroit, parking lots and ghettos cut by expressways that hurry the bankers and merchants out of the commercial areas as quickly as possible. Everywhere from Marseilles to Seattle, and maybe from Shanghai, the hearts of cities are emptying and dying. For a century now they have had no defensive value – indeed rather the reverse: they are now targets for holocausts and are totally indefensible. Castle and city walls are quaint symbols of a dead past. Nor are they the seat of organised religion, the centres of dramatic ritual, the home of priest-kings or even priests. Moscow's patriarch is an active civil servant, the mufti of Cairo is of little account, Rome is no longer the Vatican, and the Dalai Lama, the last of the priest-kings, dwells in exile. The city churches themselves can scarcely maintain an existence; with next to no congregations they steadily close. London was happy to sell a Wren church to a Missouri townlet. Nor are cities essential to government. Brazil can be governed as easily from Brasilia as Rio de Janiero and the President is equally in control from Florida, California or Air-Force One. If the Pentagon were removed to Death Valley and the Treasury to Boise, Idaho, the government of the most complex society on earth would not suffer. And even commerce and industry no longer need the city. The Port of London has decayed to the point of death – dock after dock has closed: the volume of New York's trade diminishes. Markets are also finished: Les Halles have been uprooted, Covent Garden closed; shopping centres, vast and complex, root themselves in suburbia where people dwell or long to. All that is left – and for how long? – is the world of pleasure: the restaurants, the theatres, the shops for the rich élite or stray tourists whether from the suburbs, or foreign lands. And frighteningly the majority of the commercial enterprises could move from the great cities of the Western World with no loss to themselves: improved means of communication, one of the greatest triumphs of the new industrial and scientific world, has obliterated distance and made propinquity meaningless. It is true for the time being swarms of men and women still flow in and out of cities every day, yet there is no compelling social need except that their offices and factories happen to be located there. Sooner or later, and probably sooner, this lack of social need will overcome the compulsion generated by the huge investment in real estate and commerce and industry will hive off to more appropriate social situations. Because the city was the heart of life for ten thousand years is no passport for survival in a scientific and industrial world.

But the city is still more vigorous than other institutions that are millenniums old. Organised religion with the paraphernalia of temples, priests, festivals, goes back to the first emergence of civilisation as we know it, but that, too, is now only a pale shadow of what it was. In England where, oddly enough the decay of organised religion may have gone furthest, congregations at village churches are often well under ten people. Chapels, the homes of vigorous dissenting groups in the nineteenth century — Methodists, Baptists, Congregationalists and the rest — are no better off. The chapels are being closed and sold off. Even the strongest church of all — the Roman Catholic — is in convulsions, weakened by declining priesthood and rent by a new radicalism, and also declining congregations. And the dissolution of organised religion is further reflected in the growth of half-baked mysticism, dabbling in magic and astrology, the spread of Buddhism and Christ cults amongst the middle-class hippie young. The impulse to believe still runs strong in many young men and women, but they cannot accept the forms in which belief has been encased for centuries. Interestingly enough, the major criticism hurled at what remains of organised religion, self-criticism often voiced amongst those who still participate — is that religion has lost its social commitment, coupled with a demand for Christianity's return to the early days of Christ — a time indeed when Christian belief was neither socially organised nor socially acceptable. Religion may persist, but what is unlikely to remain are the institutional forms that were part of the secular structure of society.

Equally as interesting as the decay of formal, organised, church-structured religion is the new confusion of belief; the way the revolution in sexual morality has spread like measles through the denominations — Roman Catholic priests and nuns demand marriage, so that, of all things, they can be fulfilled as human beings; the Anglican Church cautiously condemns extramarital relations and with reluctance tolerates lesbianism and homosexuality; the Quakers, at least in England, accept the entire sexual revolution so long as love dominates. As for strict belief in the Christian myth, that is no longer necessary when an Anglican bishop can state publicly that God is dead. Any clergyman, of any denomination of half a century ago would be appalled by the state of organised religion today. He would find it as baffling as an eighteenth-century connoisseur of art confronted by a Jasper Johns. For religion is not alone in collapsing into near anarchy – the same is true of all the arts.

Painting, sculpture, music, poetry and a great deal else would be incomprehensible to a cultured man of the nineteenth century; whereas an artistically inclined Greek of the fourth century BC or an Egyptian of 2000 BC or a mandarin of Han China would have had little difficulty in appreciating to the full the poetry, the painting, the sculpture, the literature and, except for the Chinaman, the music of the nineteenth century.

The new social revolution penetrates deeper, far deeper than this, into indeed the very basis of society and its most elementary institution, the family. For 10,000 years, and probably even longer, but certainly for as long as we can discern, the family has been the basis of society, its most powerful social and economic unit. In most agrarian societies wife–husband–children grouped in a family are an adequate self-supporting work unit in which there are carefully differentiated and accepted divisions of labour. And the same is true of crafts: although in crafts there might be a considerable number of child apprentices, these apprentices were always expected to accept the role of children of the family. The family, of course, was far more than an economic unit, even though this was its most powerful centrifugal force: it was a school which provided not only technical education but education for life. Most of humanity throughout history never went to any other school. It was in the family that boys and girls learned their skills as farmers or crafts-men or housekeepers. As they learned children received also from their fathers and mothers the social morality – their attitudes to secular govern-ment as well as sexual morals. In the family they were moulded by disci-pline, by propaganda and if necessary by force for their social roles. As with all human institutions it had its crashing failures as well as its suc-cesses, but it was a highly complex and powerful institution through which all human beings in all centuries of settled agrarian life had to pass.

Now the economic and social function of the family is rapidly breaking down – skills are no longer taught there and often education for life does not take place there either: schools and society at large have absorbed these functions, with the result that the family is now so weak in social and economic functions that it breaks down very easily under its material stresses. While in the past men and women often grew to hate each other in marriage, or became bored, the social and economic bands were so strong that in most societies divorce was unthinkable. A man might take concubines or other wives, in a few idiosyncratic societies a wife might be permitted to take lovers, but easy divorce was an exceptional rarity, particularly in advanced or developed societies, except for the very rich and powerful for whom the economic bonds were far less strong. But now the social and economic weakness of family life is demonstrated by the steady increase in divorce and the beginning of the social acceptance of men and women living together without marriage at all.

In the case of protection of children the family still performs an important function that society as yet cannot easily replace, but the education of children no longer takes place within it. Schools themselves, however, are in little better shape than families, organised religion or cities. There is a powerful radical movement to remove education from schools: indeed schools are constantly being denounced as prison-like 'The belief that a highly industrialised society,' writes Paul Goodman, 'requires twelve or twenty years of prior processing of the young is an illusion or a hoax.' Pupils denounce curricula as irrelevant and school-masters themselves have little faith in what they teach if one can judge by the constant soul-searching and debate that infests any conference of teachers. And yet more and more pupils are pressed into the system for longer and longer. Unhappy, frustrated, disoriented, not only do campuses flash into riot, but so do high schools. The idea of police in the corridors of a public school is enough to make Thomas Arnold, who introduced the prefect system, moan in his grave.

Increasingly it is seen that the school is unable to do what it did so powerfully and so effectively during the last three or four hundred years – and indeed what is still done in communist countries – educate for living and inculcate or strengthen social principles. The problem is that an educational system that was designed to educate an élite has lost its rationale. Faced with the task of educating the masses of industrial society for which it was never designed, it is breaking down in the attempt. An élite is willing to be disciplined, to learn seemingly arcane subjects such as Latin or medieval history or divinity if the rewards of success are obvious – high professional office, status in society. For the masses now pouring into the public schools and universities all that beckons is a job in a factory or an office and no guarantee of social status. What is available for all distinguishes no one.

We are at the end of 10,000 years of history. We are in the middle of a revolution more profound than humanity has experienced, and thus we are affected even more deeply than we realise. Not only are age-old social institutions breaking down, but there is a greater problem. Men, women and children are losing their ability to identify with society; they no longer have clear social roles to fulfil, to aspire to, to feel guilty about if they fail in them. For the last 10,000 years in any society fathers and mothers, husbands and wives, sons and daughters have had defined social roles. And the crisis of identity we hear so much about arises not so much because the individual is lost, but because society no longer defines his function.

Consider the role of children. The powers that parents exercise over children, the need for children to respect the authority and wisdom of age, was almost universally accepted for the last 10,000 years. But now with the weakening of the family, the respect and the subordination have both gone. Similarly the subordination of women; likewise the authority of men. Until recently social roles were very strongly defined. Of course, there were many who rebelled against them, many more who failed to live up to them, many who found them constricting and disagreeable, but the majority of mankind accepted their social role, even if they rarely attained it. Women's liberation, the revolt of adolescence, the decay of the patriarch is not due to a sudden fever which has gripped this generation, but the product of a social revolution, of a readjustment that man has only once previously experienced in his history.

Whether men and women can live in and found institutions for a new age, more complex than they have ever experienced before is open to doubt. Understanding the situation may help a little. Governments are always more conservative with regard to social change than society itself (witness the problem of divorce in Italy or legalised abortion here), but if they could be made to realise that the social experimentation that is going on is not due to the sickness of youth or the corruption and self-indulgence of this generation, but has profound social causes, perhaps they then might help rather than hinder experiments in adjustment.

But in the end men and women must themselves evolve new institutions and find new social roles that express the innate needs of man and also provide those necessary and very deep psychic protections and safeguards that we all require. These new roles will spring from humanity's great biological adaptability, if they spring at all. Or, of course, there may be a retreat, a very sharp retreat from highly scientific, technological urban civilisation. New York or London may become the new Nineveh and Tyre buried under vast ruins of their own detritus. And possibly, perhaps even probably, man will fail to cope: his aggressive and acquisitive greeds which are perhaps his deepest drives may prevail. We may blow ourselves up or pollute ourselves off the face of the earth. A sad end, it might seem, to the mighty hopes of scientific progress. Not so! Sooner or later there must be a last generation. Naturally one would prefer it to be later rather than sooner, but if our children or grand-children should be the last, we can take this somewhat arid consolation that the scientific progress that doomed mankind was well worth it, for during the last forty years more men and women have lived longer, lived happier and more fulfilled lives than ever before in human history, or ever could have done without that progress. This is as true of Africa, of India, of China as it is of the developed countries of the West. If there is total disaster, it will not be the fault of science and technology, but of man's incapacity to evolve socially.

All possibilities are open, but man's capacity for social evolution, as recorded in his history, is exceptional, and the human psyche is resilient and tough. If and when a new world emerges from the discords of the old, it will probably be both varied and strange. There is one thing we can be sure of – it will be little like the world that we now live in.

New Directions

My own fascination with the social apsects of history began partly accidentally in 1968. I had been asked to lecture in Chicago, not at Chicago University itself, of which I have many happy memories, but at the University of Illinois 'at the Circle'. When I arrived at O'Hare there was no one to meet me and I did not know what to do. After about twenty minutes an Englishman, Professor Maurice Bruce rushed up to me, explained that he was working at the University on a sabbatical and that he had realised that the Head of the Department had gone to Arkansas for a conference, and that no one had been delegated to meet me. An almost farcical day followed – the room that supposedly had been booked was occupied; a room was found and by some miracle or by arm-twisting an audience of about twelve was secured. Later we returned to an extremely pleasant dinner at the Drake with one or two members of the Faculty with Bruce acting as host. He drove me to O'Hare the next morning, and said that during the next academic year he was organising a conference on *The World of Lawrence Sterne* at Sheffield. Would I give a paper? How could I refuse? This crystallised my growing interest in social history and I decided to give a paper on 'The Public, Leisure and the Arts in the mid-eighteenth Century' – a theme which I developed over the next seven years in articles, lectures, particularly in the Kilham Lectures at Dalhousie University and a complex didactic exhibition 'The Pursuit of Happiness' for the opening of the Mellon Centre for British Art at Yale in 1977. Both before and after the trauma of Chicago, I had been brooding on social history, as I have mentioned before in two magazines *The Saturday Review* and *Horizon*. It seems appropriate therefore, at this point to print some of these articles which give an introduction to the way my historical interests were changing.

Terror

All London on a bomb alert, yet no war. A set battle in Los Angeles between the FBI and the self-styled Symbionese Liberation Army, a miniscule civil war may be, but civil war nevertheless. Whatever else this gang was – psychotic, fanatic, criminal – they acted as, and indeed were, urban guerrillas. And there is no reason to believe, although there may be very strong reason to hope, that they will be the last. After all, they are not the first. There were the minutemen. A middle-class girl did blow herself and her father's house sky high in Greenwich village, making bombs! She was not making toys. The conspiracy of terrorism is growing, not diminishing. Even as I write, the news has come through that the triumph of Giscard d'Estaing in the election to the French Presidency has been greeted by a French terrorist group blowing up a part of the Sacré Coeur. Assassination has become a part of the stock in trade of the politics of violence: two Kennedys, Martin Luther King, and very nearly George Wallace and Ronald Reagan. In Ireland, a Senator has been dragged from his house and slaughtered in cold blood. The attempts on De Gaulle's life were constant. Even a member of the English royal family missed being cut down by a hair's breadth.

Violence against the person would seem to be growing as fast, if not faster, than political terrorism. The incidence of rape is, quixotically, growing extraordinarily fast in western industrial society which, however, is more sexually permissive than the Western World has known since the Roman Empire. Robbery with violence reaches down into the primary schools, both in England and America. It is not the least uncommon for a twelve-year-old to rob and assault an eight-year-old.

Psychologists, sociologists, medical practitioners, lawyers, counsellors of every kind flounder about in the statistics, bemoaning the nature of our time. Certainly some of the statistics are revealing and important, and some very deviously interconnected in ways not commonly understood. Nevertheless, there is a need for perspective. The dimension of time is the dimension we all most commonly neglect – in our own lives, in the lives of others, above all in our social thinking. In our own society we very rarely see the ghosts of our grandparents or great-grandparents. They ought to be substantial, ever-present.

Terror has always been an effective social process. In many primitive tribes the initiation ceremony for boys is so prolonged, so frightening, harrowing, and physically as well as psychologically painful, that they never again lose the awe and respect for the elders of the tribe and the taboos upon which they insist. Again, in the nineteenth century, the Kabaka of Uganda, so god-like that it was an offence to look directly at him, used terror – sudden executions, mutilations, and the like – to keep his court and his subjects in abject subjection. This, however, is only a more flagrant and primitive example of what all societies in which authority is flimsily based must use. The terror employed is physical and mental. A traitor in seventeenth-century England was first hanged by the neck, taken down whilst still alive, then castrated; after a pause, disembowelled; finally his head was severed and his body quartered. This performed, of course, on a stage in full view of hundreds of men, women and children. The death of Damiens, who attempted to assassinate Louis xv of France in 1757, drew huge crowds to the Place de Grèves, mainly of the aristocracy and well-to-do, to watch Damiens' flesh slowly but inevitably torn from his body with huge pincers of red-hot iron; a performance which all the spectators watched with satisfaction, and some with glee. Louis xv and his advisors were not, of course, pathological sadists who were living out their fantasies. Terror, for them, was a necessary public weapon.

The forces of law and order were weak, the monarchy from which all authority derived was constantly at risk to a traitor or an assassin. Terror was, therefore, a deliberate form of social control. And, of course, it still exists in less open and public forms in the guise of secret police, private torture, and excessive imprisonment in régimes such as Russia or South Africa. What history does tell us, however, is that terror as a form of social control has steadily diminished this last 200 years. And there is a further factor, too, in terror used in this way – it can be counter-productive. The classic example is, of course, the Aztec regime, who terrorised their subject people by extravagent human sacrifice – only to make them eager allies of a handful of Spaniards!

Terror, of course, need not be physical. Mental terror can be equally, probably, more effective in social control than physical terror. The punishments of sin and the terrors of Hell loomed larger in western society before 1900, when the forces of social control were weak, yet social turbulence, riot and revolution were almost a commonplace. Fear of the hereafter, the gruesome tortures of the pits of Hell, were as valuable in keeping the poor subjected as the Cossack's whip or the Junker's boot. Although, from 1700, the fear of Hell fades, mental terror does not; secular ideologies can torture the mind as effectively as religious; deviation, heresy, fear of being cast out, maintain their hold. The mental anguish and self-inflicted humiliations of deviant Peking professors have a powerful resonance with religious conflicts that at times have riven Western men. Terror fertilises fear; and, of course, authority is not alone in realising how it might be exploited.

The guillotine, the noose and the firing squad might keep the authoritarian régimes of nineteenth-century Europe secure, but their opponents learned quickly enough the value of the knife, the revolver, and, above all, the bomb. Indeed, the nineteenth century bred a consistent type of terrorist, linked ideologically, as well as psychologically, with the terrorists of today. There are differences, some significant, but the resonances are greater.

As the state became more powerful in nineteenth century Europe, men began to hate it passionately – some, like William Godwin, Leo Tolstoy or Thoreau just rejected it, preached against it, and tried at times to live as if it did not exist. But it was the power of the state, the intense feeling that it inexorably crushed human freedom, that led them to their views – their hatred of all law, all authority. Tolstoy experienced his emotional and intellectual crisis after witnessing a public execution. From that time, for him, the state was a monster, an engine of evil terror. The same feelings, the same intense fear and hatred of the state, led others to action rather than withdrawal. Thinkers, such as Proudhon, Bakunin and the Nihilists, particularly Nechaev, and later Kropotkin, began to preach, and their followers to practise, a programme of revolutionary terrorism, which often took root in the minds of solitary, self-involved, unsuccessful young men who, at the same time, were obsessed by *folie de grandeur*. The result was an outburst of assassinations and bombings which terrified Europe in the last decades of the nineteenth century. And, as ever, the like-minded quickly found each other, and an Anarchist International Conference was held in 1881 which advocated 'the propaganda of the deed', the gesture of terror designed to strike fear into authority, and to awaken the oppressed. The propaganda of the deed was not to be confined to blowing up royalty, prime ministers, judges, generals, prisons and prison-keepers, essential although such acts were to anarchism; indeed, the anarchists managed to kill a not inconsiderable bag of crowned heads, grand dukes, arch-dukes, prime ministers and other assorted greats. Their panacea, however, was terror everywhere. The more unexpected, the greater the fear it would arouse. So the anarchist journals came up with schemes that bordered on the ludicrous: rats and mice were to be soaked in gasoline, set alight and let loose in buildings of importance, or just buildings. Cooks were instructed in the best ways of poisoning their masters or mistresses. Anarchists were advised to destroy crops to inflame the peasantry, and set fire to factories to inflame the workers. Readers were told how to procure dynamite, and naturally how to use it. In desperation the French police started their own anarchist journal in the hope that the subscription list would lead them to their quarry. Alas, it did not, for France was wracked by a series of outrages in the 1890s. One anarchist threw a home-made bomb into the Chamber of Deputies; poorly made, it winged several, but killed no one. Another, Rovachal, murdered a 90-year-old miser and his housekeeper, to get money for his bombs, blew up the homes of a judge and prosecutor, was betrayed, and went to the guillotine shouting 'Long live anarchy!' Within days the café where he had been caught blew up with the proprietor in it. The failure to reprieve the anarchist who had thrown his bomb into the French Parliament led immediately to the slaughter of the French President Carnot. Crowned heads and presidents naturally grew nervous when they appeared in public, for almost all of them that did not succumb had near misses, sometimes amidst appalling carnage. A bomb intended for Alfonso XIII of Spain blew twenty bystanders to bits, many of them raining down on the royal carriage.

Terrorism is contagious. Every bomb made headline news, and the slaughter was, of course, vividly photographed; such publicity provoked fantasies and made converts to the 'propaganda of the deed'. Nor was it only young pathological Frenchmen and Russians who were converted. In 1887 a bomb was tossed at the police in Chicago, killing some and creating panic. London had a shoot-out with embittered anarchists, a battle that resembles the Los Angeles battle against the Symbionese. And, of course, on it went in France – cafés, railway stations, public meetings. Nowhere seemed safe. As the French anarchist poet, Tailhade, wrote, 'What do the victims matter provided the gesture is fine?' And certainly the anarchists knew how to make one fine gesture. They died well. None wilted; all who were caught went to their deaths denouncing the state, the bourgeoisie, demanding revenge and extolling anarchy. If trapped, they shot it out or blew themselves up. They may have lacked sense, but they never lacked courage; indeed, they had an excess of it. Perhaps those who dispense terror lack fear.

Certainly, they inspired it in the authorities who, as is usual in such situations, over-reacted. When Vaillant, who had been responsible for the bomb outrage in the French Parliament, but who had killed no one, was put to death, public sympathy on the Left surged towards him, no matter how much they deplored his act. The aim of the terrorist was martyrdom, and through his martyrdom to draw attention to what he believed to be the iniquitous evil of society. As one Russian terrorist wrote: 'The revolutionary is a lost man; he has no interests of his own, no cause of his own, no feelings, no habits, no belongings; he does not even have a name. Everything in him is absorbed by a single exclusive interest, a single thought, a single passion – the revolution.'

He goes on writing, in a tone of almost religious ecstasy, to denounce all laws, all education, all conventions as evil.

Indeed, it would be salutary if our social commentators, perhaps the Federal Bureau itself, were to study the literature of terrorist activity – or even the history of it. Undeniably, terrorism spread between 1880

and 1914 in something like plague proportions; so much so that many
men of wisdom and authority felt that society might easily be
approaching a major cataclysm. This epidemic is curiously similar to
what is happening in our own times. The groups are small, highly
individualistic, but by their actions achieve vast public impact. Even
their methods and the emotional responses are very similar to those of
the terrorist today.

One lesson from history is clear, martyrdom breeds martyrdom. The
violent extirpation of a terrorist gang is unlikely to stop terrorism.
Another is that, as in religion, the terrorist is the result of sudden
personal conversion. Most of the nineteenth-century terrorists had led
very commonplace, ordinary, frequently not very successful lives, and
then one event, such as the execution of an anarchist, or the reading of
an anarchist tract, or the witnessing of a public act of state brutality,
would trigger their conversion to a total life of terrorism and martyrdom
so that they felt nothing but righteousness in robbery or murder, even
of the innocent. And again, one must distinguish very carefully between
organised political underground movements, such as the IRA or the
Palestinians, who are using violence for tactical and strategic purposes
in a precise political context. Such movements may draw to it men
and women of similar temperament to those who are attracted to the
'propaganda of the deed', but they will be few, and either absorbed into
a disciplined army, or rejected. In general, the fierce temperament of the
committed terrorist makes him a solitary or rarely more than a member
of a small band of like-minded conspirators living together as a group,
feeding each others fantasies and death wishes. And finally – as far as
the lesson of history goes – the gloomiest factor of all is that anarchist
terrorism lasted a very long time in Western Europe. It was a ferocious
social problem for thirty years. Naturally the holocaust of World War
I checked it, but, amongst the more repressive régimes of Europe, it
revived again in the 1920s.

Certainly, it was weakened by the growth of social justice, by the
steady erosion of the ghetto-like hells of the European slums which had
done so much to feed it for, in spite of their acts and their crazed
philosophy, most of the anarchist terrorists were men and women of
very deep human compassion, whose imaginations had been made raw
by the social inequalities which surrounded them. In the 1950s they
disappeared from the open, freer, more liberal nations. England, outside
Ireland, and even Wales, where there was frustration, social injustice
and a quasi-despotic ruling class, had always been relatively free from
terrorism. Most of what occurred was caused by foreign anarchists to
whom England gave shelter. And to the historian there can be little
doubt that terrorism battens on social injustice, and flourishes under

fierce repression and martyrdom. Once terrorism has gripped the imagination of paranoics and misfits, it becomes difficult to check; for certain types of temperament it possesses a compulsive attraction, and also in modern industrial society the weapons of terrorism – dynamite and guns – are too readily available. The Symbionese Liberation Army may easily be obliterated, but, like the dragon's teeth, it is likely to breed a like progeny. At least we can console ourselves with the thought that terrorism is not a social sin peculiar to our own society; it has a long as well as lengthening history.

Graft, the Ratbane of Politics

William Ewart Gladstone, the Victorian statesman, was occasionally forced to reply to a personal letter when he was sitting at his desk in the British Treasury. When he returned home he went straight to his library and tore up a penny stamp. So undeviating was his rectitude that any other course would have been impossible: enemies as well as friends expected no less of him. When he was Prime Minister he would take up his stick and hat, leave Downing Street for the raffish side-streets of the Strand, alive with old whores, child prostitutes, pimps and ponces. In these alleys flesh of every variety and age was for sale; the surroundings were as filthy as they were insanitary; violence was commonplace, blackmail rampant. Gladstone would politely raise his hat to a woman of the streets, argue with all his immense powers of persuasion and turn on his uncheckable moral fervour in order to persaude the whore to return home with him – not for dalliance, but for tea, cakes, reformation and rebirth. And although the more robust members of Parliament might roar with laughter at his antics and weave about him comic and derogatory stories, his virtue remained as unsullied as it was adamantine. Corruption of the flesh or of the pocket had no place in Gladstone's universe. In the late Victorian world, adultery, once public knowledge, ended political careers, as it did Parnell's, while peculation was regarded as immoral as the sins of the flesh.

And since Gladstone's day the British have taken a self-righteous pride in the purity of their political life. Even the suspicion of a hint about new taxation ruined Thomas, and a romp with Christine Keeler put paid to Profumo's career. Divorce is just tolerated, but it had better not be sordid; better still for the politician to be the injured party. At least one famous British statesman's reputation was saved by a friend (literally filling the breach and claiming the ignominy. The odour of self-righteousness pours from the Palace of Westminster as thick as a London fog; hence the blank incomprehension that Adam Clayton Powell could remain a Congressman year after year, hence the hands raised in pious horrow when it was learned that Nkrumah had salted away over $6 million for his personal fortune. The old colonial hands are full of a gloomy sense of prophecy fulfilled. Graft, the ratsbane of politics, ruins countries, saps the people's virtue, renders institutions corrupt and denies a nation greatness. So we are told – but does it?

After two centuries of almost unprecedented rapacity and logrolling, American politicians, it seems, are beginning to change their tune. They might note that British political purity emerged when Britain had reached the zenith of her powers and was poised for decline. In her days of growth from the age of Elizabeth to midway through the age of Victoria her politics were as corrupt as any the world has seen – a bonanza with truly noble pickings. Take Elizabeth I's famous minister, William Cecil, and his son, Robert. They shovelled public gold into their private cellars: battened on the Court of Wards and dug deep into the royal purse. Their great houses – Burghley and Hatfield – were built on the loot of office, and the ease and comfort of generations of Salisburies depended on the acumen and rapacity of their ancestors. Girls on the payroll? This is old hat. Sir Robert Walpole had his mistress paid by the Board of Customs and Excise to the tune of some $70,000 a year. And he thought nothing of using official Admiralty barges to smuggle in his liquor when he was Secretary of the Navy. As for graft – Joseph Merceron, who ran East London in the early nineteenth century – could have taught Boss Tweed many a trick. Of course, these were blatant days, when perquisites of office were not overlaid with hypocrisy, though even Walpole was careful to get his mistress's pension under a *nom de plume*.

Yet it should be remembered that William Cecil was an exceptionally fine statesman and politician. Both wise and perceptive, he laboured unceasingly at his job, as earnestly and as successfully as any Gladstone. He proved well worth his plunder. And so was Walpole. True, his pickings were gigantic – probably in modern money around $30 million (think of that, Mr Powell) – but he gave England twenty years of peace, secured her political stability for generations, and launched her well and truly on the road to riches and greatness. So, perhaps, he was cheap at the price.

Of course, all corrupt politicians are not worth their salt. England would have been no loser if the Duke of Chandos had never been born, yet he was as greedy, if not more so, than his friend Walpole. The fortunes of most of the peerage of England have their origins in political graft, but not many of their ancestors are memorable for their political distinction. And certainly the story of American politics is no less muddy. So when denouncing Nkrumah and Ghana, it is well to remember our own history. Young, raw, emergent, politically inept countries are particularly prone to corruption. Some countries, it is true, avoid it. No one can suppose that Stalin had a Swiss bank account or that Mao has pocketed a fortune. Their corruptions might be regarded as of a different order – and to my view far worse.

Nothing is more irritating in Professor Henry Bretton's *The Rise and Fall of Kwame Nkrumah* than his constant reiteration of Nkrumah's personal greed, self-indulgence, and mild plunder of his state. It is repeated on page after page, yet Nkrumah's political achievements – Volta Dam, Ghana's new port of Tema, the beginnings of its industry, its astonishing developments in education – are mentioned but briefly. Moreover, sneers at Nkrumah's pan-African idealism seem somewhat out of place when, with army coup following army coup, Africa appears to be well on the way to South American-style political systems. Indeed, from the pages of this book rises the unpleasing stench of national self-righteousness: no matter how gross or self-indulgent Nkrumah's methods may have been, his intentions and his successes cannot be regarded as negligible. I suspect that he will prove to have been well worth his graft, if not his tyranny.

Of course, there is graft and graft; and fashions change. Boss Tweed, like Walpole, could be flamboyant; the age permitted it. Today, as Adam Clayton Powell knows to his cost, graft must be grave, discreet, faceless. Mr Powell's mistake was to revel too openly in his luck: new power, like new riches, is very intoxicating and very indiscreet.

I am all for checks on politicians. I am for the most severe and restrictive rules on all forms of graft and logrolling. But when viewed in the long perspectives of history, these are the least serious of a politician's crimes. Most of them are corrupt at a far deeper, a far more tragic level. Think of their complacency in the face of scattered limbs of women and children blown sky-high; think of their indifference to hunger, to the thin-ribbed children and the lifeless eyes of worn-out women; think of their caution, their fears for their own comfort and way of life, the crimes they have committed and still commit in the name of liberty. When do they speak up for humanity, for the future – and damn the consequences to their own careers and payrolls? How often do their words burn a message into the heart of mankind? Complacency, pride, and dead imagination – these are the corruptions of politics. Most of them are moral prostitutes, randy for power; and theirs, perhaps, is the world's oldest profession. Humanity has paid over and over again in blood and suffering for its politicians. Let us remember before we condemn Nkrumah or Powell that frail as they proved to be in the exercise of power, one gave vision, the other hope, the one to a nation, the other to a race.

Echoes Across the Centuries

The sad wet Suffolk countryside is made for reflection. The hard east winds that snap the ploughed earth into a brown cement will not come for another week or so, nor will the clear pale blue skies or the thin snow flurries. Now the clouds are low and the day itself little better than a grey twilight. In my distant village there is never the sound of a vehicle and the silence is so intense you can hear a bird stir in the bushes. The house, scented with wood fires, is empty, quiet, enclosed but creaking a little with its 500 years. Until guests come in the early evening there is little to do but brood.

It is a curiously appropriate moment to meditate about age and politics – the motif of the concluding volume of my *Life of Sir Robert Walpole*. Walpole was Prime Minister for a longer time than any other man in English history – twenty-one years. This retention of power fascinates active politicians and, perhaps inevitably, they are more interested in how Sir Robert obtained and held power rather than in how he came to lose it. The effect of age on power is a theme that has haunted me for some time now. After all, the world is still littered with aged and ageing politicians.

Walpole was a consummate wheeler and dealer – the best England has ever known. He judged every man's price, pampered the rather insignificant toadies who gave him uncritical support, ruthlessly pursued those who showed him the sharp edge of their criticism. An overweening personality, he could bully, cajole, plead with, threaten, twist a man until he got his vote. His programme was stodgy, but worthy – prosperity, and, if possible, peace. As artful as LBJ at his best, Walpole so came to dominate political life, particularly the House of Commons, that he became known simply as The Great Man. Envy and exclusion provoked a vociferous opposition (the intellectuals, note, were largely against him) but he slapped it down. Year followed year and King George II succeeded George I, and on and on he went.

Then, in the middle 1730s, Walpole's friends of a lifetime began to die, and faces were changing in the Commons. The new ones were young, aggressive, hawk-like. They wanted to seize the Spanish Empire, so they magnified the dangers to British interests of Spain and its ally France. The old xenophobic arguments were trotted out. Spaniards and French were Catholics, Protestant-killers, their governments absolute and tyrannical. They threatened England's vital concerns; the English way of life. And England's mission was to save the world. Freedom must be preserved, which meant throwing the French out of Canada, the Caribbean, India, and grabbing heaps of Spanish territory. Walpole loathed the idea but he loathed losing power more. That he at 62 should give it up seemed quite intolerable; by then he felt it was his until death. So he went to war in the West Indies and made an awful mess of it. Friends deserted. He was forced increasingly to rely on men who were repugnant to the few old allies who still stuck by him; the nadir was reached when the rouged, toothless Lord Hervey was made Lord Privy Seal.

Naturally he clung desperately to the vestiges of authority, refusing to read any portents, let alone omens. He even did nothing to extricate himself from the war that would, it seemed, ruin his life's work. (It did not of course; history is never so neat as that.) Still preened, someone said, as if he were going to see his mistress, he strutted to his corner in the House of Commons, expecting, demanding the incense that had wafted before him for so long. But this huge fat man was an ageing hulk and, riddled with gout, a rotten one at that. And suddenly politicians could see him as he was; the charisma vanished, the manna disappeared. There he stood, old and grey, with only a few years left to him. He was no route to their future, only a cul-de-sac.

Of course, it wasn't merely his age. Look at De Gaulle sailing on through his seventies; however, he personifies an idea rigidly fixed in the context of the future – the Revival of France. And then there was Churchill, who, as Lord Moran has shown in those marvellous diaries, was only half a man; yet his authority was based, not on wheeling and dealing, but on historical principles, on a deeply human concept of destiny. By 1950 Churchill, like De Gaulle in the 1960s, had become a symbol to mankind. The future can still be possessed by an ageing statesman if he embodies an idea greater than himself, but not by a politician concerned merely with power. Then the stench of decay makes his underlings' nostrils twitch, and they bolt for cover to await his inevitable collapse.

History never has true parallels, although there are echoes and resonances between one era and another. Consider these facts: an escalating war without decision, a war never desired by Walpole that threatened everything he had wished for. The hawks screeched for decisive action, irrespective of consequences, whereas Walpole knew well enough that behind Spain, France was formidably strong. Slowly but certainly the hawks won. Meanwhile Walpole felt the years, each one like ten: and there he was, oscillating between illness and health like a metronome. And then came his awareness that he was a liability to his party, indeed its greatest.

There are echoes across the centuries of this in the White House. Will political death at the hands of his own party come as suddenly to LBJ? Certainly, there is a sense that time is short, of whole generations quietly deserting. Long before the final blow came for Walpole all youth had given him up as useless: he could neither focus their ambitions nor stir their hearts or minds. They had found a new idol – the young William Pitt – an orator whose biting denunciations seared Walpole's reputation; a man who risked his own future for the sake of what he so passionately felt; indeed, Pitt was consigned by his party for many years to the wilderness because of the flaming rhetoric by which he castigated Walpole. Yet his voice dominated not only his generation but his century.

More perhaps than at any time in human history we need a voice. A quarter of the world is either enjoying or is poised on the brink of fabulous affluence, affluence such as mankind has never before known. But elsewhere there is only hunger, disease, privation, which lead, naturally enough, to desperate remedies, to constriction of liberties for the sake of liberty to eat. If ever there was a time for magnanimity, clothed in a rhetoric of fire that could burn its way into the hearts of men who rule – not in the mansions of state, but in the wards, precincts and villages – it is now. The power of language, sadly enough, is fading, and the art of inspiring millions of men to aspirations beyond their necessities and indulgences is almost dead. For millennia this was the work of the great religious leaders, whose gnomic utterances seemed to unlock the significance and duties of human life. They belong to a vanished race, their last strange, feeble representative – Gandhi. And the race of revolutionaries, those hard, bleak men who reconciled generations to misery and terror for the sake of unborn generations, seem to have found their apotheosis in the poems of Mao or the four-hour harangues of Castro, which are about as uplifting as the disquisitions of Origen.

The hard historical truth is that the pursuit of power – with all that it means in terms of wheeling and dealing – has triumphed over religious inspiration, revolutionary fervour, or the vision of statesmen. In politics statesmen are as rare as politicians are common. And, when the most powerful position in the free world might come to them through the harsh realities of national politics, who will now bother to speak to and for generations not yet born? The Johnsons and the Walpoles win. After Walpole's defeat it was not Pitt who secured the prizes, but Walpole's disciples, trained in his techniques and nurtured in his arts of manipulation. All they wanted was Walpole's clothes. They kept the war, and made it global.

These are sad thoughts under sad, sad clouds in a sadder landscape: but then 1967 is a sad prospect. Increasing war, elusive victory, race riot and turmoil, an adolescent generation that is increasingly bewildered by a vision of life that contains satisfaction without hope, riches without magnanimity, and achievement without purpose. What a change in a few brief years.

A few brief years, therein lies our sole hope: the hope that a statesman will emerge who will raise the dialogue of politics, who will not be afraid to use the language either of scorn or magnanimity. Listen to the words of William Pitt to the House of Lords when he pleaded in 1775 for peace with American colonists, which, of course, their lordships rejected:

> Yet, when I consider the whole case as it lies before me, I am not much astonished, I am not surprised, that men who hate liberty should detest those who prize it; or that those who want virtue themselves should endeavour to persecute those who possess it. . . . The whole of your political conduct has been one continued series of weakness, temerity, despotism, ignorance, futility, negligence, and the most notorious servility, incapacity, and corruption. On reconsideration I must allow you one merit, a strict attention to your own interest, in that view you appear sound statesmen and politicians. You well know, if the present measure should prevail, that you must instantly relinquish your places. Such then being your precarious situations, who should wonder that you can put a negative on any measure which must annihilate your power, deprive you of your emoluments, and at once reduce you to that state of insignificance for which God and nature designed you.

Would that words such as these were heard again. Would they not waken the Senate and reverberate across the nation? Words, words, we need words as much as actions.

Inflation

Economists pontificate; sociologists pontificate; politicians promise nostrums. Treasury officials work out complex machinery of wage, price and dividend control, and from time to time they have persuaded governments to try and impose by law their intricate schemes to check inflation. Almost always to no avail. And the debate goes on and on and on, and so does inflation. Rarely does a public figure, let alone a politician or an administrator, turn from looking at the obscure future into a much clearer past, for chronic inflation has happened before in the world's history, and most particularly in Europe's. As a disease, inflation is almost as complex as cancer, and about as curable. It can affect specific countries or areas and leave the rest of the world unaffected. This has been true of Brazil and Latin America since World War II, and even the great German inflation after World War I, when a man needed a brief case to carry enough marks to buy lunch, was more of a local than an international phenomenon. The experience was chronic, devastating, yet specific. The rest of the world – at least economically speaking – was

not greatly affected financially, although the social and political consequences were to prove catastrophic by the growth of National Socialism.
However, inflation can also be long-term — an intermittent fever that
crests very sharply from time to time, but never dies away, and lasting,
may be, for a century.

This was the variety of the disease that Europe suffered from between
1530 and 1620; and this is much closer to our present circumstances
than the dramatic inflationary spiral of Weimar Germany or the
temporary, if sharp, inflation of France or England during the Napoleonic Wars. Wars usually cause bursts of inflationary fever, but our
present dilemma goes far deeper than the crisis of currency caused by
World War II.

Historians have been fascinated by the steady and continuous inflation
of sixteenth-century Europe for more than a generation, probing deeply
into its causes and, unfortunately, showing less concern for its consequences. They came up initially with a neat, simple cause — the type of
explanation, indeed, that some of our more simple-minded economists
still entertain about on our condition, that the trouble lay with the
sudden and sharp increase in money supply. In the sixteenth century,
Europe, via Spain, was flooded with bullion, first gold from the Aztecs
and Incas, and followed by vast quantities of silver from the mines of
Potosi. What further explanation was needed?

Alas, so simple an answer did not take long to disprove. A formidable
Scandinavian scholar, Gertrude Hammarstrom, showed that inflation
was hitting the tiny communities of Norway, which the bullion never
reached, as hard as it was hitting the towns of Spain, the Netherlands,
France and England. The Aztec and Inca gold was of no fundamental
consequence, and inflation was steaming ahead long before the mountain
of silver at Potosi had been discovered. Money supply was no answer,
although almost all historians would agree that the sudden influx of
huge quantities of bullion (the trade was remarkably erratic) could send
up the temperature of inflation a degree or two over a short period, but
as a fundamental cause bullion was dropped. Nevertheless, it remains
as a contributory, secondary factor, helping to sustain, rather than cause,
inflation. What did? Almost certainly the growth of population, but
growth in highly special and economic circumstances. As with our own
time, the first and strongest inflationary pressure came on food, then
clothing, then manufactured goods; indeed, food prices remained the
basic problem. Nevertheless, rapid growth of population has not always
resulted in inflation — one has only to think of Ireland in the first half
of the nineteenth century. Agriculture needs to have the capacity to
expand production, either by new techniques or extension of cultivated
areas. Yet only to a limited extent. The demand for food must continue

to put pressure on the capacity to meet it, or prices will not rise. This does not mean that fine harvests may not produce a glut, or a temporary drop in prices – one has only to think of the butter mountain or the beef mountain of contemporary Europe – but the long-term pressure must be steady. There are, naturally enough, in so complex a situation as inflation, other factors which we, today, are fully aware of. The increasing distrust of credit instruments, and the attraction of gold, silver, negotiable goods of all kinds. As trade and exchange grow more feverish, fuller of risk, so the need for credit increases, high interest rates fail to deter gambling on the future, and so increase the risk, as they increase prices. And so the fever becomes so intense that society itself becomes at risk. However, the causes of sixteenth-century inflation, fascinating and complex as they may be, are of less interest to us than the consequences. For the causes are scarcely controllable, but the consequences may be.

The consequences of sixteenth-century inflation were profound and very long-lasting. At first, inflation acted as a catalyst, stimulating farmers, weavers, primary producers of every kind to produce more, to go for the obvious profit, even if it meant hoarding grain in times of scarcity, or trying to make a corner in pepper. The prudent, intelligent, up-to-date small farmer could do well, as could the intelligent, prudent, cautiously experimental landlord. Trade was riskier, but could, and did, bring vast fortunes to men of the calibre of Sir Thomas Gresham and Lionel Cranfield. Large-scale capitalists, they spread their risks in commodities so that they could ride the gluts and exploit the shortages. Also Gresham worked intelligently the foreign exchange market, but as banks from West Germany to New York realise, in a world of inflation the risks in currency may be phenomenal and disastrous. Nevertheless, inflation can, and does, make men very rich, either on a large or a small scale. Hence there is always a powerful sector of society quite happy to let inflation pursue its course. Inflation, however, also makes far more men poor, which leads to bitter social envy. In Elizabethan times of the corn badgers (traders of grain) or the monopolists who could force up prices were the targets of bitter denunciation. There was a growing distrust of the *nouveaux riches*, a steady intensification of social bitterness that began to sour political life. This resonates with our own times when we read bitter diatribes against the Gnomes of Zurich, against the asset-strippers, against the commodity cornerers. In the sixteenth century, for every man inflation made richer, there were dozens whom it made poorer, not only labourers, whose real wages, unprotected as they were by unions, steadily fell, but also craftsmen and artisans. Wide-scale poverty drove the poor into the towns (a powerful consequence of inflation in Brazil) and so created a nightmare of anxiety for Tudor

governments. They were forced into social and economic legislation of
the most authoritarian and complex kind. Lord Burghley, Elizabeth 1's
Secretary of State, produced a complex incomes and prices policy with
formidable statutory sanctions, but it had no effect. Inflation went its
course. His poverty programmes did little better. Indeed, one of the
ironies of inflation is that it forces governments into attempting complex
remedial measures which rarely have any effect at all except to intensify
class bitterness on the one hand, and distrust of the ability of governments on the other.

One of the most fascinating consequences, however, of an inflationary
world is the strong social emotion generated about material objects.
Although it does stimulate competitive expenditure on goods that have
intrinsic and enduring value, from houses to jewels, it also provokes a
hatred of waste. Material possessions therefore become imbued with
intense, yet complex, moral feeling. Certainly in sixteenth-century
Europe there developed the attitude that, except for those demi-gods,
the aristocracy and the Court, ostentation was wicked and that riches
and a preoccupation with material things could be dangerous to the
soul. Outward show, ostentatious display became, at the worst, sinful,
at the best, anti-social; prudence, thrift, the careful use and preservation
of material things helped to avoid evil. To put the matter bluntly and
crudely, inflation helped to stimulate and foster a 'Puritan' attitude to
riches that cut right across denominational religion. It was as prevalent
in France as in England; austerity was virtuous.

This attitude certainly resonates increasingly with our own time, with
its concern for recycling and protection of resources. There is also,
today, the flight from ostentatious dress (witness our own middle-class
children's attitude to clothes – the Levis, the torn jackets and sweaters)
which echoes the cultivation of extreme sobriety and plainness that
marks the European middle class of the mid-seventeenth century. The
present attack on waste – whether in packaging or large cars – resonates
with the seventeenth-century attack on ostentatious living. We can, therefore, in our own inflationary world expect an increasingly powerful
movement towards austerity and social morality about objects. Within
a decade it may seem sinful not to dress like a Mao peasant, and one
can expect a similar attitude to develop towards food, drink and possibly
entertainment. Such a movement may well become the dominant force
in all societies, but it will probably triumph in those most desperately
affected by inflation.

If this were the only effect of inflation, the future would seem less dark.
But there are others that are more profound. The powerful reactions to
inflation which took place in the seventeenth century are mirrored in
what is happening in our own time. It is probable that there will be a

sharp decline in population growth. This may be excellent in the long term, but it will create chronic economic and social problems in the short. Certainly, this is what happened in the seventeenth century. We know now that family limitation, largely, though not entirely, through *coitus interruptus* – for condoms were probably only available in Europe's capitals by the second half of the seventeenth century – was widely practised. This reduced sharply the birth rate. Already West Germany and America have fallen below zero growth, and the cost of rearing and educating a child in advanced industrial societies has grown formidable – in America some $200,000 a child from birth to graduation – and beyond the means of many potential parents. Hence the social norm, infused increasingly with moral imperatives, is rapidly becoming two children per family, or less.

Population movements, however, are erratic, and subject to complex factors; in undeveloped countries inflation and sharp population increases may be combined, as in Brazil. Also, the attitude to children, a sense that more than a few is socially and economically disastrous, applies to the waste-conscious, standard-of-living conscious societies, not to primitive agrarian societies, whether inflationary or not. What we may be sure about is that continued and chronic inflation will have consequences for family size, particularly in those countries where the industrial middle class is strong and highly conscious of not only its own social needs, but also the life it feels that it must provide for its children.

The worst consequence, however, of inflation has always been the corrosion that it brings to political institutions, particularly democratic institutions, for it has usually intensified the desire of governments to exercise more absolute authority in order to preserve the power of traditional forces in society.

Every monarchy, in the sixteenth century, except the English, went bankrupt. War, grandiose ambitions, and civil and religious strife played their part, but war, civil and religious strife have occurred, and so too have grandiose ambitions in other centuries, but they have not always led either to bankruptcy or to absolutism. These factors acquired extra force, extra heat may be a better term, because of the inflationary world in which they took place. The cost of government and of armies soared, traditional revenues could not keep pace; as always in an inflationary world interest rates flew towards the sky, and so bankruptcy followed for bankers as well as monarchs. More frustrating for those who had a stake in social and economic stability was the incapacity of any government to check or control this inflationary process. At their wits' end for money, governments sold honours – anyone could buy an Earldom or a Baronetcy from James I. Government offices were sold to the highest bidder, extravagently by Louis XIII, immoderately by the English Stuarts, steadily by the Spanish monarchies. Licences for monopolies – the selling of playing cards, the issuing of wine licences – became a commonplace of government, and a bitter irritation to those who suffered the consequent inflation of prices. It required all the art of Elizabeth I in 1601 to quieten the rage of her Parliament at the extortions of monopolists.

Almost every financial action taken by any government or monarchy in the inflationary world of the sixteenth and early seventeenth centuries led to social and political discontent. Ministers were vilified, hated and used up with remarkable rapidity by monarchies who increasingly felt that all criticism was iniquitous and that absolute obedience as to God was the only solution to the problems of an inflationary world. Representative assemblies, no matter how limited their social base, became an anathema to them, and they began rapidly to disappear as a part of the machinery of government, again except in England. Parliament's survival, however, in England has been quite precarious. For eleven years, Charles I governed without one, and, but for an inane and unnecessary war in Scotland, he might have died in his bed without ever calling another. As it was, Parliament had to wage war to survive, and struggle for the rest of the century to maintain its survival and its privileges. Elsewhere representative institutions vanished, replaced by monarchical absolutism backed by increasingly efficient bureaucracies. Always in an inflationary world the nostrum is authority – the power to impose. And yet, Philip II of Spain, who enjoyed more direct power, perhaps, than any monarch of his time, was as powerless to check inflation as Elizabeth I of England, who was constrained to share some of her authority in finance with her Parliaments. Nevertheless, the mood amongst those men of property and authority, then, as now, was that only a great increase of power at the centre could check the rot that inflation was creating in the social fabric. The same mood was generated in the 1920s in Germany, with the consequences that we know all too well.

Few, I think, would deny that our own system of politics may be put seriously at risk by inflation. Every politician, every party, must have a programme of cure which they will attempt to sell to the electorate. Mr Wilson attempted to impose an income and prices policy, and was checked by the trade unions. Mr Heath imposed a policy by legislation and was wrecked and defeated. President Nixon's nostrums have vanished into limbo. Everybody promises solutions, but none of these can work because the inflationary forces are not national. One solution that might work is the same as that used with a patient with a highly contagious fever – isolation. A closed economy, based on considerable internal resources, such as America's or Russia's, may escape. The intricate interlocking economies of the free world, through which run the fever ducts of multinational corporations, makes isolation virtually impossible. So, as politicians' programmes fail, their promises boomerang, a fickle electorate turns to fringe parties, or extravagant nostrums, with the inevitable result of weak, usually minority governments, as we now see in Italy or Great Britain, and even Iceland. Weak central government makes even moderate control of inflationary forces improbable. And so politicians and political institutions fall further into disrepute, and the anger and rage of society grows and grows, so that political traditions, no matter how ancient, political institutions, no matter how venerable, crumble with surprising ease. Old ideologies disappear with equal alacrity. New and harsh social moods can spread with astonishing speed. An old world can be lost almost overnight. Inflation acts like the Black Death on tradition.

The same even is true of social and economic institutions. The guild system, which controlled the work of craftsmen – quality of goods, prices, the system which instituted the concept of what profit should be, and one which had grown in complexity and sophistication in the late middle ages, rather as trade unionism has in the nineteenth and twentieth centuries – collapsed or passed into desuetude under the impact of the inflationary world of the sixteenth century. And institutions as tough as unions may go the same way, or become monsters of uncontrollable power, provocative even of civil disturbance, perhaps war. What we can be sure of is that the political and social institutions will not remain as we know them.

If the resonances from the past ring clear and undistorted, what is certain is that all is at risk once inflation leaps beyond control – attitudes to life, institutions of every kind and, above all, political systems whose impotence is most clearly demonstrated; and the strain is always heaviest at the centre. The tempests are beginning to blow, and they will rage for years to come.

Famine

They stare up at us from the newspapers; they haunt the weekly magazines – children with distended bellies and glazed, bulbous eyes; old people dying. Sometimes a skinny hand is held out without hope. Those in the photographs are dead, are dying, will be dead. Dead from one cause only: not enough to eat. Dead of starvation. Occasionally the *New York Times* prints a horrifying story of an old man or woman found dead of starvation in a Manhattan apartment, alone, unfed, a victim of the vast anonymity of urban life. Yet how rare it is for anyone in our cities to die that way – and how common elsewhere. The media bombard us with documentaries about the doom-laden areas south of the Sahara,

where the desert steadily advances and the people die. Africa lives with
famine: more people every year, more hunger every year. In India famine
is endemic, kept not at bay, only barely in control, by massive injections
of American grain. Two years ago China, perhaps Russia, were saved
from Africa's fate only because they had the money to empty the gran-
aries of the Middle West and Canada.

The harrowing pictures stir our conscience, for the children, the list-
less, downhearted adults, the pathetic elders, are always black or brown,
never white. And we are told over and over again that famine will
spread, that hunger will reach millions more every year. If we in the
West gave up meat on just one day each week, we would release enough
grain to stem the tide but, alas, not for long – half a year, a year may
be. Famine will persist. It will grow worse. The pictures of the doomed
will continue to haunt us. But this is not new; it is only the return of a
familiar visitor. Famine and mankind have lived together for millennia.

It is hard for us to believe that famine used to sweep through the
towns and villages of Western Europe almost every decade, garnering
the young, the old, the weak. Europe, indeed, has known an abundance
of food for a very short time, far shorter than America. Indeed, apart
from Australia and New Zealand and a few tiny underpopulated parts
of the world, the United States is the only society in human history to
lack the traumatic experience of famine. Even Europe did not defeat
famine until the late nineteenth century, and then only in the West.
France was one of the richest agricultural nations in Europe – vast
cornlands in the Champagne, olive groves and vineyards in the south,
lush beef pastures and great mountain plateaus for thousands of sheep;
fertility everywhere, yet everywhere endemic starvation.

Pierre Goubert, who has carefully analysed the condition of the peasantry in the Beauvaisis in the seventeenth century, has shown that the
great majority of families scarcely possessed enough land to stave off
starvation even in the best of times. Food was simple and bad – mainly
gruel, a little cheese, and, more rarely, meat. So marginal was existence
that four wet summers, from 1649 to 1652, brought devastating famine.
Within ten years, in 1661, even greater disaster swept France: hundreds
of thousands died of starvation in the worst famine of the century.
Inevitably, famine bred pestilence as virulent diseases leapt from one
enfeebled body to the next. Such great harvests of death were not,
however, without their macabre recompense: bad times ended, and
plenty, once returned, had fewer mouths to feed. But man, fertile as ever
in the most gruesome times, replenished the population and thus created
the prospect of renewed decimation.

So it was in most of Europe: only the Netherlands and England fared
better. Further east, conditions were worse. No decade passed without

famine stalking the land. By 1750, only England and the Netherlands had defeated famine: improved agriculture, an admirable transport system by the standards of the day, and relatively small populations made them the first countries anywhere to escape the scourge of famine. But not, of course, hunger: that still abounded, often desperate enough, as in Bristol in 1812, to drive men and women to riot.

But if England escaped famine, the British Isles did not, for Ireland, supporting too large a population on a single too precarious crop – the potato – experienced not the worst but one of the most publicised famines of the nineteenth century – the Great Hunger of 1846. Over a million people, out of a population of some eight million, perished. Many were so desperate that they resorted to cannibalism – the usual by-product of desperate hunger. The misery was so profound, so traumatic, that it affected generations of Irishmen, breeding a deep hatred for the English, who, as absentee landlords, became the mythic fathers of the famine.

Yet the Irish famine was something of a turning point, for the British Prime Minister, Peel, spent large sums of government money to import maize from America to relieve the distress. Hitherto famines had run their course, alleviated by small government benefactions and private charity. Direct government intervention to secure large grain supplies, combined with planned relief programmes, was novel. Alas, the Irish did not know how to grind maize, and in any case were deeply suspicious of it, while the relief programmes were hedged about with prohibitions. Nevertheless, in spite of its shortcomings, the operation became a model, later modified and improved, for the famine relief organisations that were a prominent feature in nineteenth- and twentieth-century western societies.

By 1900, in Western Europe the battle was largely won; hunger there was in plenty, but no longer were tens of thousands of peasants dying. Eastern Europe fared less well, and of course even the precarious plenty of Western Europe could be, and was, destroyed by war. Germany and her satellites, as well as Russia, experienced famine after both World Wars, and in 1919 the scourge of disease that goes with it swept through the West, killing more people by influenza than had been killed by bullets.

Along with organised relief went improvement in food production – a steady 'green revolution' that began in Flanders in the early seventeenth century, burgeoned in England in the eighteenth, spread elsewhere thereafter, and still, thank God, possesses momentum. It was not merely an attempt to develop new land or improve crops and husbandry, it was a deliberate effort to increase yields, to experiment and disseminate the results. In England in the eighteenth century, technological development, of crops and machinery, was the self-conscious pursuit of an elite of landowners and farmers eager to improve yields and exploit new sources of food, such as the potato and the sugar beet. In the nineteenth century, America took the lead in agrarian advance, and the world's food supply, especially since the brilliant successes after World War II, has almost kept pace with the exploding population. In 1960 the people of the world were probably better fed than ever before.

Yet it was to prove but a moment of illusion, a mirage of plenty that the world is unlikely to know again. One sinister aspect of famine has always been that it only temporarily checks the pressure on a society's food supplies. The fertility of man, persisting amid the most terrible disasters and deprivations, soon obliterates the effects of famine relief and makes its recurrence ever more likely. Alas, a comparative abundance, combined with superior medical services, has had a like effect. Once more population growth, as in the past, has out-distanced not the good harvests but the bad, and bad there always are and will be. Drought in the Sahara, poor monsoons, crop failure in Russia and China – all have eaten up the world's reserves, and in Africa and India large-scale famine is once more reaping its harvest. And so humanity returns to the condition it has lived with for millennia.

Food shortage not only kills people, it corrodes social institutions, breeding rebellion, violence and locust-like migrations. Liberty and freedom are not born in hunger: it was famine that gave Lenin and the Bolsheviks their mass appeal. The constant peasant riots of seventeenth-century Europe served only to strengthen the power of the state, for they confirmed the need for professional standing armies, as much to keep a brutal peace at home as to make war abroad. Social turmoil usually leads to a strengthening of power at the centre – sometimes in a monstrous form.

Observed in the light of the past, the prognostications are not good. Famine will stalk the world for the foreseeable future. And yet we should not be entirely without hope. The potentials for increased food production are not exhausted, and they are the preoccupation of men backed by government resources to an extent hitherto unknown. At least the problem is not left to Fortuna, the fairy godmother of famine. The horrors of Africa, the hideous pictures of starving Indians, these should not blind us to the fact that the world's largest population, the Chinese, have not suffered severe famine for a decade or more – a miracle by the standards of the past. And it is not impossible that these more desperate times may provide a greater effort, a more relentless fight against one of the oldest enemies of man.

What we can be sure of is that the dream of plenty is over. It was scarcely ever more than an illusion. Man's drive to breed, so necessary for survival in a world of pestilence, war and famine, becomes in a world of increasing supplies and improving health the procreator of the evils it formerly surmounted. In the seeds of birth lie the harvest of death.

Heroes

How often we hear that we lack heroic leaders. Where are the Churchills and the Roosevelts, or the Gladstones and the Lincolns? Even the communist world, at least in the West, has given heroes up and denounced the cult of personality. Yet some men and women still hunger for an authority that they can idolise, for a personality that they can transform into someone greater, someone finer than a common mortal. They are having a hard time with the present run of politicians. After all, is it possible to imagine chain-smoking, handbag clutching, grand-motherly Golda Meir as Jeanne d'Arc? How would a sculptor place her on a monument? Or Harold Wilson with his baggy trousers and homely pipe? Could one wrap him in a toga or set him astride a prancing stallion in bronze or stone? Can we bring ourselves to contemplate Richard Nixon by Canova – the sculptor who made Napoleon look heroic in the nude? Today's statesmen are simply not cast in the heroic mould; many of them have lives as brief as butterflies: who can name, for instance the last ten Prime Ministers of Italy?

Even the heroic gesture is at a discount: the assassins of our time are nondescript psychopaths – mad and motiveless except in their own wild dreams. Terrorists blow up the anonymous and the innocent. Sarajevo is no more. And yet, only a generation ago heroes abounded – though the few of them that remain are now ageing and fading: Tito and Mao, Haile Selassie and Chang Kai-shek.

And were the World War II heroes really heroes? Stalin was a paranoid madman. De Gaulle, the male incarnation of Jeanne d'Arc, founded the most chauvinistic and disruptive foreign policy pursued by any nation since the war. Many of Churchill's acts were petty, stupid and dangerous. His faults were small, of course, compared with those of Hitler, Napoleon and Alexander the Great. Each of these men was in pursuit of a dream too large for human life. Each had a heroic vision of himself that he persuaded his countrymen to share, visions leading to genocide, slaughter, endless war and carnage. No – better to have tough men of limited vision, pursuing the possible. Men lost in a dream of power or drunk on the thought of loyalty to a Leader are politically and socially dangerous.

This fear of heroes is very recent. Only a hundred years or so ago

Thomas Carlyle was trumpeting the virtues of heroes and hero worship, extolling Cromwell and Robespierre. Maybe in this present age we are watching, as with so many aspects of the past, the death of the hero. Is that a blessing or a tragedy? Are heroes part of the dream life of mankind from which we cannot and should not escape? Or will they go for good?

The hero has always been a strange phenomenon, not only in personal lives but in society. Obviously the worship of heroes is keenest in adolescence; we have discovered that our parents have feet of clay but still yearn to identify with someone. Adolescents today are as idolatrous as their fathers and grandfathers were: they worship Walt Frazier, Jane Fonda, Bob Dylan, or perhaps Noam Chomsky, just as their parents worshipped Babe Ruth, Joan Crawford, Frank Sinatra, or perhaps Bertrand Russell. Heroes and heroines will never die for adolescents — they merely change their names.

We tend to assume that the need for heroes dies with adolescence, and we look upon an adult who is prone to hero worship as childish or retarded. It may not be fair to do so, however. Daniel Levinson and Roger Gould, American psychologists, have recently made some very subtle studies, stemming from Erik Erikson's work, on the stages of adulthood, which they believe to be full of crises every bit as violent and disturbing as adolescence.

One of the most fascinating of these studies touches on the hero. Males (we know less as yet about females) tend to acquire mentors in their late adolescence — men older and more experienced than themselves. Often the need for these mentors, who receive confidences and give advice, continues into early adulthood. At about forty, however, the need suddenly vanishes. At that age most men stop growing — or, rather, realise with an intense and shattering personal vision that they are growing old. At thirty, life's possibilities are still almost infinite; for most men at forty, the rut, whether rough or well-upholstered, is as unalterable as the Grand Canyon. For most men life henceforth has one direction, leading inevitably to ageing and death. Without the soaring possibilities of adolescence and early manhood, what need is there for a hero or even a mentor?

Now the importance of this goes far beyond the psychology of the individual. It throws great light on social psychology as well, and may even help to explain some odd but recurring historical manifestations. Mentors, of course, are not necessarily heroes. Far from it. Yet there may be a psychological relationship between mentor and hero: given the right personal and social circumstances, the desire for a mentor may easily be transmitted into the worship of a hero. This might help to explain why societies have regularly been swept by hysterical tornadoes of hero worship. And why — since this trait appears to be more deeply

embedded in the masculine psyche than the feminine one – male-domi-
nated societies, particularly those with a powerful warrior class, are
more prone to hero worship than others. One has only to name a few
heroes – Julius Caesar, Augustus, Washington, Napoleon, Hitler, Mao,
Lenin – to realise that war is often linked with them. Indeed, they seem
sometimes to seek it: Napoleon's desire for a heroic destiny for France,
symbolised in his own person, drove him to battle, and finally to the
disastrous campaigns in Spain and Russia.

Of course, not all national heroes lead their countries to disaster. At
times of crisis, national heroes can help a society achieve a sense of
identity. Hence it is natural that societies, and minorities struggling for
freedom, should crave heroes through whom they can acquire confidence
and identity. It is not surprising that when the blacks began to struggle
free in America during the 1950s and 1960s, they wanted their own
black history, and their own black heroes. No more surprising, indeed,
than that a crowd of heroic martyrs, with their heads severed, their
bodies scarred by red-hot gridirons, should populate the early history of
Christianity. Nor should it astonish us that after the Reformation in
England, Foxe's *Book of Martyrs* should be read as keenly as the Bible.
The fortitude of these martyred men and women, heroes of the Protestant
faith, helped fortify and strengthen Protestantism, as well as breed
example. But who reads, or needs, Foxe now? Who but some scholarly
monk turns to the *Acta Sanctorum*? Religious revolutions, the great
crisis of faith and belief, are probably a thing of the past.

Yet in distant ages heroes were abundant. Indeed, the further one goes
back in time, the more the world is peopled with demigods. They struck
so deep a chord in the human psyche that they lived not only for
generations, but for centuries. Hercules is still strangling serpents in the
statuary of sixteenth-century Italy: the infant Hercules is still being
modelled in bronze in eighteenth-century France. Only in the nineteenth
century does he begin to fade, and in the twentieth century he vanishes.
Hercules portrayed the physically heroic side of man; not a symbol
merely of virility and sexuality, but of man's muscularity, his capacity
to dominate the animal world, to kill lions, to strangle serpents. But the
deep social need for Hercules and his like has faded into the heroes of
the football field, or been transmogrified into Tarzan for small boys. His
social base has evaporated.

Because the heroic is so deeply involved in personal fantasy, there has
usually been a subculture of anti-heroes or, rather, heroes of the poor
and deprived. Robin Hood, as far as English society is concerned, has
been one of the most persistent. Century after century he has deprived
the rich and insensitive, avenging the poor for their bad luck in the
lottery of life. He was a hero to the wretched poor of the Middle Ages,

to the stern Puritans, and to the Levellers and the Diggers of the English revolution in the seventeenth century, sects that wanted social justice. And he was still a hero in the days of the Luddites, when craftsmen struggled to push back the oncoming tide of the Industrial Revolution. But, Robin Hood has gone the way of Hercules – or rather, he has joined Disneyland. He entertains small children. His social force, his heroic stature, have vanished with the forests that gave him birth.

Almost all the heroes of antiquity symbolised deep social, as well as individual, needs. It is hard for us, bred on science and rationalism, to grasp how fearsome, how magical, the universe appeared to earlier societies, how full of wonders and portents it was. It could only be controlled by men and women larger than life. Heroes were necessary both as gods and as a part of the ritual that kept the external world secure and tolerable.

Heroes were closely linked with the unknown. The earliest hero in recorded literature was Gilgamesh, the Sumerian whose desire to fathom the mysteries of life plunged him into heroic conflicts with the monsters of the sea. The epic poem that tells his story is a masterpiece of poetic literature because his words as well as his actions touch the deepest springs of human hope and despair. Does good triumph over evil, can the wall of death be breached and hope of a future given to men and women fearful of the brevity of their lives? Time and time again, in epic literature, the hero goes through the darkness to the gates of death, though rarely emerging with the secret in hand.

Danger, tribulation, success in the face of monsters – this is the heroic world of epic poetry and legend. And we need not seek far for the reasons, though they are not easy for us today to grasp. How can we understand the fears that haunted people who lived on the edge of great primeval forests and swamps, or the loneliness of small communities isolated in the gray and treeless coves of the wild Icelandic shores. Into these coves sailed high-prowed ships filled with ferocious men hungry for women and cattle. Or the grey rocks could split and erupt in the volcanic outbursts that spoke of the anger of cruel gods. No wonder people sat by their fires in the endless nights of winter, listening to tales of their heroes – of Grettir, who fought and killed monsters yet died a cruel death: of the boundlessly courageous Njal, who was burned alive with his sons; of Aud the Deep-Minded, heroine of sagas, who triumphed over all tribulation. These tales not only offered comfort and a kind of hope, they also strengthened the will to survive in a wild, bleak world. Hope and heroes were close relations; in all epics – whether in the tale of Gilgamesh exploring the underworld, or Odysseus wandering from peril to peril over the waters, or Eric the Red braving the arctic seas –

they return, and so long as they are greater in spirit than ordinary men, they triumph.

But epic heroes such as these essentially belong to rural worlds, to societies living near the wildnerness. And no wonder then that they are dying, particularly in the Western World, where nature has become benign. In Western Europe and the United States there is very little untamed nature left – scarcely room for a goblin, let alone a giant, even in the well-patrolled national parks. The control of natural forces; the conglobulation of humanity in metropolises, cities, towns; the end of isolation through newspapers and television; the elimination of personal and tribal vendettas; the abolition of hand-to-hand, face-to-face war – these are the reasons for the dwindling role of the hero. But are there deeper causes at work too? Apart from the occasional anti-hero, like Robin Hood, heroes have usually belonged to ruling aristocracies and the warrior class. They were exemplars of the ruling castes of noblemen, mandarins, and Brahmins, Odysseus, Beowulf, Grettir, Roland – all are aristocratic images. And they decline as aristocracy declines. King Arthur of legend lives on in the Camelot of musical comedy. They are a part of an aristocratic past that western society has rejected.

Further, the age structure of society may also be a determinant of the social role of heroes. After all, early societies – Homeric Greece, Vedic India, the Vikings of Iceland – were young societies where men were old at forty. France was a young man's world during the Revolution and the Napleonic era. The hordes who worshipped Hitler were not the aged but the idolatrous young. As social psychologists have revealed, men need mentors until they step across the threshold of middle age. In societies like our own, where the mature and the ageing outnumber the young, the need for heroes may be weaker.

The history of social processes – the decline of the family, the change of attitudes towards animals or children – is always difficult to understand; indeed, they present perhaps the most difficult problems that an historian has to face. And so, too, with the decline of the hero. Our grandfathers read Plutarch; we do not. How rarely now do our leaders have the charisma of a Napoleon or an Alexander the Great – Kennedy for a moment, Churchill for a few years. Yet how quickly they fade. And we should not regret it: there may have been less romance in a Truman or an Attlee, but there was also more hardheaded realism. And that is the stuff that heroes were never made of.

Private Lives and Public Faces

Old Cato. The trouble began with him. After all, he symbolised all the Roman virtues, in him all the principles of an honourable citizen were fulfilled. Called from his farm, he saved his country, yet sought neither riches, nor honours, nor power. Not for him the Roman triumphs of a victorious general nor the dubious future of a politician knee-deep in graft. His service done, back to his farm, his integrity as unsullied as his courage. So old Cato hangs, like the morning star, in the dark world of politics. Time and time again his memory has been revived to revile the stark realities. The bitterest journalist to oppose the corruption of Sir Robert Walpole called himself Old Cato: and his letters were used again and again by those Americans who revolted against George III. Their idol was, indeed, Old Cato – a simple farmer of integrity, patriotic, forthright, incorruptible. Is this image of Old Cato a fatuous chimera that the public pursues in its longing to be governed by men of virtue? Would it not be wiser to accept more stoically and more ironically the frailties of man's nature; to accept that private lives and public faces may tell very different stories?

In fact, the hunger, the longing in the public for virtue in its governors, has been very intermittent through the course of history. Naturally enough it is most prominent in democracies, whether of small towns and countries or in the representative democracies of the great modern western states. Monarchies and aristocracies rarely notice the problem. Wise, benevolent, god-fearing monarchs were naturally preferred to the dissolute. But a King such as Henri IV or Louis XIV could run through mistress after mistress without the awe and majesty of their public image being damaged in the least. Elizabeth I of England could swear like a fishwife or frolic in her bedroom with the Earl of Leicester without her majesty being diminished one iota. And as with the monarchs, so with their relations and courtiers. In Louis XIV's France, men were executed for homosexual affairs, but no harm came to the King's brother and his minions. The court might sneer and gossip, but when *Monsieur* appeared, all was reverence and obeisance. A little gossip might trickle through to scandalise the Parisians, but for the majority of Frenchmen the sexual antics of the Court were as remote as those of the gods on Olympus. Not for them to question the wisdom of God in providing them with such rulers. Indeed, by the eighteenth century sexual high-jinks were almost *de rigueur* for any monarch: to be without a mistress was almost unthinkable. George II of England loved his wife, Caroline, deeply, both emotionally and physically, yet he felt that it was essential for him to take a mistress. And his wife, in no way nonplussed, made the King's choice, the charming but slightly deaf Mrs Howard, one of her ladies-in-waiting. Later, when the King took a more succulent German mistress in Hanover, he wrote enormously long letters describing Madame Walmoden's most intimate charms to his wife, so that she might relish his success. Again, no way nonplussed, she gave these letters to the Prime Minister, Sir Robert Walpole, to read. Not that sexual immorality bothered him overmuch. Everyone knew that he kept a mistress who had already given him a bastard. The whole House of Commons knew it. But, of course, no one dreamt of asking him to resign. Nowadays the Lords Lambton and Jellicoe had to withdraw immediately from politics the moment it was discovered that they had made use of a call-girl. Indeed, a solemn judicial committee was immediately set up to see if national security had been threatened. The gulf between the eighteenth century and the twentieth in this regard is vast. Nor can it be explained that this is the result of aristocratic manners and habits being replaced by middle-class morality. That is both naïve and uninformed. After all, the worthy Benjamin Franklin, the epitome of middle-class attitudes, fathered and publicly acknowledged his bastard son without making anyone in Philadelphia, or later indeed during the Revolution, fear that such a blot should exclude him from politics. Nor can one dismiss the eighteenth century as an age that was extravagantly permissive. It was not. Aristocratic society was lax, as it always has been. But middle-class society, which was both numerous, vociferous and influential, certainly was not. But there is no suggestion at all from one end of the century to the other that anyone should be hounded from politics for sexual peccadilloes. There was the unquestioned assumption that such matters were private, between a man and his God; and nothing to do with whether he was an excellent administrator or a good or bad Whig or Tory. Private sexual practices were not a public matter. They became so in the nineteenth century; not, however, rapidly. The Lord Chancellor, Brougham, could still send his footman for a whore when he felt like one without being tumbled from office. Disraeli refused to consider making publicity at the time of a general election about his rival Palmerston's having fathered a bastard at eighty on the prudential grounds that it might win him the election. Yet a generation later Parnell's adultery with Kitty O'Shea ruined his career, so did the adultery of Charles Dilke, a most gifted liberal statesman; a homosexual in the cabinet later in the century shot himself as the only decent way out when discovery seemed imminent. Another went into life-long exile. Human nature, of course, did not change; statesmen, politicians, even headmasters skipped in and out of bed. Lloyd George's exploits rivalled Casanova's. But public hypocrisy was essential. The public face, that of the stern moralist Old Cato, must always be maintained; discovery

meant political death. This attitude has, of course, been nothing but
harmful. Men of ability have been destroyed, and this is as true of
America as of England or Europe, and worse still, a potential web of
blackmail has been created, not necessarily monetary, for fear of
exposure can close a mouth as well as open a pocket. It might be
healthier if the sexual habits of our political masters were ignored unless
so outrageous and unbridled as to be dangerous to the safety and welfare
of the state. This boundary of danger, naturally, is hard to define. As
public mood changes, so will our demands change; at least in the matter
of sexual practices. English society can now accept adulterers in political
life, but not, it would seem, the use of call-girls.

Money is a different matter. Old Cato returned to his farm not a
penny richer for his service to the state. And how rare it is for any
politician in the Western world to return from public affairs no richer
than when he entered them. In recent centuries, in countries which
possessed representative institutions, the acquisition of money through
the use of political power has rarely been brazenly and openly admitted.
Ministers of state expected monarchs to make them lucrative gifts of
offices and sinecures, as well as lands and honours. Colbert, a man of
middle-class origins, became immensely rich in the service of Louis
xiv. Burghley House and Hatfield House – two of England's greatest
Elizabethan mansions – were built out of the pickings of office by
Elizabeth i's two Cecils. The elder Cecil, William, exhorted every penny
he could from his Mastership of the Wards, and no method was too
nice for him. Indeed, England's statesmen and politicians went on looting
the till for the next two centuries. Sir Robert Walpole put the cost of
his mistress on the Customs and Excise, took kickbacks on any contracts,
pocketed bribes from men seeking office, played the Stock Exchange on
inside information, and smuggled a great deal of his brandy. He was a
splendid statesman, giving Britain such peace, prosperity and stability
that the country had never known before. It might be argued that he
was cheap at the price. A century later Disraeli's financial dealings were
not so spectacularly corrupt as Walpole's, but they were dubious enough,
and today they would have cut his career short before it had begun.
And yet Disraeli's qualities as a statesman, particularly in foreign affairs,
were accepted as distinguished and for his country's good. The acquisition of money by such means was always regarded as corrupt,
Walpole's dealings were skilfully hidden. Disraeli's so carefully concealed
that even now the truth cannot be discovered. Lloyd George's fiddles
with party funds still cannot be properly assessed. Lloyd George, after
all, was the architect of England's victory in World War I, yet throughout
his life he was in danger of exposure for sexual high-jinks as well as
financial and political corruption. It would seem that amongst the most

gifted leaders of the world the public image and the private face rarely match. And yet against the long list of corrupt yet brilliantly useful statesmen, there is another list. William Pitt embracing poverty and spurning even sinecures; Gladstone, who would tear up a postage stamp at home if a private message had been despatched through official channels. And a host of others, American as well as English, who have spurned all temptation; men whose private and public images have never been at variance. By and large they are narrow, rigid men, committed ideologues.

In a world of mass media, of universally used copying machines, such men will increasingly be the winners. As privacy vanishes, the public and the private man have to become one. Although there may be certain gain in public morality as hubris catches up with the guilty and the delinquent, some men and women of exceptional capacities may be lost. A world of Woodrow Wilsons, honourable surely, chills the spirit to contemplate. As yet that seems but a distant prospect, but as disaster follows disaster to politicians in America and Britain, when public faces are torn aside to reveal greed and lechery, it may come more quickly than we think. Even if it does, corruption will remain at a deeper level.

Lechery and greed are venal sins, but not mortal. More grievous, more dangerous to the public good, is double-talk, where men preach high-minded morality, yet practise another. Men and governments create a public image out of their ideas. They pose as guardians of liberty, the pillars of law and authority; and yet they may in their private and secret life suborn witnesses, commit perjury, conspire to thwart those very laws about which they prate. At its worst, this is found in traitors, in men like Kim Philby, who lived as a dedicated servant of British society and betrayed it to Russia. But morality can be betrayed as well as countries – not merely sexual or financial morality, but the morality of law without which the individual becomes the victim of the state. And such betrayal of society is never easy to lay bare; the public image is often a careful and deliberate hypocrisy; and exposure much more difficult than for sexual peccadilloes or financial graft. And, alas, the deepest drive of men who enter public life is usually the hunger for power which corrupts more absolutely than warm blood or an empty pocket.

And so the sanctions should be far more savage, the punishments more condign, the rejection of such men by society were absolute. In handling power integrity is all: here, at least, public image and private behaviour must never diverge; if they do, democracy and justice are at risk, and there can be no compassion.

Gifts

We all know the story of the Trojan horse. The way the wily Greeks deceived the besieged citizens of Troy with a huge wooden horse. Struck with wonder and cupidity, the Trojans dragged it within their citadel only to find it full of death-giving Greeks. A story of ancient mythology, not very believable, suitable only to beguile young children, for no longer does it contain much significance for the mature. We are not gripped by the story; it does not touch the strings of fear and dread that lie buried deep within us, as it was meant to. But the Greeks and Romans, living close to the gods, knew well enough that gifts were complex matters, touched with danger as well as delight, death-producing as well as life-enhancing. Perhaps we are too unaware of the emotion-charged nature of gifts. We should open our eyes for even if they cannot kill, they can tempt and destroy; societies as well as individuals, parties as well as politicians.

Gifts have always fulfilled a complex social function: perhaps less complex today than in times past, although that may be due to our own lack of realisation of what we are doing when giving. Almost all gifts are placatory – even toys to children: that is why, even in the earliest times, gift-giving, particularly to the gods, was widespread, down to the humblest peasant who would give an ear of corn, a few beans and olives to his household gods, to the deities of the woods. On occasion, he might slaughter what he could ill afford, a young kid as an offering to the god of a natural spring so that it might continue to flow – an action which Horace immortalised in one of his most beautiful odes – 'O fons Bandusiae.'

Such gift-giving to the gods was, of course, sacrifice: after all, sacrifice means merely to make something holy by giving it absolutely to the gods. A holy place was land given up entirely to the gods, into which no human might go without special rites and propitiations. People as well as animals could be, and were, given to the gods, but as the gods were ever-living, the embodiment of eternal life, so, too, the gifts should contain life, whether locked in a seed of corn or ebulliently present in a nubile virgin. And the sooner despatched to the gods, the better. And what greater gift could there be to the gods than one's own child, and if accepted by a perfect death, what glory to the family. Doubtless many a Mayan heart passed through a torment of emotion – sorrow, pride and joy – as mothers and fathers watched their young daughters being cast into the sacred waters at Chichen Itza.

But as we all know, giving a present is fraught with anxiety – will it please, will it seem too little or too great, imposing greater demands than the recipient might wish to bear? And so, too, the gifts to the gods were riddled by a little anxiety. Obviously a gift to them should be perfect; and, of course, it had to be despatched to them in the correct fashion. Hence the priests conducting the sacrifice rapidly inspected the entrails to see that the animal was perfect. It surprised no one when Roman Emperor Caligula was assassinated, because a few months earlier a part of the liver of an animal he was sacrificing to the gods was missing. Naturally the gods spurned his gift, and punished him.

In gifts to God's representatives – the Kings and Princes and noblemen – there was of course a similar motive, a similar anxiety. As with the gods, a gift can outrage the man it is meant to charm. Samuel Pepys, whose conscience never fell into a deep sleep, was often troubled by the presents which came to his desk in the Navy Office where he was Secretary. He could swing contracts, not always, but often, so he was a target for merchants. He loved the silver flagons and dishes as well as the gold coins that came his way, but they were dangerous: they created at times obligations he did not want; so he devised elaborate rules to protect himself. The contract had to be excellent for the Navy; the amount given must be appropriate for the contract; and, most difficult of all, and so rarely achieved, gifts should not necessarily imply future kindnesses. And then, as Pepys realised, as politicians and statesmen were to realise generation after generation, gifts were honey-covered; in spite of all rules they stuck to their conscience.

From ancient days to recent times, the most sensitive area of gift-giving has naturally been with men of power. Deep down in the human heart there is a need to placate, to win over. It is stupid not to recognise the strong emotional base and discuss all gift-giving to men of power as beady-eyed corruption. There is deep symbolism in gift-giving at all levels. Corruption may be there, but there is much else; indeed very ancient ways of behaviour. When Prime Minister Heath presents President Pompidou with a gold decanter on an official visit to Paris, he is doing exactly what the heroes of Homer were doing when they gave each other 'glittering cauldrons' of bronze. They symbolise peaceful intent; discussion rather than war, friendship instead of enmity. This national placatory gesture is still permitted. No head of state proceeds abroad without his trunk of gifts.

Alas, gift-giving in politics does not stop with the antique and stylised conventions of heads of state. The power exercised by secretaries of state or presidential aides is nearly as great as that of the ancient gods. They, alas, can waive punishment, stop indictments, fiddle contracts, provide honours, make men millionaires or destroy them with rumour and vilification. Indictments die in the Justice department. Texaco provides air planes for Mr Connally. ITT dispenses largesse. Legal, may be; dubious, certainly: the altars of modern gods give off the stench of corruption as much as any sacrificial altar to the ancient gods of Aztec and Mayan.

All advanced societies have tried to eradicate the practice – so that men's careers have been blighted by the gift of a vicuna coat; or recently in England even a large gift to a theatrical charity run by a wife damaged a powerful politician's career.

The corruption of political gifts are like a deep-rooted cancer, no sooner cut out than it springs up elsewhere. The only cure is to prevent politicians and administrators from exercising personal power. It is the power that draws the gifts and the corruption; the delight in using it that inflames cupidity. The only safeguard is to diminish and delete power. The corruption is ultimately in those who dispense power, not in those who offer money.

The gift-giving goes on, and will go on, in more subtle, more devious ways. It is very rare for a successful politician to die poor, even though he may have been born destitute. There are cunning methods that no legislation can possibly check, even if there was felt to be the need. For example, the gift of advice. A prudent investment suggested from time to time can make a politician's future secure. How could that be excised? Certainly, the gift of advice can be most lucrative, for how else could Prime Minister Heath, born in the humblest circumstances, (his family had to take in lodgers for the summer holidays in their sea-side home), afford a yacht for £45,000, and no yacht is cheap to maintain, yet this is his third. And, of course the advice need not be direct, and I am sure in Prime Minister Heath's case certainly was not – the device of the blind trust removes all personal involvement. And, remember, politicians in Britain are poorly paid, and perhaps the most fiercely protected from corruption. British politicians have been ruined for accepting even a holiday in slightly dubious circumstances. Yet it is hard to think that sound and generous advice does not breed a small seed of obligation, a need to make a return. It would be inhuman to be without such feelings. And the friends of men of power rarely go without their rewards. And yet the borderline here must be thick with dangerous booby-traps. And some prefer to eschew the man and give to him, as it were, sideways to his party. Men, after all, want to stay in power, and gifts to their parties that enable them to do so are hardly likely to be spurned. Lloyd George crudely showed the way; men poured their money into a Liberal Party fund which he controlled. They got knighthoods and baronies. Crude, but, for a time it worked. The methods of President Nixon's friends were more subtle. $200,000 dollars passed in cash are not paid without a thought for the future. Knighthoods may not be for sale, but protection often is. So gift-giving, and the dangers of corruption, so keenly felt by Pepys, move crab-wise. But undeniably the corruption is there; it would be naïve to think otherwise. As Pepys himself realised in his gloomier moments, he did not get his silver dishes for nothing. Like the gods, he could not ignore an appropriate sacrifice. He had to put away his thunderbolts and sign the contract. A party may be the recipient of funds, but men handle its power.

Although the dangers of gift-giving, the potentiality for corrupting a human relationship, or the relationship between men and power, is most obvious in politics; the dangers, many and varied, are implicit in almost all gifts. Few give out of sheer *joie de vivre*. The hurried purchase of a toy, the quick choice of a bit of costume jewelry in the airport shop, is usually meant not only to please but to placate. When we give, we demand; when we accept, we yield. The human sacrifice at Chichen Itza, the black bull sacrificed to Mars, the rich Christmas gift to the head of a corporation, are all linked by a common human emotion. The desire to capture the future at any price and ward off disaster. The same deep-seated emotion lurks even in the oddest forms of gift-giving that some societies have devised – the gift by eskimos of their wives to a stranger; a habit which is also found amongst the Bedouin. Strangers to such isolated groups of the tundra and desert are menacing portents that can only be defused by the closest intimacy.

Most of us hunger for love, for power, for security; many need the regard, even the interest, of their fellow men and women; to a few the debt of another's kindness is too much to bear, so gifts flood the world, and so long as they do some hearts, some minds, some men of power will be corrupted. If gods could be diverted from their purpose by a timely sacrifice, how could we expect mere mortals to be untouched? That men should offer gifts is human and not culpable. The danger always lies in acceptance, for all gifts may be Greek.

The Vanishing Servant

Master and servant: for millennia this has been an intense human relationship, sometimes short-lived, sometimes life-long, but rarely casual, indifferent or uncharged with emotion. A few rare human beings can easily play the role of master or subordinate, but the majority find the first role uneasy and the second unpleasant. It requires, therefore, strong social forces, combined with powerful economic needs, to keep the master–servant relationship viable.

At one time, of course, it was a relationship that most people experienced, one way or another, particularly in the older societies of Europe and the East, although the servant class was widespread in eastern and southern America during the nineteenth and early twentieth centuries.

But now, everywhere, servants are vanishing; a multi-millionaire in the Middle West may, on occasion, have to mow his own lawn, drive his own car, fetch his own newspaper, shop for drink; likewise, his wife may have to cook a meal, stack the dishwasher and adjust the thermostat. In any case, servants or no, she would expect to draw her own bath water and dress herself.

What a contrast with a Victorian woman of similar riches, who, seeing that the drawing-room fire was lack-lustre, would ring for a footman to wield the poker and put on fresh fuel. As for filling her own bathtub, the idea would have horrified her as much as the thought of getting on her knees and scrubbing the floor. No matter what time she might get back from a ball or a party, she would expect her maid to be awake to help her undress. In the 1930s there were still many upper-class English girls who had not the slightest idea of how to make a cup of coffee or boil an egg. Within a generation such luxurious dependence on others had vanished, and even in the 1930s the servant class was on the decline.

High wages, greater opportunity for other employment, are the quick and trite explanations for the disappearance of the footman, and the lady's maid. But this is not true. Unemployment is high in the United States and in Britain, and still servants do not abound. High wages obviously do not tempt, for the wages currently offered a butler, maid, or gardener are astronomical by the standards of previous generations. Want-ads lure servants with promises of free apartments, colour television, the use of a car, long holidays, and limited hours – but to little avail. When dining with the upper middle class in England it is as well to know a few words of Spanish or Portuguese, otherwise one has to channel one's wants through the hostess-interpreter. Nor will you find many blacks, or Indians, or Pakistani, desperately poor as many of them are.

What has happened? Why is the servant class vanishing? Why is it that what once was so comfortable and so secure has become alien and distasteful?

The authority of the master and the devotion of the servant were at their most absolute in the earliest civilisations we know of. When Sir Leonard Woolley found the entrance to the Royal Tombs at Ur, he discovered that the deep passage leading to the burial chamber was lined with the remains of slaughtered girls who had been decked out in finery. There had been no struggle. They had sat quietly waiting for death to transport them to an eternity of service to their dead mistress, for how could she manage without them? Nor was this a quirk of the Sumerian Kings: the recent discovery of the royal Han tombs with their jade-clad bodies of Prince and Princess revealed a similar custom. Servants continued to follow their masters through the doors of death even into late Roman times, when an aristocrat would mark his death with funerary games, bequeathing a clutch of gladiators or some of his own slaves for the killings.

With the disappearance of slavery and, it may be, with the spread of Christianity, masters no longer held the power of life and death over servants, but there were few other restrictions in the relationship. Samuel Pepys, displeased by an act of carelessness committed by his young maidservant, thought nothing of beating her with a broom and locking her in a damp, rat-infested cellar for twenty-four hours. Even so, servants were better placed than apprentices, who, because they were bound for seven years, could suffer terrible brutality at the hands of their masters and mistresses; they were flogged, starved and imprisoned, and if they ran away, they were more often than not hauled back and delivered up to their tormentors. Such subordinate relationships could be exploited by sadistic appetites, and in a world full of brutality, pain and misery, few cared. Occasionally, a particularly brutal master or mistress was brought to retribution, but most went scot-free.

One of the keys to the problem of the disappearing servant, perhaps, is to be found in the treatment of children. Even into the late Middle Ages English families rarely kept their children at home. The sons of noblemen were sent to act as esquires to Princes, while gentlemen sent their sons and daughters to noble households to serve as pages, maids, and the like. Poor children, too, were sent off; not all, of course, but thousands were dispatched to slave for the well-to-do. Most of Pepys' servants were children or adolescents; his boy, Tom, who ran his errands and accompanied him on the lute, was but fourteen when he entered the household. His maids were usually very young girls. In earlier centuries in Europe, people married late – nearer 30 than 20, for men and women alike. So the servant class was largely a youthful class.

This remained true in the nineteenth century, when the population grew so fast that the developing Industrial Revolution could not always absorb it. Indeed, nineteenth-century England probably saw a greater extension of the servant class than any other western country, for England was rich and had a large population, of which a considerable section was very young. Furthermore, a declining agriculture meant that many girls and boys could not be absorbed into the farms. There was no compulsory education and no social welfare. But there was a tradition of servitude for children, and into service they went.

Of course, not all servants were children: the life generated a sense of security and family loyalty, and many were happy to live out their lives in service. Boys and girls, after all, became servants at a deeply impressionable age. But more important, service provided a roof, clothing, and above all, food in a world that was drenched in poverty and abounded in slums. How else could a poor, illiterate boy or girl acquire the necessities of life except by slaving in another's home? And the slavery could be mild. In big households, duties were rigidly divided and an ambitious boy or girl might rise through the elaborate hierarchy – from pantry boy to butler, from under nursery-maid to nanny, from kitchen maid to cook, or even to housekeeper, and then one had one's *own* maid. In sickness a servant was looked after, in old age provided for. Naturally, conditions varied from household to household, but it was often terror of the world without that kept servants within.

The world within could be rich and varied, evil or saintly, chaste or passionate, and occasionally, but rarely, dull. For one thing, servants could live their masters' and mistresses' lives vicariously. If valet or maids, they travelled, not only abroad, but to house parties and weekend junkets; in other servants' halls they were known by their master's name and given his precedence – a rich field here, not only for social snobbery but also for easing the sense of subordination that haunts a servant's life. But perhaps the richest rewards in the servant's world were offered by the triangular relationships between master, servant and the master's children.

The English nanny was, in a sense, the animal mother of the young child: she fed it, cleaned it, spent days and nights with it, and gave it the warmth, the physical affection, that all young animals need; whereas the true mother was, more often than not, an idealised and glamorous creature living in a different world. Indeed, many would argue that nineteenth-century upper-class Englishmen were addicted to working-class girls because all the physical warmth they knew had come from their lower-class nannies. For the boys, again, there could be another odd servant–master relationship; it was from grooms, gamekeepers and young footmen that the sons of the house learned about sex, and their first attempts were frequently made on the servant girls of the household.

There was exploitation at all levels, from mistresses tyrannical through illness to masters tyrannical through sensuality or senility. There was exploitation of loyalty and of lust. The servants might be fed well and used kindly, but they were always *used*. And their resentment took its revenge in subtle ways, from dilatoriness to 'accidental' breakages to sexual seduction.

The master–servant relationship is rapidly vanishing, and the reasons therefore are complex – as they always are when an age-old human institution begins to crumble. Education of the young is one reason, and the spread of industrial society, with its opportunities, another. The sharp decline of a rural population is yet a third. Yet none of these quite gets to the heart of the matter. Why should there be far more domestic servants in Moscow than in New York? Why did female domestic service continue unchanged during the war-years in Nazi Germany and almost disappear in Britain?

These are not easy questions to answer, but one factor may provide the leading clue: the less patriarchal a society is, the less easy its members find it to accept the master–servant bond. The most satisfactory servants in Europe today still come from regions where the authority of the family and the father remains strong – Portugal, Spain, Southern Italy, France. And this might help us explain why black men spurn such work, no matter how lucrative. Whatever the reasons – profoundly sociological or superficially economic – the servant class is following the dodo into oblivion.

Yesterday – Interpreter of Human Experience

The world is out of joint. It has been so since man first contemplated it, an object of lamentation long before Jeremiah. As in one's personal life, how rare it is for the present to compare favourably with the past. Every civilisation, almost every nation or tribe, has created a golden legend; sometimes an age when the gods strode the earth, sometimes when heroes larger in spirit and prowess than ordinary men lived and loved on a superhuman level, or in our own Judaeo-Christian tradition a time when man was free from sin, when – how odd we are – nakedness was pure. Even the more realistic Chinese regarded their past with reverence, looking back to an age when due honour was given to ancestral wisdom, when retribution came to those who failed to show a proper filial respect, when, in fact, justice prevailed. Only recently has history ceased to be Heaven, or the awful reminder of God's wrath. For golden ages do not last, and the recent past is streaked with blood like an angry, storm-rent sky. The forces of evil stride history. The devil snaps up the frail who drift weakly into ungodliness or Nemesis looms over the thoughtless, the wanton, the carelessly happy. Elsewhere, calamity overwhelmed those who forgot their dutes to the wise dead. History was a long lost bliss but a recent terror, like a childhood lost in the horrors of adult living.

As John T. Marcus shows in his admirable discussion of historical thought, *Heaven, Hell and History* (Macmillan, 1967) much of this moral, indeed religious, interpretation of the past reappears in a different guise in the secular interpretation of history which has gained currency since the first great historical revolution of the Renaissance. Marx, methodical and earthbound as he was, remained caught up in the conflict of good and evil, in an apocalyptical vision of man's struggle in Time. For Marx and his early disciples, there was still a golden past of primitive equality, an uncorrupted communism before private property corroded the generous instincts of man and rendered him gross and grasping. Drugged with gain, he became indifferent to the suffering mass of mankind. But, as ever, retribution would come; the spirit would triumph over the flesh, when the class struggle was resolved the golden age would return, heaven replace hell. True in some of its dimension Marxism might be, but beneath was the old legend, the old sad story of man's fall and man's coming salvation.

Often national history was no more realistic, indeed a good deal worse. We all remember those marvellous Teutons of Tacitus, so virile in their northern forests, electing their chieftains, living the strong, satisfying, martial life. Such splendid animals to be ancestors of a nation God-chosen to be a *Herrenvolk*. Whatever tribulations may have buffeted and torn the poor German nation apart, the suffering was a part of the mysterious necessities of that inevitable process which would lead the *Volk* to its predestined glory. And even if the insanities of Nazi history are easy enough to scoff at, they are but the lunatic end product of that same nationalist history that generations of nineteenth- and twentieth-century Britons, French, and indeed, Americans, were fed on. After all, think of the pioneer spirit, of those log cabins, of those upright Puritans in the wilderness, and cannot one see destiny being made manifest? This, of course, in history for the masses, whether Capitalist or Communist, Chinese or French. Maybe these historical attitudes have been necessary; at least the leaders of mankind, or rather its rulers, have always felt the need of history to explain the past to their own satisfaction and to steel their subjects to the rigours of the present. True history has been rare, as rare as Auk's eggs and it is easy, and not entirely unjust, to dismiss it all with Henry Ford as 'bunk'. And yet. . . .

There are varieties of truth and man's explanation of reality has only in recent centuries turned towards the accurate delineation of the experience of mankind. He was too totally absorbed in his environment to bother overmuch about his past except as a sort of social and moral glue, used in order to make his community cohere. Whereas in the last three hundred years the revolution in historical studies has been as great as the revolution in science, there has been no historical equivalent of the technological revolution. With dwindling social authority, the historian has found it difficult to impress his knowledge of the social experience of the past on either the governors or the governed. The difficulties have been partly professional and partly due to a resistance in the general intellectual climate to historical truth. It is far easier for intellectuals to accept interpretation of life through literary studies or sociological surveys than through historical enquiry. As the historian's

THE PERSPECTIVE OF HISTORY

tools have grown more refined, and his interpretation more accurate, he has, ironically enough, lost intellectual authority.

To take but one example, it is staggering how easily intellectuals have accepted the Lawrence–Leavis attitude to the growth of industrial society. They insist that it has debased the moral nature of man, led to a shrinking of his intuitive life and denied him the deep satisfaction that rural life brought, when man lived so much closer to nature and so kept to her rhythms. The satisfaction of making a cartwheel with primitive tools is regarded as realising the whole nature of a man at at much deeper level than putting a computer together. Great segments of historical truth, which all demographic history proves over and over again, are brushed aside – or rather not brushed aside, for one cannot brush aside what one does not know. The findings of historians are ignored, yet a little reading would teach the Leavis school that agrarian communities were riddled with hunger, disease, violence and the most abject poverty; they provided a world of little hope and infinite toil in which anxiety about the harvest was constant – as true of pre-industrial England as of India. Indeed the bulk of mankind have found little satisfaction in rural life until they became rich and affluent.

History is not wanted as evidence. Intellectuals have preferred to use it as a family album of fading photographs, a provocative for nostalgia, a dream world to which they can flee from the demanding and frightening present. In the nineteenth century, appalled by the implications of industrial society, with its demagogy, corruption and vulgarity, the upper class intellectuals of both Old and New England created a never-never land of medieval history, inflating the spirituality of a world that festered with human misery – a world as barbarous as medieval Tibet. Mont St-Michel, built out of the blood and bones of starving peasants, became a symbol of genteel sensitivity. What bogus nonsense. Nor is it only intellectuals who are pervaded by social nostalgia: so are many professional historians and by far more writers of history whom the public read with attention and approval. And this, of course, is as true of East as of West. The over-size heroic figure of Peter the Great comes and goes in Soviet historiography like a recurring dream. But this is no more absurd than the history that turns Washington into a moment or Nelson into a schoolboy's hero. A clear vision of the past is very rare.

Strictly professional history, of course, is in far better shape. Concerned with very limited issues and problems, the degree of accuracy achieved is remarkably high: indeed, the facts of history have rarely been so carefully judged. Gradually too they are being given great quantitative weight and within the limits of their own relevance, discussion of their interpretation can be as exacting as that which goes on at the frontiers of science. Some of the problems of history are not only at least as exceedingly complex as certain of the profounder biological problems, but equally important. And, obviously many have immense pertinence to our own time and situation: the factors that have brought about the industrialisation of primitive communities, those which inhibit or stimulate the growth of population and – perhaps, even more exciting in the history of ideas – the gradual discovery and acceptance of the habit of truth. All of these matters have a direct bearing on our own social and political situation, whether it be *vis-à-vis* Vietnam, Israel or Soviet Russia. Historians with this trained sense of human reality and of the cause of social change ought to be one of the clearest voices in educating and informing the masses. They ought to be as pressing with advice to governments as economists or scientists. Yet they are silent or unheeded. History, which has ceased to be the interpretation of heaven and hell should take its rightful place as the interpreter of human experience. It is time the statesmen listened.

Progress of the Protestant

We rarely realise how completely steeped we are in western culture: born in it, bred in it, educated in it, we accept it and believe in it, and rarely give it the long cool look that so many of its oddities deserve. And religion, the Christian religion, is one. Yes, an oddity. If we glance for a moment at the other great religions of the world – Buddhism, Confucianism, Hinduism, the Taoism, the followers of Zen, the poly-theisms of Greece, of Rome, of Sumer, of Egypt, we find tolerance, a continuing tolerance of other Gods and of divergent beliefs; Buddhism grows as many branches as the banyan tree, but no one is called a heretic. Heresy, and all its murderous consequences, is only to be found in Christianity, or in its first cousin, Islam.

And heresy appears quite late, even in Christianity. The first three centuries passed without the deliberate massacre of other Christians who differed only on a point of dogma. The Donatists in the fourth century were, in a sense, the beginning of the long cruel story of heresy, of the slaughter of men, women and children, often done with deliberate and extravagant horror, that has stained the history of Christianity with gallons of blood. Its history reeks of burning, tortured flesh. And yet this is the religion of brotherly love.

That the infidel might be fair game for slaughter has been an occasional aberration with other religions, but with its ancestor Judaism and its close relation Islam, it has been the compulsive neurosis of Christianity for centuries. It is as well to remind ourselves that European civilisation, from which America stems, has been one of the bloodiest and most aggressive in man's history. It has been the epicentre of all the major global wars. Indeed, war, as a totally destructive force, was born on the battlefields of Europe. How far the European's aggression was fed by his ideological ferocity is a difficult yet necessary question. Whatever the answer may be, this unholy combination of cruelty and religion is an inescapable fact.

It is brought home vividly by *The Progress of the Protestant, A Pictorial History of Early Reformers to Present Day Ecumenism,* by John Haverstock: a book which should be by anyone's bedside who believes his own view of life to be so absolutely true that it should be imposed on others with napalm, TNT and firing squads. John Haverstock has brought together a splendidly varied collection of illustrations, many of them little-known woodcuts from the martyrologies of Catholic and Protestant. They are carefully organised under subjects and strung together in a long chain; the effect is cumulative, exciting and highly educative.

The late medieval origins of Protestantism, based largely on anticlericalism, are followed by the tremendous and savage conflicts of the Reformation and Counter-Reformation. Here the woodcuts drip with holy gore. We see the starved Catholics of Amboise, stripped naked, drawn forcibly over a taut rope and then slowly roasted. Not that the Catholics treated their victims more sweetly: the Inquisition was no more sparing of the rack than Elizabeth I's Protestant torturers, and the smell of burning Protestant flesh floated in the days of her father and sister across the quiet market square of Cambridge. All done, of course, from the highest of motives – the service of truth. Even though the fires died out and the racks grew rusty, life did not get much jollier. Gaol, whopping fines, second-class citizenship, interspersed with occasional outbursts of sadistic violence, remained the lot of the unorthodox in either Protestant or Catholic countries. And yet, as Protestant sects multiplied and proved indestructible, toleration grew and Europeans prided themselves on the discovery of what the East had practised for millennia.

However, the restless old-Adam of dogmatic truth needed fresh fields now the old battle-grounds at home were no longer so readily available. Protestant and Catholic missionaries fought their battles anew over the souls of the primitive peoples of Africa or America or the misguided ones of India and China. It is odd to realise that the last, bitter war between Protestant and Catholic was fought out by the black adherents of these faiths in Uganda in the nineteenth century. The pictures and the woodcuts become, however, a little milder – baptisms of chiefs, or the impressive piety of the black brands plucked from burning, with only here and there a picture of a Baptist missionary being clubbed to death. Naturally Haverstock does not neglect the internal history of Protestantism – its manic obsession with the devil and all his works, its crude manifestations in the camp meeting or the wilder heresies that flourished in the semi-literate frontier society. To whatever aspect of the subject he turns his sharp and piercing eye, he always has something pertinent to say and a batch of illustrations to illuminate his story. My one complaint about this beautiful, impressive and frightening book is that many of the pictures are not dated. Some of the illustrations are imaginative reconstructions made some 200 years after the event which they depict and there is nothing to tell one so anywhere in the book.

And although Haverstock is fair and judicious, he does, perhaps, gloss a little the more fearsome aspects of Protestantism. True, he draws attention to their preoccupation with the devil's agents – witches (but here they were neither better nor worse than their Catholic protagonists), and produces a splendid woodcut of the Salem witches dangling on their gibbets. And yet, perhaps, he is a little too gentle with the Protestants' myth-dominated intellectual world, with their grey pride and their hatred of the world's delights.

Nevertheless, these pictures are so vivid and the coverage so comprehensive that it cannot fail to stir the imagination and make one think again about the strangeness of our past. Because it is *our* past we tend to accept it as normal, as the most natural experience for men and women. We have been taught to revere our martyrs, those brave misguided creatures who suffered the torments of hell for a point of dogma: for a phrase or even a word. In the West, we have come to regard persecution for belief as an almost ineradicable feature of human life – forgetting Greece, forgetting India, forgetting Imperial China. The harsh intolerance of Communism after all stems from Marx and from Lenin, therefore from the West. To most liberal humanists since Erasmus this aspect of Western intellectual life seemed utterly deplorable.

And yet I suspect that the very ferocity of the dogmatic battle may have heightened the part played by ideas, and strengthened the concept that lies at the heart of Western science, as well as Western philosophy, that truth can be discovered, that it is no illusion but an absolute of reality. And here the Protestant world was at an advantage over the Catholic. The Protestants placed their emphasis on the individual's need to discover the truth. Once, discovered, it could become a prison of the mind, but almost from the moment Luther nailed his thesis to the door of Wittenburg church, Protestant truth became multiple, sects sprang up like weeds, and peasants and craftsmen had to practise their dialectical skills on the gritty knots of dogma – baptism, trans- or con-substantiation, the sacraments, the authority of bishops, all required to be argued about as well as believed in.

Philistine, dogmatic, violent, the Protestant world might be, but basically, Protestantism, like the Catholic reaction which followed, was intensely literate. And may be the chaotic, strident, theological conflicts, and the social and political problems which they pose, and the constant arguments which they provoked, were a curiously fertile seed-bed for natural science. Certainly theological dispute cannot have been inimical, for the majority of the great scientists of the seventeenth century were, like Newton, deeply religious men, as interlocked in the theological structure of their world as any other believer. This juxtaposition, however, of science with religion in the seventeenth century will always amaze.

And here again we touch on one of the more remarkable aspects of the Western intellectual tradition. The time when these dogmatic battles and their attendant cruelties, so luridly illustrated in this book, were at their most ferocious was also the age of magnificent art, of the springtime of music, of the rebirth of philosophy and of the foundation of modern science. Indeed it is extraordinary how the West has managed to combine, even in modern times, great barbarity and intellectual splendour within the same ideological framework, often indeed, within the same society.

Indeed, cruelty and barbarity, philosophically and intellectually justified, remains a part of our world. And one of the most terrifying aspects of Haverstock's book is its modern relevance. As one turns over the pages, glancing at the burning martyrs, the victims on the racks, the clubbed misssionary, one feels satisfaction that such a world has passed into oblivion. No one is going to sear my flesh because I believe in no part of the Christian myth. And yet . . . are not men and women and children being blown to shreds, burnt alive and mutilated for myths equally a matter of faith and not of argument? 'Freedom' for a communist or a capitalist is as explosive as faith was to Catholic or to Protestant. Aggressive economic and social forces can still marshall themselves behind dogma that attracts like a magnet the idealism and self-sacrifice of individual men and women. However, buy Haverstock's book. It will give you a disturbing weekend. It should trouble your mind and haunt your imagination. Above all, make you question the nature of our past, the world we have created. And what better function can a book have than this?

The Emperor Constantine

Seen from the distance of centuries, turning points in the world's history appear sharp and dramatic, and few more so than the conversion of the Emperor Constantine to Christianity after the Cross appeared before him at the Battle of the Milvian Bridge, which he won against the odds. Only a few years previously the Tetrarchy, of which his father was a member, had conducted, particularly in the East, the most savage and ruthless persecutions the Christians had endured in their existence. Within a few years all was changed. At Nicea the Emperor sat at the head of a Synod of Christian Bishops deliberating on the nature of the creed and the substance of the Trinity. What could have been more miraculous? What more dramatic?

Naturally the great Christian historians Lactantius and Eusebius of Caesarea highpoint this dramatic time of change when the Devil and his works received so singular a rebuff. And yet under the eye of a skilful, shrewd and realistic scholar how inevitable it all seems. As Ramsay Macmullen demonstrates in *Constantine*, the Emperor was compelled to take the actions he did by the very nature of his circumstances, and how very cautiously the Emperor moved from paganism to Christianity. Before Constantine Christianity had deeply penetrated the imperial courts, the ferocity of the Great Persecution was due to the strength and ubiquity of the Church in the East and, indeed, so strong and so ubiquitous that the persecution could not prevail against it. And so toleration possessed political value as the rival emperors struggled for power and played for popular support. The multitude of Christians in the East gave to Constantine, once Christian, a powerful fifth column in his struggle against his great rival, Licinius. But once gained, the Emperor remembered pagan Rome and the strength of its traditions. His public acts and public statements are ambiguous and vague. He went on employing pagans at Court until his death. The Church certainly was no longer persecuted, indeed richly endowed with churches, lands, jurisdictions and authority. Orthodoxy received state backing, heresy was persecuted and paganism discouraged.

Seen through Macmullen's eyes this, once one of the most dramatic turning points of the history of the Western World, appears so cautious and so slow that the ordinary men and women in the Western Roman Empire can scarcely have realised what had taken place. The lesson would seem to be that great revolutions often steal on societies almost unawares.

There are other fascinating points of interest in Ramsay Macmullen's book; the most pertinent for our own time is this. A point in social development arrives when, although the forces of reaction abetted by government authority can be whipped up into quite furious persecution, the apathy, indifference or secret sympathy of the mass renders such persecution useless and nugatory. There are tides in human affairs that can never be stopped by any government once they have swept a significant segment of society into their current. Any attempt to stop a fundamental change in belief is as hopeless as Canute ordering the waves to retreat. Spiro Agnew might brood on this with profit.

History never loses its cunning and today's dissidence too often becomes tomorrow's authority and proves a poor exchange. The Christianity that triumphed with Constantine soon became a harsh, persecuting, monolithic Church, hell-bent on extirpating heresy and paganism and as capable of Emperor adulation as any decadent Roman Senate. It quickly learnt to render unto Caesar. Not content with this, its scholars attempted to change the whole ideology of the Western world. Pagan beliefs were rooted out or transmogrified: temples were razed, oracles destroyed.Pagan history was forced into Judaeo-Christian chronology. The past became the sole property of the Church. Yet the task of obliteration proved beyond even the Church's powers, even in the diminished literacy of the Dark Ages. (And here would be a powerful lesson for Kosygin, Brezhnev and the rest – if they were capable of learning – for Russia alone has attempted an ideological revolution as vast as that initiated by the Christian Church in the fourth century.) In the Dark Ages monks and nuns surreptitiously read and copied their Ovid, turned to Horace for solace: true the losses were colossal – Tacitus hung on the tenuous thread of one manuscript, but sufficient pagan literature survived to haunt the imagination of men. So also did the ruins – the broken arches, amphitheatres, the crumbling walls, creating a sense of a lost past, more complex, more civilised, more cultivated than the mean existence that the men of the medieval West had to endure. And a past that will not die, that entrances men with a sense of greater artistic achievement is a threat to any closed world of authority: a ghostly criticism of the present that nothing can exorcise. In the end not even the massive authority of the medieval Church could prevent the rebirth of the ancient pagan world which gave Europe's intellectuals renewed confidence. It led to that recovery of nerve, that belief in the validity of the natural world and human happiness which Peter Gay has written about so perceptively in the concluding volume of his masterpiece on the Enlightenment. This duality of Europe's past – pagan and Christian – essentially the result of Constantine's conversion, did more. It helped to create history as we know it, for it posed an historical problem of a magnitude that no other civilisation has faced – the contrast which Gibbon seized upon in an immortal image – the bare-foot friars praying in the ruins of the Temple of Jupiter. How could it have happened, the collapse of such greatness into such poverty – a question still not answered.

These two books – Macmullen's and Gay's – have provided me with the best kind of historical reading, for they are concerned with momentous changes in human destiny and thought. Both deal exquisitely with precise and fascinating historical situations, as well as illuminating with their deep sense of realism complex human charactsrs – a Constantine or a Voltaire. And yet both books provoke one to think far beyond their confines: for revolutionary changes in attitude to human life resonate long, long after they are originally made. Even today we are still entangled in the world of Constantine as well as of the eighteenth-century *philosophes*. Belief and unbelief are still in conflict and these books are curiously appropriate, and will be particularly relished by those who enjoy the ironies and surprises of history.

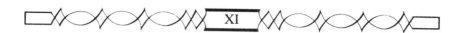

Final Words

Throughout the 1960s, 1970s and 1980s my career had been successful. True I had missed the Chair in Modern History but a personal chair had followed shortly afterwards. I was elected to the British Academy at a reasonably early age if deduction is made for the lost war years and I had been singularly blessed with pupils, graduate and undergraduate, young men whose exceptional distinction was confirmed by their careers – starting just before the war with A. R. Hall, the outstanding historian of science. Of my first three Christ's pupils after the war, one became a Vice-Chancellor, another a Bishop and the third a Reader at a provincial university. Eric Stokes and F. C. Spooner followed and J. P. Kenyon trod on their heels along with the late Lord Crowther-Hunt, my first research student. Five of my best – Simon Schama, Geoffrey Parker, John Brewer, Derek Hirst and Linda Colley – have become a part, alas, of the brain-drain and now J. P. Kenyon has followed them. Fortunately others have remained – Neil McKendrick, John Vincent, John Burrow, Michael Bush, Roy Porter, Joachim Whaley and so one might go on. My delight at their success has been strengthened greatly because their field of work has been distinct from my own. Occasionally I may have sparked an interest in them through an article or a book but I have never regarded research students or bright undergraduates as fodder for my own researches. They are all independent scholars in their own right, owning nothing to me but talk and encouragement. And yet so paranoiac are some other scholars, that there has been talk of a 'Plumb school' and a 'Plumb conspiracy'.

I had neither the time nor the desire to create either. Although I liked my work, I did not enjoy most professional activities outside teaching and lecturing. Most academic conferences I find a waste of time and decided early to go to as few as possible. Even worse were the so-called seminars – a sort of intellectual cricket net, rarely deadly, giving rise to a flood of mutual admiration in public, mixed with a little venom in private when the seminar was ended. I could see no reason to waste hours in conferences or seminars which could be spent in creative writing. I only held one seminar as a professor. It was in a year that I had students – John Brewer, Roy Porter, Linda Colley, Derek Hirst, Richard Tuck, Keith Wrightson – of such extraordinary brilliance that I thought they should be brought together – but they did the speaking, I did not – wisely – thinking of the competition. Had that been repeatable in other years I might have become a seminar addict.

In fact I became so bored with academic chores that, independent financially of what I was paid as a professor, I resigned early in 1974. As a professor one had to sit on the Faculty Board and its committees. I had done my time as Chairman in the 1960s. All obligations discharged I found it almost unbearable to listen to the never-ending dialogue between Professor Elton and Professor Finley, who saw eye to eye on nothing but modern architecture. (They were responsible for the disastrous Faculty Building. How could anyone have thought of putting a library into a conservatory tall enough for palms?) That was one recurring nightmare. The other was the never-ending programme of Tripos Reform – an unstoppable and disastrous activity. The younger historians, hell-bent to prove the singular importance of their own piece of turf, chopped the subjects into smaller and smaller pieces or added tiny pebbles from the wilder shores of the Third World. If these aspects of the History Faculty fatigued me, the appointments which the Board made filled me with a sense of doom. How could any body of rational men pass over Simon Schama or Geoffrey Parker, or get rid of Hugh Brogan? As for professorial appointments, apart from Eric Stokes, and the miracle of Quentin Skinner after I had resigned, they filled me with disquiet and a sense of hopelessness.

For decades nothing exciting, nothing original, nothing creative has been attempted in the teaching of history. Scarcely any of the leading historians in the Faculty have given any thought for its future or considered what contribution the Faculty of History might be making to the intellectual life of the University as a whole, let alone the world at large. A drop in student numbers, chronic overstaffing in obscure fields of history and a rapidly dwindling supply of cash is now driving it into crisis. But the tide of failure may turn, often a tide does before it reaches its greatest ebb. And it would be ridiculous to give the impression that the Faculty was wholly without distinction. It is not.

Sir Geoffrey Elton is a very considerable historian. He is energetic, industrious, a scholar whose capacity as a writer has slowly improved; indeed he now writes an authoritative prose with less pomposity and his technical equipment has always been exceptional – a precise scholar and a steamroller in argument. His weaknesses lie in a kind of implacability of vision and total rigidity in commitment to an idea. *The Tudor Revolution in Government* was a gross overstatement, natural enough in a young scholar eager to make his mark but he has, until very recently, been adamant in its defence. His stature, however, has been diminished from what it might have been by a lack of magnanimity towards fellow historians and by a kind of paranoia to some. His endless denigration of Lawrence Stone, an historian of wonderfully stimulating if over-optimistic creativity diminishes him, not Stone. And apart from the objects of his paranoia, he often reveals a warm and supportive nature, especially to his faithful research students.

Sir Owen Chadwick who began life as an historian very modestly indeed, has with a combination of energy, charm, ruthless ambition brought such distinctions on himself and his University that borders on the miraculous. His books are innumerable, some surprisingly good and neat but some indifferent when not downright bad. He and Elton, however, have not used their distinction and success with any true benefit to their Faculty.

C. P. Snow always maintained that even men most inclined to favour the second-rate could never withhold recognition from supreme talent. And this is certainly true of the Faculty, and on these the future of history at Cambridge lies. It would be invidious for me to name them, indeed it might even do them harm to suggest that I approve of them but in the history of ideas, in medieval studies and in seventeenth-century social history there are historians of exceptional quality – soon the leadership must be theirs. Sir Geoffrey is going through the traumatic agonies of departing; Sir Owen is soaring into the empyrean; Maurice Cowling, an endearing, comic figure but intellectually disastrous, is about to enter limbo. Fresh winds must blow, and may be history as education, history as wisdom, history as a part of high culture will once again take its rightful place at Cambridge; and one hopes that if a new school of history, bent on change, comes into being, it will reach out to other faculties not only in the humanities but also in the sciences. This could be helped by a radical change in the university's faculty and examination system. But, I am afraid, so radical a change would require direct govern-ment intervention through a Royal Commission.

The last years of my professional life had, at least, one element of surprise. Trevelyan, Churchill, Bryant had died and I thought that their version of the British past which had at times become a vital factor in the world of politics and diplomacy had gone the way of the empire. I did not think that a generation reared with no memory of World War II, for whom Churchill was just a name, could respond to the 'patrician' version of history – Britain as the protector of freedom, liberty and the rule of law. The immense upsurge of patriotic feeling at the time of the

Falklands crisis which united for a time Labour, Liberal and Alliance with the Conservative Party's actions surprised me. The greatest distrust and criticism of the Falklands War was probably to be found amongst intellectuals and academics, not the nation at large. In 1983 I was asked to give the Winston Churchill Memorial Lecture at Washington College in Fulton Missouri where Churchill had made his great Iron Curtain speech. The Falkland crisis was still very fresh in everyone's memories and I dealt with it at the beginning of the lecture.

The British reaction to the Falklands crisis astonished many Americans, astonished all Germans, and indeed most other Europeans except the French whose historical experience is also concerned with the struggle for liberty. Many feared that Mrs Thatcher's furious belligerence would be inflamed in the future by similar threats to Hong Kong or Gibraltar. Such reactions betrayed a lack of historical judgement and complete ignorance of the role that history has played in Britain's sense of itself. A similar lack of historical empathy has bedevilled understanding of the French by any American president since the war. None of them could respond with warmth to De Gaulle, Pompidou, Giscard d'Estaing and now Mitterrand: the French, like the British, are gripped by their past. Churchill, of course, would have understood instinctively why the overwhelming majority, left or right, supported Mrs Thatcher, just as he found it easy to understand why French men and women acclaimed De Gaulle: even though he, himself, found him unbearable. Or why so much of Mitterrand's policy has his nation's, as well as his party's, support.

The reason, of course, lies in the dominion of history. The British people are still entangled in their past, far less may be than they were, but still very deeply. And so are the French. Memories of their greatness still influence Mitterrand just as they did De Gaulle: hence their common attitude both to NATO and the independent nuclear deterrent. Any past, however, is multi-faceted: at times liberating, at times dangerous. In Ireland William III and Oliver Cromwell are real presences, bloodying the present in the most tragic and desperate way. And, even in the Falklands crisis, the legality of the past was endlessly and uselessly argued about. Whether John Smith first sighted the islands seemed to matter to some English intellectuals far more than the fact that an entirely British community had lived there for generations, displacing no one. That history should matter comes as no surprise to most Britons, nor it would seem to most Argentinians, although the majority of the world's governments were bewildered. No historians, however, commented with much sense on the historical dimension of the Falkland crisis. Those who did largely confined themselves to a legalistic investigation of the nature of territorial sovereignty. Mrs Thatcher had a much firmer grasp – and history told her that the British stood for the liberty of free Britons and the rule of law. For her, as for Churchill; that was what British history had been about, especially English history, from Magna Carta to the defeat of Hitler. In this crisis of the Falklands the latter mattered more than the former, particularly to anyone over fifty. But undoubtedly there was a very real sense of the past which Mrs Thatcher rightly sensed and used.

Indeed the patrician's past or 'The Whig Interpretation of History' is still the only past that a statesman can use at times of crisis to arouse the nation's sense of itself. More than fifty years have elapsed since Butterfield's book – professional historians whatever their political commitment have accepted Butterfield's view – but as yet the public have not.

The only alternative social attitude to history, even today, is the Marxist and radical interpretation, that English history only makes sense in terms of class struggle, first bourgeois rising against feudal aristocracy and destroying it, the longer, tougher and unfinished struggle between the emerging working class against the middle class linked with the relics of aristocratic power. During my lifetime this Marxist attitude has made great strides in the universities and in an increasing number of schools. It led to a great deal of distortion of history – Christopher Hill attempting to maintain that the English Revolution was a bourgeois revolution leading to modernity; Eric Hobsbawm arguing in the cost of living debate that the Industrial Revolution led to the degradation and impoverishment of the working class. His thesis could only be made plausible with a carefully selected period of short duration but was utter nonsense over the nineteenth and twentieth centuries, or by E. P. Thompson creating a self-conscious and radicalised working class in the early nineteenth century but forgetting that a great slab of the proletariat were intensely patriotic and jingoistic. At one time it looked as if a new distorted past for Britain would be forged and widely accepted. Professional historians first dislocated and then began to destroy their interpretation. Most of these Marxist historians were born to some affluence and they failed to realise that most of the proletariat preferred a refrigerator to a revolution. Between the bourgeoisie and the proletariat the Marxists thought was a huge unbridgeable chasm, forgetting the cultureless, respectable, dumb petit bourgeoisie whose small comforts lured the prosperous proletariat to buy their council houses, get one car and then another, and settle for holidays in Spain. The picket lines dwindled, the workers opted for capitalism. But the final horror for the Marxists must be the sight of a world hell-bent on privatisation from the backyards of the Semipalitansk to Crewe, from Kunching to Shanghai. For seers who get the future so wrong, who never realised that capitalists run after the proletariat as keenly as any Marxist – how could they ever have got the past right? The Marxists were just as disastrous as the atomisers, as the Namierites, but they wrote better and were far more widely read. And they appealed to adolescents longing to be free of the materialism of goods. Nevertheless one of the joys of my professional life is to have witnessed their failure. Yet their failure does not obliterate materialism which does not demand the support of Marxist ideology any more than psychological studies of historic figures need the absurdities of crude Freudianism.

An optimist by nature I cannot but believe that the present disarray in thinking about history, its nature, its purpose, its right to life, is for the subject's good. Yet the crisis in history remains. Academic history is hugely overstaffed, is uncertain what to teach, has a declining number of men and women who want to be taught and faces a growing public indifference to its fate.

I think that a sharp decline in the number of professional historians will do the subject no harm. Take my own field – eighteenth-century studies. From calculations made at the Fifth International Conference on Eighteenth-Century Studies over 6000 men and women teach it, write it, lecture about it and derive their livelihoods from it. At that conference 35 scholars read long papers on one topic – 'The portrayal and condition of women in eighteenth-century literature'. When printed, the translation of the five-day conference was longer than the Bible, some 2040 densely printed pages. Other historical periods have identical situations – Renaissance Studies, Reformation Studies, Early Modern Europe, History of Science, and so on – conferences take place every year with their thousands of historians. Almost certainly there are more historians alive today than the total sum of historians of all other generations added together. As I said in my Fulton Lecture

> There is an even greater decline in the number of university students who become teachers of history in schools. Before the war, about 50 per cent of all undergraduates reading history became schoolmasters; now it is less than ten per cent. This, of course, is due to the decline of the amount of teaching of history in schools. Up to 1950, history in schools was a major subject as central as mathematics or English. Now in almost all secondary schools in Britain it is optional or subsumed in social studies. In very few schools indeed is history taught as Churchill learned it or I did. Nothing is taught simply and directly. Instead of teaching the history of the nation, in Britain or in America, it is thought to be too nationalistic, too chauvinistic, too Eurocentric, and so what is taught instead are historical themes. Indeed one of the themes offered for teaching in the New York City schools is 'The Position of Women in Imperialist Nigeria', which I think must be rather baffling to the most clever and expert twelve-year-old New Yorker.

Such an approach leads to a decline in demand for history This is an aspect of my profession which none of us really foresaw when Kitson Clark bullied us to add two or three papers (all large in scope) to the Tripos 40 years ago.

There is one aspect of history that has not changed very much over the last 40 years – history of entertainment. Some books by highly qualified professionals can be included in this category, books such as

Garrett Matlingly's *The Defeat of the Spanish Armada*, for example. A number of Lawrence Stone's books come into this category as well, as do the superb essays of Hugh Trevor Roper. Few, if any, however, reach an audience of Trevelyan's proportions – probably only A. J. P. Taylor and myself have done that, except for Hugh Trevor Roper's *The Last Days of Hitler*. Far more successful – in terms of audience – are historians such as Alistair Horne, Antonia Fraser, Barbara Tuckman or Elizabeth Longford, all of whom have been exceptionally successful. Others such as Christopher Hibbert, a good, undervalued writer, have produced a steady stream of interesting historical studies with the regularity of an established novelist. And as with literature, there is an undergrowth, wild and luxurious, of lurid history that drifts through the bookshops fulfilling a need – rather like the romantic novels of Barbara Cartland or Catherine Cookson.

Naturally a subject that provides so much entertainment has attracted television and through television historians have reached audiences of astonishing magnitude. A variety of methods have been tried for television and the field is still open for experiment. A. J. P. Taylor mastered the 'face-to-face' approach, talking to camera and holding a respectable audience for twenty minutes or so – a difficult task requiring great artistry in presentation as well as an intuitive sense of the level of intellectual discourse the audience could take. But there has been no one to take his place. Occasionally historians appear in discussion programmes but not frequently enough. There seems to be a curious blockage about the use of historians not only in television but also in government – economists and sociologists, often remarkably ignorant of the historical processes behind the problem on which they pontificate, are preferred. Indeed one would like to see a few young aggressive historians pushing their way into public recognition. There is a half-baked attempt in the television series called *Time Watch* but again the programme lacks direction – the good, the bad, the indifferent are lumped together, some illuminating, some interesting but most dull with no attempt made to discover who was or who was not good before the camera. No producer would trust an amateur actor into a West End production and just hope for the best. That is why the finest historical series have owed their success to their professional anchormen. Kenneth Clark was a consumate lecturer, his series *Civilisation*, one of the best historical series yet made, heightening the intellectual consciences of millions of viewers through the world: the same is true of Alistair Cooke's *America*, Jacob Bronowski's *Ascent of Man* and Huw Wheldon's *Royal Heritage*. Worldwide, each of these series found audiences of well over 20,000,000. *Royal Heritage* has been repeated five times in Britain and is shown year in year out in America on cable or closed circuit television – likewise *Civilisation*. There is a vast and hungry audience longing to know about the past, vaster than any historian has ever been able to reach before. The satisfying of this hunger is in its infancy and there are great problems. Television, as I found when I wrote the scripts for *Royal Heritage*, requires skills that writers do not naturally possess – a high visual sense and a very direct intellectual approach – not simplistic but direct and clear. And I am sure that there is a great opportunity for professional history. Here once again the French are leading the way with a television version of *Montaillou*, not an entirely successful experiment but better than almost any other historical programme, except for the great BBC series.

The passion for history remains. A great deal of professional history will always and must be written for other professionals providing the raw material for the creative historians who still have remarkable opportunities to instruct, to illuminate and to encourage wisdom: a knowledge of the dimension of time without which neither a society nor an individual nor the universe itself can be understood.

Appendix One:
Date and Place of Publication

Part I

1 'Anguished Historian' – a review of *Lewis Namier; a biography* (London, 1971) by Julia Namier – *The Observer*, 16 May 1971.
2 'The Atomic Historian'; *The New Statesman*, 1 August 1969.
3 Introduction to *Absolute Liberty: a selection from the articles and papers of Caroline Robbins* (Hamden, Connecticut: Arden Books for the Conference on British Studies and Wittensberg University, 1982); ed. Barbara Taft.
4 'Edmund Burke and his Cult' – a review of *Burke and the Nature of Politics* (2 volumes, Louisville Kentucky, 1957 and 1964) by Carl B. Cone – *In the Light of History* (Penguin, 1972).
5 'The Elections to the Convention Parliament of 1689'; *The Cambridge Historical Journal*, Volume V, No. 3, 1937.
6 'Political History, 1530–1885'; *The Victoria Histories of the Counties of England: Leicestershire* Volume II (London, 1954) ed. W. G. Hoskins and R. A. McKinley.
7 'The Organisation of the Cabinet in the Reign of Queen Anne'; *Transactions of the Royal Historical Society*, 5th series, Volume 7, 1957.
8 'Walcott' – a review of *English Politics in the Early Eighteenth Century* (Oxford, The Clarendon Press, 1956) by R. R. Walcott – *The English Historical Review*, lxii, 1957.
9 'Owen' – a review of *The Rise of the Pelhams* (London, Methuen, 1957) by John B. Owen – *The English Historical Review*, lxxiii, 1958.
10 'Namier and Brooke' – a review of *The House of Commons 1754–90 (History of Parliament Volumes I–III)*, (London, HMSO, 1964) by Sir Lewis Namier and John Brooke – *The Spectator*, 22 May 1964.
11 'The Growth of the Electorate in England from 1600 to 1715'; *Past and Present*, Number 45, November 1969.
12 'Political Man' – a paper given at the symposium 'Man versus Society' at the University of Delaware, October 1966 – *Man versus Society in Eighteenth Century Britain* (Cambridge University Press, 1968), ed. James L. Clifford.

Part II

1 Introduction to the series *History of Human Society*:
Graham Clark and Stuart Piggott, *Pre-Industrial Societies* (Hutchinson, 1965)
C. R. Boxer, *The Dutch Seaborn Empire 1600–1800* (Hutchinson, 1965)
J. H. Parry, *The Spanish Seaborn Empire* (Hutchinson, 196)
John R. Alden, *Pioneer America* (Hutchinson, 1966)
Raymond Dawson, *Imperial China* (Hutchinson, 1972)
Anthony Andrewes, *The Greeks* (Hutchinson, 1967)
C. R. Boxer, *The Portuguese Seaborn Empire, 1415–1825* (Hutchinson, 1969)
Donald Dudley, *The Romans* (Hutchinson, 1970)
Jacquetta Hawkes, *The First Great Civilisations* (Hutchinson, 1973)
J. D. Fage, *A History of Africa* (Hutchinson, 1978)
Jerome Chen, *China and the West: Society and Culture 1825–1937* (Hutchinson, 1979).
2 A review of *The History of the Idea of Progress* (London, Heinemann, 1980) by Robert A. Nisbet; *The New Republic* Volume 182, 23 February 1980.
3 'The Historian's Dilemma'; *Crisis in the Humanities* (Pelican, 1964) ed. J. H. Plumb.
4 'G. M. Trevelyan'; *Men and Places* (London, 1963) by J. H. Plumb.
5 'The True Voice of Clio' – a review of *George Macaulay Trevelyan: A Memoir by his Daughter, Mary Moorman* (London, Hamish Hamilton, 1980) – *Times Literary Supplement*, 2 May 1980.
6 'To cover two and a half millennia in 300 pages takes a brave man' – a review of *Social Change and History: Aspects of the Western Theory of Development* (Oxford University Press, 1969) by Robert A. Nisbet; *New York Times Book Review*, 15 June 1969.
7 'Oswald Spengler'; written for *The Observer* series 'Great Blunders'.
8 'Toynbee: Prophet rather than historian' – a review of *A Study of History* (3 volumes, Oxford University Press, 1962) by Arnold Toynbee – *Paperback Review*, March 1962.
9 'It Took a Lot of Doing for Man to Get On in the World' – a review of *Prehistory and the Beginnings of Civilisation* (*History of Mankind* Volume I) (London, 1963) ed. Jacquetta Hawkes and Sir Leonard Woolley – *New York Times Book Review*, 23 May 1963.
10 'A Great Story Left Untold' – a review of *The Ancient World, 1200 to 500 (History of Mankind Volume II)*, ed. Luigi Pareti – *New York Times Book Review*, 1 August 1965.
11 'Most History – in 500,000 words' – a review of *The Columbia History of the World* (New York, 1972) ed. John A. Garraty and Peter Gay – 'Book World', *Washington Post*, 30 April 1972.
12 'Churchill the Historian'; *Churchill: Four Faces and the Man* (Penguin, 1969).
13 'Thomas Babington Macaulay'; *Men and Places* (London, 1963).
14 A review of the *Selected Letters of Thomas Babington Macaulay* (Cambridge University Press, 1982) ed. Thomas Pinney; *The Spectator*, Volume 232, 15 June 1974.
15 'The Good Old Cause' – a review of *Macaulay's Essays* (London, 1964) ed. H. Trevor-Roper; *British History in the Nineteenth Century and After,*

1782–1919 (Pelican, 1965) and *Britain 1688–1815* (London, 1965) by Derek Jarrett – *The Spectator*, 23 July 1965.

16 A review of *The Story of England; Makers of the Realm* (London, 1953) by Arthur M. Bryant; *Times Educational Supplement*, 1 January 1954.

17 A review of *The Elizabethans and America* (London 1959) by A. L. Rowse; University of Cambridge Trevelyan Lectures 1958; *The Sunday Times*, 18 Ocrober 1959.

18 A review of *The King's Peace* (London, 1955); *The King's War* (London, 1958) and *The Trial of Charles* (London, 1964) by C. V. Wedgwood; *The Spectator*, 28 August 1964.

19 'History and Tradition' – *Great Ideas for Today*; Encyclopaedia Britannica (Chicago, 1974).

20 A review of *The Mediterranean and the Mediterranean World in the Age of Philip II* (London, 1972–3) by Fernand Braudel (translated by Siân Reynolds); *New York Times Book Review*, 31 December 1972.

21 A review of *Capitalism and Material Life 1400–1800* (London, 1973) by Fernand Braudel (translated by M. Kochan); *The New Statesman*, 26 May 1973.

22 'The End of An Epoch' – *Horizon*, Volume 14, Summer 1972.

23 'Terror' – *Prism*, 1974.

24 'Graft, the Ratbane of Politics' – 'Perspective', *Saturday Review*, 29 February 1967.

25 'Echoes Across the Centuries' – 'Perspective', *Saturday Review*, 28 January 1967.

26 'Inflation' – *Horizon*, Volume 17, Spring 1975.

27 'The Persistence of Famine' – *Horizon*, Volume 17, Autumn 1975.

28 'Disappearing Heroes' – *Horizon*, Volume 16, Autumn 1974.

29 'Private Lives and Public Faces' – *Horizon*, Volume 16, Spring 1974.

30 'Gifts' – *Horizon*, Volume 15, Autumn 1973.

31 'The Vanishing Servant' – *Horizon*, Volume 15, Summer 1973.

32 'Yesterday – Interpreter of Human Experience' – 'Perspective', *Saturday Review*, 26 August 1967.

33 'The Protestants' – 'Perspective', *Saturday Review*, 27 April 1968.

34 'Constantine' – 'Perspective', *Saturday Review*, 27 December 1969.

Appendix Two: Notes

The Elections to the Convention Parliament of 1689

1 The majority of historians, writing of this period, have based their opinion of the election on the uncritical eulogy of Edmund Bohun, in his *History of the Desertion* (edn 1689), p. 122, and the main evidence quoted in its support is the order of 5 January 1689, by which all troops were to withdraw from towns where elections were to take place. This order was to safeguard William's own interest as much as to secure the freedom of elections; for the soldiers, deserted by James, were not enamoured either of William or his supporters. Cf. Bodleian, Rawl [inson] MSS. D. 1079, fo. 91; [Hon. Anchitell] Grey, *Debates [of the House of Commons from the year 1667 to the year 1694]*, IX, 112, 169. There has never been any detailed examination of the question.

2 See below, where this is amply illustrated by a description of the dual corporations of William's reign, also by the riots at Nottingham, cf. [Sir George] Duckett [Bt., *Penal Laws and Test Act in 1687–8*], II, 116.

3 The opposition of Winchester is glowingly described by Macaulay, *Hist [ory of England from the Accession of James]*, [edn 1856], II, 336.

4 Macaulay, *Hist.* II, 334–7.

5 Duckett, II, 236, 228, 221–53.

6 Duckett, II, 221–55.

7 It is a difficult number to compute as the franchise at this time was often altered in particular boroughs by the decision of the House of Commons. The usual number given in 38, making 76 seats; see [L.B.] Namier, *Structure of Politics [at the Accession of George]*, vol. I, and A. E. Porritt, *Unreformed House of Commons.*

8 Quoted in Duckett, I, 288.

9 For example Gatton, which was owned by Sir John Thompson and Thomas Turgis; neither favoured James.

10 Duckett, I, 196. S[tate] P[apers] Dom[estic], J[ames] II, Bundle 7, No. 405.

11 Duckett, I, 196.

12 Duckett, I, 196; II, 219. The agents report that, 'We also find that Mounsr. Fagel's letter and other pamphlets are industriously spread through all parts.' They say that they have not sufficient books and pamphlets to meet this.

13 Duckett, I, 198.

14 Ibid.

15 Ibid., II, 220.

16 All but those for Hertfordshire and Warwickshire are extant; they are to be found in Rawl. MSS. A. 139B.

17 Duckett, I, 97n., 103. Darcy was son of Conyers, Lord Darcy, and heir to the Earl of Holderness.

18 B[ritish] M[useum] Add[itional] MSS., 34, 516, ff. 50–4.

19 This is obvious from the histories of various boroughs, especially Nottingham, and from the debates on the Corporation Bill later in the year. Cf. Grey, *Debates*, IX, 510–20.

20 One strange result of this return of charters was the existence for years in many places of dual corporations, transacting corporation business and returning different members to Parliament. This division, or multiplication, of corporations was strongest in Suffolk, where at Dunwich the anomaly was not removed until 1698. There are cases in other counties, but all of them occur in small boroughs where this duality hampered patronage and caused a number of contested elections. For Dunwich see H[istorical] M[anu]scripts] C[ommission], *Var[ious] Coll[ections]*, VII, 104–6. Dunwich had a contested election 1688–9, 1689–90, 1691 (by-election), 1695, 1698; but as soon as the charter differences were settled, there are no contested elections, e.g. 1699–1700 (bye), 1700–1, 1702. Other dual corporations were: Oxford (H.M.C. *Var. Coll.* II, 270–2); Aldeburgh (H.M.C.*Var. Coll.* IV, 279 *et seq.*); Thetford (H.M.C. *Var. Coll.* VII, 147–9); Plympton (J. Brooking Rowe, *History of Plympton Erle*, pp. 82–5), and possibly Tewkesbury (H.M.C. *Downshire MSS*, II, 550).

21 Duckett, I, 198.

22 In a negative manner, i.e. no one was proposed to oppose them and they were able to consolidate their interest.

23 Most of Dr Charlett's letters are in the Ballard MSS. For Harrington, cf. D[ictonary of] N[ational] B[iography] and Add. MSS. 36,707. For Sarre cf. Ballard MSS. 45, fo. 23.

24 B.M. Add. MSS. 36,707, fo. 62. A.M. to James Harrington. A.M. is well informed on Parliamentary affairs.

25 These were Sir John Brownlow, bt., Thomas Masters, Francis Morley, and Thomas Babington.

26 K. Feiling [*History of the*] *Tory Party*, App. II, pp. 496–8, and Rawl. MSS. D. 1079, fo. 22.

27 Macaulay, *Hist.* III, 523.

28 An exact number cannot be given because in one or two cases no Christian name is mentioned by Sunderland, and at the time there were two or three holders of the same surname.

29 Duckett, I, 103.

30 Ibid.

31 William Stockdale and William Palmes were the only Yorkshire members to vote for the Sacheverell Clause.

32 B.M. Add. MSS. 24,475, fo. 133.

33 Ibid.

34 Thirteen minus the two dissenters and then adding Lord Fairfax. Dissenters or friends of dissenters are fairly easy to trace as the King's agents usually state the fact or if they voted for the Sacheverell clause and had in September

1688 received the support of James II, there is then little doubt that they belonged to this group,

35 Dcukett, II, 228.

36 Sir Robert Davers, who voted against the vacancy. Feiling, *Tory Party*, App. II, p. 497.

37 There is no direct evidence that he recommended anyone to Andover or Portsmouth. In January 1688–9, Francis Gwyn was writing to Lord Dartmouth about Portsmouth (H.M.C. *Dartmouth MSS*. p. 142), and Dartmouth might then be looked upon as the agent of the government and the two candidates who were suggested were returned: both of these men, Henry Slingsby and Richard Norton, had been favourable to James' three question (Colonel Richard Norton not entirely so), and I think they may be counted as men whom James would have supported. Cf. also Duckett, I, 424–5.

38 Duckett, I, 430.

39 Charles, Earl of Wiltshire, son of the Marquis of Winchester, afterwards Duke of Bolton; Henry Wallop, MP for Whichurch.

40 Thomas Bilson, MP for Petersfield.

41 Sir Benjamin Newland, MP for Southampton, a London merchant.

42 John Pollen, who voted against the vacancy.

43 A number are to be found in Danby's lists printed by E. S. de Beer in the *Bulletin of the Institute of Historical Research*, 1933–4, XI, 1–25. The number is calculated partly from this source and partly from the list of members opposing the first Exclusion Bill, printed as App. I, Feiling, *Tory Party*, pp. 494–5.

44 B.M. Add. MSS. 36,707, fo. 62, quoted *supra*, p. 240.

45 This is substantiated by a letter of William written to Danby immediately after James' flight. Cf. J. H. Plumb and Alan Simpson, 'Letter to the Earl of Danby from William, Prince of Orange', *Cam[bridge] Hist[orical] Jo[urnal]*, V, 107–8; also B.M. Add. MSS. 28,053, fo. 375.

46 Mr F. F. Smith in his *Parliamentary History of Rochester*, p. 123, says that William recommended Sir Joseph Banks and Sir Roger Twisden, but I have not been able to substantiate this.

47 The Declaration is printed in Corbett, *Parl[iamentary] Hist[ory]*, V, 4–13.

48 The Lord Warden's right to nominate one member was abolished by Act of Parliament, 1690, 2 Gul. et Mar. c. 7.

49 After James IIs detention at Faversham, he named the Earl of Winchelsea Lord Warden, but the gentlemen of Kent asked Winchelsea to refrain from using the title until he received a patent for the office. He agreed to do this but, owing to the rapid development of events, he never received a patent. B.M. Add. MSS. 33,923, fo. 433 (Sir Edward Knatchbull's Diary).

50 Thomas Papillon, London merchant, was of Huguenot descent and one of the leaders of the revolt against the Old East India Company. MP for Dover 1673–80, 1689–90; London 1695–8. Cf. *Memoirs of Thomas Papillon*, ed. by A. F. W. Papillon.

51 Although the lack of government interference in the Cinque Ports is not typical of preceding elections, it was of those that were to follow.

52 Cf. Lord Cutt's memorandum, printed in H.M.C. *Mrs Frankland-Russell-Astley*, p. 77.

53 Sir Robert Holmes, kt., MP for Winchester, 1669; Newport (Isle of Wight) 1678–9, 1685, 1690; Yarmouth (Isle of Wight) 1688–9. He had consented

to the three questions concerning the Penal Laws, proposed by James II: Duckett, I, 474. For his life, cf. *D.N.B.*

54 B.M. Add. MSS. 34,516, fo. 564. The Earl of Sunderland recommended: *Yarmouth*: William Hewer and Edward Roberts; *Newport*: Sir Robert Holmes, kt., and Mr – Netterville; *Newton*: William Blathwayt and Thomas Done. Hewer, Holmes, Blathway and Done were all in government employment. Of Edward Roberts and Mr – Netterville, I have no information. Thomas Done and Sir Robert Holmes secured seats in the Convention, the former for Newton, the latter for Newport.

55 *Newport*: ' 'Tis the only corporation of the three that has (in effect) a free election.' Lord Cutt's memorandum: H.M.C. *Mrs Frankland-Russell-Astley*, p. 7 Dillington was 'of Knighton, Isle of Wight'. Opposition to the proposed government candidates had begun in September. Sir Robert Holmes to Samuel Pepys, Rawl. MSS. A. 179, fo. 44.

56 Richard Jones, Earl of Ranelagh of the Irish peerage, MP for Plymouth, 1685–6; Newton (Isle of Wight) 1688/9–95; Chichester 1695–8; Marlborough 1698–1701; West Looe 1701–5. He declined Castle Rising in 1701. The variety and type of his constituencies show clearly that he had no established interest and that he was a government candidate. See a letter of his to Lord Cutts, H.M.C. *Mrs Frankland-Russell-Astley*, p. 93.

57 Fitton Gerard, MP for Yarmouth (Isle of Wight) 1688/9–90; Clitheroe 1693/4–5 (by-election); Lancaster 1696/7–8 (by-election); Lancashire 1698–1700/1. He usually had difficulty in procuring a seat in Parliament. For his methods, see C[ommons'] J[ournal], XI, 77–8.

58 Viscount Weymouth to Robert Harley, 7 October 1701. H.M.C., R[eport] 15, p[ar]t IV, p. 26: 'Chatham has a great stroke in that election [i.e. Rochester] which the admiralty may direct.'

59 Cf. *ante*, pp. 245–6, for the suggestion that William recommended them. The Minute Book of Rochester Corporation only states that they were unanimously elected.

60 H.M.C., R. 11, pt. IV, p. 237; H.M.C., R. 15, pt. 1, p. 142. Gwyn was secretary to the assembly of peers which directed affairs during the interregnum. He was elected for the Earl of Clarendon's pocket borough of Christchurch. For details of his career, cf. *D.N.B.*

61 Pepys had written to Sir Robert Holmes in September asking him to secure a seat for him in the Isle of Wight. Holmes gave a half-hearted promise but said that he had a great number of King's servants to provide for. Rawl. MSS. A. 179, fo. 44. Holmes and Pepys had never been on friendly terms since their quarrel over Cooper, Pepys' old mathematical master who became the inefficient master of Holmes' ship on Pepys' recommendation. Bryant, [*Life of Samuel Pepys*], I, 193–4.

62 Rawl. MSS. A. 174, ff. 210, 212 *et seq.*

63 Pepys, it is true, was a friend of James, but so were many other officials and civil servants of whom William made use. Also all of Pepys' offices were confirmed by the Prince. (Rawl. MSS. A. 174, fo. 165) and it was not until several months after the settlement that Pepys fell into disgrace.

64 H.M.C., R. 11, app., pt. XII, pp. 31–7. The Leeds MSS. are now deposited at the British Museum but are not available to readers; the calendar indicates a number of letters that would throw a great deal of light on Yorkshire and Lincolnshire elections.

65 'I rode with many others to York where next morning my Lord Fairfax and

Sir John Kay were unanimously elected Members of the Convention', *Diary of Ralph Thoresby*, p. 191.

66 Sir John Lowther was the 1st Viscount Lonsdale; cf. *D.N.B.*

67 Sir Christopher Musgrave, a well-known Parliamentary figure; cf. *D.N.B.*

68 Henry Wharton was brother to Thomas Wharton, afterwards first Marquis of Wharton.

69 Cf. H.M.C., R. 12, pt. VII, p. 226.

70 H.M.C., R. 13, pt. VII (Lonsdale MSS.), p. 98.

71 Ibid., p. 99.

72 H.M.C., R. 12, pt. VII (Le Fleming MSS.), p. 232.

73 *Letters and Diary of Henry, 2nd Earl of Clarendon*, ed. S. W. Singer, II, 219, 221–2. William Harbord was elected for Launceston, Thetford and Scarborough; he elected to serve for the first.

74 At Wootton Bassett, which was under the influence of the Earl of Rochester. At this election Henry St John the father of Viscount Bolingbroke, and John Wildman, the son of Major Wildman, the well-known republican, were returned. It is impossible to conceive of Wildman being a nominee either of Rochester or the St John family and he must have been elected in opposition to the wishes of the patron. In other boroughs where high Tories had patronage, no Whig crept in, e.g. Christchurch, under the patronage of the Earl of Clarendon (later a non-juror), returned two well-known Tories, Francis Gwyn and William Ettrick.

75 These are to be found in the *State Tracts*, published in 1706, and in *Somers Tracts* and the *Harleian Miscellany*.

76 *Diary of the Time of Charles* , ed. R. W. Blencowe, II, 288–91. The original paper is to be found in B.M. Add. MSS. 32,681, where there is also another memorandum of Burnet, written a short time afterwards, in which he sets down the people whom he expected to fill the administration. This has not been published.

77 B.M. Add. MSS. 29,594, fo. 139.

78 Ballard MSS. 45, fo. 22.

79 H.M.C., R. 12, pt. VII, pp. 233–4; B.M. Add. MSS. 33,923, fo. 429 *et seq.*; The Diary of Sir John Knatchbull, bt., MP for the county of Kent 1685–7; 1689–95. Extracts, concerning the flight of James II, were published by P. Vellacott, *Camb. Hist. Jo.*, II, 49 *et seq.*, but there is a great deal of value concerning elections in Kent and dealings between Knatchbull and Nottingham which ought to be published.

80 Rawl. MSS. A. 174, fo. 140.

81 Carte MSS. 130, fo. 239.

82 Duckett contains the answers to the three questions concerning the Penal Laws and Test Act made by practically every country gentleman of importance.

83 B.M. Add. MSS. 33,923, fo. 45 (b).

84 Sir John Stonhouse, 3rd baronet of Radley, was 2nd son of Sir George Stonhouse, who had disinherited his eldest son and who had represented Abingdon from 1661 to 1675, when he was succeeded by his son who represented it from 1675 to 1688. In 1679, Stonhouse was reported to be supported by the 'Catholic interest'. V[ictoria] C[ounty] H[istory], Berks[hire], II, 164; but he was one of the four justices in 1688 who were reported as being dangerous to James' cause. Duckett, app. p. 237. Stonhouse died in 1700. His son obtained a seat for Berkshire 1701 and 1702.

85 Thomas Medlicot, son of a London dyer, was appointed Recorder in 1675 but dismissed by James II in 1686; and later in that year defended the Baptist congregation at Abingdon. He was reinstated December 1687, but was removed by the Corporation in October 1689. Cf. J. and J. A. Venn, Al[umni] Cant[abrigiensis]; Bromley Challenor, *Selections from the Records of the Borough of Abingdon*, pp. 179–211, and A. E. Preston, *St Nicholas of Abingdon and Other Papers*, pp. 138–9. For his speech, see Grey, *Debates*, vol. IX. For his descendants, cf. Namier, *Structure of Politics*, II, 494.

86 For Southby , cf. Duckett, app. p. 237. For elections, *C.J.* X, 123–4, 326.

87 Elections for Weobley, Reading, Colchester, Harwich, Norwich, etc.

88 Sir Pury Cust was the son of Sir Richard Cust, 2nd bt., High Sheriff of Lincolnshire, 1695, and Commissioner for collecting the arrears of taxes in 1698. For his relationship with Sir John Brownlowe (MP Grantham) and William Brownlowe (MP Peterborough), see *Records of the Cust Family*, 3 vols, ed. Lady Elizabeth Cust.

89 Bertie was the fifth son of Montagu, Earl of Lindsey, brother of the Earl of Lindsey of this date. He voted against the vacancy of the crown: Feiling, *Tory Party*, app. II.

The Political History of Leicestershire, 1530–1885

Scholars requiring a more detailed footnoting of this article should consult *The Victoria County History of Leicestershire*, vol, II.

1 Between 1547 and 1628 seven members of the Hastings family represented Leics. From 1807 to 1888 a Manners represented the county: *Return of Members of Parl.*, H.C. 69 (1878), lxii (1).

2 *L. & P. Hen.* , xix (1), 146. Only 2 counties, Hants and Suss., were called on to provide fewer ox-wagons, whereas the demand on horses from Leics. was very high indeed, only three other counties providing more.

3 Strype, *Eccl. Mem.* iii (2), 171–2. Hen., the 3rd earl, was married to the sister of Lady Jane's husband. He did homage to Jane as Queen, but deserted her as soon as he could: *Complete Peerage*, vi, 656–7.

4 *D.N.B.*; *Complete Peerage*, vi, 656–7; Neale, *Elizabethan Ho. of Commons*, 39. M. M. Knappen, *Tudor Puritanism*, 411, quotes a rather extravagant eulogy, *The Crie of the Poor*, on his death in 1595. The least happy stanza from a Leics. point of view was the following:

> No groves he enclosed nor felled no wood,
> No pastures he paled to do himself good;
> To commons and county he lived a good friend,
> And gave to the needy what God did him send.

5 W. Notestein, F. H. Relf and H. Simpson, *Commons Debates, 1621* (Yale, 1935), ii, 49, 50–1. Sir Geo. Hastings was said to have had an annuity of £300 a year, which some argued was the equivalent of a freehold. Sir Edw. Coke took a large part in the debate on the constitutional issue.

6 *Return of MPs.* Sir Wolstan Dixie married Frances, dau. of Sir Thomas Beaumont of Stoughton, and his son was married into the Beaumonts of Gracedieu: J. Nichols, *Leices.* iv, 506.

7 Cf. L. A. Parker, 'The Agrarian Revolution at Cotesbach, 1501–1612', *T.L.A.S.* xxiv, 72–3; E. F. Gay, 'The Midland Revolt and the Inquisitions of Depopulation of 1607', *Trans. R. Hist. S.* (2nd ser.), xviii, 195–237; J. Stow, *Chron.*, 889.

8 Information about Leics. parliamentarians and royalists is derived from *Cal. S. P. Dom., Acts and Ord. of Interr.* (ed. Firth and Rait); *C.J.* for parliamentarians, Cal. of Proc. of Committee for Compounding, 1643–60, for royalists.

9 *Return of MPs; Complete Peerage*, vi, 175–6, for Grey of Ruthin. His father Anthony, 9th Earl of Kent, was rector of Aston Flamville (with Burbage), 1590–1643). He was 82 when he succeeded his distant cousin Hen., 8th Earl of Kent. His son had no right to the title Grey of Ruthin, which he used: *C.J.* ii, 2.

10 Belvoir Castle became a royalist stronghold in Jan. 1643, although the 8th Earl of Rutland was a parliamentarian. See p. 113, and Nichols, *Leics.* ii, 51.

11 *C.J.* ii, 641, 646, 649, 654–5; B.M. Pamphs., E. 154 (4), E. 134 (43), for the commissioners' report of their treatment at Leic.: *L.J.* v, 193, 195, 202, 203, 208; Nichols, *Leics.* iii, App. iv, 26.

12 Nichols, *Leics.* iii, App. iv, 39.

13 W. C. Abbot, *Letters and Speeches of Oliver Cromwell*, i. 228. 'I perceive Ashby-de-la-Zouch sticks much with him', wrote Cromwell.

14 Nichols, *Leics.* iii, App. iv, 36–9; B Whitelocke, *Mem. of Engl. Affairs* (1682), 105.

15 B.M. Pamphs., E. 289 (6) ('Narration of the seige and taking of the town of Leicester').

16 Ibid., E. 288 (4) ('Perfect Relation of the taking of Leicester'); H. Symonds, *Diary*, 179.

17 Hist. MSS. Com., *Hastings*, ii, 70, 141.

18 *Return of Members of Parl.*, H.C., 69 (1878), lxii (1). The Faunts had played a discreet part in the Civil War. In 1660 Geo. Faunt was worth more than £2,000 p.a. and was a prospective Kt. of the Royal Oak: Nichols, *Leics.* iv, 170. He was also a commissioner of the Leics. militia in 1660: *Acts and Ord. of Interr.*, ed. Firth and Rait, ii, 1434.

19 *C.J.* ix, 577, 596–7, 598; *Cal. S.P. Dom.*, 1679–80, 120. Voting was: Lord Sherrard 2,585, Lord Roos 2, 389, Sir John Hartopp 1,831.

20 Theophilus, 7th Earl of Huntingdon, was made Captain of the Band of Gentlemen Pensioners 27 June 1682, and a Privy Councillor 28 Feb. 1683; Hist. MSS, Com., *Hastings*, ii, 349, 173: *Hastings*, iv, 220. Cf. also *D.N.B.* In 1685 the Huntingdon influence once more made itself powerfully felt in Leic.: Leic. City MSS., Hall Bks. xix, Nos. 197, 200, 202.

21 Return of MPs; Complete Peerage (1896 ed.), 152. The Earl of Rutland was asked by the King to manage the county election: Hist. MSS. Com., *12th Rep.*, App. v, *Rut.*, ii, 85–6.

22 Charles II was so certain of Leic. that the franchise was in fact widened: cf. R. W. Greaves, *Corp. of Leic.*, 1689–1836, 8.

23 K. Feiling, *Hist. of Tory Party, 1660–1714*, 497. T. Babington's politics were rather unstable. He had been Huntingdon's candidate in 1685 (Leic. City MSS., Hall Bks., xix, no. 202); in Feb. 1688 he refused to support the repeal of the Test Act (Duckett, *Penal Laws*, i, 104), yet a year later he supported James II; but once more in 1690, he turned militant Whig and

voted for the Sacheverell Clause. He lived at Rothley Temple and was the ancestor of Lord Macaulay.

24 On 2 May 1721 the county presented a petition demanding punishment of the South Sea directors: *C.J.*, ix, 533; whereas in 1753 the county members were very attentive over the Ashby Turnpike Bill: *C.J.* xxvi, 531, 536, 543, 597, 622, 633.

25 *Return of MPs.* Wilkins was married to Rebecca, dau. of Wm. Wollaston of Shenton, whose mother was a Cave and whose grandmother was the widow of Villiers: Nichols, *Leics.* iv, 541. Wilkins was one of the first to exploit the Leics. coalfield on a large scale: *ibid.* iii, 932–3, 1125.

26 Duke of Rutland MSS., at Belvoir Castle, vol. xxi, letters of Geo. Ashby to Earl of Rutland, 17–19 Nov. 1701. Ashby received half a doe from Rutland on 19 Nov.

27 Duke of Rutland MSS., at Belvoir Castle, vol. xxi, letters of Ambrose Phillipps to Earl of Rutland, 18 Nov. 1701, and Geo. Ashby to Earl of Rutland, 19 Nov. 1701. Probably because Winstanley had Tory leanings.

28 Immediately afterwards, no doubt out of pique, the Earl of Rutland refused to recommend Beaumont for a deputy-lieutenancy: *Cal. S.P. Dom., 1702–3*, 339.

29 If we are to believe his memorial tablet in Hungerton ch., he was elected 'without any expense to himself or family'.

30 Margaret, Lady Verney, *Verney Letters of the 18th Century*, i, 325. 'Bird is supplied from above, for to be sure he has not of his own, his interest is the Duke of Rutland's and Lord Sherrard's so they must support him.'

31 Ibid., i, 329. Cf. also 'A True State of the Proc. at the Leics. Election', B.M. Historic Tracts, T. 1700 (1), probably written by Cave: Verney, *loc. cit.*

32 *C.J.* xviii, 22. Sir Thomas Cave's account of the election is to be found in Margaret, Lady Verney, *Verney Letters*, i, 327–30.

33 Hist. MSS. Com., *14th Rep.*, App. i, *Rut.*, iii, 1. 'Sir Thomas Cave interceding for Mr Wright of Eaton says that he is to be discharged from the lands he holds of the Duke because he would have voted for Cave at the last election': 19 Dec. 1771.

34 *C.J.* xix, 217, 251; Hist. MSS. Com., *12th Rep.*, App. v, *Rut.*, ii, 193. The contest was extremely close. Manners polled 2,691, Mundy 2,684: Leics. County Rec. Off., *Poll Bk. of 1719*.

35 *C.J.* xx, 39. Wigley obtained his revenge in 1737 when he was elected for Leic., defeating the Whig aristocrat's candidate, T. Ruding of Westcotes: Greaves, *Corp. of Leic.*

36 Lady Verney, *Verney Letters*, ii, 253. The poll was: Smith 2,722, Cave 2,536, Ashby 1,744. In 1734 two Tories were returned, Lord Wm. Manners being defeated. No doubt this was because of his support of Walpole and excise. For the election, cf. Leic. City Mun. Room, Hastings MSS., Bundle 18, Ambrose Phillipps to the Earl of Huntingdon, 9 Dec. 733.

37 There was only one stocking-frame in the town to every six in the county: cf. W. Felkin, *Hist. of Machine Wrought Hosiery and Lace Trade*, 177.

38 S.P. 41/30, ff. 369–70; S.P. 41/31, ff. 13, 25; W.P. 4/759, ff. 16–21. In 1758 and 1759 Rutland received insufficient support in Leics. to create a militia regiment.

39 F. O. Darvall, *Popular Disturbances in Regency Engl.*, 184; Felkin, *Hist. of Machine Wrought Hosiery*, 237 et seq.

40 *Leic. Jnl.* 3 July 1818; this was before his son became an ardent Roman Catholic: cf. G. B. Pagani, *Life of Revd. Aloysius Gentili*, 192–7;

41 C. J. Billson, *Leic. Memoirs*, 32–3; *Return of Members of Parl.*, H.C. 69 (1878), lxii (1). The voting was: Keck 3,517, Lord Robert Manners 3,000, Paget 2,203: Leics. County Rec. Off., *Poll Bk. for 1830.*

42 *Leic. Jnl.* 16 Jan. 1835. Lord Althorp's Ch. Rate Bill proposed to abolish ch. rates in return for a charge of £250,000 on the land tax: E. L. Woodward, *Age of Reform,* 492.

43 B.M. Add. MS. 40522, f. 15. Duke of Rutland to Robert Peel 1 Jan. 1843. His son, the Marquess of Granby, resigned his post in the Prince Consort's Household as a protest against the repeal of the Corn Laws. He was MP for the Northern Division at the time: B.M. Add. MS. 40583, f. 217.

44 For the growth of Roman Catholicism in north Leics., cf. Pagani, *Life of Gentili,* 178, 182, 192–4, 197, and *Dublin Rev.* xxxi, 381–2.

45 For the condition of the stockingers in the 30s and 40s, cf. T. Cooper, *Life of Thomas Cooper written by Himself,* 133–42. Also H.O. 52/24.

46 H.O. 52/26. Magistrates of Leic. to Home Sec. 13 Jan. 1835, stating that 70 special constables were sworn in for preservation of peace during the election for the southern division of the county. Also Revd. J. Dyke to Home Sec. 5 Jan. 1835.

47 Cf. his election address, printed *Leic. Jnl.* 15 Apr. 1859. 'I should oppose with a watchfulness and jealous resistance the unbounded pretensions of the Church of Rome', also *biid.* 29 April 1859, where Hartopp is described by the Revd. E. Stevenson as 'a religious tyrant'.

48 *Leic. Advertiser,* 14 Nov. 1867. Paget had twice as many votes in Leic. itself: cf. Leics. County Rec. Off., *Poll Bk. for 1867*: Paget 1,060, Pell, 504.

49 Cf. Paget's speech at Kibworth in June 1870, reported in *Leic. Advertiser,* 4 June 1870: 'The £12 voters did not give their own votes but their landlords', as they were tenants at will.'

The Organisation of the Cabinet in the Reign of Queen Anne

1 A preliminary sketch of this paper was read to the Anglo-American Historical Conference in 1955.

2 Harley's notes are to be found Brit. Mus., *Portland MSS*, List 4, 29/9: Sunderland's at Blenheim, C1-16; Dartmouth's at The William Salt Library, Stafford. I am indebted to the Duke of Portland, the Duke of Marlborough, and the Earl of Dartmouth for permission to use, and to quote from, these documents. Harley's and Dartmouth's notes are chronologically arranged and references to these are by date only; Sunderland's are not chronologically arranged, so reference is given below by the Blenheim class mark. E. R. Turner glanced at Dartmouth's notes but failed to realise their importance, and subsequently he made the remarkable statement that no sequence of minutes of either the cabinet or the committee had survived. E. R. Turner, *The Cabinet council of England in the Seventeenth and Eighteenth Centuries, 1622–1784* (Baltimore and Oxford, 1930–2), i. 168 n. 53, 188.
    [Since writing this note the Blenheim archives have been sold to the British Library where they are now deposited.]

3 *Blenheim MSS* C1–16, D67.

4 There is a serious gap in Harley's notes from 8 September to 10 November 1706. In 1707 the bulk of Harley's notes deal with cabinet business, yet Sunderland's memoranda make it clear that he was present at the committee. His notes for these meetings must be lost. Sunderland often refers to meetings for which there are no notes surviving.

5 *Blenheim MSS* C1–16, E35, F3.

6 Ibid., C4, 24, 34; D2, 4, 17, 36–7, 71, 81; E42–3. For the most recent account of this expedition *cf.* Gerald S. Graham, *The Walker Expedition to Quebec* (Navy Records Soc., 1953).

7 Ibid., B8, 10; E29–30; F4–6; for Peterborough, D31–3; for Greg, F12.

8 Ibid., B38; A. Browning, *Thomas Osborne, Earl of Danby and Duke of Leeds, 1637–1712* (Glasgow, 1951), does not mention either these rumours or the investigation.

9 E. R. Turner, *Cabinet Council*, ii. ix–xiv, lists the literature of the controversy up to the date of its publication. Cf. also Stanley Pargellis and D. J. Medley, *Bibliography of British History, The Eighteenth Century*, pp. 65–6.

10 Wolfgang, Michael, *Englische Geschichte im Achtzehnten Jahrhundert* (Leipzig, Berlin and Basel, 1896–1955), i. 440; iii. 546–92. Michael was in substantial agreement with F. Salomon, *Geschichte des Letzen Ministeriums Königin Annas von England* (Gotha, 1894), p. 356. Turner's criticism of Michael and Salomon is *op. cit.* i. 355–61, and Michael's of Turner, *Englische Geschichte*, iii. 551 *et seq.*

11 E. Trevor Williams, 'The Cabinet in the Eighteenth Century', *History*, N.S. xxii (1937), 240–52; 332–4.

12 References to these sources will be found scattered throughout Turner's footnotes. Nottingham's notes are in Brt. Mus., *Add. MS* 29591: Bolingbroke's, P.R.O., *S.P. Dom.*, 34/3.

13 The principal cause of confusion arose because the formal name of the members of the cabinet was 'Lords of the Committee of the Privy Council' and all ministers had to be sworn members of the privy council before they could sit in the cabinet. In casual speech and writing reference was often to 'The Lords', 'The Lords of the Committee', 'The Lords of the Cabinet' or, more rarely, 'The Lords of the Council', but even Turner recognised that men in business kept mostly to a uniform usage. 'Lords of the Committee' or 'Lords' referred in the vast majority of cases to meetings without the sovereign, and this practice became much more uniform as Queen Anne's reign progressed. Nottingham, whose experience dated from the early part of William's reign, was the most careless of all. The difficulties caused by this somewhat casual nomenclature disappear when the organisation of the two bodies and their functions are understood.

14 *Dartmouth MSS.*

15 Brit. Mus., *Add. MS* 29588, fo. 265; *Cal. S.P. Dom.* 1702–3, p. 239.

16 E.g. meetings of 6 July 1704 and 18 August 1704 were held at secretary Hedges' house. Brit. Mus., *Portland MSS*, List 4, 29/9.

17 *Cal. S.P. Dom.* 1700–2, p. 242; 1702–3, p. 725.

18 *Dartmouth MSS*, 30 October 1710. 'Mr de Torcy and Marshall Tallard's letters were read and ordered to be reconsidered when my Ld. Privy Seall comes to town.' Harley, too, begged him to take a more active interest and tried by flattery to draw him closer to the ministry. Hist. MSS Com. (13

Rep., app., pt. ii), *Portland MSS*, ii. 223–6. Newcastle was not ill during this period; his death in July 1711 was quite unexpected.

19 Ibid., p. 223. Somerset attended his last meeting of the cabinet at Kensington Palace on 17 September 1710. *Dartmouth MSS*. Jonathan Swift wrote on 13 August 1711, 'The reason why the cabinet council was not held last night was because Mr Secretary St. John would not sit with your duke of Somerset. So today the duke was forced to go to the race while the cabinet was held. *Journal to Stella*, ed. H. Williams (Oxford, 1948), i. 332 and n. 6. Erasmus Lewis, who was Dartmouth's under-secretary, denied this rumour, but historians have uncritically repeated it. If there was any substance in Swift's rumour, it can only mean that Somerset was trying to force himself back into the cabinet after nearly a year's absence, which is improbable, for such an action would have given rise to widespread comment.

20 *Townshend MSS*, Raynham Hall, Norfolk. I am indebted to the Marquess Townshend for permission to use these manuscripts, 'Cabinet memoranda' of Charles, 2nd viscount Townshend. Also, Turner, *Cabinet Council*, ii. 1–2. Archbishop Tenison did his major stint of committee work during the summer months when other cabinet ministers were often on vacation.

21 *Portland MSS*, ii. 200.

22 J. Swift, *Journal to Stella*, ii. 434, 436–7.

23 Brit. Mus., *Portland MSS*, List 4, 29/9. *Portland MSS*, ii. 208.

24 E. Trevor Williams, 'The Cabinet in the Eighteenth Century', 242–3.

25 *Dartmouth MSS*, 24, 25, 26 August 1710.

26 Brit. Mus., *Portland MSS*, List 4, 29/9. *Cal. S.P. Dom.* 1702–3, p. 21.

27 References are too numerous to give. Almost every memorandum relating to the committee mentions such interviews and discussions.

28 E. R. Turner, 'The development of the Cabinet 1688–1760', *American Hist. Rev.*, xviii (1913), 766–7.

29 *Dartmouth MSS*, 11 February 1711. Argyll was summoned to attend by letter from Dartmouth, E. R. Turner, *Cabinet Council*, i, 181–2 and n. 114.

30 *Blenheim MSS* C1–16, D42, D71.

31 Brit. Mus., *Portland MSS*, List 4, 29/9, 2–9 July 1704.

32 Brit. Mus., *Add. MS* 29589, fo. 96. Godolphin wrote to Nottingham 19 August 1703, 'Yor Lordship knows that a resolution taken in the cabinett councill ought not to be altered but in the same place'.

33 *Dartmouth MSS*, various dates.

34 Ibid. 26 September 1710, cabinet, 'The petition of Balthasar St. Michell rejected'. For St. Michell, *cf.* Helen Truesdell Heath, *The Letters of Samuel Pepys and his Family Circle* (Oxford, 1955), pp. xxiv-xxviii, 228–9.

35 Ibid, 17 November 1710. Other surprisingly trivial matters to reach cabinet level were the condition of the lions in the Tower (*Blenheim MSS* C1–16, F 29) and the affair of Lord Stanhope's French cook, who has been brought to England without authority in 1710. Dartmouth's memoranda refer to this vexed question time and time again.

36 Palatines: *Blenheim MSS* C1–16, D44–7, *Dartmouth MSS* 18 January 1711 *et seq.*; parliamentary bills: *Dartmouth MSS* 19, 26 November 1710, 2 January and 4 February 1711; East India Company: *biid.* 1 and 2 April 1711, *Blenheim MSS* C1–16, D72; plantations: ibid., C1–16, D71, *Dartmouth MSS* 19 September 1710, 25 February 1711; judges: ibid. 24 February 1711; proclamations: *Blenheim MSS* C1–16, C12, F27, F37. This list is not, of course, comprehensive: it could be greatly enlarged.

37 *Blenheim MSS* C1–16, A1, B51, C1, D53; *Dartmouth MSS* 18 April 1711.

38 *Blenheim MSS* C1–16, D28–9. John Chudleigh finally obtained his commission in the Coldstream Guards on 25 October 1707. C. Dalton, *English Army Lists*, vi. 55.

39 *Dartmouth MSS* 16 March 1711.

40 Ibid., 26 November 1710.

41 *Dartmouth MSS* 11 March 1711; cf. also *Blenheim MSS* C1–16, F15, for a suggestion that there might be secret matters about strategy that were not disclosed to the entire cabinet.

42 For a discussion of the different attitudes of Harley and St. John concerning the Quebec expeditions, cf. W. T. Morgan, 'Queen Anne's Expedition of 1711', *Queen's Quarterly*, XXXV (1928), 464–6.

43 Brit. Mus., *Add. MS* 29591, fos. 29, 32–4, 128–31, 135–6.

44 Many such meetings are reported by Swift: e.g. 19 January 1712, 'I dined today with lord treasurer; this is his day of choice company; where they sometimes admit me, but pretend to grumble. And today they met on some extraordinary business; the keeper, steward, both secretaries, lord Rivers, and lord Angelsey.' *Journal to Stella*, ii. 467.

45 These have been deposited by the Marquess of Downshire at Berkshire Record Office. I am indebted to Mr Peter Walne for drawing my attention to them.

46 *Townshend MSS* (Raynham); P.R.O. *S.P. Dom.* 35/23, 29, 31, 32.

47 For further discussion of this question cf. J. H. Plumb, *Sir Robert Walpole*, i. 201–3.

48 An exact and lucid account of the cabinet in the late 1739s will be found in R. Sedgwick, 'The Inner Cabinet from 1739 to 1741', *Eng. Hist. Rev.*, xxxiv (1919), 290–302.

49 In addition to the memoranda scattered throughout the *State Papers Domestic* at the Public Record Office and the *Newcastle MSS* (particularly Brit. Mus., *Add. MSS* 32993–33002, 33004), there are others, made both by Townshend and by Spencer Compton, in the possession of Mr H. L. Bradfer-Lawrence, who has very kindly permitted me to use them.

50 E. R. Turner, *Cabinet Council*, i. 345–87. In these pages Turner very fairly sets out the difficulties and confusions caused by the slight and secondary nature of his evidence and by the absence of any continuous series of minutes or memoranda.

The Growth of the Electorate in England from 1600 to 1715

This article is based on a paper given at the Conference of British Studies held at the University of Kansas in October 1968. It first appeared in *Past and Present: A Journal of Historical Studies* no. 45 (November 1969) pp. 90–116. World Copyright: The Past and Present Society, 175 Banbury Road, Oxford.

1 See Bernard Bailyn, *The Ideological Origins of the American Revolution* (Cambridge, Mass., 1967); also his *The Origins of American Politics* (New York, 1968), and J. R. Pole, *Political Representation in England and the Origins of the American Republic* (London, 1966).

2 [Thomas Gordon and John Trenchard], *Cato's Letters*, 3rd edn (London, 1733), iii, p. 11. For Trenchard, see Caroline Robbins, *The Eighteenth-Century Commonwealthman* (Harvard, 1959), pp. 115–25.

3 Quoted by Michael Walzer, *The Revolution of the Saints* (London, 1966), p. 259.

4 The growth of the political pamphlet in the first half of the seventeenth century and its proliferation in the second still awaits its historian.

5 Nineteen pamphlets were printed in February 1715, all directed at the freeholder's vote in the imminent general election: *The Monthly Catalogue 1714–17*, repr. by the English Bibliographical Society, 1st ser. (1964), pp. 57–63.

6 It was not always pamphlets that were distributed. In 1721, with an eye on the 1722 election, the Earl of Sunderland had C. King's, *The British Merchant or Commerce Preserv'd*, 3 vols sent to every parliamentary borough for the use of the inhabitants; Godfrey Davies, *Bibliography of British History, Stuart Period, 1603–1714* (Oxford, 1928), p. 186. The past was also readily invoked. In preparation for the Yorkshire election in 1734, the Tories published, suitably edited, Sir John Reresby's *Memoirs* to justify Tory policy since the reign of Charles II; not to be outdone the Whigs published *The Revolution in Politics*, in serial form, eight cheap parts so that the poorer freeholders could afford to buy them: *Memoirs of Sir John Reresby*, ed. A. Browning (Glasgow, 1936), p. x, n. 1; J. H. Plumb, *Sir Robert Walpole* (1960), ii, p. 314.

7 L. B. Namier, *The Structure of Politics on the Accession of George III*, 2nd ed. (London, 1957), p. 73; R. R. Walcott, *English Politics in the Early Eighteenth Century* (Oxford, 1956), pp. 9–10.

8 Principally Dr W. A. Speck of Newcastle University, but the subject is huge and the pastures as plentiful as they are lush.

9 F. F. Jacob, *The Fifteenth Century 1399–1485* (Oxford, 1961), p. 415. Also M. McKisack, *Parliamentary Representation of English Boroughs during the Middle Ages* (Oxford, 1932); J. S. Roskell, *The Commons in Parliament in 1442* (Manchester, 1954). There is also a very valuable short article by K. N. Houghton 'A Document Concerning the Parliamentary Election at Shrewsbury in 1478', *Trans. of the Shropshire Arch. Soc.*, lvii (1961–4), pp. 162–5, where it is argued that there was a growing recognition 'by the end of the fifteenth century that the electors might be faced with a choice of candidates, to be determined by a majority decision'. However, this appears in a number of the cases cited to be a widening *within the corporation*, not an extension to voters outside it. For example, two corporations quoted by Mr Houghton – Exeter and King's Lynn – were in fact closed and narrow electorates throughout the sixteenth century. The freemen in Exeter had no vote until 1627 (see below, pp. 101–2). King's Lynn did drop an elaborate procedure in 1525, when the twelve leading burgesses gave up the right to elect, but that right remained limited to the two corporate bodies – the twenty-four and twenty-seven. the freemen (about 200) did not secure the right to vote until the Long Parliament. *Hist. MSS Comm., 11th Report*, iii, pp. ix–x, 179. However, the extension, even if small and mainly within the corporate body, is worth more detailed study.

10 In the Parliament of 1621: see Wallace Notestein, Francis Helen Relf, Hartley Simpson, *Commons Debates 1621* (New Haven, 1935), pp. iv, 421–2 and below.

11 J. E. Neale, *The Elizabethan House of Commons* (London, 1949), pp. 261–72.

12 Patrick Collinson, 'John Field and Elizabethan Puritanism', in *Essays Presented to Sir John Neale*, ed. S. T. Bindoff, J. Hursfield and C. H. Williams (London, 1961), p. 159. Michael Walzer, ;*v11cit*., p. 135, points out that these early Puritan divines, Cartwright, Rogers, Field, etc. were sons of skilled craftsmen or yeomen, typical forty-shillings freeholders in fact.

13 Neale, *The Eliabethan House of Commons*, pp. 250–4.

14 Collinson, *op. cit.*, pp. 153–5.

15 For example, irregularities at Shrewsbury were dealt with in April 1604: the following resolution was passed on 25 June 1604 'that from, and after the end of this present Parliament, no Mayor of any City, Burrough or Town corporate should be elected, returned or allowed to sit as a Member of this House'. *House of Commons Journal* (hereafter cited as *HCJ*), ii, p. 201; p. 296. For Goodwin's Case, see J. P. Kenyon, *The Stuart Constitution* (Cambridge, 1966), pp. 25, 27.

16 The only recent work of value on this subject is by Richard L. Bushman, 'English Franchise Reform in the Seventeenth Century', *JL. of British Studies*, iii (1963), pp. 36–56. However, the appendix to this article is inadequate.

17 Not all corporations succumbed to the gentry or even shared their representation with them. Of the members who represented Exeter between 1537 and 1640 only eight were from gentry families and these were elected in the sixteenth century: Wallace T. MacCaffrey, *Exeter, 1540–1640* (Harvard University Press, 1958), pp. 224–5.

18 *HCJ.*, ii, pp. 556, 570–1, 677–8, 687, 801–4. For the ill of 1621, see Notestein, Simpson, Relf, *Commons Debates 1621*, iv, pp. 421–2.

19 *HJC.*, ii, p. 884. The Committee of Privileges 'held it inconvenient to have them set down their names: because notice might then be taken of them, to their prejudice'.

20 Notestein, Relf, Simpson, *Commons Debates 1621*, iii, p. 412; iv, p. 446.

21 *HCJ.*, ii, pp. 158–60, 509. This attitude had a long history: see Neale, *The Elizabethan House of Commons*.

22 *HCJ.*, ii, p. 161: Bucks. Co. 1604. The sheriff 'desired every gentleman to deal with his freeholders', which indicates clearly enough the relationship between gentry and freeholders; and this was always to be true of the majority, but see pp. 104–7.

23 Neale, *The Elizabethan House of Commons*, pp. 140–5. Over 50 per cent of the boroughs in 1689 with electorates of less than 500 votes, that is the most manageable part of the Commons, were the results of Tudor revival or enfranchisement, i.e. the rotten part of the Constitution was a Tudor creation.

24 For the revival of parliamentary boroughs, see the very valuable article by Lady Evangeline de Villiers, 'Parliamentary Boroughs Restored by the House of Commons 1621–41', *Eng. Hist. Rev.*, lxvii (1952), pp. 175–202. Lady de Villiers, however, does not discuss the question of franchise. James I, who thought that there were far too many decayed boroughs sending representatives and refused to consent to the enfranchisement of Durham until Old Sarum was disenfranchised, nevertheless revived or created a few boroughs. They were:

1604 Evesham; Harwich

1605   Bewdley
1610   Tewkesbury
1614   Bury St Edmunds
1615   Tiverton

Lady Villiers points out that, apart from Bewdley, these were all towns of economic and social importance and she thinks that the boroughs restored by the Commons compare very unfavourably with them. The Commons boroughs, she considers, were 'rotten' from the start (ibid., p. 183). However, in this she is mistaken. The franchise tells a different story. Harwich had 32 electors; Bewdley (until 1679) thirteen; Tewkesbury (until 1640) probably 24; Bury St Edmunds 37 and Tiverton 25 – very convenient elections to control. I am uncertain about Evesham, where the franchise may have been in the freemen from its revival in 1604 which, if this is so, would have given it an electorate of around 250, about the same as Hertford. The boroughs revived by the Commons, however, had wide franchises, comparatively large electorates and were strongly contested. In these contests, the inhabitants played their part – unusual activities in a 'rotten' borough. See M. R. Frear, 'The Election at Great Marlow in 1640', *Jl. of Modern History*, xiv (1942), pp. 433–48. In 1640, the inhabitants of Great Marlow wanted to be represented by two opposition members whom they could trust, namely Peregrine Hoby and Bulstrode Whitelocke. As their leader Toucher Carter, 'a country fellow in plain and mean habit', told Whitelocke, 'it being no corporation, all the inhabitants had their votes in the election, and most of the ordinary people would be for Hoby and Whitelocke' (ibid., p. 438). So perhaps the boroughs revived by the Commons were not so rotten as they seemed. They certainly proved less manageable than James I's revivals. Once a wide franchise has been created and there are more than a 100 voters, the problems of patronage become more difficult, particularly in times of political crisis.

25 *HCJ.*, ii, p. 568.
26 Ibid., p. 686.
27 Ibid., p. 714.
28 Ibid., p. 792; also John Glanville, *Reports* (London, 1775), pp. 107–8.
29 *HCJ.*
30 See J. H. Plumb, *Growth of Political Stability* (London, 1967), pp. 48–9.
31 Shrewsbury was probably the largest at about 450. Attempts, however, were made to enlarge this further in 1604 when the sheriff tried to poll the inhabitants: *HCJ.*, ii, p. 201.
32 MacCaffrey, *Exeter 1540–1640*, pp. 223–4. For other boroughs, particularly Reading, see E. C. Whitworth, 'The Parliamentary Franchise in the English Boroughs during the Stuart Period' (London Univ. M.A. Thesis, 1920). For Hakewell's part in the revival of the Buckinghamshire boroughs, see Lady de Villiers, 'Parliamentary Boroughs Restored by the House of Commons', pp. 175–90. Hakewell possessed an estate in Buckinghamshire.
33 MacCaffrey, *Exeter, 1540–1640*, pp. 199, 223, 273; J. J. Alexander, 'Exeter Members of Parliament', pt. iii, *Report and Trans. of the Devonshire Assoc.*, lxi (1929), pp. 195–6; Frances Rose-Troup, 'An Exeter Worthy and His Biographer', ibid., xxxiv (1897), p. 252.
34 MacCaffrey, *op. cit.*, p. 218; Ferdinando Nicolls, *The Life and Death of*

Ignatius Jurdain (London, 1654). Jourdain had experienced conversion as an adolescent whilst living in Guernsey. He had been 'new borne'.

35 D'Ewes' views were based on what he regarded as constitutional legality. He argued strongly on behalf of the right of the poor of Great Marlow to vote. 'I moved that the poorest man ought to have a voice that it was the birthright of the subjects of England and that all had voices in the Election of Knights etc.': *The Journal of Simon D'Ewes*, ed. Wallace Notestein (New Haven, Yale University Press, 1923), p. 43. On the other hand, he disapproved very much of the fact that the Commons in 1640 had accepted as valid many writs signed by the commonalty and not by the mayor or bailiff, who for D'Ewes were the only legal returning officers. For D'Ewes, as I suspect for most, it was not a question of extending the electorate, but declaring ancient rights. D'Ewes was a precisian, not a politician.

36 *The Journal of Simon D'Ewes*, ed. Notestein, pp. 431–2; D. Brunton and D. H. Penington, *Members of the Long Parliament* (London, 1954), p. 136 for Oldsworth; also Violet A. Rowe, 'The Influence of the Earl of Pembroke in Parliamentary Elections, 1625–1640', *Eng. Hist. Rev.*, 1 (1935), pp. 242–56. Naturally the opposition did not wish to upset so powerful an ally as Pembroke: political necessity was stronger than their dedication to principles relating to the franchise. Yet there were others, apart from D'Ewes, who put them first. They were a minority.

37 It is remarkable that there is, as yet, no general study of the growth of political propaganda in England. By the time Thomason's collection starts in 1640, it is fully fledged, but its origins are obscure. Its growth must be related to an awareness of opinion and a desire to influence it: that is, an electorate to sway. On this subject see Godfrey Davies, 'English Political Sermons', *Huntington Lib. Quart.*, iii (1939), pp. 1–22. And, of course, there was just as much awareness by Charles i and Archbishop Laud of the need for propaganda.

38 Neale, *The Elizabethan House of Commons*, p. 135.

39 Alan Everitt, *The Community of Kent and the Great Rebellion* (Leicester, 1966), pp. 76–83.

40 Frank W. Jessup, *Sir Roger Twysden, 1597–1672* (London, 1965), p. 141, n. 1, refers to the existence of this MS. which had been bought by Sir Thomas Phillips (Phillips MS. 16083) in 1858. It was sold in the Phillips sale in 1967 and found its way, via a Kentish bookseller, to the Bodleian Library where it is now: MS. Top. Kent e.6. The detailed lists deserve analysis.

41 It should be noted that Dering did not blame a landlord or one of the gentry for this default.

42 By 'obscure' Sir Edward meant, of course, men of obscure birth, of low social standing.

43 Bodl., MS. Top. Kent e.6.

44 Ibid.

45 For these counties see C. A. Holmes, 'The Eastern Association' (Cambridge University PhD thesis, 1969), pp. 42–53.

46 Jessup brings out clearly the tangle of family and political issues that were involved in these elections: *op. cit.*, pp. 137–44.

47 Brit. Mus., Egerton MS. 2646, fo. 142. I am indebted to my colleague, Dr C. A. Holmes, for this reference.

48 See Holmes, *op. cit.*, pp. 70, 82–4.

49 Valerie Pearl, *London and the Outbreak of the Puritan Revolution* (Oxford, 1966).
50 A. S. P. Woodhouse, *Puritanism and Liberty* (London, 1938), pp. 52–85.
51 Vernon F. Snow, 'Parliamentary Re-apportionment Proposals in the Puritan Revolution', *Eng. Hist. Rev.*, lxxiv (1959), pp. 409–92.
52 Of course, the nature of the franchise was only one aspect of elections which troubled the opposition, whether it was the parliamentary puritans of the 1620s or the Levellers of the 1640s; they were concerned about the freedom of elections. The Levellers, unlike the parliamentary opposition of the 1620s, were also concerned with the distribution of seats. There is no indication that this greatly troubled members in the 1620s; indeed the reverse is true. In their Bill for 1621, they accepted that there would be boroughs with less than 24 voters: Notestein, Simpson and Relf, *Commons Debates 1621*, iv, pp. 421–2.
53 Plumb, *The Growth of Political Stability*, pp. 40–1.
54 Ibid., pp. 41–5.
55 Ibid., p. 43, n. 1.
56 These figures are based on the Suffolk poll books for the general elections of 1701, 1702, 1705, 1710: in the possession of the West Suffolk Rec. Off. (1701, 1702 [Cullum Library]), the East Suffolk Rec. Off. (1710) and the Society of Genealogists (1705). I am indebted to Dr W. A. Speck for the loan of his copy of the latter.
57 Cockermouth Castle, Leconfield MSS.
58 *The Poll Books for Nottingham and Nottinghamshire, 1710*, ed. Myrtle J. Read and Viet W. Walker (Thoroton Soc. Rec. Ser., 1957), p. xviii. The biographical index by Miss Walker is the only fully detailed analysis of a poll book that we possess as yet. Norwich poll books for 1710 and 1715 are in the Guildhall Library, London.
59 All the following details are taken from the poll books listed above.
60 The smaller the number of voters in a village, the more likely they are to vote Whig or Tory as a bloc. It is very rare for a village of more than six or seven voters to be unanimous in its politics.
61 The franchise at Mitchell was in the inhabitants paying scot and lot.
62 See also the valuable computer analysis of Hampshire by W. A. Speck and W. A. Gray to be published in the *Bull. of the Inst. of Hist. Res.* I am grateful to the authors for allowing me to see this.
63 *The Growth of Political Stability*, esp. chap. iii.
64 See my 'Political Man', pp. 135–149.

Political Man

1 For a fuller discussion of the growth of the electorate in the seventeenth century and its consequences for the politics of the period 1689–1715 see J. H. Plumb, *The Growth of Political Stability in England, 1675–1725* (London, 1967), pp. 34–47.
2 Ibid., pp. 66–97.
3 John Smith (1655–1723) of South Tedworth, Hants. A leading Whig, a friend of the Junto who was a Lord of the Treasury from 1694 to 1702; Chancellor of the Exchequer 1699–1701, 1708–10; Commissioner of the Union with Scotland 1706; Speaker 1705–8. A close friend of Sir Robert

Walpole, he sat in Parliament 1679–81, 1691–1723. (*Dictionary of National Biography*.) William Bromley (1664–1732) of Bagington, Warwickshire, a leading Tory who was Commissioner of Public Accounts 1696–1705; Speaker 1710–13; Secretary of State 1713–14. MP 1689–98, 1701–32. (*Dictionary of National Biography*.)

4 W. A. Speck, 'The Choice of a Speaker in 1705', *Bulletin of the Institute of Historical Research*, XXXVII (1964), 20–35.

5 Camb. Univ. Lib. C(*holmondeley*) H(*oughton*) MSS, Charles Turner to Robert Walpole, 31 October 1705.

6 The votes of the House of Commons were printed; totals of divisions were given, not names of voters.

7 A seat at Amersham (Bucks) was under dispute. This is described as a pocket borough of the Drakes (Tories, by Walcott (Robert Walcott, *English Politics in the Early Eighteenth Century* (Oxford, 1956), pp. 13, 40). However, in 1705 party division reared its head. Sir Samuel Garrard, one of the Tory members, afterwards the Lord Mayor of London who invited Sacheverell to preach in 1710, had supported the Tack, and Sir Thomas Webster, an ardent and rich Whig, decided to oppose him. Two polls were taken because Webster insisted that all inhabitants not receiving alms had the right to vote: the Tories maintained only those paying church rates had the right. The two polls were:

	Inhabitants	Ratepayers
Viscount Newhaven (T)	90	58
Sir Samuel Garrard (T)	84	54
Sir Thomas Webster (W)	91	41

The interesting fact here is the very considerable support given to Sir Thomas Webster in a tiny town dominated by the great estate of Shardeloes which belonged to the Drakes. Doubtless Webster's money helped to strengthen some Whig sentiments, but he also possessed a solid voting base. This is an excellent illustration of the strength of party in a closed borough (see *Hist. MSS Comm.* XV, app. 4,180), but there are many others.

8 These figures refer to the division on the choice of Speaker: Smith won by 248 to 205. Seymour had led the opposition to Smith.

9 C(*holmondeley*) H(*oughton*) MSS, John Turner to Robert Walpole, 7 December 1705.

10 For these and further examples, see J. H. Plumb, *the Growth of Political Stability in England, 1675–1725* (London, 1967), pp. 66–97; L. B. Namier, *The Structure of Politics at the Accession of George III* (2nd ed, London, 1961), pp. 102–4; G. Rudé, *The Crowd in History* (New York, 1964), pp. 47–64.

11 Plumb, *op. cit.* pp. 78f. For Buckingham, F. P. and M. M. Verney, *Memoirs of the Verney Family during the Seventeenth Century*(London, 1907), II, 380–8.

12 For the way votes were carefully scrutinised, see J. H. Plumb, *Sir Robert Walpole* (London, 1960), II, 322.

13 In 1784 Chester cost the Grosvenors £8,500 for food and drink for 3,000 electors: Gervas Huxley, *Lady Elizabeth and the Grosvenors* (London, 1965), pp. 85–6. Essex in 1763 is said to have cost both sides over £30,000:

L. B. Namier and J. Brooke, *History of Parliament 1754–90* (London, 1964), I, 4.

14 L. B. Namier and J. Brooke, *op. cit.*, I, 9. At six general elections during this period there were only 37 county contests out of a possible 240.

15 Ibid., I *passim.*

16 C(*holmondeley*) H(*oughton*) MSS, John Wrott to Robert Walpole, 31 May 1710; G. Rudé, *The Crowd in History*, p. 35. He cites riots in South Yorkshire and Nottinghamshire in 1791 and 1798 respectively.

17 Leon Radzinowitz, *A History of English Criminal Law* (London, 1948), I, 4–5. 'Broadly speaking, in the course of the hundred and sixty years from the Restoration to the death of George III, the number of capital offences had increased by about one hundred and ninety.'

18 L. W. Hanson, *The Government and the Press* (Oxford, 1936), p. 85. Also, C(*holmondeley*) H(*oughton*) MSS, 74, folios 12, 13, 64.

19 J. H. Plumb, *Sir Robert Walpole*, II, 142.

20 John Loftis, *The Politics of Drama in Augustan England* (Oxford, 1963), pp. 63–127.

21 Nicolas Hans, *New Trends in Education in the Eighteenth Century* (London, 1951).

22 G. A. Cranfield, *The Development of the Provincial Newspaper, 1700–1760* (Oxford, 1962), pp. 215–16.

23 Ibid., pp. 168–206.

24 The only copy of this newspaper is in my possession. Many issues contain detailed reports from America, for example 4 August 1768, which prints three and a half columns on riots in Boston; pro-American arguments were printed and so too were the arguments of 'Scrutator', who followed 'the Pennsylvanian Farmer's insidious epistles' and wrote to refute them (4 August 1768). The paper was much more strongly biased towards Wilkes than towards the American colonies, although again the paper was careful to print an occasional satirical thrust at Wilkes himself (e.g. 18 August 1768 – the Strutter to J. Wilkes, Esq.). There were at least two debating societies in Liverpool at this time, the Conversation Club and the Debating Society, which concerned themselves with politics, the latter being the more radical. A similar awareness of political issues and widespread public interest in politics existed throughout the West Midlands, particularly Birmingham.

25 Ann Finer and George Savage, *The Selected Letters of Josiah Wedgwood* (London, 1965).

26 R. S. Fitton and A. P. Wadsworth, *The Strutts and the Arkwrights* (Manchester, 1958).

27 G. Rudé, *Wilkes and Liberty* (Oxford, 1962), pp. 220–3; Also 'The Middlesex Electors', *EHR* (1960), pp. 601–17.

28 J. H. Plumb, *Sir Robert Walpole*, II, 251–67; E. R. Turner, 'The Excise Crisis', *EHR* (1927), pp. 34–57.

29 Anthony Lincoln, English Dissent, 1763–1800 (Cambridge, 1938); Eugene Charlton Black, *The Association* (Cambridge, Mass., 1963), pp. 174–212.

30 *The Diary of Sylas Neville 1767–1788*, ed. Basil Cozens-Hardy (Oxford, 1950), pp. 90–1, 149. See also Caroline Robbins's pioneer work, *The Eighteenth Century Commonwealthman* (Cambridge, Mass., 1959).

31 Black, *op. cit.* pp. 31–130; H. Butterfield, *George III, Lord North and the People 1779–80* (London, 1949), pp. 229–68.

32 César de Saussure, *A Foreign View of England in the Reigns of George I and George* (London, 1902), p. 162.
33 G. Rudé, *The Crowd in History 1730–48*, particularly chapter IV, 'Labour Disputes in Eighteenth-Century England'.
34 Nicolas Hans, *New Trends in Education in the Eighteenth Century* (London, 1951), p. 177.
35 P. S. Foner, *The Complete Writings of Thomas Paine*, ed. P. S. Foner (New York, 1945), II, 910. 'At least one hundred thousand copies of the cheap edition were sold in England, Ireland, and Scotland' (ibid., I, XXX).
36 Quoted by James T. Boulton, *The Language of Politics in the Age of Wilkes and Burke* (London, 1963), p. 138. Also M. G. Jones, *Hannah More* (Cambridge, 1952), p. 133, where it is reported that pt II was found 'lurking at the bottom of mines and coalpits'. And A. Temple Patterson, *Radical Leicester* (Leicester, 1959), p. 72.
37 Of course some rich men stayed loyal to their reformist principles, more it would seem in the provinces than the metropolis. Josiah Wedgwood welcomed the French Revolution, as did Thomas Walker of Manchester to his cost. See Frida Knight, *The Strange Case of T. Walker* (London, 1957).
38 *The American Correspondence of a Bristol Merchant 1766–1776*, ed. G. H. Guttridge (Berkeley, Calif., 1934), p. 6; Namier and Brooke, *History of Parliament 1754–1790*, I, 206–7; W. E. Minchinton, *Politics and the Port of Bristol in the Eighteenth Century* (Bristol, 1963), p. xxxi.
39 *Wedgwood MSS* (Barlaston). Josiah Wedgwood to Thomas Bentley 7 August 1779. Wedgwood remained unconvinced by those radicals who opposed raising a regiment of militia in Staffordshire in order to free troops for America. 'I am not at present fully convinced by them, that it is better to fall a prey to a foreign enemy rather than defend ourselves under the present ministry. Methinks I would defend the land of my nativity, my family and friends against a foreign foe, where conquest and slavery were inseparable, under any leaders – the best I could get for the moment, and wait for better times to displace an obnoxious minister, and settle domestic affairs, rather than rigidly say, I'll be saved in my own way and by people of my own choice, or perish and perish my country with me.' I owe this quotation to Mr Neil McKendrick.
40 For Hannah More, see M. C. Jones, *Hannah More* (Cambridge, 1952). For the growth of working-class literacy, R. K. Webb, *The British Working Class Reader 1790–1848* (London, 1955); Donald Read, *Press and People 1790–1850* (London, 1961).
41 Temple Patterson, *op. cit.*, pp. 146–55, 186–8.

The Historian's Dilemma

1 Hans Meyerhoff, *The Philosophy of History in our Time* (New York, 1951), p. 22.
2 Not all generalisations, of course; one of the favourite pastimes of professional historians is the creation of the doubtful hypothesis, usually in a field where the data of argument is sufficient for plausibility but completely inadequate to settle the question: two examples from British history – the rise of the gentry of the late sixteenth century; the increased fertility of marriage after 1750. Both have stimulated massive research, full of fasci-

nating detail; neither hypothesis has been proved or disproved or is likely to be.

3 Indeed too much satire. The philosophers of the Enlightenment were neither wildly optimistic nor unaware of the tenuous nature of human progress – material or cultural. They were as aware of the passionate, instinctive and destructive sides of human nature as all intelligent men must be.

4 One might ask oneself what is all science but contemporary science, never fixed, never final.

5 Yet it must be stressed once again that the philosophers of the Enlightenment hoped that man might do this; they had confidence in man's intellectual powers to secure a more rational and just world, and hope and confidence are not the same as blind faith.

6 Sir Lewis Namier's attitude was somewhat ambivalent. He would seem to have considered the main value of history as mainly personal and psychological. He believed it could deepen the wisdom of the wise, breed a healthy scepticism in the learned, and even, on occasion, teach a lesson. In general, his position was first cousin to Veronica Wedgwood's. His sympathies, however, were deeply conservative and he was mightily suspicious of general concepts.

7 'Providential' historians might argue that goodwill triumphs over evil, and that mankind will slowly and painfully achieve a higher state of spiritual awareness and that material progress need not be inimical to much spiritual improvement: few do.

8 This, of course, is not to deny the existence of either brutality or victimisation. There was plenty of both.

9 See P. Geyl, *Debates with Historians* (The Hague, 1955), pp. 18–34.

G. M. Trevelyan

1 Cf. Trevelyan's essay 'The Middle Marches' in *Clio: a Muse* (1913).

2 Not the same, as Trevelyan is careful to stress in his admirable memoir of his father, *Sir George Otto Trevelyan: A Memoir* (1932).

3 Winston Churchill has said that Somervell taught him his mastery of English. To have helped produce two such masters of our language as Churchill and Trevelyan is indeed a claim to fame.

4 Of course, Trevelyan was a young man of means, and could afford to quit an assured position. In any case he could easily have maintained himself by his writing, but whether the choice would have been so easy had he been without private means is an interesting speculation.

5 The battle of Dunbar is dealt with in five lines.

6 *English Historical Review*, vol. 20, pp. 403–4.

7 Theodore Macaulay Trevelyan, who tragically died in 1911, aged five.

8 What Italy meant to men of culture in the nineteenth century is described by Trevelyan himself in his essay: 'Englishmen and Italians', published in *Clio: a Muse*.

9 Cf. *Autobiography*, p. 34: 'I used to look askance at Gibbon's dreadful saying that history is "little more than the register of the crimes, follies and misfortunes of mankind". Nor do I even now wholly subscribe to it. But the war of 1914–1918 enlarged and saddened my mind, and prepared me to write English history with a more realistic and less partisan outlook. Yet,

even after that war, the Reign of Queen Anne and the History of England up to the end of Victoria's reign, still seemed to me, when I came to write them, to be stories of happy endings.' This, too, was written in 1949!

10 Over 200,000 copies have been sold, but in schools copies are used time and time again, and, of course, many schoolmasters base their lessons on it.

11 Cf. his Romanes Lecture, *The Two Party System in English Political History*, delivered at Oxford in 1926 and reprinted in the *Autobiography and Other Essays* (Longmans, 1949), pp. 183–99.

12 Unused fragments of the projected earlier part may probably be detected in two essays in the *Autobiography and Other Essays*. They are: 'Social Life in Roman Britain' and 'The Coming of the Anglo-Saxons'.

Thomas Babington Macaulay

1 Sir George Otto Trevelyan: *Life and Letters of Lord Macaulay* (World's Classics edn), II, p. 173.

2 In this context it is worth noting Acton's dictum, 'Resist your time – take a foothold outside it.' G. L. Kochan, *Acton on History*, p. 36.

3 Macaulay did write one poem which displays a certain tender, heartfelt sensibility of both thought and language – a poem about a Jacobite, whose theme, appropriately enough, is the poignancy of exile from home:

> To my true King I offered free from stain
> Courage and faith; vain faith and courage vain,
> For him, I threw lands, honours, wealth away,
> And one dear hope, that was more prized than they.
> For him I languished in a foreign clime,
> Grey-haired with sorrow in my manhood's prime;
> Heard on Lavernia Scargill's whispering trees
> And pined by Arno for my lovelier Tees.

4 Trevelyan: *Life*, II, p. 87.

5 T. B. Macaulay, *Critical and Historical Essays* (Everyman edn), II, pp. 375–6.

6 P. Geyl, *Debates with Historians* (The Hague, 1955), p. 27.

7 There were exceptions. The works of Archdeacon Coxe, a far too neglected historian, were quite scholarly biographies, and these works mark the beginnings of the modern historical biography as Macaulay's essays mark the beginning of popular biography. And, of course, Johnson's *Lives of the Poets* are in a sense precursors of Macaulay's biographical essays.

8 T. B. Macaulay, *Essays*, I, pp. 332–3.

Index